Japan's Imperial House in the Postwar Era, 1945–2019

HARVARD EAST ASIAN MONOGRAPHS 432

Japan's Imperial House in the Postwar Era, 1945–2019

Kenneth J. Ruoff

Published by the Harvard University Asia Center
Distributed by Harvard University Press
Cambridge (Massachusetts) and London 2020

Printed in the United States of America

The Harvard University Asia Center publishes several monograph series and, in coordination with the Fairbank Center for Chinese Studies, the Korea Institute, the Reischauer Institute of Japanese Studies, and other facilities and institutes, administers research projects designed to further scholarly understanding of China, Japan, Vietnam, Korea, and other Asian countries. The Center also sponsors projects addressing multidisciplinary and transnational issues in Asia.

Cataloging-in-Publication Data is on file at the Library of Congress

Library of Congress Control Number:2019948116

ISBN 9780674244474 (hardcover : alk. paper)
ISBN 9780674244481 (pbk. : alk. paper)

Index by Jac Nelson and Cornelia Robert

♾ Printed on acid-free paper
Last figure below indicates year of this printing
29 28 27 26 25 24 23 22 21 20

For Jean, Carolyn, Megan, and Patrick,
who have brought me such joy

Contents

Figures

Acknowledgments

Some twenty years ago, I wrote *The People's Emperor: Democracy and the Japanese Monarchy, 1945–1995*. Now, with the ascension of a new emperor and the dawn of the Reiwa era, the time seemed ripe to expand and update the study of the monarchy's role as a political, social, and cultural institution in contemporary Japan.

The first six chapters of this volume, covering the history of Japan's postwar monarchy through 1995, are based largely on the corresponding chapters of *The People's Emperor*, updated as needed. Chapters 7 and 8 bring us along through the remainder of the Heisei era (1989–2019) to the early days of the Reiwa era, including the abdication of Emperor Akihito and the ascension of Emperor Naruhito in 2019. In these new chapters, I devote particular attention to the heir crisis, stressing the fragility of the imperial line under the current legal system.

Between the time that *The People's Emperor* was published and the preparation of this updated volume, I continued to receive guidance from many of the individuals cited previously. But along the way, more people helped me. Words cannot express my gratitude for all the advice I have received from Professor Hara Takeshi of the University of the Air over the past fifteen years. He is a remarkable scholar, and I profit from every communication with him.

More recently, Inoue Makoto, a journalist for the *Nihon keizai shinbun*, has been a source of much advice and has been very kind about making introductions for me in Japan. He is a man of great dignity and character and is widely trusted, giving his introductions special weight. He also recommended the photograph used as the basis for the cover of this book.

Kimura Takahisa, now retired from Kyodo News, has continued to translate into Japanese so many of my writings, including my recent study of the Heisei monarchy. He is a constant source of sage advice. Much of the new material in this edition was first published in Japanese in a book titled *Tennō to nihonjin* (The Emperor and the Japanese). I am grateful to my editor in the Publications Division of the Asahi Newspaper Company, Nakajima Mina, for skillfully guiding me through the publication process.

A series of invitations following Emperor Akihito's rare television address in 2016 indicating his desire to abdicate drew me back to the topic of the Japanese monarchy. Dr. Tristan Grunow invited me to give a lecture about the imperial house at the University of British Columbia. This was followed by an invitation by Professor Susan Pharr to speak about the monarchy at Harvard University, and then an invitation from Professor Melissa Dale to lecture about the same topic at the University of San Francisco. I also lectured at Portland State University. Finally, Professor Helen Hardacre invited me to lecture again at Harvard University. Slowly but surely, with much help from questions asked and feedback provided in conjunction with these lectures, I began to update my understanding of the postwar monarchy to include recent developments.

Meanwhile, various mass media outlets in Japan were asking me for commentary about dramatic new imperial developments, which also required me to think through topics such as abdication. I eventually concluded that this might be the basis of a new book. First, the Asahi Newspaper Company and I reached an agreement to publish a book about the Heisei monarchy. Subsequently, Bob Graham, director of publications for the Harvard University Asia Center, agreed, after consulting various Harvard faculty, that an updated and expanded version of the original English edition was in order. I acknowledge his skillful guiding hand in bringing this new volume to fruition.

While preparing new material for this book, Professor Sasahi Hiroo of Ryukoku University (then in residence at Portland State University as a visiting scholar) provided advice on which new photographs to include. Portland State University's Friends of History underwrote the cost of reproducing those photographs. Generous supporters of the Center for Japanese Studies at Portland State University have continued to nurture a stimulating intellectual environment in the face of a bizarre national neoliberalist trend whereby state governments (including Oregon) are disinvesting from public universities. Who would have thought we would reach a point in the United States when higher education is not seen as a public good? My heartfelt gratitude goes to all the community members who have stepped up to support the Center for Japanese Studies and the Friends of History.

Between the time when *Tennō to nihonjin* was published in January 2019 and this new volume was prepared, NHK World brought me to Japan twice to serve as a studio analyst for television coverage of Akihito's abdication and Naruhito's enthronement. Suffice it to say that television news is a high-pressure, time-sensitive endeavor. It is time sensitive not only in the sense that one must report the news as it happens, but also because one must make use of extremely limited on-air time to transmit important points in a concise way. This experience forced me to refine with utter precision my thoughts on various issues related to the contemporary imperial house. Although I must dutifully stress that this book is in no way endorsed by NHK World, I am grateful to them for providing me with an experience that I credit for improving parts of this monograph.

For my wife, Jean; daughters Carolyn and Megan; son, Patrick; and family dog, Chip, who sometimes kept me company when I was writing, I have good news. The updated book is done! Thanks so much for all your support.

• • •

Acknowledgments for *The People's Emperor*

Carol Gluck, David Cannadine, and Henry D. Smith II provided valuable guidance from the time that this project was in its earliest stage through to its completion. The Department of History at Columbia University was an excellent place at which to study when I underwent the doctoral program there between 1990 and 1997. In addition to Carol Gluck and Henry D. Smith II, Sheldon Garon, Michael Tsin, and Frank Upham participated on the Ph.D. defense committee and provided numerous suggestions for revising the dissertation into a book. Both Andrew Gordon and David Titus read versions of the manuscript and offered extensive and valuable suggestions for fine-tuning the final product. I was privileged to work with these scholars, and it is my great pleasure to acknowledge their assistance.

During research stays in Japan, Takami Katsutoshi and Furuya Jun of Hokkaido University, Takahashi Hiroshi of Kyodo News Service, and Takagi Hiroshi, formerly of Hokkaido University and presently of Kyoto University, provided assistance, for which I am grateful. The Faculty of Law at Hokkaido University hired me as a research associate and then as a lecturer between 1994 and 1996, allowing me to complete the research for this book in a supportive environment. In addition to Hokkaido University faculty members already mentioned, I am indebted to Kawasaki Osamu, Matsuura Masataka, Nakamura Ken'ichi, Nakano Katsurō, Ozaki Ichirō, and Yamaguchi Jirō for regular assistance on numerous fronts. Fellow graduate students Iwabuchi Sachiko and Yamazaki Mikine also were always willing to help. I also express thanks to Mark Levin and Isabelle Landreau, who during my stay in Sapporo provided many laughs, in English and French, respectively. It was truly enjoyable to be affiliated with the dynamic Faculty of Law at Hokkaido University.

John Ziemer, executive editor of the Harvard East Asian Monograph series, was kind and astute in guiding me through the various stages of preparation of the earlier book, and I thank him for his efforts. At Portland State University, the chair of the History Department, Lois Becker, and my departmental colleagues provided a congenial working environment for which I am grateful. My research assistant, Lisa Griffen, helped me with many tedious tasks related to completing this book, and I acknowledge her diligence. It is my pleasure to acknowledge Bruce and Cindy Brenn, Sandy and Akiko Lynch, and Tim and Martha McGinnis for their strong support of the Japanese Studies program at Portland State University.

During the course of researching this project, many individuals at numerous libraries on both sides of the Pacific helped me, sometimes with quite difficult requests, and I am able to thank only a few by name. Takada Naoko and Adachi Yoshie of the Political Science Resource Room at Hokkaido University found ways to put even the most obscure sources into my hands. Kobayashi Shiori assisted me with computer questions. At Columbia University, Amy Heinrich, Yasuko Makino, Ria Koopmans-de Bruijn, and the staff of the Starr East Asian Library provided assistance beyond the call of duty.

During a return trip to Japan for research in the summer of 2000, in addition to many of the individuals mentioned above, I received kind assistance from Professor Tomino Kiichirō of Ryukoku University, Mayor Asoda Yutaka of Kashihara City and his staff, Nishino Keiichi of Kashihara Shrine, Yamagami Yutaka of the Nara Prefectural Library, Fukushima Mutsuo of Kyodo News Service, and Koide Izumi, librarian of the International House of Japan.

Between 1994 and 2000, parts of original edition were presented as papers at the following institutions and conferences: Portland State University; Columbia University; Harvard University; Nissan Institute of Japanese Studies, Oxford University; Japan Centre, Cambridge University; Hokkaido University; German Institute for Japanese Studies (Tokyo); Association for Asian Studies Annual Conference (1996, 1998); American Historical Association Annual Meeting (1999); the "Competing Modernities in Twentieth-Century Japan: Empires, Cultures, Identities" conference held at the University of California at San Diego; and the International House of Japan's Seventh Annual Ph.D. Kenkyukai Conference. I thank the many individuals who made helpful comments regarding those presentations. I also want to mention that while I never had the opportunity to work with Professor Watanabe Osamu, I profited from his scholarship on the monarchy in postwar Japan.

Research and writing were made possible through generous financial support from several institutions. Between 1990 and 1997, the Department of History and the East Asian Institute at Columbia University awarded me several fellowships. Hokkaido University provided me with comprehensive support for my field research between October 1994 and March 1996. I profited from a postdoctoral appointment at the Edwin O. Reischauer Institute of Japanese Studies at Harvard University (1997–98). Grants from the Northeast Asia Council of the Association for Asian Studies, the Faculty Development Committee at Portland State University, and the Friends of History at Portland State University allowed me to return to Japan in the summer of 2000 to conduct further research, especially about the 2,600th anniversary celebrations, and to purchase the photographs included in this book. I express my heartfelt thanks for all the financial assistance that this project received.

I am grateful to Enid Ruoff for proofreading several versions of the manuscript. From the time that I began to study Japanese in the summer of 1985, I received dedicated instruction in this language at Cornell University, Harvard University, Keio University, and Indiana University.

I also was privileged, in the spring of 1987, to be taken in by the warmest and, in the area of learning Japanese, most demanding of host families. The Suzuki family—Hidenori, Yoko, and Akiko—played an instrumental role in teaching me Japanese, and for the past fourteen years they also have provided countless insights into life in Japan. I was one of the nine foreign exchange students hosted by the Suzuki family between 1986 and 1995, of whom seven achieved fluency in Japanese. I thank them for this admirable grassroots contribution to internationalization.

Abbreviations

The following abbreviations are used in the text and notes:

CCP	Chinese Communist Party
CIE	Civil Information and Education Section (SCAP)
DPJ	Democratic Party of Japan
DSP	Democratic Socialist Party
JCP	Japan Communist Party
JSP	Japan Socialist Party
LDP	Liberal Democratic Party
NLC	New Liberal Club
PARC	Policy Affairs Research Council (LDP)
SCAP	Supreme Commander for the Allied Powers
SDF	Self Defense Forces

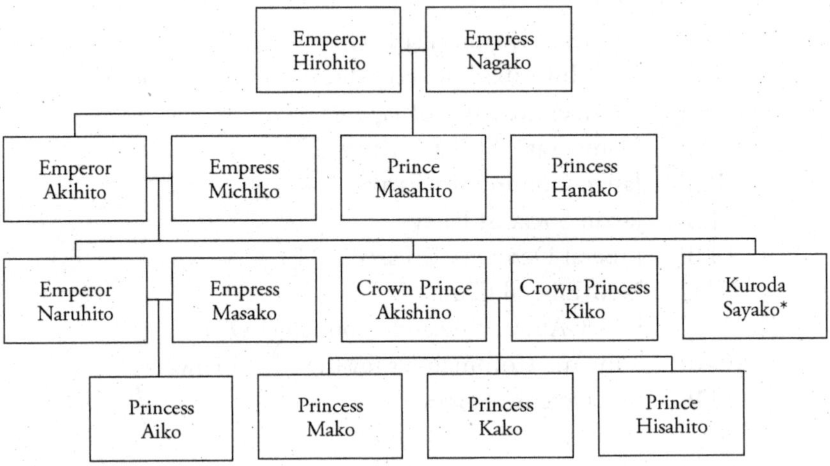

FIGURE 1. A chart showing some members of the royal family to help illustrate, in particular, the heir crisis as of 2019.

* Kuroda Sayako, formerly Princess Nori, lost her royal status upon marriage in 2005.

Introduction

The Constitution of the Empire of Japan (Meiji Constitution, 1889)

Chapter I. The Emperor

Article I. The Empire of Japan shall be reigned over and governed by a line of Emperors unbroken for ages eternal.

Article III. The Emperor is sacred and inviolable.

Article IV. The Emperor is the head of the Empire, combining in Himself the rights of sovereignty, and exercises them, according to the provisions of the present Constitution.

Article XI. The Emperor has the supreme command of the Army and Navy.

The Constitution of Japan (Postwar Constitution, 1946)

Chapter I. The Emperor

Article I. The Emperor shall be the symbol of the State and of the unity of the people, deriving his position from the will of the people with whom resides sovereign power.

Article III. The advice and approval of the Cabinet shall be required for all acts of the Emperor in matters of state, and the Cabinet shall be responsible therefor.

Article IV. The Emperor shall perform only such acts in matters of state as are provided for in this Constitution and he shall not have powers related to government.

Few institutions are as well suited as the monarchy to provide a window on Japan. For the first seven decades after the end of World War II, this national symbol of Japan experienced momentous change. Throughout the modern period (1868–present), Japanese supporters and opponents of the throne have used it to define themselves and their nation. The monarchy, which is also a family, has been significant as both a political and a cultural institution. Indeed, an examination of the monarchy requires that we abandon a strict division of the political from the cultural and of the symbolic from the political. The emperor has embodied the modern Japanese nation-state,[1] and nationalism is a phenomenon that belies the compartmentalization of politics, culture, and symbols.

Japan's defeat in 1945 represented a critical turning point not only in the history of the nation but also in the history of the monarchy. The Meiji Constitution led to a particular form of emperorship, which was reformed after 1945. The monarch of the Meiji Constitution enjoyed imperial sovereignty; the Postwar Constitution, which is premised on popular sovereignty, redefined the emperor as a symbol with no "powers related to government." In many critical respects, the postwar emperorship differs from the prewar version. At the same time, the prewar form has continued to structure postwar expectations of the monarchy and the nature of the Japanese "polity," a term that can mean simply the form of government but in a broader sense includes fundamental values as well. Although this study highlights continuities between the pre- and postwar eras, 1945 was enough of a disjuncture in imperial history to justify examining the postwar era as a distinct period.

The monarchy remained a delicate subject into the twenty-first century, as evidenced by the controversy that followed then–Prime Minister Mori Yoshirō's (1937–) clumsy remark in May 2000 that Japan was a "divine nation centered on the emperor";[2] the debates that preceded the passage of a bill making *Kimigayo*, with its celebration of the imperial line, the national anthem in 1999;[3] and, most of all, by the violence and terrorism that have sporadically been part of the contest over this national symbol. One example of such violence was the Motoshima Incident. In December 1988, as Emperor Hirohito (1901–89; r. 1926–89) was dying, Nagasaki Mayor Motoshima Hitoshi (1922–2014) publicly remarked, "I think that the emperor bears responsibility for the war." Motoshima's interpretation of Hirohito's wartime role was neither new nor extreme, yet he was ostracized by the political establishment and threatened by violent right-wing groups. In January 1990, a member of one such group shot Motoshima for his statement made at a time of national "self-restraint" invoked to show respect for the emperor.[4] Motoshima survived and even went on to win reelection in 1991, but his experience is a reminder of how emotional the topic of the emperor remained decades into the postwar era.

For conservative Japanese, the monarchy is the symbol of Japan's timeless culture, the embodiment of "traditional" customs and beliefs. Immediately after the war, three scholars argued that the "symbolic" monarchy represented a return to the tradition of emperors who served ceremonial, cultural roles and remained above politics. The interpretation that the postwar monarchy is a return to premodern tradition, though not fanciful in broad terms, brushes over the fact that the present monarchy has little in common with its premodern ancestor. But even though the postwar version of the monarchy differs considerably from its prewar antecedent, it has far more in common with the prewar monarchy than with the premodern one. As I will argue in this book, politically and culturally, the monarchy has been profoundly shaped by the Occupation-era constitution and seventy years of societal evolution. Rather than being traditional, what characterizes the monarchy today is its "postwarness."

In theoretical terms, the existence of a hereditary royal family seems antithetical to democracy, the founding principle of postwar Japan. For some Japanese, the throne represents all that is "undemocratic" about the nation. For still other Japanese, the throne is a powerful symbol of democracy; they point to the 1959 marriage of the recently retired emperor and then–crown prince, Akihito (1933–; r. 1989–2019) to a "commoner," in what was interpreted as a "love match" (as opposed to an arranged marriage). At a time when the government was considering revisions in the constitution, the popularity of Crown Prince Akihito's "democratic" marriage served to remind politicians of the people's attachment to the principle of equality (Article 14 of the Postwar Constitution) as well as to the principle that "marriage shall be based only on the mutual consent of both sexes" (Article 24).[5] As this study shows, the monarchy has become thoroughly embedded in Japan's postwar culture of democracy, and to a great extent, its postwar evolution has been driven by the society itself.

Until recent years, historical studies of postwar Japan have focused overwhelmingly on the Occupation (1945–52). But did the postwar "settlement" take place during the Occupation or after the Japanese regained their independence and the power to shape their polity? In the case of the throne, the symbolic monarchy created by the Postwar Constitution gained legitimacy only in the decade after the Occupation's conclusion in 1952. This is not to say that this process was smooth. Furthermore, even after gaining acceptance, the symbolic monarchy has continued to evolve. The focus on the period 1952 to 2019 distinguishes this book from other studies of the postwar monarchy.[6] Addressing the period from Japan's surrender to 2019 permits a comprehensive analysis of the significance of prewar institutions and practices, the Occupation reforms, and social evolution in shaping the monarchy. The most important reason that this study was extended through to the end of Akihito's reign is that the full flowering of the "monarchy of the masses," a concept central to this book, could take place only after Hirohito's death. An endpoint of 2019 also draws attention to ongoing struggles of the Japanese to conclude the postwar era. This book addresses the period from 1945 to 2019 to question whether, even as we approach the seventy-fifth anniversary of the end of World War II, the "postwar era" has come to an end in Japan. From the 1990s through to the present, the Japanese have contentiously debated how to remember the war. The very breadth of this discussion calls into question assertions that the postwar era concluded, at the latest, with the death of Emperor Hirohito in 1989. Emperor Akihito devoted much of his reign to bringing closure to the postwar era, but it is not clear that he succeeded in helping conclude it.

As surrender became imminent in the summer of 1945, Japan's leaders, including the emperor, grew obsessed with "preserving the national polity." To most Japanese, that meant not simply ensuring the survival of the "line of Emperors unbroken for ages eternal" but also maintaining imperial sovereignty. The Japanese authorities' fixation on the national polity is evidenced by the dialogue between Japanese and U.S. officials regarding Japan's acceptance of the Potsdam Declaration. Japanese authorities initially indicated, on 10 August, that they would surrender provided that the "declaration does not comprise any demand which prejudices the prerogatives of His Majesty as a Sovereign Ruler." Japan's Supreme War Council, led by the emperor, drafted this conditional reply in an attempt to guarantee the monarchy's survival, even though council members had reason to assume that U.S. leaders might authorize the further use of atomic bombs and destroy Japan's cities one by one. The U.S. Secretary of State, James F. Byrnes (1882–1972), soon put an end to Japanese hopes for conditional surrender. The next day, he replied: "From the moment of surrender the authority of the Emperor and the Japanese Government to rule the state shall be subject to the Supreme

Commander of the Allied Powers who will take such steps as he deems proper to effectuate the surrender terms."[7]

The Japanese authorities then surrendered unconditionally. They would later insist that there had been a tacit understanding about preserving the monarchy. This was not necessarily the case. The Potsdam Declaration stipulated that "the Japanese government shall remove all obstacles to the revival and strengthening of democratic tendencies among the Japanese people. Freedom of speech, of religion, and of thought, as well as respect for the fundamental human rights, shall be established."[8] It was not exactly clear what the declaration, which did not mention the monarchy, meant for the future of the throne. Emperor Hirohito was recognized throughout the world as the symbol of Japanese militarism, a fact weighing against the survival of the monarchy. Japan's defeat in 1945 was as devastating as any suffered by a country in the twentieth century, and domestically the throne potentially faced indictment by the Japanese people for the national disaster.

How, then, did the monarchy survive? For a few months after the surrender, the Japanese throne's fate was debated inside and outside Japan. After the laws regulating discussion of the monarchy were suspended in October 1945 at the orders of the U.S. occupation forces, criticism of the monarchy and Emperor Hirohito, already strong in the Allied countries, surfaced in Japan as well. On 2 December 1945, many Japanese were shocked when the national radio station, NHK, broadcast a debate about the future of the "emperor system" (*tennōsei*). The moderator of the debate, Murobuse Kōshin (1892–1970), opened the proceeding by remarking, "I think that the first step for our country's democracy is to encourage a lively debate about this problem."[9] The broadcast popularized the Marxist term *tennōsei*, which came to be used by individuals of all political colors to describe the monarchy in both positive and negative ways.

The participants in the NHK debate differed over the "essence" (*honshitsu*) of the emperor system. Japan Communist Party (JCP) leader Tokuda Kyūichi (1894–1953), only recently released from prison, voiced his party's position that the "repressive" monarchy should be abolished.[10] The JCP also labeled Hirohito and other imperial family members "war criminals." The previously limited, underground criticism of the monarchy achieved a wide audience. This was a radical change from the days of Imperial Japan (1890–1945).

Eric Godal in the Newspaper PM, New York, Sept. 12, 1945

FIGURE 2. This cartoon mocking the concept of democracy under Emperor Hirohito, the symbol for most Americans of Japan's militarism, provides commentary on popular American animosity toward the emperor and on racist feelings toward the Japanese in general (note how the cartoonist drew the pupils' faces). (*Amerasia* 9, no. 16 [Sept. 1945], 242.)

In early 1946, just months after the surrender, the U.S. occupation authorities settled the monarchy's fate by pressuring a conservative Japanese government to accept a draft constitution authored by the Government Section of the Supreme Commander for the Allied Powers (SCAP) that ensured the throne's survival but radically redefined the emperor's position.[11] The American-written constitution has been a source of political controversy from its inception, and initially nothing was more contentious than the reform of the emperor's position from sovereign to symbol. When Foreign Minister Yoshida Shigeru (1878–1967) saw SCAP's draft constitution for the first time on 13 February 1946, he characterized it as "revolutionary" and "outrageous."[12]

General Douglas MacArthur's (1880–1964) announcement on 6 March 1946 regarding the proposed constitution neglected to mention the pressure that SCAP had exerted on the reluctant Japanese authorities:

> It is with a sense of deep satisfaction that I am today able to announce a decision of the Emperor and Government of Japan to submit to the Japanese people a new and enlightened constitution which has my full approval. This instrument has been drafted after painstaking investigation

> and frequent conference between members of the Japanese Government and this headquarters following my initial direction to the Cabinet five months ago.[13]

As he would throughout the Occupation, MacArthur invoked the emperor to legitimize reforms initiated by SCAP, including the revision of the emperor's constitutional position.[14] In this, MacArthur was following domestic precedent: Japanese politicians had used the emperor to legitimize decisions throughout the modern era. In essence, the U.S. occupation authorities invoked the emperor's authority to legitimize a new constitution that rendered it constitutionally insupportable to use the emperor to legitimize policy.

There were other possible scenarios for the throne. The monarchy could have been maintained but without Hirohito, whose responsibility for the war in at least a moral sense seemed evident to many inside and outside Japan. Had the Occupation authorities decided to abolish the monarchy, it is questionable whether the Japanese would have mounted much resistance (and one can only speculate on the restorationist movements that might have arisen after the Americans returned home). Accounts that posit the Japanese people's immutable affection for their throne even in the face of cataclysmic national defeat fail to recognize the impact of the sweeping campaign undertaken after the surrender by Japanese authorities, with the help of their U.S. overseers, to distance the emperor from the war and to remake the throne to match the pacified and democratized Japan. If the Americans had indicted the emperor for his role in the war and demonized the throne as the primary agent of the national disaster, public opinion might have evolved quite differently.

Not only was MacArthur under orders from Washington to preserve the monarchy, he personally found both the monarchy as an institution and Hirohito the individual useful in carrying out his reforms. Other leading Occupation figures such as General Bonner Fellers (1896–1973) defended the throne and Hirohito as necessary bulwarks against communism.[15] Fellers's faith in the power of monarchy to stifle communism was shared by British leaders, who were determined to restore and then protect the Greek monarchy during that country's bitter civil war in the aftermath of World War II.[16] Whether or to what extent the monarchy played a role in preventing the communization of Japan is open to debate.

However, the throne's continuing resonance is evidenced by the fact that more than seventy years after the emperor was constitutionally transformed into a symbol, individuals seeking to exert political and cultural influence in Japan continue to invoke the monarchy in support of their positions.

A word about terms. Although "people's emperor" is not a phrase that Japanese frequently employed to describe their monarch at the time the earlier version of this book was published, I use it because it aptly describes two fundamental aspects of the postwar throne. First, according to the popular-sovereignty Constitution of Japan, the continuing existence of the monarchy is dependent on the will of the people. Second, as a result of the emperor's constitutional position, in the postwar era the imperial house has labored to maintain its popularity more than at any other time in Japanese history. This is not to suggest that the people necessarily have had a say in shaping all aspects of the monarchy, but the fact that the imperial house's survival is predicated on the people's desire to keep their monarchy has greatly influenced the royal house's operational style.

Throughout the book I use another term to describe the monarchy. The Japanese have come to refer to the constitutionally redefined monarch as the "symbol emperor" (*shōchō tennō*) and to the monarchy as the "symbol emperor system" (*shōchō tennōsei*). I use the term "symbolic monarchy" primarily because it is understandable to nonspecialists. These terms capture Japanese expectations for their monarchy: that its role be only symbolic and ceremonial. Although these terms imply a contrast with a prewar monarchy that was at the center of the political process, they are problematic. Implicit in these phrases is a suggested contrast between a prewar monarch who was political but not symbolic and a postwar monarch who is symbolic but not political. Yet the boundaries between the symbolic and the political cannot be so easily drawn, as we shall see.

The symbolic monarchy exists in the context of Japan's postwar democracy, and in the sense used in this book democracy is structurally a political system characterized by a popular, representative government chosen through free elections supported either by a constitution or by tradition (or some combination of both). It is also distinguished by the extensive legal protection of civil liberties, such as the right to dissent, the freedom of association, and the freedom of the press. The Postwar Constitution explicitly provides for all of these, and in practice civil liberties have enjoyed comprehensive protection in postwar Japan. An ethos supportive of democratic values, such as equality and liberty, is also an important aspect of democracy. Finally, democracy is also a debate about what democracy is. In Japan's case, the monarchy has often featured in this debate, especially in the decades after the surrender.

The postwar monarchy is distinguished by impassioned public debates about its symbolic nature, issues that fit an expanded definition of what is political. Many of the emperor's symbolic acts have carried political significance, although measuring their resonance is a far more imprecise enterprise than computing the increase in governmental revenues that resulted from the change in the sales tax. Precisely because of its symbolic role, the monarchy has retained a certain centrality in postwar Japan. At the extremes, left- and right-wing groups have both resorted to violence over the throne. In fact, Japanese of all political inclinations have contested the meaning of the monarchy, and thus of Japanese national identity, throughout the postwar era.

There are many ways to periodize the postwar history of the monarchy. One could divide this history into three periods of (1) reform, 1945–47; (2) the shaping of the symbolic monarchy even while its legitimacy remained in question, 1947 to the late 1950s, early 1960s; and (3) ongoing contestation over the contours of the symbolic monarchy, late 1950s, early 1960s to the present. Both 1945, the year of Japan's defeat, and 1947, the year the Postwar Constitution went into effect, were major disjunctures. It is difficult to be more precise regarding when the symbolic monarchy provided for by the Occupation-era constitution achieved legitimacy. Other important turning points, such as the Occupation's conclusion in 1952, Crown Prince Akihito's wedding in 1959, and Emperor Hirohito's death in 1989, further complicate this periodization.

Although Japan has undergone rapid change since 1945, it is still possible to speak of a "postwar system" because the 1947 Constitution has remained unchanged for more than seventy years. Thus an understanding of postwar Japan commences with the constitution. Why has the Occupation-era constitution, especially the chapter on the emperor that so riled Japanese authorities in 1946, survived unrevised, and how has it changed the emperor's role?

Chapter 2 examines how constitutional reform reshaped the emperor's public role. The new constitution rendered every public act of the emperor subject to open constitutional debate for the first time in Japanese history. How did the Japanese interpret the public role of a living symbol? In Japanese as in English, the word "symbol" has a connotation of passiveness, as in a sign that represents or expresses something else. Although the most common symbol of nation-states, a flag, simply flies from a pole, a symbol emperor walks and talks. This can be a problem, for it is not so easy for a person to be neutral. Furthermore, a totally neutral emperor serves no positive function.

By the early 1960s, a consensus about the emperor's new public role had emerged. After the new constitution went into effect, it was the political left, which had never enjoyed control of the imperial symbol, that demanded most forcefully that the emperor be kept outside politics. The left—represented for most of the postwar period by the JCP and the Japan Socialist Party (JSP)—was particularly adamant that the emperor's public neutrality be maintained. Was the left successful in making the conservatives in the Liberal Democratic Party (LDP) who have ruled Japan for most of the past seventy years abide by the constitution in shaping the emperor's public role? To what extent was postwar policy regarding the emperor shaped by the law, which is so crucial to healthy democratic systems?

Even as the Japanese were faced with interpreting the emperor's new, symbolic role, the validity of the Postwar Constitution remained in doubt for a decade after Japan regained independence. Why did the constitutional revision movement that arose after the Occupation fail? One important reason for the movement's failure was the spirited defense of the postwar system by the left, but did all the forces on the right agree, for example, on the necessity of revising the emperor's position? As this book will show, the political right has been far from united on the various issues related to the monarchy during the past seven decades. Too often portrayed as monolithic, the right often has disagreed about the monarchy, seemingly one of its core issues. What does this suggest about divisions within the right regarding other matters? The left also has by no means been monolithic, but it is the plurality of the right that often has been overlooked. The political views of the right wing, far from being static, have evolved over time.

In terms of views of the monarchy, it is possible to separate the political right roughly into extreme right, far right, and right-of-center factions. The extreme right has been defined by its willingness to employ violence to achieve its anti-establishment goals. (One must avoid assuming that the left is anti-state and the right pro-state, for radicals on both the left and right are anti-establishment.) One important example of an extreme right group was the DaiNihon Aikokutō (Greater Japan Patriot Party) as led by virulent nationalist Akao Bin (1899–1990). For most of the postwar period, the far right's defining characteristic has been its hostility toward the reformed imperial system and the postwar system in general. Unlike the extreme right, the far right has worked within the democratic system to achieve its ends, even though elements of the far right have opposed fundamental features of the democratic system. The Association of Shinto Shrines (Jinja honchō) has been an important representative of the far right. The right-of-center faction has been the broadest and also the most difficult to define with precision. Representatives of this faction have not been enthusiastic supporters of certain aspects of the reformed imperial system, especially in the decades immediately following the Occupation, but at the same time they have not been as reactionary as the far right or not reactionary at all. Nakasone Yasuhiro (1918–), a politician active throughout the postwar period and prime minister from 1982 to 1987, was right of center, especially during his years as prime minister. This division of the right is based foremost on views of the monarchy and does not necessary hold when expanded to other issues, although it sometimes proves useful in other areas as well. The boundaries between these factions are often fuzzy. For example, the quiet complicities between the far right and the extreme right is a topic deserving of further examination.

Supporters of the constitutional symbolic monarchy reached both abroad and back into their own country's history to legitimize what seemed so radically new to many in 1946. Many Japanese saw Britain, a constitutional monarchy, a bedrock of democracy, and the example employed by the U.S. drafters of the constitutional chapter on the emperor, as a logical model to emulate in developing their own symbolic monarchy in the decades after the war. The director of education for Emperor Akihito, for example, placed the British model at the center of the crown prince's education.

According to another interpretation of the symbolic monarchy, the system of imperial sovereignty created after the Meiji Restoration of 1868, whose retention so occupied Japan's leaders in 1945 and 1946, was in fact an aberration in the sixteen-centuries-long history of the throne. According to this interpretation, the present symbolic monarchy represents a return to the past. The weaknesses of this simplistic interpretation of the postwar throne are examined in chapter 2.

Chapter 3 addresses the clash between the new constitution and the long-standing custom of government ministers briefing the emperor on political matters behind closed doors. Nowhere has the tension between imperial practices developed under the Meiji Constitution and the limits placed on the emperor by the new constitution been greater than with regard to the legitimacy of briefings. An analysis of this practice allows us a glimpse into the views of Emperor Hirohito, whose role in the shaping of the postwar monarchy needs to be underscored.

When the Postwar Constitution destroyed the imperial prerogative, what became of the political role of the emperor as an individual? It was Emperor Hirohito who insisted that briefings continue, and this practice survives today as a result of his authority during the four decades he occupied the throne under the new constitution. Was Hirohito involved in politics even under the Postwar Constitution? If so, what does this tell us about his role under the Meiji Constitution? Although these briefings correspond to a similar practice in Britain, is this custom constitutionally justified in the case of Japan? Why has such a gap developed during the postwar era between public expectations of the emperor's symbolic role and his actual role in politics? These and other questions are addressed in chapter 3.

Chapter 4 traces three themes that came together in a dramatic manner in the 1990s as a result of Emperor Akihito's apologies to Japan's neighbors for his country's wartime actions: war responsibility, the political right's endorsement of the symbolic monarchy, and definitions of the emperor's public role. To understand why Emperor Akihito, who was eleven when the war ended, devoted considerable energy during the first decade of his reign to "disposing of the postwar" (*sengo shori*) through apologies and other symbolic acts, one must trace the failure of Emperor Hirohito to address these matters. Beginning on the day of the surrender, Emperor Hirohito was disassociated from the war through a campaign undertaken by Japanese crafters of the imperial image and the U.S. occupiers. Not only was he distanced from the war, astonishingly, he was also recast as a pacifist.

Efforts to absolve Emperor Hirohito of war responsibility centered around claims that in practice under the Meiji Constitution (with a few exceptions) he had been a limited monarch who dutifully sanctioned the decisions of his ministers even when he disagreed with them. His pacifist nature, as the postwar mythmakers would have it, was revealed by his rare and courageous intervention into politics to end the war. The postwar removal of Hirohito from the political process in Imperial Japan has lent a particularly ironic edge to the role played by his son, groomed to be a symbolic monarch, in confronting politically volatile questions of war responsibility.

The reign of the reconstructed Hirohito lasted four decades into the postwar era. Even as the one-time sovereign remained on the throne, more and more representatives of the political right came to accept the Occupation-era reform of the sacrosanct national polity that had so shocked the political elite in 1946. In fact, interpreting the present symbolic monarchy as a return to tradition provided conservatives with a face-saving way not just to accept the symbolic monarchy but to champion it. By the 1990s, the interpretation that the emperor as symbol represented tradition had gained a certain orthodoxy. Is it possible, however, to disentangle the symbolic monarchy from other postwar principles, such as popular sovereignty? Conservatives speak of the symbolic monarchy as a return to the past, but is this merely a mechanism to draw attention away from the sweeping nature of the postwar democratic reforms?

One might have expected the legitimization of the symbolic monarchy to have dampened the controversy surrounding the emperor's public role, but this was not the case. No acts by an emperor under the Postwar Constitution breached the public neutrality of the throne more than the apologies issued by Emperor Akihito. These apologies were the subject of antagonistic debates over their constitutionality. Apologies may be symbolic acts, but they can have strong political overtones. An examination of the groups that protested against the imperial apologies not only reveals shifts in interpretations of the throne on the right but also undermines simplistic interpretations that continue to portray the throne as, by definition, a bulwark against the left.

Chapter 5 examines popular political actions regarding measures related to the monarchy. In addition to abolishing state support for Shinto and rewriting the constitution, the Occupation authorities enacted other reforms that affected the monarchy's position in Japanese society. When the Imperial House Law was revised in 1946, SCAP ordered Japanese authorities to delete a provision for choosing a new reign name upon the accession of an emperor. The reign-name system thus lost its legal basis.[17] However, the popularity of the reign-name system was demonstrated by the fact that most Japanese continued to count years according to Emperor Hirohito's reign name, Shōwa, the system to which they were accustomed. There have been five emperors and thus five reign names in modern Japan: Meiji (1868–1912), Taishō (1912–26), Shōwa (1926–89), Heisei (1989–2019), and Reiwa (2019–). The official name of Emperor Hirohito became Emperor Shōwa upon his death, but I use Hirohito in this book since it is familiar to Western readers. Along the same lines, after his abdication the official title of Akihito became emperor emeritus, but I use Akihito because it is more familiar.

Occupation authorities also pressured the Japanese government to abolish Foundation Day, the national holiday that celebrated the supposed foundation in 660 BCE of the Empire of Japan by Emperor Jimmu. In 1948, Prime Minister Katayama Tetsu (1887–1978), both the first socialist prime minister and the first prime minister under the new constitution, indicated his intention to include Foundation Day on the list of proposed postwar national holidays. Katayama was responding to a government poll that showed overwhelming popular backing for Foundation Day. Among the national holidays most favored by the people, it garnered an 81 percent approval rating, finishing third in popularity only to the New Year's holiday and the emperor's birthday.[18]

Occupation authorities, however, demanded that the Japanese government terminate this holiday. Dr. William K. Bunce, chief of the Religions Division of the Civil Information and Education Section (CIE) of SCAP, met informally on 28 May 1948 with members of the House of Councillors Cultural Affairs Committee. His purpose was to transmit SCAP's wish that Foundation Day be removed from the list of national holidays. Bunce stressed that Foundation Day lacked a historical basis and had been established by the state during the Meiji era to encourage feelings of superiority among the Japanese race. He dismissed popular support for the holiday as the result of misguided education.[19] The Diet, Japan's parliament, and Katayama's successor as prime minister, Ashida Hitoshi (1887–1954), reluctantly bowed to SCAP pressure. Foundation Day was not included among the national holidays established that July.

Nationalistic reaction against these reforms of the imperial system not only varied in strength but also produced different results. Piecemeal efforts to recriminalize insulting the dignity of the throne (lèse-majesté) left little lasting mark. In contrast, movements to reestablish Foundation Day as a national holiday and perpetuate the reign-name system succeeded (Foundation Day, however, was reformed greatly to suit the postwar polity, and it is open to debate whether renewed observance of this holiday has in fact served to unify the Japanese). In contrast, the equally well-organized movement to restore state support for the Yasukuni Shrine failed (the spirits of Japanese war dead are enshrined at this Shinto shrine). What explains the success of some movements and the failure of others?

Critics of the prewar emperor system have accused the government of restoring Foundation Day as a national holiday and the legal basis of the reign-name system "from above" to reestablish emperor worship. Was this the case, or to an extent not previously understood were these movements broad in nature? If so, then the postwar monarchy has been more society-driven than is usually thought. What were the motivations behind the widespread endorsement of Foundation Day and the reign-name system? These and other questions are addressed in chapter 5.

Chapter 6 traces the reform of the imperial house's style of operation to remake the monarchy to suit the postwar polity. Like the citizens of other democracies, who can contest the meaning of their national symbols, the Japanese have been free to invest their monarchy with a meaning that corresponds with their national vision. One characteristic differentiates symbolic monarchies from inanimate national symbols, however. Americans may argue over the meaning of the Stars and Stripes, but the flag has no influence over whether it is interpreted as a symbol of freedom or of a checkered history that includes racial discrimination and the extermination of Native Americans. In contrast, the emperor himself (and the monarchs in Britain, Spain, and other countries with largely symbolic royal houses) and the palace bureaucracy still play an active role in shaping the throne's symbolic meaning.

To operate successfully in a mass, democratic society, a monarchy must wed itself to the core values of that society. Before Japan's surrender, the monarchy had been the pinnacle of an unquestioned political and social structure; after the war, it recast itself as the symbol of the postwar culture of democracy—of Japanese beliefs, attitudes, values, ideals, and sentiments about what constitutes democracy. Over the past seventy years, the Japanese have disagreed over the precise definitions of the values central to the postwar system, but in broad terms one can speak of a set of principles that contrasts with the values dominant in Imperial Japan. The Postwar Constitution provided for equality, in contrast to the previous aristocratic and patriarchal system. Another important postwar principle was liberty, as symbolized by the extensive rights provided by Chapter III of the constitution. The Japanese also gained greater freedom to express skepticism about the need for individual sacrifice for the good of the state, a sacrifice demanded in the name of the emperor in Imperial Japan.

The principles of peace and international cooperation replaced the military values glorified especially in the 1930s. The rapidity with which the military and military values were discredited after Japan's surrender cannot be overstated. The military was abolished outright for several years after the surrender, and certainly the military's thorough removal from politics throughout the postwar period has aided the cause of democracy in Japan. The Japanese typically cite popular sovereignty, the no-war clause, and the fundamental human rights guaranteed in Chapter III as the distinctive features of the Postwar Constitution. Constructed in the aftermath of the war, the so-called postwar values came to enjoy predominant popular support only in the late 1950s and 1960s.[20]

Beginning on the day of Japan's surrender, the emperor and his advisors engaged in a campaign to remake the imperial house to suit the "New Japan" and keep the throne in tune with the emerging postwar value system. It proved easier for the imperial house to align itself with certain postwar values than with others, but clearly the throne worked to position itself as a symbol of the reformed polity. Emperor Hirohito dismounted his white horse, abandoned his military uniform, and was transformed into not only a pacifist but also a family man who democratically walked among the people.

It was Akihito, however, who emerged as an untarnished symbol of democratic and pacifistic Japan. Akihito's choice of a bride from outside the former aristocracy (which was abolished by the Postwar Constitution) symbolized the thorough defeat of the prewar authoritarian and aristocratic order and the emergence of an egalitarian mass society. The inviolate monarchy "above the clouds" was transformed into something with no precedent in the imperial house's long history: the "monarchy of the masses" that reaches out to citizens in ways that suggest that a social contract exists between the imperial house and the sovereign people.

The monarchy of the masses developed, even matured, while Emperor Hirohito was on the throne, but it has primarily been associated with Akihito. Still a powerful symbol, the monarchy is shaped by and is used to shape changing definitions of Japanese identity. This book is more a study of the monarchy in society rather than, for example, an institutional history of the Imperial Household Agency, although topics such as the relationship between the throne's gatekeeper and the mass media are addressed.

Chapter 7, to stress further that individual imperial family members have agency in spite of the extremely strict restrictions under which they operate, examines the Heisei era in depth, when the first emperor enthroned under the Postwar Constitution, Akihito, with the empress almost always at his side, pursued an especially active interpretation of the role of a symbol emperor. Although the emperor operates under significant constitutional constraints, Akihito nonetheless put an indelible stamp on the monarchy and on Japan during his thirty years as emperor. Emperor Akihito and Empress Michiko developed an unusually close partnership, an interesting new development, and together they vigorously pursued an agenda in the emperor's role as symbol of the state and of the unity of the people.

The agenda or symbolic essence of Akihito and Michiko was characterized by five themes analyzed in chapter 7: (1) an unabashed support of the postwar system characterized by pacifism, democracy, and internationalism; (2) efforts to compress the margins of society by reaching out to the most vulnerable members and also by extending a hand to others marginalized by geography and other factors; (3) efforts to bring closure to the postwar era by trying to heal the festering wounds of the war and of the imperial era in a more general sense; (4) demonstrations of pride in the best that Japan has to offer, but a pride tempered with a cosmopolitanism that clashed with simplistic nationalism, including in reference to views of Japan's history; and (5) the unusually active and important role Michiko played. Chapter 7 introduces the present emperor, Naruhito, who will surely put his own stamp on the monarchy and society going forward. The new emperor faces many challenges, arguably the greatest of which is maintaining national unity as Japan diversifies on many fronts.

Chapter 8 addresses Emperor's Akihito's abdication and, in a broader sense, the present fragility of the imperial line. Although Akihito's abdication should be seen as his attempt to stabilize the imperial line by keeping it in tune with society (by having his son Naruhito assume the emperorship before Naruhito became a senior citizen), it also drew attention to the peril the imperial line faces going forward as the result of the paucity of heirs (this was also probably one of the reasons for the abdication).

At the time of Emperor Akihito's abdication, the imperial house enjoyed its greatest popularity of the postwar era, which is significant considering that royal houses and democracies (and modernity in general) are somewhat tenuous grafts even though there are several successful examples of this blend worldwide. The problem Japan's imperial house faces is a scarcity of eligible heirs. The postwar Imperial House Law limits eligibility to male imperial family members of patrilineal lineage. As the result of postwar reforms eliminating the concubine system and narrowing the number of collateral families eligible to provide heirs, the size of the imperial family overall is small and by coincidence (but a coincidence that was going to happen sooner or later) there have been very few male children born lately.

It is no exaggeration to say that unless reforms are instituted, the future of the imperial line rests on the shoulders of Prince Hisahito (2006–), the only boy among the current generation of imperial children. Possible reforms include allowing women to become emperor (*tennō*; historically this term has also been used to reference to the eight regnant empresses that Japan has had) or steps to increase the presently limited number of collateral families eligible to provide an heir.

But there is an intense minority in Japan that insists what makes Japan's imperial line unique is the (supposedly) unbroken male imperial bloodline (*bansei ikkei*). As the result of this intense minority's stubborn resistance, it is not clear that reforms will be forthcoming in spite of the urgency of the situation. Debates about the future of the monarchy have exposed the racialist underbelly of Japan, for many on the right continue to cling to the notion that the imperial line epitomizes a pure race. In the face of gender equality becoming a global standard in the twenty-first century, proponents of maintaining patrilineal lineage have been cornered into making the curious claim that the issue of imperial lineage is completely separate from that of gender equality. The ongoing delay in addressing the scarcity of heirs has already resulted in a situation whereby discussion about whether to reform the system to allow women to serve as *tennō* could be construed as personal (and it may end up being personal). Is it to be Princess Aiko (b. 2001) or Prince Hisahito as *tennō* down the road? This complicates an already contentious issue.

Because debates over the imperial house's "essential" role throughout its 1,600-year history (or, according to legend, 2,600-year history) shaped the monarchy after 1945, knowledge of certain aspects of the imperial house's lengthy history is necessary to understand the postwar monarchy. It is especially important to understand the invention, after the Meiji Restoration of 1868, of the modern monarchy and its development until 1945. The monarchy of 1889, the year the Meiji Constitution was promulgated, was considerably different from the monarchy of 1868, and the monarchy of 1940, when the Japanese commemorated the putative 2,600th anniversary of the "unbroken imperial line," was different from the monarchy of 1889. The extent and nature of the 2,600th anniversary celebrations in particular must be understood to grasp how the monarchy of postwar Japan differs from its immediate predecessor. Chapter 1 examines the imperial house's history from "660 BCE" to 1945.

CHAPTER 1

The Monarchy, "660 BCE"–1945

Empirical evidence indicates that Japan's monarchy originated around the fifth century CE. Historian Herschel Webb has identified two features of the imperial house that differentiate it from other monarchies. First, the Japanese have placed tremendous stress on dynastic legitimacy, on the necessity of continuing the bloodline by keeping the throne within one family. Second, since its origin, the monarchy's primary function has been largely ceremonial, with the exception of two relatively short periods in its 1,600-year history.[1] The throne was the sacred aspect of the government.

The first exceptional period began in the seventh century, when the monarchy was reformed to give the emperor an important "political" role in the making of governmental policy, in addition to his sacerdotal functions. This reform was based on the Chinese model of government. During this period of direct imperial rule (*shinsei*), Emperor Temmu (r. 673–86) sponsored the compilation of the *Kojiki*. At a time when the imperial line was still relatively new, this mythical account invented a 1,300-year history of imperial rule over Japan that supposedly began with Emperor Jimmu's enthronement in 660 BCE. According to the *Kojiki* (published in 712) and the *Nihon shoki* (720), Jimmu culminated his eastward military expedition by founding the Empire of Japan.

The *ritsuryō* administrative system established early in the eighth century formally vested further political power in the emperor in the Chinese manner. The emperor became the chief administrator in addition to his religious role as officiant in the rice harvest rituals.[2] Direct imperial rule in ancient Japan proved short-lived, however. Only a few emperors are thought to have actually ruled. By the tenth century, the emperor again was distanced from policymaking, and his role was once again ceremonial.

The only exception during the next 900 years was the Kemmu Restoration of imperial rule carried out by Emperor Go-Daigo (r. 1318–39), who seized power from the Kamakura shogunate for a few years in the early fourteenth century before he was overthrown by Ashikaga Takauji (1305–58) in 1333. What followed is remembered as one of the most sensitive periods in imperial history. Ashikaga installed a competing line of the imperial house on the throne in Kyoto (the Northern dynasty). Go-Daigo fled to Yoshino, where he and his descendants (the Southern dynasty) continued to claim the throne. This volatile situation was eventually resolved by compromise in 1392, and today the imperial line is descended from the Northern line.[3]

After the monarchy lost its political power, emperors continued to perform certain ceremonial functions such as granting court ranks and offices. This was the case even during the Tokugawa period (1600–1868), when the imperial house was particularly impotent in political matters.[4] Although the imperial house always played a role in elite society, it is open to debate whether, before the modern period, peasants had even a vague knowledge of the emperor's existence. In other words, the emperor was either unknown or largely irrelevant to the vast majority of the population before the construction of Japanese nationhood after the Meiji Restoration of 1868.

Although the modern Japanese nation-state is largely a product of the Meiji era (1868–1912), the intellectual foundations of modern nationalism centering on the throne can be traced to the seventeenth century. It was during the three centuries of Tokugawa rule that nativist (*kokugaku*) scholars defined the throne as the distinctive feature of Japanese identity. Aizawa Seishisai (1781–1863) wrote in his *New Theses* of 1825: "Our Emperors, descendants of the Sun Goddess, Amaterasu, have acceded to the Imperial Throne in each and every generation, a unique fact that will never change. Our Divine Realm rightly constitutes the head and shoulders of the world and controls all nations."[5] The shogunate recognized the imperial house's increased stature by such acts as "identifying" Emperor Jimmu's tomb in 1863.[6]

Toward the end of the Tokugawa era, when the shogunate appeared too feeble to meet the threat of encroaching Western powers, "imperial loyalists" invoked the emperor to challenge the shogunate's legitimacy. The monarchy was gradually drawn into politics, to some extent as an individual agent but to a much greater extent as a symbol. Emperor Go-Daigo's Kemmu Restoration five centuries earlier served as a model for the imperial loyalists who carried out the Meiji Restoration of 1868 that toppled the shogunate. These imperial loyalists proclaimed the "restoration of imperial rule" (*ōsei fukko*). The Meiji Restoration was a political coup carried out by court nobles and low-ranking samurai. More important than the transfer of political power was the new leadership's prompt institution of a far-reaching program of modernization. Thus the Meiji Restoration marks the beginning of Japan's drive toward modernity.

The Making of the Modern Monarchy

Although politics were carried out in the emperor's name in the early years of the Meiji era, direct imperial rule was in fact largely a symbolic concept. Men such as Ōkubo Toshimichi (1830–78) and Itō Hirobumi (1841–1909) exercised decisionmaking authority, and they oversaw the rapid modernization of Japan during the Meiji era. Ōkubo, Itō, and other members of the Meiji oligarchy invoked the emperor as the symbol of the national unity that they were trying to achieve. Although at the time of the Meiji Restoration people in Japan shared, to a high degree, a common ethnicity and language, it was during the Meiji era that the majority of people gained a sense of being Japanese.

The small group of men in control of the government oversaw the remaking of the young emperor into a Western-style sovereign, a figure of towering authority who bestowed on his subjects a constitution, sternly inspected Japan's modernized army and navy, and presided over various imperial ceremonies designed to impress Western nations with Japan's modernity and rising international stature. Historian Takagi Hiroshi has demonstrated that just as Emperor Meiji was remade to suit the needs of the new nation-state, so, too, was Emperor Jimmu. Infrequent Tokugawa-era images that pictured a Buddha-like Jimmu were replaced with a wealth of images showing a Westernized Jimmu leading the eastward military expedition to unify the empire.[7]

Although the monarchy of Imperial Japan came to be defined by the Meiji Constitution, the imperial institution constructed during the Meiji era was as much a cultural and ideological invention as a politico-legal system. Virtually all aspects of the monarchy were reinvented and modernized. New imperial "traditions" or practices "which seek to inculcate certain values and norms of behaviour by repetition, which automatically implies continuity with the past,"[8] were invented, and old traditions were manipulated to suit the modern age.

In 1868 the Japanese government issued an edict requiring that years be counted according to imperial reigns, thus reforming the era-name system.[9] A system of counting years borrowed from China in the seventh century, era names had been used in Japan for 1,200 years. Even during the Tokugawa period, the emperor selected era names. But for most of Japan's history, era names did not necessarily correspond to the reigns of emperors. Before the Meiji Restoration, era names were changed to mark not only the accession of a new emperor but also, in the classical Chinese manner, auspicious or inauspicious events. For example, the last emperor of the Tokugawa period, Kōmei (r. 1846–66), had seven era names within his reign.

Under the modern reign-name system, 1868 became year one of Meiji, the name by which Mutsuhito (1852–1912), the first emperor of Japan's modern era, has been called since his death. In 1872, Japan adopted the Western solar calendar, also referred to as the Gregorian calendar. Rather than adopting the practice of dating years according to the Christian era, however, the Japanese dated them according to the reigns of emperors. This was one of many efforts by the Japanese to maintain a distinct identity even as Japan borrowed heavily from the West.

Another ancient tradition that was modernized was the imperial award system. The practice of the emperor bestowing court ranks and titles dates from the *ritsuryō* system and has continued for centuries regardless of the political impotence of the throne. The modern award system, based on European models, was developed during the first decades of the Meiji era. Article 15 of the Meiji Constitution provided the emperor with the authority to confer "titles of nobility, rank, orders and other marks of honor." The Imperial Household Ministry took a leading role in selecting individuals who merited recognition from the emperor. In Imperial Japan, three categories of awards, each with several ranks, were issued regularly. Special awards included the Order of Culture (*Bunka kunshō*) and the Order of the Golden Kite (*Kinshi kunshō*). The most prestigious honor a member of the military could receive, the Order of

FIGURE 3. According to the *Nihon shoki*, during a crucial battle in Emperor Jimmu's eastward expedition, a golden kite appeared from nowhere and landed on the end of Jimmu's bow. The kite was so dazzling that it frightened the enemy soldiers, allowing the imperial army to achieve victory. The Order of the Golden Kite, the highest honor a member of Japan's prewar military could receive, commemorated Emperor Jimmu's exploits. (Photograph courtesy Kyodo Photo Service.)

the Golden Kite (established in 1890), commemorated Emperor Jimmu's foundation of the empire. Most regular awards went to either military men or bureaucrats, servants of the emperor. Commemorative medals were issued to mark special national occasions, such as the annexation of the Korean Peninsula in 1910.[10]

The national holidays that the Meiji government established also reflected its emphasis on the monarchy. In a study of the "mnemonic sites" (rituals, including national holidays, and "material sign[s] on the physical landscape") that the political elite constructed during the Meiji era to place the emperor at the symbolic center of the new nation, historian Takashi Fujitani traced the establishment of eleven new national holidays between 1873 and 1927.[11] Each of them commemorated an aspect of the monarchy.

One important new holiday was National Foundation Day (*Kigensetsu*). The Meiji government invented Foundation Day in 1872 to celebrate the founding of the unbroken imperial line, and thus the Empire of Japan, exactly 2,532 years previously by Emperor Jimmu, as supposedly indicated by the *Kojiki* and *Nihon shoki*. These two mythical accounts of the imperial line's origin assumed an importance in modern Japan that they had never enjoyed previously. Although the practice of celebrating Jimmu's accession on 11 February would eventually be portrayed as historically accurate, this day was not the first selected by the Meiji government. In 1873, Emperor Meiji celebrated Foundation Day on 29 January. But later that year, 11 February was selected as the day for celebrating the first emperor's accession.[12] One eminent prewar Japanese scholar translated *Kigensetsu* as the "Festival of the Accession of the First Emperor and the Foundation of the Empire."[13]

From 1872 to 1885, the government sent Emperor Meiji, relocated to the shogun's former palace in Tokyo, on a series of tours to teach people throughout Japan that they were subjects of the emperor and citizens of the new nation. (Many accounts of Imperial Japan emphasize the people's role as subjects rather than as citizens; in contrast, almost all accounts of postwar Japan interpret the people as citizens.) The Meiji government also designed the tours to enable the emperor to perform symbolic acts useful in popularizing the ideology of the unbroken imperial line and edifying imperial landmarks; in 1877, for example, Emperor Meiji celebrated Foundation Day at Emperor Jimmu's tomb.

In the late Meiji period, the person of the emperor was replaced by his official portrait (*goshin'ei*). While the emperor retreated into the palace, copies of a portrait that showed the emperor as a generalissimo dressed in a Western-style military uniform were distributed to government offices and schools throughout Japan. Historian Iwamoto Tsutomu has documented cases of eight schoolteachers and principals who were "martyred" between 1896 and 1945 trying to rescue the imperial portrait from burning school buildings.[14]

During the first decades of the Meiji era, Shinto was recrafted into a state religion with the emperor as its high priest.[15] The emperor was said to be a deity in human form (*arahitogami*). The Meiji government assumed the responsibility for the financial support and supervision of ancient shrines, such as the one at Ise, whose association with the imperial house predates the modern era. The hallowed character of Ise Shrine derives from its housing of the sacred mirror, which, along with the sword and curved jewel, constitute the sacred regalia of the imperial family. According to imperial mythology, the mirror houses the "*kami*-body" of the Sun Goddess Amaterasu, progenitor of the imperial line.

Before the promulgation of the Meiji Constitution in 1889, the government invented locations for the tombs of all emperors whose burial sites were not recognized already and sponsored the construction of new shrines to make the monarchy prominent in Japan's physical landscape.[16] In 1888, the Meiji government certified a spot in Nara prefecture as the place where Jimmu's enthronement had taken place 2,548 years earlier. Meiji political leaders repeatedly invoked Emperor Jimmu as they went about modernizing the throne and building a modern nation-state. Kashihara Shrine, consecrated to Jimmu, was completed two years later, in time for the 2,550th anniversary of Jimmu's enthronement. Takagi has described Kashihara Shrine as the "device that allowed the people to participate in the myth of Jimmu."[17] In 1890, Kashihara Shrine consisted only of a small compound and two buildings, both of which had been moved from the imperial palace in Kyoto. The expansion of Kashihara Shrine into the huge compound it occupies today was the product of the continuing sanctification of Jimmu between 1890 and the banner year 1940, when millions of Japanese visited Kashihara Shrine and the nearby mausoleum of Jimmu in commemoration of the 2,600th anniversary of the first emperor's enthronement.

The decade leading up to Emperor Meiji's promulgation of the constitution on 11 February, Foundation Day, in 1889 was contentious. After the Meiji government issued an imperial rescript in 1881 that promised the establishment of a parliament by the end of the decade, the activity of various political parties intensified. Between 1881 and 1889, the cliques in control of the government labored to produce a constitutional and administrative system that would safeguard their political power. For example, a new nobility, comprising former samurai lords and court nobles as well as individuals who had rendered outstanding service to the country, was created to serve as the backbone of the throne. The Peerage Act of 1884 established a five-rank aristocracy modeled on the

Prussian system. The peerage consisted of approximately 500 families. Ancient *ritsuryō* court titles were replaced with European titles, such as prince, viscount, and baron. The aristocracy provided members for the House of Peers, intended to serve as a conservative check on the House of Representatives of the Diet.

During the 1880s, some Japanese proposed polities more liberal than that eventually established by the Meiji Constitution, although there were few republicans in Japan at the time.[18] The famous liberal (and nationalist) Fukuzawa Yukichi (1835–1901), in two tracts on the imperial house, "Teishitsuron" (On the imperial family; 1882) and the later and essentially similar "Sonnōron" (On reverence for the emperor; 1888), called for a monarchy unsullied by politics.[19] Fukuzawa favored the creation of a polity broadly modeled on that of Great Britain.

In writing "Teishitsuron," Fukuzawa drew on his considerable knowledge of Japanese history and culture, as well as of various Western scholars' writings, including those by English commentator Walter Bagehot (1826–77), whom he cited at one point. After the Meiji government's announcement that a parliament would be established, parties aligned with the government, to Fukuzawa's dismay, began to invoke the imperial house in the hope of justifying their platforms.

Fukuzawa began "Teishitsuron" with the simple statement "The imperial house is something outside politics" (*Teishitsu wa seiji shagai no mono to nari*)[20] and stressed: "Judging from history from ancient times, there are no examples of the people of the country of Japan using the sacred dignity of the throne to make an enemy of [other] Japanese people, or of the Japanese people joining together to make the imperial house their enemy."[21] He proceeded to scold those who involved the monarchy in politics. The result of the "imperial house descending into the dust of political society" was "damage to its dignity." He prayed for the "independence of the imperial house," one "without bias" and "without party."[22] Fukuzawa did not cite Bagehot at this point, but the similarities to a statement in the English writer's 1867 tract *The English Constitution* are apparent: "The nation is divided into parties, but the crown is of no party."[23]

Fukuzawa noted that there were those who wondered what role the crown could play if it were not involved in the important work of the country's politics. He characterized this as a "shallow view" of the monarchy. He divided human life into "form" (*keitai*) and "spirit" (*seishin*).

According to Fukuzawa, politics could regulate the form of a society but could never satisfy its spiritual needs. A parliament could do many things, such as establish a country's laws, but it could not "win the admiration of the people." In contrast, "Our imperial house is the center (*chūshin*) that wins over (*shūran suru*) the spirit of the Japanese people."[24]

Fukuzawa proceeded to detail critical functions best undertaken by the monarchy. He wrote that only the imperial house could "support moral customs"; the government was not up to this task. "In Western languages," Fukuzawa approvingly remarked, "it is said that the royal house is the source of honor."[25] He also suggested that the imperial house should play the vital role of promoting scholarship and the arts. Fukuzawa cited the example of Prince Albert (1819–61), husband of Queen Victoria (1819–1901). While refraining from direct involvement in politics, Prince Albert encouraged both high art and the work of common artisans. His support of the latter, Fukuzawa noted, had contributed to the prosperity of Great Britain.

Fukuzawa argued that the monarchy could play a crucial role in the introduction of Western civilization (*bunmei*) to Japan. He also concluded that only the imperial house could be entrusted with the equally critical role of preserving Japanese civilization (*bunmei*). Fukuzawa thus employed the term often used during the Meiji period to describe the civilization of the West to speak of Japan's own civilization. Fukuzawa listed various Japanese arts, from sumo to the tea ceremony, that were in need of imperial support. Writing at a time when the imperial house was still relatively poor, Fukuzawa suggested that its finances be improved so it could carry out the important tasks he had enumerated. He observed that there were large tracts of government forest and suggested that some of them be turned over to the imperial house for eternity. Soon thereafter, the Meiji government transferred vast tracts of land, stocks, and other forms of wealth to the imperial house to establish its financial independence.[26] This included much of the forest land in the newly colonized northern prefecture of Hokkaido. Fukuzawa's advice that the emperor be kept out of politics went unheeded, however. The Meiji Constitution subsequently placed the emperor at the center of the political process.

Itō Hirobumi, principal author of the Meiji Constitution, gave this interpretation of Article 1 in his *Commentaries on the Constitution of the Empire of Japan* (1889):

> At the outset, this Article states the great principle of the Constitution of the country, and declares that the Empire of Japan shall, to the end of time, identify itself with the Imperial dynasty unbroken in lineage, and that the principle has never changed in the past, and will never change in the future, even to all eternity. It is intended thus to make clear forever the relations that shall exist between the Emperor and His subjects.
>
> By "reigned over and governed," it is meant that the Emperor on His Throne combines in Himself the sovereignty of the State and the government of the country and of His subjects.[27]

More than providing for direct rule by the emperor in practice, the principle of imperial sovereignty continued to justify oligarchic rule by men like Itō. This explains the governing elite's attachment to imperial sovereignty. The emperor was by no means a powerful king along the lines of France's Louis XIV. Even though the emperor might actively engage in making policy, he was most of all the source of authority to legitimize decisions made by others.

Article 4 of the Meiji Constitution symbolized its hybrid nature. The term used to define the emperor's position as sovereign head of the empire, *genshu*, was a translation of the German term *Staatsoberhaupt*. The drafters of the Meiji Constitution located in ancient Chinese texts a character compound to express the sense of the term *Staatsoberhaupt*.[28] The term *genshu* itself was not used in Japanese political or legal discourse before the Meiji era.

The emperor's prerogatives under the Meiji Constitution included military command, civil administration (the broadest of his prerogatives), administration of awards, and authority over the imperial house. Political scientist David Titus has described how the decisionmaking process in Imperial Japan was legitimized through the principle of imperial prerogative:

> The strategy was to bring the decision-making process into the corridors of the 275-acre palace in which the emperor's prerogatives were castled, sealed off by walls and moats and guarded by the gatekeepers of the Imperial Will. The separation of court and government, palace autonomy, and the fusion of rites and court were devices to enhance the transcendental immutability of imperial prerogative, to make the palace an inviolable sanctuary for the resolution of political conflict, and thus to make conflict among political leaders invisible.[29]

Once policy was announced as the imperial will, it became difficult, even dangerous, to question that policy. Rescripts were the official mechanism for publicizing the imperial will. The "emperor in public" equaled the imperial will. The imperial will—policy—was, however, a collective product, not the product of the emperor individually. The emperor's personal will could and did influence the imperial will, but as a rule it was not allowed to be the imperial will on its own. Some emperors had strong wills and sought to act on them politically, but emperors were also regularly manipulated for political ends.

Just as the Meiji administrative and constitutional structure was a product of the 1880s, so were the various official rescripts and rituals that formally defined citizenship in terms of loyalty to the emperor. Edicts such as the Imperial Rescript on Education (1890), which three generations of Japanese schoolchildren were made to memorize, stressed loyalty to the throne:

> Our Imperial Ancestors have founded Our Empire on a basis broad and everlasting and have deeply and firmly implanted virtue; Our subjects ever united in loyalty and filial piety have from generation to generation illustrated the beauty thereof. This is the glory of the fundamental character (*kokutai*) of our Empire, and herein also lies the source of Our education. . . . Should emergency arise, offer yourselves courageously to the State; and thus guard and maintain the prosperity of Our Imperial Throne coeval with heaven and earth.[30]

Although precise definitions proved elusive, Japan's national polity (*kokutai*) was said to be a family-state (*kazoku kokka*) of blood relatives headed by the sovereign emperor, a notion explicitly enshrined as official ideology in the 1930s. Just as the loyalty of a family toward the father was seen as natural in the Confucian worldview, so was the people's obedience to the emperor.

Popularization of the modernized emperor continued throughout the Meiji era. Modern Japan's first international war served to disseminate the emperor's position as supreme commander. During the Sino-Japanese War (1894–95), the press reported that Emperor Meiji, relocated to Hiroshima to be closer to the theater of war, arose early each morning. After donning his uniform as supreme commander, he supervised the military operations while sharing the spartan life of the troops. In the aftermath of Japan's victory over China, German doctor Erwin Baelz (1849–1913) observed the following in his diary: "The position of the imperial family was strengthened by the crisis. The personality of the Emperor came more and more to the front. His portrait hung on the walls of every office, every school, and on ceremonial occasions all those present solemnly bowed their heads before it."[31] A decade later, the empress emerged as a model for Japanese women in times of national crisis. During the Russo-Japanese War (1904–5), which resulted in great numbers of casualties for the eventually victorious Japan, the empress visited the wounded in hospitals and even personally applied bandages.

B. H. Chamberlain (1850–1935), a British professor of philology at Tokyo Imperial University, was an especially astute observer of what he called "the invention of a new religion" in Japan at the turn of the century:

> Schools are the great strongholds of the new propaganda. History is so taught to the young as to focus everything upon Imperialism, and to diminish as far as possible the contrast between ancient and modern conditions. The same is true of the instruction given to army and navy recruits. Thus, though Shinto is put in the forefront, little stress is laid on its mythology which would be apt to shock even the Japanese mind at present day. To this extent, where a purpose useful to the ruling class is to be served, criticism is practised, though not avowedly. Far different is the case with so-called "historical facts" such as the alleged foundation of the Monarchy in 660 b.c. and similar statements paralleled only for absurdity by what passed for history in mediaeval Europe, when King Lear, Brute, King of Britain, etc., etc., were accepted as authentic personages. For the truth, known to all critical investigators, is that, instead of going back to a remote antiquity, the origins of Japanese history are recent as compared with that of European countries. The first glimmer of genuine Japanese history dates from the fifth century after Christ. . . . From the late Prince Itō's grossly misleading *Commentary on the Japanese Constitution* down to school compendiums, the absurd dates are everywhere insisted upon.[32]

Portrayed as utterly traditional, the civic religion of loyalty to the emperor was as recent as the Japanese nation-state itself:

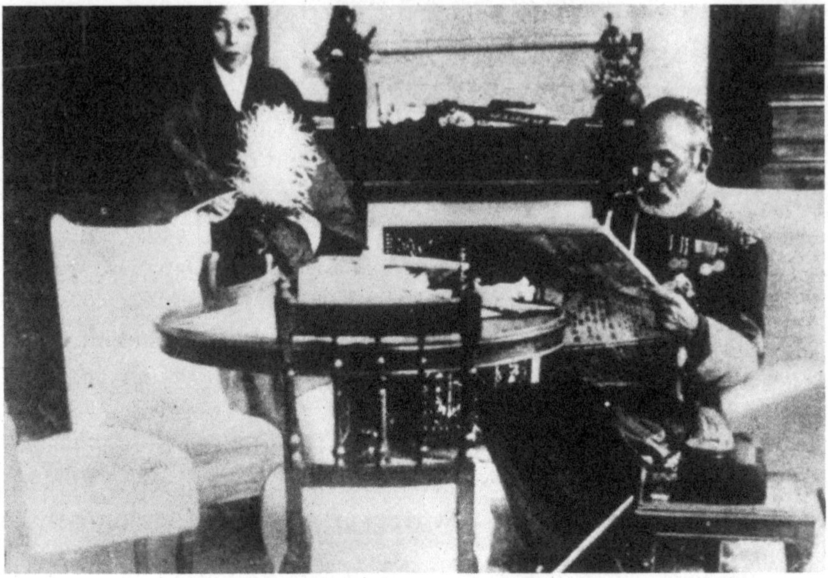

FIGURE 4. As headmaster of the Peers School, General Nogi Maresuke strictly supervised Hirohito's education from age seven to eleven. This photograph shows Nogi and his wife at the breakfast table on 13 September 1912, the day they committed ritual suicide to follow into death their lord, Emperor Meiji, whose funeral took place that day. (Photograph courtesy Kyodo Photo Service.)

> The new Japanese religion consists, in its present early stage, of worship of the sacrosanct Imperial Person and of His Divine Ancestors, of implicit obedience to Him as head of the army (a position by the way, opposed to all former Japanese ideas, according to which the Court was essentially civilian); furthermore, of a corresponding belief that Japan is as far superior to the common ruck of nations as the Mikado is divinely superior to the common ruck of kings and emperors.[33]

The Meiji era saw Japan adopt not only railroads and other material features of modernity but also a modern national ideology: the cult of the emperor. Historian Carol Gluck has described eloquently how, by the end of the Meiji era in 1912, this new religion had achieved an unprecedented level of orthodoxy. This was in part the result of efforts by provincial officials and local notables to convince the masses to accept, as common sense, the emperor-centered ideology.[34]

The Meiji era concluded with one of the most spectacular events of modern Japanese history. On 13 September 1912, the evening of Emperor Meiji's funeral, General Nogi Maresuke (b. 1849) and his wife committed suicide in front of the imperial portrait in their home. The concept of following one's lord in death was based on samurai ideals. The suicides riveted the Japanese, who debated their propriety, in the context of modern Japan, at length.[35] As the headmaster of Gakushūin (Peers School), Nogi had strictly supervised Hirohito's education for the previous four years. Indeed, three days before following his lord in death, Nogi had quizzed Hirohito, then eleven years old, at length about his studies and then lectured the boy about emperorship for approximately fifty minutes.[36] Hirohito is thought to have revered Nogi. The general's suicide was yet another in a series of stern lessons about duty for the future emperor, who assumed official responsibilities at age twenty due to the poor health of his father, Emperor Taishō (1879–1926).

The Monarchy after World War I

Some historians label the post–World War I period in Japan the era of "Taishō Democracy," but one must avoid portraying the 1920s in isolation from the preceding and following decades. Just as the 1920s owed much to the consolidated Meiji system, there were many continuities between the 1920s and the 1930s, a decade historians label variously as militaristic, authoritarian, or fascist. But it is true that democracy became a powerful concept among certain influential circles in Japan in the 1920s, whereas by the late 1930s it clearly had lost its appeal.

Since the opening of the Diet in 1890, the Meiji oligarchs had struggled with political parties over who was to dictate government policy. The increasing influence of the parties is demonstrated by the fact that leading oligarchs such as Itō eventually accepted leadership roles in parties. In 1918, for the first time in Japanese history, an individual who had risen through the ranks of a political party, Hara Takashi (1856–1921), became prime minister. Between 1918 and 1932, with the exception of the years 1922 to 1924, Japan's government was led by "party" cabinets.[37] The prime minister came from the majority party in the Diet, and the emperor was expected to affirm the decisions of the Cabinet even though he maintained supreme authority.

During this period of parliamentary government, the constitutional theories of Minobe Tatsukichi (1873–1948), a professor at Tokyo Imperial University, came to the forefront. Minobe interpreted the Meiji Constitution in a manner that, although not questioning imperial sovereignty, legitimized the centrality of the Diet in decisionmaking. In simple terms, Minobe's interpretation held that the emperor was one of several organs of the state in which governmental power was vested. Other state organs included the Diet, which, according to Minobe, was superior to all other organs except the emperor. Although the Diet was inferior to the emperor, the "autocratic organ" of government, the constitution nonetheless placed checks on the emperor's authority.[38] In practice the Diet was to be the primary decisionmaker.

Historian Banno Junji has shown that Prime Minister Hara endeavored to keep the monarchy out of politics during his tenure in office (1918–21). Hara wrote in his diary in September 1920:

> It is the role of constitutional government to assume full responsibility without implicating the imperial family, and that, in my view, is best for the emperor, too. I believe that the imperial family would be more secure if its members refrain from getting directly involved in politics and engage mainly in charitable work, granting rewards, etc., and my policy is directed toward this.[39]

Hara's interpretation shows that there was support even at the highest levels of the prewar government for a ceremonial monarchy. This was true even if imperial sovereignty remained inviolate even in the eyes of most liberals.

During the 1920s, Hirohito came of age. In 1921 he became regent for his mentally enfeebled father. That year he also undertook an extended trip to Europe. When World War I swept away the Prussian, Russian, and Habsburg monarchies, the British royal house emerged as an especially important example for Japan's monarchy. The highlight of Crown Prince Hirohito's six-month tour was a state visit to Great Britain. Japanese commentators interpreted the welcome received by their future emperor at Buckingham Palace as an indication that Japan had achieved the status of a first-class world power.

Not all Japanese believed that the British monarchy was a worthy reference for the young crown prince, however. In the year of Hirohito's European tour, Nagata Hidejirō (1876–1943), a member of the House of Peers and future mayor of Tokyo who was known for his strong nationalistic views, published a short book in English, *A Simplified Treatise on the Imperial House of Japan*. Nagata, who early in his book expressed his dissatisfaction with Fukuzawa's two treatises on the throne, argued that Japan's imperial house was superior to the British royal house: "King George V is of the Hanoverian family of Germany, which ascended to the British throne in 1714. . . . Compared with the Japanese Imperial Family, which is over two thousand years old, it can not be said to be a very old [dynasty]."[40]

Nagata noted that the "British people respect their King as the symbol of the nation," but then posed a question: "Are the devotion and attachment felt by the Japanese for their Imperial Family the same as those felt by the British people for their King?" Nagata's answer was short: "Certainly not." He insisted that it was impossible to regard the imperial family as the symbol of the people because this suggested that the imperial family and the people were independent of each other.[41] Nagata's twisted reasoning regarding the indivisible unity of the Japanese people and the imperial family is not the issue here. What is significant is Nagata's attempt to elevate Japan's imperial house above the British royal house at a time when some Japanese liberals were holding up the British polity as a paradigm.

In 1924, Hirohito, still regent, married Kuni-no-miya Nagako (1903–2000), daughter of a collateral house of the imperial family. As was appropriate at the time, the marriage between Hirohito and Nagako was arranged by formal introduction rather than being a "love match."[42] Emperor Hirohito made one important break with custom regarding married life, however. During the Occupation, the concubine system at court was abolished. Hirohito, with his commitment to monogamy, did not miss the ladies-in-waiting.[43] No one ever has been able to provide evidence that he was anything but a faithful husband to Nagako during more than fifty years of married life. Even when his advisors, after Nagako had given birth to four daughters but no son several years into their union, urged him to make use of the concubines to produce an heir to the throne,[44] Hirohito refused. Nakago gave birth to Akihito, the heir, on 23 December 1933.

Hirohito ascended to the throne in 1926 on the death of Emperor Taishō. The Cabinet, with the approval of the Privy Council, selected the reign name Shōwa. During Hirohito's regency and the early Shōwa period, Japanese authorities faced the first cohesive revolutionary challenge to the consolidated Meiji system, from the JCP, which was formed in 1922. The analysis by the Communist International (Comintern) of Japan's stage of development concluded that Japan remained backward enough to require a two-stage revolution, first a bourgeois-democratic revolution and then a proletarian-socialist one. The JCP eventually accepted this analysis and the prescription of the Comintern that one of the JCP's most urgent goals was the abolition of the monarchy.

The JCP's 1932 Theses, as had the 1928 Theses, employed a term, "emperor system" (*tennōsei*), that became commonly used to describe the monarchy after Japan's defeat in 1945. At the time, however, "emperor system," a translation of the English term "absolute monarchy," was a pejorative designation for the entire Meiji political system, which the JCP sought to overthrow. The 1932 "Theses on the Situation in Japan and the Tasks of the Communist Party" issued by the Comintern argued:

> The first starting point to estimate the concrete situation in Japan consists of the character and the relative role of the monarchy.
>
> The absolute monarchy which was formed in Japan after 1868 has maintained its full power in spite of all changes of policy, and has all the time increased its bureaucratic apparatus of coercion and oppression of the working masses. It based itself chiefly on the feudal parasitic class of landlords on the one hand and on a rapacious bourgeoisie that is rapidly becoming wealthy, on the other hand. It was constantly in a close bloc with the upper ranks of these classes and represented the interests of these two classes in a fairly flexible manner. At the same time it maintained its independence, its relatively great role and its absolute character, only slightly concealed by pseudo-constitutional forms. In order to protect its power and income, the monarchist bureaucracy exerted every effort to maintain in the country the most reactionary police regime, to preserve everything which was most barbarous in the economic and political life of the country. The monarchy is the main pillar of political reaction and all the relics of feudalism in the country. The monarchist state apparatus forms the firm backbone of the present dictatorship of the exploiting classes, and its destruction must be looked on as the first of the fundamental tasks of the revolution in Japan.[45]

The Japanese establishment, including the major political parties, reacted strongly to threats to the Meiji polity, even as the Diet extended democratic rights to the people. In 1925, three years after the formation of the JCP, the Diet passed the Peace Preservation Law and instituted universal male suffrage. Article 1 of the Peace Preservation Law reads: "Anyone who has formed an association with the objective of altering the *kokutai* or the system of private property, and anyone who has joined such an association with full knowledge of its object, shall be liable to imprisonment with or without hard labor for a term not exceeding ten years." This marks the first appearance of the term *kokutai* in law. Most communists in Imperial Japan were eventually imprisoned for violating the Peace Preservation Law.

Many analyses of the modern cult of the emperor, penned after Japan's attempt to dominate Asia militarily ended in disaster, have viewed the efforts of the Meiji political leaders who constructed the modern monarchy as motivated by sinister ends. Fujitani reminds us that this was not necessarily the case:

> Control through official culture was not understood in the negative images familiar to most students of Japan's so-called emperor system—such as shackling, enslaving, blinding, and making submissive, frustrating the development of modern subjectivity—but rather in positive terms, as a means of sweeping away ignorance, inflexibility, or darkness, and thus as knowledge in the positive sense.[46]

The local elites who competed in the 1880s to have their prefecture be the first to receive a copy of the imperial portrait were in a contest to be the most modern. Furthermore, the monarchy and the monarchy's role were not static, for Japan evolved rapidly. The particularly jingoistic national culture of the 1930s was, as is true of culture generally, the product of a specific time, although it naturally drew on Japan's existing cultural capital, both modern and premodern.

The Emperor System and the Fifteen-Year War, 1931–45

Although many scholars have found the roots of Japan's militarism in the Meiji era, in a more immediate sense the Manchurian Incident of

1931 was an important turning point. That year, the Japanese army, with the complicity of the government in Tokyo, began to extend its control of Chinese territory, thus souring relations not only with China, where nationalism was on the rise, but also with the United States and Britain. Domestically, only years after Hirohito became emperor, a series of terrorist acts carried out by elements within the military destroyed the fragile system of party government. Party governments had clashed with the army and navy on various issues, especially on the funding of the military. After the assassination of Prime Minister Inukai Tsuyoshi (b. 1855) in 1932, no head of a political party would serve as prime minister until after Japan's surrender.

The Cabinets of the 1930s claimed to transcend parties and partisan politics. Military leaders insisted that based on the constitutional principle of the emperor's right of supreme command, they answered to the emperor, not to the Cabinet or the Diet. Nationalists at the forefront of the "movement to clarify the national polity" (*kokutai meichō undō*), which emerged in 1934, targeted liberal supporters of parliamentary government for attack in a deliberate strategy to destroy parliamentary government. Even party politicians invoked the *kokutai* ideology to denigrate their opponents in the Diet. This proved a dangerous strategy because the *kokutai* ideology soon came to be used to question parliamentary government itself.

In 1935, Minobe was accused of contradicting the sacrosanct national polity for, in the eyes of his critics, holding that the emperor was "merely" an organ of the state rather than the state itself. Although Minobe was never jailed, he was driven from public life. According to his accusers, he had infringed on the limitless power of the emperor by distinguishing the emperor from the state. He was the most famous academician to be hounded by *kokutai* ideologues. Minobe's ordeal symbolized the defeat of the fragile experiment of broadening the parliament's policymaking role. Discrediting the parliament provided greater leeway to individuals and organizations that sought to monopolize the emperor's authority for their own political ends. What emerged more and more as the 1930s progressed was an environment unfriendly to those who might question, for example, the military's claim that its policies represented the imperial will.

After Japan commenced full-scale war with China in 1937, the state increased its efforts to inculcate the imperial ideology. The manner in which Foundation Day was celebrated mirrored the prevailing trends. Historian Andrew Gordon has shown that during the first decades of the twentieth century, especially during the period after World War I, various groups contested the meaning of Foundation Day. Democratic parties used the holiday to celebrate suffrage, democracy, and constitutional government.[47]

In contrast, by the late 1930s the state had appropriated Foundation Day as an exclusive celebration of emperor and empire. Debate over its meaning was no longer permitted. As the war with China continued and relations with the United States deteriorated, the 2,600th anniversary celebrations scheduled for 1940 assumed an especially important role in rallying people to the cause of the state. In December 1939, the Spiritual Mobilization Headquarters issued a set of rules that the Japanese were to observe in celebrating Foundation Day the following year. The first of the seven rules stated that at precisely 9:00 a.m. on 11 February, whistles, sirens, and bells were to sound throughout the Japanese empire, alerting all subjects to begin to "worship from afar" (*yōhai*) the imperial palace.[48] This holiday also marked the intensification of Japanese efforts to make colonized peoples into imperial subjects. It was on 11 February 1940 that the Japanese colonial authorities ordered all Koreans to replace their original names with Japanese ones within six months.[49]

The most ceremonial year in Imperial Japan was 1940; elsewhere I analyzed the various 2,600th anniversary celebrations.[50] More than 12,000 events were held to commemorate the anniversary, and 15,000 projects were completed, most of them in 1940 but also in the years preceding and following the anniversary itself.[51] Many of these events and undertakings involved extensive public works projects. In certain concrete ways, the emperor system was an economic issue in Imperial Japan.

It is misleading to portray the 2,600th anniversary celebrations as something simply foisted on the people by the central government. Several years before the Cabinet-level 2,600th Anniversary Celebration Bureau was formed in 1935, local notables in prefectures such as Nara that were rich in imperial sites were already at work lobbying the government regarding proper commemoration of the anniversary.[52] In 1936, the 2,600th Anniversary Celebration Bureau responded by announcing six major projects:

FIGURE 5. This stone monument is said to mark the spot in Okayama prefecture, recognized as authentic by a Ministry of Education committee in 1939, where the Palace of Takashima stood. According to the *Kojiki*, Emperor Jimmu spent eight years at Takashima during his eastward expedition. (From the *Kigen nisen roppyakunen shukuten giroku*, vol. 15 [Naikaku insatsukyoku, 1943]; reprinted with permission from the National Archives of Japan.)

1. improvement of the roads leading to the Kashihara Shrine and Emperor Jimmu's mausoleum;
2. investigation and preservation of sacred vestiges (or relics) of Jimmu;
3. improvement of roads leading to imperial tombs;
4. support for an international exposition;
5. construction of a national history museum; and
6. completion of a definitive study of Japanese culture.[53]

In 1938, the bureau also approved monies for the improvement of roads leading to the Miyazaki Shrine, which was also consecrated to Jimmu. Following is a tiny sampling of the flurry of activities and projects related to the anniversary celebrations.

The government's decision to grant official recognition to sites mentioned in accounts of Jimmu's exploits energized notables in localities along the route Jimmu was said to have followed in his eastward

FIGURE 6. Young volunteers at work in 1940 improving road access to the tomb of Emperor Junna (r. 823–33) in Kyoto prefecture. Although Junna was an actual emperor, there is no evidence that the tomb officially designated his is authentic. (From the *Kigen nisen roppyakunen shukuten giroku*, vol. 16 [Naikaku insatsukyoku, 1943]; reprinted with permission from the National Archives of Japan.)

expedition. In some cases, local men of influence had been working since the Meiji era to have their village recognized as the place where, for example, the appearance of a golden kite had tipped a critical battle in favor of the imperial army. Villages compiled pamphlets to make their case, often in competition with as many as eight other villages that also claimed to be the location a particular event involving Jimmu had taken place.[54] In late 1939, a committee of experts appointed by the Ministry of Education that included historians such as Hiraizumi Kiyoshi (1895–1984) of Tokyo Imperial University recognized nineteen additional sites in seven prefectures as having an authentic relationship to Jimmu.[55]

The government also underwrote extensive projects to upgrade the existing imperial landscape. The projects themselves were important, but also significant was the mechanism employed to achieve mass participation in these undertakings. Today in the city of Kashihara, near the baseball stadium, one can still find a stone monument commemorating the work of the 1,214,081 individuals who came in groups from throughout the empire in 1939 and 1940 for stays of a few weeks to broaden and beautify the Kashihara Shrine compound and improve the roads to the shrine and to Jimmu's mausoleum.[56] Much of the work to widen and lengthen the roads leading to the other 122 imperial tombs (of which many were of dubious validity, including those for the more than 20 emperors now regarded as legendary) was also carried out by people who labored for free in service to the throne.

The term "volunteers" may not be accurate to describe the members of numerous school groups that worked to better the imperial landscape, but representatives of groups such as the Greater Japan National Defense Women's Association (DaiNihon kokubō fujinkai) went to work at Kashihara Shrine and other imperial sites on their own initiative. The Women's Association was one of several mass organizations that provided women with a means to participate politically. The extent to which participation was enlisted from above or emerged from below is a difficult question to answer with precision, but what is significant is the number of people—several million—who took part, with their own hands, in sanctifying the myth of the unbroken imperial line dating from Jimmu. There were also less physically taxing ways for individuals to commemorate Jimmu's enthronement. When the 2,600th Anniversary Celebration Bureau sponsored a competition to select the "People's 2,600th Anniversary Song," 17,487 people submitted entries.[57]

Governmental and business organizations published a wealth of guides for individuals interested in visiting the new or improved imperial sites.[58] The response by tourists nearly overwhelmed certain localities in 1940. More than 1.25 million people made the Kashihara Shrine the site of their New Year's visit that year, a twentyfold increase over 1939. Another 700,000 tourists came to the shrine on 10 November, the day that Emperor Hirohito, in Tokyo, presided over the most important public celebration of Jimmu's accession held in 1940.[59] Tokyo and Kashihara were the sites where the most august commemorations of Foundation Day were held, but virtually no area of Japan was left untouched by Jimmu that year. Areas particularly significant on the imperial landscape, such as Kashihara, benefited not only from government largesse in the form of public works but also from the heightening of their stature on the national tourist landscape. The anniversary celebrations were staged the same year that Japan signed the Tripartite Pact, allying itself with the fascist dictatorships of Germany and Italy, countries whose spectac-

FIGURE 7. An enlarged version of the postmark issued in Kashihara on 11 February 1940, a day celebrated in Japan as the 2,600th anniversary of Emperor Jimmu's accession and the foundation of the empire. The top part of the postmark reads, "In commemoration of the 2,600th year of the era [that began with Jimmu's accession]." The bottom part, "15.2.11," refers to 11 February in the fifteenth year of Shōwa (the name of Emperor Hirohito's reign). In the middle is pictured the *Yatagarasu*, or crow with three claws, supposedly sent by Amaterasu to guide Jimmu through a particularly difficult part of his eastward expedition. (From the *Kigen nisen roppyakunen shukuten giroku* [Naikaku insatsukyoku, 1943], 9: 271; reprinted with permission from the National Archives of Japan.)

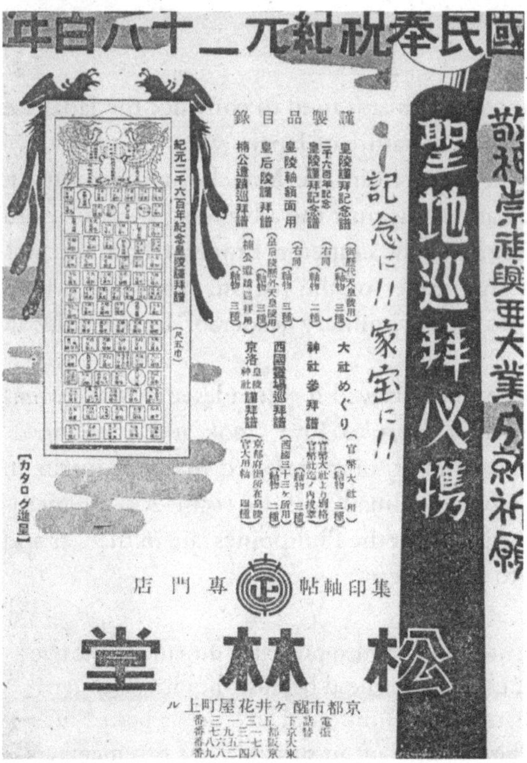

FIGURE 8. This advertisement by Shōrindō for memorabilia to commemorate holy visits to imperial sites was published in a government-issued guide to shrines. Tourists could have the table that appears on the left stamped upon visiting a particular imperial tomb. At the apex of the table appears the place for a stamp marking a visit to Emperor Jimmu's mausoleum. (Kigen nisen roppyakunen shukuten jimukyoku, *Jinja* [Naikaku insatsukyoku, 1939].)

ular mass demonstrations of nationalistic fervor had inspired Japanese planners.

The year 1940 was exceptional, but each Foundation Day celebrated from 1938 until the end of the war was the occasion for politicians to "clarify" Japan's "unparalleled" national polity. In a speech on 11 February 1941, Home Minister Hiranuma Kiichirō (1867–1952) reminded primary-school teachers that:

> Japan's national polity (*kokutai*) is unique in the world. Heaven sent down Ninigi-no-Mikoto [grandson of the Sun Goddess] to Kashihara in Yamato Province with a message that their posterity should reign over and govern Japan for ages eternal. It was on this happy day, 2,601 years ago, that our first Emperor, Jimmu, ascended to the Throne. Dynasties in foreign countries were created by men. Foreign kings, emperors and presidents are all created by men, but Japan has a Sacred Throne inherited from the Imperial Ancestors. Japanese Imperial Rule, therefore, is an extension of Heaven. Dynasties created by men may collapse, but the Heaven-created Throne is beyond men's power.[60]

The holiday was one of many mechanisms used to convince the Japanese of their uniqueness and of the holy nature of Japan's wars.

In Japan, fifteen years of war—from the Manchurian Incident in 1931 to the desperate suicide attacks against the advancing U.S. forces in 1945—were fought in the name of the emperor. Emperor Hirohito was the spiritual and constitutional leader of the nation. Numerous visual images of Emperor Hirohito as the military leader of Imperial Japan endure.

Memories of his wartime role survived for decades after the surrender. The Japanese interviewed in Haruko Taya Cook and Theodore F. Cook's *Japan at War: An Oral History* often referred to the emperor in speaking of the war. Naval officer Kojima Kiyofumi (1919–2002) remembered facing starvation in the jungle in the Philippines late in the war and leading a group of soldiers to surrender:

> As we came down from the mountains and approached the enemy, the two army men urged the rest of us to go on ahead because they had such terrible diarrhea. I suggested that we all rest instead. Later, they repeated their request. Finally they said they didn't want to surrender. As two members

FIGURE 9. Emperor Hirohito, Supreme Commander of the Army and Navy, at a military review in 1942. He appears in the center, holding binoculars. (Photograph courtesy Kyodo Photo Service.)

> of the Imperial Army, they'd rather "die for the sake of the Emperor." They asked me to leave them a hand grenade as we left them.[61]

Japanese soldiers were forbidden by imperial rescript from surrendering, and the few who did often brought shame on their families. As Japan's losses mounted in the summer of 1945, the most common image of Emperor Hirohito broadcast in newsreels showed him, in a benevolent gesture to bereaved families, visiting the Yasukuni Shrine to honor the war dead.[62] The Meiji government sponsored construction of the shrine, completed in Tokyo in 1869, to honor the souls of Japanese who died fighting for the nation.

After the bloody invasion of Okinawa (the only prefecture in Japan proper to suffer a land battle), the atomic bombing of Hiroshima, the Soviet Union's entry into the war against Japan, and the atomic bombing of Nagasaki, Japan's attempt to subjugate Asia came to a catastrophic end. On 15 August 1945, the government's decision to end the war was broadcast by radio to the people. Emperor Hirohito himself made the announcement (in fact, what was broadcast was a recording of the emperor's announcement, but listeners believed that they were hearing a live broadcast). It was on this occasion that millions of Japanese heard their emperor's voice for the first time. The experience remains etched in the memory of the Japanese who listened that day, and the broadcast represented the first step in the postwar remaking of the throne. Within less than a year, the Meiji system, most notably the Meiji Constitution, to which seventy million Japanese had become accustomed, would be swept away by the reforms of the Occupation.

CHAPTER 2

The Constitutional Symbolic Monarchy

In the aftermath of Japan's devastating defeat, the palace's campaign to remake the throne proceeded on several levels at once. It included reconceptualizing the imperial house as an institution similar to the British royal house. The Japanese could point to the example of Britain, a constitutional monarchy widely viewed as one of the world's most stable democracies, to argue that the imperial house was not necessarily an impediment to the development of parliamentary democracy. Six weeks after the end of the war, Emperor Hirohito, coached by his advisors, publicly announced his vision of the postwar monarchy. During his first postsurrender interview, with two U.S. journalists, the emperor called for Japan to become a constitutional monarchy like that of Britain.[1]

The Occupation reforms are widely interpreted as having made the Japanese monarchy similar to the British monarchy. But in constitutional terms only a tenuous link exists between those Japanese who cited the British monarchy as a model in the immediate postsurrender period and the symbolic monarchy that resulted from the Constitution of Japan. In the six months between the surrender and the release of SCAP's draft constitution, many prominent Japanese invoked the British monarchy to defend imperial sovereignty. And the essential lesson that many Japanese in late 1945 and early 1946 saw in the British monarchy was not that the king was the symbol of the nation, but that the king retained legal sovereignty.

In a January 1946 essay "Democracy and Our Parliamentary System,"[2] Minobe Tatsukichi, arguably the preeminent Japanese constitutional scholar at the time, addressed the question of whether Japan's present parliamentary system was compatible with democracy, and, if not, what reforms were necessary. Minobe pointed out that although people in all democracies accepted the principle of popular sovereignty, there were many diverse forms of political organization: "There are countries where as a concept the principle of popular sovereignty (*kokumin shukenshugi*) is accepted, but the monarch as a representative of the people exercises sovereignty (*tōchiken o okonau*)."[3]

Minobe stressed that the sovereign imperial house was "our country's greatest strength." In reference to the ongoing debate about the terms of surrender in the Potsdam Declaration, Minobe articulated the form of democracy that he considered suitable for Japan: "Even when one speaks of the democratization of the [Meiji Constitution] . . . one must interpret this as meaning democracy under a monarchy. [In the case of Japan, democratization] is not the people themselves as supreme power-holders, but rather that supreme power, namely sovereignty, is vested in the monarch; the monarch exercises sovereignty."[4] Minobe emphasized that it was entirely possible to democratize Japan without changing the emperor's constitutional position. Representative of much of Japan's political elite (at least the part of the elite that favored or at least accepted the concept of parliamentary democracy), Minobe sought a return to the period of Taishō Democracy, when the Lower House, or House of Representatives, of the Diet emerged as a key player in decisionmaking. Minobe's stalwart defense of imperial sovereignty may seem surprising in light of the persecution he suffered during the 1930s, but he believed that parliamentary democracy could prosper in Japan under his interpretation of the Meiji Constitution.

The most explicit comparison between the Japanese and British monarchies that appeared in the Government Section's two-volume official history of the Occupation political reforms can be found in a February 1946 document submitted by the Japanese government in support of a constitutional draft compiled by its constitution committee. Chaired by State Minister Matsumoto Jōji (1877–1954), the Matsumoto Committee included Minobe, Kiyomiya Shirō (1899–1989), Miyazawa Toshiyoshi (1899–1976), and other eminent constitutional scholars.[5] The "General Explanation of the Constitutional Revision Drafted by the Government" stressed that even while maintaining imperial sovereignty, some minor reforms to the Meiji Constitution would give Japan "a system similar to that of England wherein the so-called 'parliamentary democracy' has complete sway."[6]

JCP leader Miyamoto Kenji (1908–2007), who had been released in

October 1945 after thirteen years of imprisonment, belittled the use of the British monarchy to protect the emperor system:

> So long as sovereignty rests with the monarch, it will be a privileged system of rule as before, a conception in opposition to democracy. . . . Supporters of the emperor system often cite the British structure of rule, but we must acknowledge the following. In the present war, Britain, with the United States, the Soviet Union, China and other countries, was on the side of those fighting European fascism and the Japanese emperor system.[7]

In fact, the Matsumoto Committee's suggestion that parliamentary democracy could develop under a constitutionally sovereign monarch was not inconceivable in light of British history. Today, the British monarch retains legal sovereignty, but decisionmaking is centered in Parliament. However, the Matsumoto Committee's suggested revisions struck Occupation authorities as providing Japan with a grossly insufficient base for democracy, given that country's recent history. During the 1930s, the principle of imperial sovereignty had been used to stifle parliamentary politics. By adopting the actual functioning of the British constitutional monarchy as their model, Occupation authorities sought to prevent a recurrence of the throne being used against democracy; their solution was to align the constitutional position of the emperor with the symbolic role they intended him to play in practice.

The Symbolic Monarchy as Japanese Tradition

Although the British royal house served as reference for the postwar Japanese monarchy, many Japanese today, especially conservatives, tell a different story of how the symbolic monarchy developed in Japan. They argue that the postwar monarchy represents a return to the true Japanese tradition of a symbolic imperial house that existed before the Meiji Restoration of 1868. This interpretation emerged in the months before the Government Section constitutionally redefined the emperor as a symbol.

Shortly after Japan's surrender, the editors of the newly founded intellectual journal *Sekai*, eager for essays critical of the emperor system, asked Tsuda Sōkichi (1873–1961) to submit a piece about the monarchy. *Sekai* was a journal devoted to creating "New Japan." Liberals in postwar Japan shared with their counterparts in Germany a wish for a thorough rupture with the shameful past. Tsuda, it seemed to the editors, had good reason to be an opponent of the monarchy. In some of his prewar writings, Tsuda had suggested that the *Kojiki* and *Nihon shoki*, canonical texts of Japan's official imperial history, were largely mythological. In the context of the ideological mobilization that Japan underwent after its simmering conflict with China escalated into full-scale war in 1937, he came under attack for contradicting the national polity.

In 1939, Tsuda, a professor at Waseda University, was appointed guest lecturer in Oriental history in the Faculty of Law at Tokyo University. As a result of this appointment, Tsuda attracted further attention from right-wing ideologues, who accused him of undermining the national polity.[8] In February 1940, Tsuda's major writings were banned. In March of that year, he was charged with infringing Article 26 of the Publication Law, which protected the dignity of the imperial house. Tsuda spent the next four years entangled in court battles until the charges were dismissed in 1944.

In 1946, to the surprise of *Sekai*'s editors and much of the intellectual world, Tsuda submitted an essay supportive of the monarchy's role in Japan's long history. Tsuda wrote the first version of his essay in January 1946, before the initial drafting of the new constitution. Before publishing his essay, the editors of *Sekai* wrote Tsuda a long letter in which they expressed their concern about his defense of the imperial house. They were afraid that Tsuda's essay would play into the hands of conservatives who sought to maintain the national polity defined by imperial sovereignty. In response, Tsuda added a few pages at the end of his essay critical of the Meiji emperor system. Only in these last pages did Tsuda use the terms *kokutai* and *tennōsei*. According to Tsuda, both words as used in contemporary debates about the monarchy were misleading. Throughout his essay, he used the term "imperial house" (*kōshitsu*) to describe the premodern monarchy and distinguish it from the modern emperor system.

Sekai published the essay in its April 1946 issue, along with the lengthy letter of concern that the editors had sent.[9] Tsuda began the essay with his version of how the Japanese state (*kokka*) was formed. According to him, rather than resulting from the dramatic military campaign of the mythical Emperor Jimmu, the Yamato state came into being in the Kyushu area around the second century CE. This state established by the imperial ancestors gradually and peacefully incorporated neighboring states into its domain over a period of two or three centuries. By the sixth century, if not the fifth, the monarchy's authority was solidified over most of "Japan." According to Tsuda's account of the monarchy's extension of its rule, "There were no circumstances in which the people plotted resistance against the imperial house."[10] Tsuda stressed that emperors refrained from directly involving themselves in military affairs and emphasized that the true work of emperors was not politics in the usual sense of the term. In other words, emperors reigned, others ruled.

According to Tsuda, the monarchy played a cultural role, especially in the introduction of superior Chinese culture. The monarchy's authority, Tsuda wrote, was spiritual:

> The imperial house, for the powerholders in the imperial court and the local elites, was something with which one should be intimate, should esteem; by entrusting themselves to the imperial house, they were able . . . to protect their lifestyle and position. . . . Among them a feeling of being one ethnic group (*minzoku*) was created, and they regarded the imperial house as a symbol of this feeling.[11]

Tsuda's word for "symbol," *shōchō*, was the same word later used to define the emperor's position in the Postwar Constitution.[12] There is no evidence, however, that this interpretation influenced the U.S. drafters of the constitution.

Tsuda insisted that serving as a symbol was the "essence" (*honshitsu*) of the monarchy and that this was the reason that the institution was able to survive century after century. In the latter part of his essay, Tsuda argued that the Meiji oligarchs had perverted the monarchy's essence:

> [They] isolated the imperial house from the people and placed it in a high position in order to demonstrate its dignity; along with Chinese ideas there was another model: at the time it was necessary to import European ways. With the [imported] concept of opposition between the sovereign and the people as a basis, they strengthened the authority of the Emperor vis-à-vis the people, and as far as possible suppressed the people's political role. . . . The [Meiji] Constitution was established under those conditions.[13]

Then, during the 1930s, militarists and bureaucrats further adulterated the monarchy by invoking the emperor for their policies:

> The militarists and the bureaucrats who followed them used the fond feelings the people have toward the imperial house as well as the provisions of the [Meiji] Constitution, and employing distorted national history as proof, they insisted that politics had to be carried out according to the direct rule (*shinsei*) of the Emperor.[14]

The militarists and bureaucrats were then able to invoke the imperial will to propel Japan into war against the United States and Britain.

Tsuda stressed that if the monarchy's position reverted to that of a symbol, the institution's survival would not contradict the new democratic system. In addition, it could play a positive role in Japan's democracy:

> To state it concretely, the significance of the imperial house's survival lies in [its role] as the center of the people's unity, as the living spiritual symbol (*shōchō*) of the people. . . . In the present period when the people themselves are supposed to direct all the affairs of the nation, the imperial house is the people's imperial house (*kōshitsu wa kokumin no kōshitsu*), and the Emperor is "our Emperor" (*tennō wa "warera no tennō"*).[15]

In their letter to Tsuda, the editors of *Sekai* warned him of the potential influence of his essay: "Make no mistake that [conservatives seeking to support the national polity] could not have imagined in their dreams that a thesis in support of the imperial house could come from a scholar of national history like yourself."[16] The editors stressed that the political left, for different reasons, would also be astonished. The editors sought to clarify Tsuda's intentions for readers by drawing a distinction between the emperor system and the imperial house: "To use the definition of Nosaka [Sanzō] and Yamakawa [Hitoshi],[17] one might say that a thesis in support of the imperial institution is not the same as a thesis in support of the emperor system. If that is the case, then the professor's essay by no means supports the reactionary forces that seek to minimize reform of the present system."[18] In a conversation with the editors, Tsuda indeed had emphasized that his purpose was not to support the emperor system that was a construct of the Meiji period.

Tsuda's interpretation went against the conservative line that sought to maintain or reestablish the Meiji system in the years immediately after the war. At the same time, it worked to preserve the monarchy. Tsuda's interpretation eventually would provide the nascent symbolic monarchy with legitimacy by linking it to Japan's past. In 1946, however, the release of a revised constitutional draft seemed, to many Japanese, to have turned the world upside down.

Left-wing intellectuals who sought to abolish the throne singled out Tsuda's essay for attack. Takakura Teru (1891–1986), a writer who had spent the decade before Japan's surrender in and out of prison, reacted with dismay to the parts of Tsuda's essay that were supportive of the monarchy. He published his rebuttal in the August 1946 edition of *Chūō kōron*.[19] This respected journal received more letters about Takakura's essay than about any other piece it published that year. Near the beginning of his essay, Takakura implicitly called for further study of the people's feelings (*kokumin kanjō*) toward the monarchy throughout history. Takakura pointed out that in Aizu prefecture, an area that had resisted the imperial army at the time of the Meiji Restoration, some people continued to hope for the restoration of the shogunate even into the early twentieth century. According to Takakura, there were people in Aizu, where during the Boshin War (1868–69) the imperial restorationist forces had treated the defeated Aizu side with brutality, who welcomed the outbreak of the Russo-Japanese War in 1904 because they assumed that Japan would lose and that a loss would topple the emperor and lead to the restoration of the Tokugawa shogunate. When Japan was victorious, the Aizu contingent was disappointed. Such anecdotes called into question Tsuda's assertion of a long history of fond feelings between the people and the monarchy.

Tsuda was not the only person arguing that the symbolic monarchy represented a "return" to previous practice. Watsuji Tetsurō (1889–1960) also interpreted the emperor's new constitutional position as rooted in domestic tradition. Whereas Tsuda had been accused during the 1930s of undermining the national polity, Watsuji, a professor of ethics at Tokyo University, had played a role in propagandizing imperial myths. He had been a member of the committee that compiled the *Kokutai no hongi* (Cardinal principles of the national entity of Japan), the handbook distributed to teachers in 1937 to reiterate the throne's centrality to the national polity. According to historian Robert Bellah, Watsuji argued that "the core of ethical value in the Japanese tradition and the reason for its superiority to other traditions lies in the Way of Reverence for the Emperor."[20]

After the war, Watsuji, in spite of his close connections to the prewar state, drew conclusions about the emperor's role in premodern Japan that lessened his attachment to the Meiji system. He reacted to the redefinition of the emperor's constitutional position with what one of Watsuji's biographers has called "indifference" (*mutonjaku*).[21] Watsuji's lack of interest in the demise of the Meiji political system was no less surprising to some observers than Tsuda's defense of the monarchy. Scholars including Bellah have argued, however, that Watsuji's view of the emperor's role in Japanese society was consistent across the divide of 1945, since Watsuji always saw the emperor in ethical and cultural terms and not from a political perspective.

As early as November 1945, Watsuji was arguing that the emperor's political role under the Meiji system represented a break with previous practice.[22] In response to a 1946 essay by Sasaki Sōichi (1878–1965), a constitutional scholar and member of the House of Peers, Watsuji articulated his view of the national polity in the context of the new constitution. Sasaki argued that the Postwar Constitution, by changing the locus of sovereignty, had altered the national polity. Sasaki thus opposed the new constitution. Watsuji sought to refute Sasaki's claim that the national polity had been modified.[23]

Watsuji argued that the new constitution had merely changed the "form of government" (*seitai*) developed during the Meiji era, whereas the essential Japanese characteristic of revering the emperor remained unaltered. Watsuji noted that "the tradition of the emperor dates from the origin of the country and is not limited to Meiji and after. Thus doubts arise as to whether what [Sasaki] calls the 'conception of the national polity (*kokutai*) . . . ' is a product of history from the origin of the country, or [only] a product since Meiji."[24] Watsuji pointed out that "for a long time before Meiji the emperor was not the superintendent of sovereignty (*tōchiken no sōransha*)."[25] "At the time of the Meiji Restoration, people recognized this, as indicated by the slogan 'restoration of imperial rule.'"[26]

Watsuji stressed that the original term for the emperor, *sumerano-mikoto*, expressed the traditional function of the emperor, which was "to unify" (*tōitsu suru*). In contemporary terms, Watsuji noted, this role could be expressed by the phrase "the symbol . . . of the unity of the people," the words used in the new constitution. Watsuji chided legal scholars that if the "conception of symbol is missing from the usual jurisprudence, then it would be good if it were incorporated from philosophy, where it has long been used."[27] Watsuji used the term "essence," as had Tsuda, to describe the emperor's position as a symbol. Watsuji insisted that the emperor's role as the "symbol . . . of the unity of the Japanese people" was not necessarily related to the state: "This unity is not a political unity, but a cultural (*bunkateki*) unity. The Japanese people, according to language, history, and customs, and all cultural activities, have formed a cultural community (*bunka kyōdōtai*)."[28] Watsuji argued that people's consciousness of this unity was based on the tradition of revering the emperor. For Watsuji, the demise of the Meiji political system in no way threatened this tradition.

Watsuji's and Tsuda's interpretations were buttressed by the work of Ishii Ryōsuke (1907–1993). When the war ended in 1945, Ishii was professor of premodern Japanese legal history at Tokyo University. The foremost scholar in his field, Ishii had not suffered persecution for his writings under the imperial system as had Tsuda (Ishii had been one of the scholars who submitted a petition in support of Tsuda to the Tokyo District Court in 1942).[29] And unlike Watsuji, Ishii had refrained from lending his support to official efforts to propagate imperial mythology.

Like Tsuda and Watsuji, Ishii turned to Japan's long history to analyze the monarchy. Ishii's scholarship was known for its meticulous attention to empirical details, and his book *Tennō* (Emperor; 1950), which analyzed the emperor's historical role from a legal perspective, was no exception. Ishii saw the monarchy's lengthy history, which he divided into six periods, as an ongoing story of continuities and discontinuities. Ishii stressed that the postwar principle of popular sovereignty was a significant rupture. The emperor long had served as a symbol to the Japanese, but never before had his position been based constitutionally on the will of the people. Ishii nonetheless drew conclusions about the emperor's historical role that were broadly similar to those of Tsuda and Watsuji.

Ishii began his concluding chapter by emphasizing the two periods before 1945 when the imperial house had borrowed models from abroad: "The form of the emperor system that developed naturally was not one of direct rule (*shinsei*) by the emperor. It was only in the Nara era [710–84] . . . and the modern era [1868–1945] that direct rule by the emperor was advocated and took place; however, both these periods were characterized by the importation of law."[30] According to Ishii, the original system was characterized by an emperor (or, in rare cases, an empress) who reigned but "did not rule" (*shissei suru koto wa nai*).[31] In other words, although the emperor was the "source of the right to rule," he "did not actually govern."[32] Throughout the 700-year-long feudal period (1185–1868), direct imperial rule (with one extremely short-lived exception) was not known in Japan.

Ishii pointed out that although many people thought that the new constitution had brought Japan into line with the development of monarchies throughout the world, this was not necessarily the case:

> One must say that [the fact that the monarch did not rule throughout most of Japanese history] is the unique characteristic of the emperor system as a monarchy. One cannot deny that when monarchies continue for a long time, the general tendency is for the original autocratic form to give way gradually to a form that does not rule. There is the . . . theory that Japan is nothing more than another such example. . . . However, in the case of Japan, the original form was for the emperor not to rule.[33]

Ishii decried the simplistic debates as to whether the new constitution had altered the national polity: "If the issue of the national polity is who is the superintendent of sovereignty, then one must say that the national polity has changed. Even a three-year old child can understand this."[34]

However, Ishii disputed the notion that the Meiji Constitution incorporated a timeless national polity by instituting direct imperial rule. The empirical evidence put forth in his book strongly called into question such a claim. In the concluding paragraphs of the book, Ishii emphasized the need to view the emperor's new position in the context of Japan's lengthy history:

> According to the establishment of the Constitution of Japan, the position and function of the emperor, compared to the period of the Meiji Constitution, has undergone a revolutionary change. It is impossible to deny this. It also cannot be denied that . . . this caused a great shock to

> people who thought of the national polity as rule by the emperor. . . . However, the national polity that these people had in mind has no historical basis. . . . The author interprets the original form (*honrai no sugata*) of imperial rule as the "principle of entrusting matters to others" (*suikyōshugi*) and for this reason [the imperial institution] has been extremely flexible.[35]

Ishii's final sentence stressed that the emperor's new position was not revolutionary after all: "It is not necessary to interpret the emperor system established by the Constitution of Japan as a great reform expressed by the phrase 'change in the national polity.'" Along the same lines as Tsuda and Watsuji, Ishii interpreted the emperor's new position as symbol as rooted firmly in Japan's tradition.

Interpreting the Emperor's New Role

Constitutional scholar Koseki Shōichi has reinterpreted the Occupation-era reform of the Japanese legal system to have been far more of a cooperative endeavor between the Americans and the Japanese than previously understood.[36] It is nonetheless true that in the case of Chapter I of the constitution, "The Emperor," the U.S. drafters, in the face of particularly stern resistance from Japanese authorities, redefined the emperor's position more radically than even the JSP had proposed, meeting the JCP's demand for popular sovereignty while stopping short of the communists' call for the monarchy's abolition.[37] Until the Spanish constitution of 1978 defined that country's king as the "head of state, the symbol of its unity and permanence," Japan was the only country in the world whose constitution explicitly defined the monarch—a human being—as the "symbol" of the nation. It still is not entirely understood why the U.S. drafters selected this term, although their model was undoubtedly the British monarchy.[38]

Whereas the British monarch's role had gradually become limited to largely symbolic functions even while it retained its historical legal sovereignty, the Constitution of Japan transformed the emperor into a symbol overnight. In spite of the arguments put forth by Tsuda, Watsuji, and Ishii, most Japanese legal scholars found the word "symbol" to be alien. But the term was not necessarily more opaque than *kokutai*, the mystical term used so often in Imperial Japan to describe the monarchy's sacrosanct position as the core of the national polity. The American

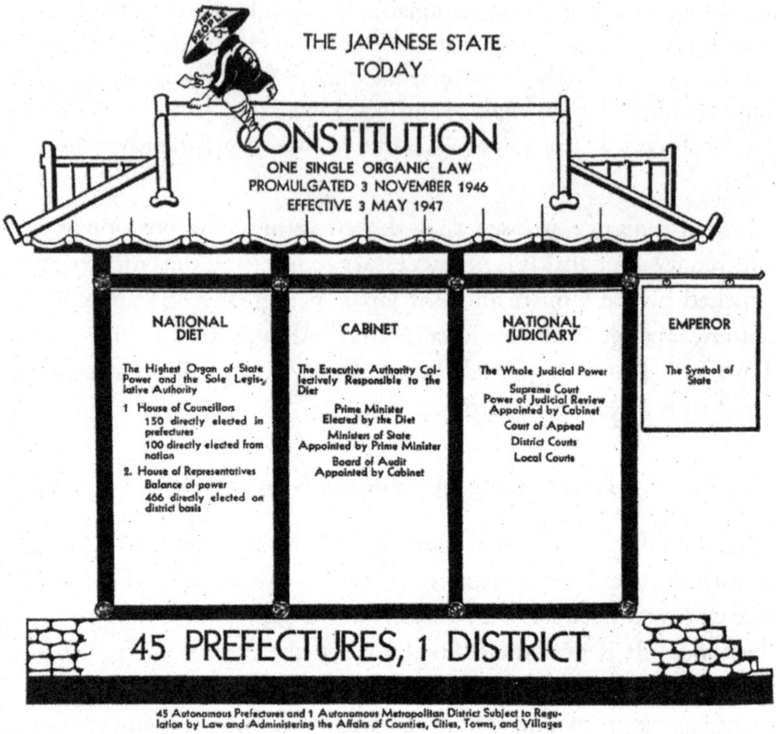

FIGURE 10. The U.S. drafters of the Constitution of Japan drew this chart to explain how the revamped Japanese governmental system would function. In comparing the emperor to a flag, the Americans no doubt had in mind their own national symbol. However, unlike an inanimate flag, a symbolic emperor walks and talks, and thus is a far more complex symbol to manage (as well as analyze). (Supreme Commander for the Allied Powers, Government Section, *Political Reorientation of Japan, September 1945 to September 1948* [Washington, DC: U.S. Government Printing Office, 1948], 1: 144.)

drafters were themselves unsure of how to articulate what they meant by a symbolic emperor. The Government Section's official history, published in English in 1948, specified:

> The Emperor's role would be that of a social monarch, no more.
>
> The plain language of the document itself makes it perfectly clear that the imperial institution is no longer the source of any authority whatsoever, can exercise no powers, and is certainly not indestructible. The Emperor is now no more than the crowning pinnacle of the structure, bearing no functional relation to the frame itself.[39]

A SCAP chart of Japan's reformed polity even pictured the emperor as a flag hanging from the governmental structure.[40] This chart suggested that the emperor was a passive entity, no more than a mirror that reflected the sentiments of the people. Nonetheless, Richard A. Poole, who was a navy ensign assigned to the Government Section who codrafted the chapter on the emperor, stressed in an interview fifty years after the constitution went into effect that "we did not intend for the emperor to sit in the palace and do nothing."[41]

Poole recalled that he and the other members of the Government Section broadly used the British monarchy as a model. However, the model the British throne provided for separating the symbolic from the political was imperfect, as recent British history had demonstrated.

In 1938, King George VI (r. 1936–52) appeared on the balcony of Buckingham Palace with Prime Minister Neville Chamberlain (1869–1940) to celebrate in front of cheering crowds the signing of the Munich Agreement.[42] The Munich Agreement resulted in dividing Czechoslovakia. Chamberlain's policy of appeasement, while popular at the time in Britain, was by no means uncontested. The king's action, to the disgust of Winston Churchill (1874–1965) and other opponents of appeasement, indicated the crown's support for placating Adolf Hitler. Even if the king had no formal decisionmaking authority, his ceremonial acts could have great political meaning. In postwar Japan, this area of ceremonial acts also was to be controversial, as the Japanese sought to define the role of their symbolic emperor.

The Postwar Constitution's unusual origins not only served to undermine its legitimacy but also shaped the manner in which it was interpreted subsequently. Once it became apparent that SCAP would insist on the passage of its constitutional draft, the Cabinet headed by Shidehara Kijūrō (1872–1951) first tried to win modifications in the wording of the text. Its next tactic was to offer, during the Diet debates, interpretations that minimized the changes in the emperor's position. The Diet played no role in the initial drafting of the Postwar Constitution, but some revisions, mostly minor, suggested by representatives were incorporated into the final version. The Diet was also the arena in which the new constitution was first officially interpreted. SCAP initially refrained from publicly clarifying interpretations to maintain the fiction that the draft was mostly a creation of the Japanese government. Politicians outside the Cabinet, legal scholars, and all other Japanese who did not have access to SCAP were confused about the emperor's new position.

A burning issue in the Diet was whether the proposed constitution would alter Japan's national polity, understood by most people at the time to be defined by imperial sovereignty. The interpretations of Tsuda and Watsuji were largely unknown then, and that of Ishii appeared later.[43] The conservative Shidehara Cabinet found itself in the unenviable position of claiming that the national polity had been maintained even though the Postwar Constitution's preamble begins, "We, the Japanese people . . . do proclaim that sovereign power rests with the people." To assert that the national polity had not changed, the Shidehara Cabinet deliberately blurred the locus of sovereignty by including the emperor in its definition of the people (*kokumin*). Under interpellation, Kanamori Tokujirō (1886–1959), the main government spokesman, acknowledged that sovereignty lay with the people. But he then argued that in the proposed constitution the term *kokumin* "refers to the whole of the Japanese people, including the emperor."[44]

The Diet, especially the House of Peers, included several of Japan's leading scholars. Critics of the government's attempt to downplay the constitutional modifications such as Nanbara Shigeru (1889–1974), president of Tokyo Imperial University, could not accept Kanamori's line of reasoning about the locus of sovereignty. Although Kanamori's interpretation sparked a series of debates among constitutional scholars, it did not last even a few years. A consensus soon emerged among scholars that popular sovereignty and monarchical sovereignty were incompatible.[45] But for decades thereafter, the left remembered the government's attempt to muddle the locus of sovereignty.

The Shidehara Cabinet's effort to preserve a measure of imperial sovereignty was the most blatant of its mostly unsuccessful attempts to obfuscate the constitutional change that had taken place. Shidehara's successor as prime minister, Yoshida Shigeru (1878–1967), sought in December 1946 to maintain the provisions for lèse-majesté in the revised criminal code. This led General MacArthur to clarify publicly that the emperor enjoyed no special legal protection under the new constitution.[46]

Many of the government's constitutional interpretations minimizing change proved untenable. But the government's attempt to muddle the significance of the new constitution created a polemical environment in which politicians and scholars seeking to emphasize reformation proposed equally puzzling interpretations of the constitution and Japan's national polity. In an essay written in late 1946, Minobe wrote that it was sophistry for the government to insist that Japan even remained a monarchy under the new constitution:

> Since the concept of popular sovereignty is opposed to the sovereignty of the monarch, if one recognizes that sovereignty belongs to the people, then one can do nothing else but deny that sovereignty belongs to the monarch. It is meaningless to say that sovereignty belongs to the people including the emperor.
>
> Since there is no doubt that popular sovereignty becomes the basis of the state, to claim that to a certain degree monarchism has been preserved is, I think, a lie to try to deceive the people.[47]

Minobe also found ridiculous the government's claim that the constitution was based on the will of the people, since the people had played no role in drafting it.

Within a year, however, Minobe reversed his opinion on the question of Japan's polity. This time, he argued vehemently that Japan remained a monarchy even if the people were sovereign. "I believe that there is no doubt that Japan's form of government did not become republican but remains monarchical as before."[48] Minobe was responding to a question exercising constitutional scholars at the time: had Japan become a republic?

Minobe's disciple, Miyazawa Toshiyoshi (1899–1976), a pillar of Tokyo University's Faculty of Law after the war, also found the government's attempt to minimize the extent of the constitutional modifications absurd. But whereas Minobe was a prewar liberal who had supported parliamentary government under the Meiji Constitution and who opposed constitutional revision, Miyazawa became a champion of the new constitution and emerged as one of its leading first-generation interpreters.

In responding to the government's line about sovereignty and the national polity, Miyazawa insisted that the people, which did not include the emperor, were sovereign. Miyazawa argued that the new constitution so limited the emperor's role that the "natural conclusion was that Japan was no longer a monarchy but had become a republic (*kyōwakoku*)."[49] Later, philosopher Katsube Mitake (1916–2005) wrote of the popularity that Miyazawa's interpretation enjoyed after the war: "The way of thinking that 'Japan was no longer a monarchy but had become a republic' (Miyazawa Toshiyoshi, *Kenpō*) has been taught for twenty years in college classrooms throughout the country."[50]

How could Japan be a republic when it retained a monarchy? Today, Japanese scholars rarely describe their country's polity as "republican." Seven decades after the Constitution of Japan was promulgated, Miyazawa's interpretation seems, at least on first examination, no less dated than Kanamori's claim that the emperor maintained a measure of sovereignty. The debate over whether Japan had become a republic symbolized the confusion that the foreign-authored chapter on the emperor sparked among Japanese.

Contentious debates over the locus of sovereignty cooled by the end of the Occupation because most scholars rejected the view that the constitution retained imperial sovereignty.[51] Defining the emperor's public position and role nonetheless would remain problematic throughout the postwar era. It was not clear to the Japanese whether the emperor remained "head of state" (*genshu*) under the new constitution. Another constitutionally ambiguous area was the extent and nature of the emperor's public acts. Today, the government recognizes three categories of acts by the emperor: (1) private acts; (2) the thirteen public acts in matters of state provided for in the constitution; and (3) public acts in his position as symbol (which are not acts in matters of state).[52] The first two categories were recognized when the Diet reviewed the draft constitution; the third was defined explicitly only in 1952.

The term *genshu* does not appear in the Postwar Constitution, which is vague regarding the identity of the head of state. There is no question that the domestic head of government is now the prime minister, as is the case in Great Britain. One could argue that the prime minister, as the highest elected representative of the sovereign people, should also represent Japan to the outside world. Complicating the matter, however, is the constitutional provision that the emperor ceremonially performs functions usually reserved for heads of state, such as receiving foreign ambassadors and ministers (Article 7.9). Yet the emperor carries out his limited acts in matters of state only "with the advice and approval of the

Cabinet." Some scholars have argued therefore that the Cabinet, collectively, is the "head of state."

The confusion dates back to the SCAP Government Section's attempt to incorporate two seemingly contradictory constitutional principles: (1) the first of the three points that MacArthur directed the Government Section to follow in drafting a new constitution: "The Emperor is at the head of the State";[53] and (2) popular sovereignty. The constitution, in providing for popular sovereignty and a monarch as head of state, represented an amalgam that, to the Japanese, seemed unprecedented. The confusion that it engendered among the Japanese was only heightened by their initial ignorance of MacArthur's intention to make the emperor head of state. Diet representatives asked the Shidehara Cabinet to explain why the term *genshu* was not used in the constitutional draft to describe the emperor's position and whether the emperor remained head of state. Kanamori's responses to these questions were generally vague, but at one point he ventured the following interpretation: "The Emperor will be treated as a head of state (*genshu*) on the ceremonial plane of international relations."[54] Ignored in all the controversy was the fact that there was, and still is, no international standard for designating a head of state. Every country is free to designate whomever it pleases as its international representative.

Defining the extent and nature of the emperor's public acts was a more complex matter, however. The Occupation authorities sought to establish an explicit distinction between the emperor in public and the emperor in private. Shortly after the surrender, Japanese authorities asked SCAP if the emperor could make a trip to the Ise Shrine to report the end of the war to the imperial ancestors. SCAP gave its permission, but only for the emperor to make the trip to this most sacred imperial shrine as a private act.[55] In this case, SCAP was particularly concerned with establishing the principle of separation of state and religion. Today the emperor remains the high priest of Shinto, but only in his private capacity.

During the Diet debates on the constitutional draft, Kanamori explained that the revised constitution was designed to draw a boundary between the emperor in private and the emperor in public: "The basic way of thinking underlying the drafting of this constitution was to distinguish clearly between the emperor's public position and his purely private position; therefore in this constitution his . . . public position is clearly written."[56] Kanamori confirmed that the emperor's public position was limited to thirteen acts in matters of state: "In this constitution, the emperor's functions (*kennō*) are concentrated in Articles 6 and 7. . . . The emperor's functions are only those listed. There are no other functions [for the emperor]."[57] An example of an act in matters of state would be the emperor's ceremonial appointment of the chief justice of the Supreme Court. If the emperor's public functions were limited to the thirteen acts in matters of state provided for by the constitution, then the corollary was that all other acts of the emperor were private.

It soon became evident that in practice the constitution provided the emperor with little to do publicly. Under the Meiji Constitution, the emperor had the legal authority to open the Diet; the Postwar Constitution includes no such provision. In June 1946, however, officials from the Cabinet Legislation Bureau and the two houses of the Diet decided, out of respect for tradition, that the emperor would attend the opening ceremony and make a statement.[58] This maintained the appearance that nothing had changed.

On 23 June 1947, Emperor Hirohito—in what certainly appeared to be his public role as emperor—attended the opening of the first Diet session under the new constitution. This practice then became a precedent (*senrei*) in the Diet.[59] This act was not necessarily justified constitutionally, however. Similarly, in February 1946 Hirohito began a series of domestic tours in his public position as emperor that, by 1954, were to see him visit virtually all of Japan. But such tours are not among the thirteen acts in matters of state stipulated in the constitution.[60]

The first indication that the government would formally interpret the emperor as having a public role beyond the thirteen acts in matters of state was provided by the Imperial House Office Law (Kunaifuhō) of April 1947. Drafted by Japanese officials, this law, which has been revised several times, specifies the duties of the palace bureaucracy. Article 1 of the 1947 version indicated that state affairs relating to the imperial house were not limited to acts in matters of state: "The Imperial Household Office shall take charge of state affairs relating to the Imperial House *and* the emperor's acts in matters of state" (emphasis added).[61] The underlying premise of the law was that since certain private acts of the emperor such as domestic tours influence the maintenance of the emperor's position as symbol, official administrative assistance should be provided to the emperor to help him perform such acts.[62] This interpretation suggested that there was a gray area between explicitly private acts and the thirteen public acts in matters of state specified in the constitution.

We might speculate that if the government had been forthright about the extent of the constitutional transformation, then more scholars might have been able to accept the slight broadening of the emperor's ceremonial public role, as well as use of the word *genshu* to indicate that the emperor remained head of state, albeit in a new and limited sense. The conservative government sought to downplay change, however, and this led many scholars to greet the government's interpretation of the emperor's new position and role with considerable skepticism. The 1948 version of the *Chūkai Nihonkoku kenpō* (Annotated Constitution of Japan), compiled by the staff of the Faculty of Law at Tokyo University (relying largely on the work of Minobe and Miyazawa), concluded that the prime minister was head of state: "*Genshu* . . . is domestically the chief of administration . . . and the organ that represents the country vis-à-vis foreign countries. . . . Since under the new constitution . . . all authority in foreign affairs [i.e., the authority to conclude treaties] rests with the Cabinet, one can only say that the prime minister is head of state."[63] This commentary acknowledged the emperor's ceremonial role in foreign affairs through his promulgation of treaties and the attestation of ministers but stressed that it was wrong in legal terms to employ *genshu* to describe the emperor's new, constricted role. The commentary also mentioned nothing about a second category of public acts in addition to acts in matters of state which, the commentary emphasized over and over, were limited to those specified in the constitution. With regard to the vaguest act in matters of state—"performance of ceremonial functions" (Article 7.10)—this commentary simply stressed that the "emperor . . . can perform state ceremonies" but said nothing as to whether he could attend state ceremonies performed by others.[64]

The question of the emperor's position and role under the new constitution became a public issue soon after Yoshida Shigeru became prime minister in October 1948 for the second time during the Occupation. Yoshida's return to office inaugurated more than four decades of conservative rule. Yoshida would remain prime minister until 1954, and he worked to preserve as much of Imperial Japan as possible in the face of what he considered SCAP's radical reforms. During Yoshida's prime ministership an act of the emperor was questioned in the Diet for the first time. In December 1948, a message that the emperor sent to President Harry Truman through Joseph Keenan became a public issue. Keenan was chief prosecutor at the Tokyo War Crimes Trial. Before he returned to the United States, the emperor asked him to deliver a message to President Truman, the gist of which Keenan shared with reporters in the United States: "The Emperor desires in his position as constitutional monarch to do all he can to foster the development of democracy, such as we have in this country [the United States], among his own people of Japan."[65]

Newspapers in Japan promptly published the emperor's message in translation, and opposition parties made an issue of it.[66] The communists and the socialists had a different vision of their country's future, and not all of them wished for their country to become a U.S.-style democracy. At the time the Japanese already were divided over whether their country, on regaining independence, should align itself with the United States or adopt a nonaligned stance in the emerging Cold War world system. The left was unified broadly in calling for Japan to be nonaligned.

In a meeting of the House of Representatives Foreign Affairs Committee on 6 December, representatives from the opposition parties demanded an explanation from Prime Minister Yoshida about the emperor's message. As soon as the meeting began, socialist Wada Toshiakira launched into an interpellation of Yoshida. Yoshida responded that if the emperor had sent such a message, about which he was ignorant, it must be considered a personal communication between him and President Truman and not an official communication between heads of state.[67] Yoshida did not argue that the emperor had the authority to send such a message as Japan's official representative. Although he refused to address the concerns of the opposition parties directly, he seemed to understand that from a constitutional perspective the emperor's message was problematic.

Wada continued to press Yoshida: "I think that it is a serious matter that the newspaper's report [of the message] gives the people the impression that the emperor continues to hold political power as before."[68] As Yoshida grew evasive, Wada's anger only increased. At one point he told the prime minister, "[If such a message were sent,] then I think that the emperor should be warned. The emperor has been stripped of all political power, and he is not in a position to do such a thing. I think that you have a responsibility at this time to sternly warn the emperor."[69] Yoshida continued to stonewall. It was the first time since the Diet opened in 1890 that the emperor had been called to task during an interpellation. This was indeed a dramatic change from prewar practices.

One week later, the government acknowledged that the emperor had sent the message but emphasized that it was of an extremely personal nature and not at all official.[70] Nosaka Sanzō (1892–1993) of the JCP demanded to know what measures the government was taking regarding the matter, and several other representatives of the opposition parties vehemently supported the interpretation that the emperor's message was improper under the new constitution. Although these representatives received little satisfaction from the government's responses, they made their point: the emperor's involvement in politics was unacceptable. In reaction to these protests from the left, conservative parties, the palace, and government agencies strove to maintain the public neutrality of the emperor.

Debates about the emperor's position and role continued among constitutional scholars. Although the new constitution had terminated the imperial prerogative in legal terms, it was not clear whether the imperial will, out of custom, retained a force that could be employed by conservative governments. Yokota Kisaburō (1896–1993), a professor of international law at Tokyo University and another leading first-generation interpreter of the constitution, stressed in his 1949 study of the emperor system, "[The emperor] is no more than a symbol (*shōchō ni suginai*). The corollary of the fact that the emperor is a symbol is that the emperor is neither sovereign nor head of state (*genshu*)."[71] But consensus on this issue as well as on the extent and nature of the emperor's public acts was not soon forthcoming. The title of a 1951 essay by legal philosopher Tsunetō Kyō (1888–1967) of Kyoto University mirrored the confusion in the academic community: "Is There a Head of State in Japan?"[72]

The gray area of public acts became a political issue when a statement by Emperor Hirohito in the Diet just before Japan regained independence in 1952 angered opposition parties, who remained sensitive about the political use of the emperor by the Yoshida Cabinet. The Cabinet is responsible for all public acts by the emperor. Emperor Hirohito said: "The fact that the Peace Treaty has already been approved by the Diet, ratified, and soon will go into effect gives me endless joy." Representatives who favored a nonaligned Japan expressed concern that the emperor's statement affirmed the peace treaty signed the previous year in San Francisco. The treaty established what came to be called the San Francisco system, in which Japan was aligned with the anticommunist West and specifically with the United States. Not only did the peace treaty place Japan firmly in the U.S. camp, but the U.S.-Japan Security Treaty signed with the peace treaty also provided for the continued basing of U.S. troops in Japan. Thus, the three most contentious political issues of the postwar era came together with the emperor's remark: the constitution, the emperor, and the alliance with the United States.

When Japan regained its sovereignty in April 1952, the Yoshida Cabinet decided in practice to maintain the emperor as the nation's international representative. The Cabinet Legislation Bureau worked to preserve as much continuity with prewar practices as possible in preparing diplomatic papers to present the emperor to foreign countries as Japan's head of state.[73] In 1953, the Japanese government sent, as a representative of the emperor, Crown Prince Akihito to attend the coronation of Queen Elizabeth II (b. 1926; r. 1952–). During this first trip abroad, the crown prince, then nineteen, visited fourteen countries and was hosted by several heads of state. Foreign countries followed the Japanese government's cue and provided the crown prince with a welcome befitting a head of state. Later, Emperor Hirohito would play host to numerous heads of state who visited Japan.

In response to a question from Representative Namiki Yoshio in the Diet about the legal nature of the crown prince's trip, Usami Takeshi (1903–1991), vice-director of the Imperial Household Agency, proposed the following interpretation, which also served to clarify the government's interpretation of the extent and nature of the emperor's public acts:

> As you said, the emperor's acts in matters of state in Article 7 are limited, and the last act, "Performance of ceremonial functions," is interpreted to mean the emperor's performing ceremonies. Therefore I think that the emperor's attending another country's ceremony, or the sending of a representative, does not from a constitutional perspective correspond to an act in matters of state. Nor is it [an act] in his private position, but *a public action in his position as symbol*; to give an example, [the emperor's] replying to a telegram received from a foreign head of state, or to give a domestic

> example, [the emperor's] attendance at the Diet's opening ceremony sponsored by the Diet . . . are not [acts] of the Emperor in his private position, but [acts] carried out from his public position. (emphasis added)[74]

The government had adopted the line that there were three categories of acts by the emperor, of which two were public: (1) acts in matters of state, and (2) acts in his position as symbol.[75] This exchange between Namiki and Usami continues to appear in the *Kokkai no kenpō rongi*, which presents the official interpretations of the Constitution of Japan.

Scholars soon joined the debate over the legitimacy of this second category of public acts. The 1953 version of the *Chūkai Nihonkoku kenpō*, in a modification from the 1948 edition, acknowledged the fuzzy legal nature of some of the emperor's acts: "Regarding the emperor, the distinction between public and private is not necessarily clear; among the private acts of the emperor, there are those with extremely important political significance (domestic tours, for example)."[76] It was becoming apparent that it was not so easy to draw boundaries between the emperor in public and in private, and between the political and the symbolic.

In 1953, the Japan Public Law Association focused at its annual conference on the emperor's constitutional position and role. The proceedings of this symposium were published in volume 10 of *Kōhō kenkyū* (Public law review). Even today, this volume is considered a landmark in the debates about the emperor's constitutional status because it presented the basic lines of possible interpretations. Kuroda Satoru (1900–1990), another respected first-generation interpreter of the Postwar Constitution, spoke first at the conference. He began by noting that so much debate had focused on the locus of sovereignty that

> the emperor's constitutional position has not undergone an in-depth investigation. As a result, even today there are questions that remain unsettled, such as the meaning of the emperor as "symbol," and the character of the emperor's acts in matters of state. Even points such as whether or not the emperor is a monarch, whether or not the emperor is head of state, and whether Japan is a monarchy or a republic create problems.[77]

Some issues, such as what constituted a symbolic act, never would be settled definitively.

By 1953 Japanese scholars benefited from access to SCAP documents about the drafting of the constitution. Kuroda was aware of MacArthur's intention to make the emperor head of state but argued that the constitution had failed to give the emperor that position. He stressed that the emperor had no "power to moderate," and performed only "passive" (*shōkyokuteki*) roles but no "constructive" (*sekkyokuteki*) ones. Kuroda cited the cases of various European monarchs who enjoyed such legal powers as the right to sanction constitutional revisions. His intent was to highlight just how limited the role of Japan's emperor was. Kuroda, who favored increasing the emperor's constitutionally defined role, concluded: "Since the emperor has no powers related to government nor the right to represent the country externally, one cannot call him the head of state. If we suppose that the emperor is a monarch, then a monarch who is not head of state must be termed a new type of monarch."[78] Most scholars agreed with Kuroda's interpretation that the emperor's independent will in no way entered into the acts that he performed ceremonially, but opinions differed as to whether his position could be called that of a head of state. The government nonetheless continued to position the emperor as Japan's official representative vis-à-vis the outside world.

Some constitutional scholars angrily rejected the government's broad interpretation of the emperor's public role. Hasegawa Masayasu (1923–2009) insisted that the emperor could perform only two categories of acts:

> Supposing that there are acts besides acts in matters of state that the emperor can do, then they are private acts with passive meaning. Therefore, so long as the emperor's domestic tours and visits to the Ise Shrine,[79] which are not provided for in the constitution, are not interpreted as private acts, then Articles 4, 6, and 7 of the constitution are being violated, especially by the latter [the visits to the Ise Shrine], which also, as anyone can recognize, violate paragraph 3 of Article 20, which provides for the separation of church and state.[80]

One constitutional scholar at the conference would soon issue an interpretation of the emperor's public acts that buttressed the government's stance, however. Kiyomiya Shirō (1898–1989), professor of constitutional law at Tohoku University, was, along with Miyazawa, Yokota, and

Kuroda, a respected first-generation interpreter of the new constitution. In his widely read 1957 study of the Postwar Constitution, Kiyomiya addressed the emperor's role as a symbol:

> [The emperor's] position as a symbol . . . is generally recognized as a public position; in order to demonstrate this function no particular acts are necessary. In the constitution, too, there are no provisions about the emperor's acts as a symbol. The function of a symbol usually is recognized as static, but with a symbol that is human . . . acts become a problem. As actual examples, there are the [emperor's] attendance and statement at the opening ceremony of the Diet, the [emperor's] exchange of telegrams with foreign heads of state, and the [emperor's] domestic tours, which had a public coloring. These are neither purely private acts by the emperor nor acts in matters of state by the emperor as an organ of the state, but should be seen merely as [public] acts of the emperor as a symbol. And these acts by their nature, of their own accord, have constitutional limits. Even though they are public acts, they must not, from the perspective of Article 4 of the constitution, be acts "related to government" or "in matters of state."[81]

Kiyomiya affirmed that the second category of public acts by the emperor in his position as a symbol were valid as long as they were ceremonial.

The Postwar Constitution succeeded in creating the expectation that the emperor's public role would be no more than symbolic, a sweeping change from the Meiji system of imperial prerogative. As has been the case with the British monarchy, it has proved difficult to draw absolute boundaries between the symbolic and the political. However, the expectation that imperial acts be symbolic is itself an important check on Cabinets and all other agents that seek to use the emperor for political ends. The most significant interpretation of Chapter I of the constitution developed by conservative governments in the critical years after the constitution went into effect was to insist that the emperor could perform public acts in his position as a symbol. Over the years, the government's stance, which justified the extension of the emperor's public role to acts such as hosting palace garden parties, has evolved little from the interpretation offered by Usami in 1952. However, government representatives stress, along the lines of Kiyomiya's interpretation, that the test for judging the emperor's public acts is the degree to which they are ceremonial and nothing more than that.[82] This interpretation has broadened the emperor's ceremonial role, but it does not blatantly contradict the underlying principles of the constitution. Conservatives could wiggle around strict constitutional interpretations, but they could never ignore the constitution completely.

The JCP rejected this second category of public acts altogether, and the JSP maintained a wary watch on conservative Cabinets' interpretation of "public acts by the emperor in his position as a symbol." Few Japanese voiced complaints about the emperor's annual attendance at the opening ceremony of the National Athletic Meet, but other public acts have generated more controversy. Ironically, this broadening of the emperor's public role, combined with the government's long-standing insistence that the emperor was head of state, eventually would return to haunt elements of the right in the 1990s with regard to the issue of imperial apologies, as we shall see in chapter 4.

The Imperial Decoration System

The drafters of the Postwar Constitution intended for the attestation of honor to be a central function of the symbolic monarchy.[83] Curiously, however, the imperial decoration system was suspended between 1946 and 1963. In 1946, the Shidehara Cabinet discontinued the regular awarding of imperial decorations with the exception of the Order of Culture, which is given to individuals who have made artistic or scholarly contributions. The government decided that all other decorations would be awarded posthumously. The Shidehara Cabinet intended the suspension to be brief and give the government a chance to reevaluate the system, which had played an important role in a war that had ended disastrously for Japan.[84] As a result of ideological battles over the emperor system, however, the decoration system remained in limbo for nearly two decades. Thus, for the first twenty years of the postwar era, the recrafted monarchy was handicapped severely in performing perhaps its most basic function.

Shidehara resigned in May 1946, and each of the three subsequent prime ministers, whose tenure spanned the next decade, labored to establish a decoration system suitable to postwar Japan. In 1948, the moderately conservative Prime Minister Ashida Hitoshi (1887–1959), who headed a centrist coalition Cabinet, proposed that the prewar system be abolished

FIGURE 11. In 1948, the Ashida Hitoshi Cabinet proposed replacing all prewar decorations with a single type of decoration, the Order of Peace. Here is a design of the proposed Order of Peace, with a dove in the middle. The order was never adopted. (Sōrifu shōkunkyoku, *Shōkunkyoku hyakunen shiryōshū* [Ōkurasho insatsukyoku, 1979], 2: 200.)

and that all awards given under it be rescinded. This represented a sweeping symbolic negation of Imperial Japan. Ultimately, Ashida sought to create from scratch a simplified decoration system appropriate to New Japan. In submitting the Ashida Cabinet's bill regarding the decoration system to the Diet in June 1948, Attorney General Suzuki Yoshio (1894–1968) called for the establishment of an Order of Peace (*Heiwa kunshō*) with five classes that would recognize individuals who had made contributions toward "peace, democracy, and culture."[85] In one version of the proposed Order of Peace decorations sketched by the Decoration Bureau, all five classes, though different in size and design, had an image of a dove in the middle.[86] The collapse of the Ashida Cabinet later that year derailed this bill.

The imperial decoration system continued to be embroiled in the debates over the emperor system. Between 1948 and 1954, but especially after Japan regained independence in 1952, Prime Minister Yoshida worked unsuccessfully to recommence the award system. He initially added a five-rank Order of Culture to the five-rank Order of Peace in his proposal for a new system. After several additional redraftings, the Yoshida Cabinet finally submitted its proposal to the Diet in December 1952. The bill no longer called for the establishment of an Order of

Peace. Instead, it proposed to reestablish prewar decorations, excluding special military decorations. Among the honors was an Order of Industry (*Sangyō kunshō*) to recognize those who had contributed to the "development of industry."[87] This proposed decoration was probably modeled on the Queen's Award for Industry in Britain. During the next several months, this bill was hotly debated in the Diet. The opposition parties eventually defeated it. Yoshida was driven from office in 1954, and his successor, Prime Minister Hatoyama Ichirō (1883–1959), also a conservative, was no more successful in this area during his two years in office. The years 1954 to 1956 were three of the most ideologically contentious of the postwar era (the battle lines regarding many issues that continue to divide the Japanese ideologically in the twenty-first century were first drawn in the 1950s), and the question of the decoration system became embroiled in battles over the legitimacy of the constitution and other Occupation-era reforms. The decoration system would not be revived until the new constitution had survived the revisionist challenge.

Contesting the Symbolic Monarchy

When Japan regained independence in 1952, the validity of the constitution became the central political issue. Some Japanese rejected the new constitutional principles and considered it disgraceful that their country's constitution had been authored by foreigners. Elements of the political right spoke of it with derision as the "MacArthur Constitution." In fact, even today, the constitution's foreign origins hamper it from serving as a unifying symbol for the Japanese to the same extent that the U.S. Constitution has functioned for Americans. Other Japanese supported the principles of the Postwar Constitution but thought that, as an autonomous act, the Japanese should draft their basic law. Article 9, the no-war clause, has occupied the constitutional revision movement ever since its inception, but in the 1950s the status of the emperor was also a chief concern of the movement.

One must distinguish between the goal of democratizing Japan and the means employed by the Occupation authorities, which often were not democratic. As a matter of fact, the U.S. Occupation authorities often set undemocratic examples in the name of protecting democracy. In 1953, in response to a suit over SCAP banning the JCP's newspaper *Akahata* as part of the purge of communists that followed the outbreak of the Korean War in 1950, the Supreme Court of Japan ruled that throughout the Occupation, SCAP "held legal authority outside the constitution" to enact the articles of surrender.[88] In a sense, Japan's postwar democracy began with the end of the military occupation in April 1952, for only then did the constitution become the highest law. With independence, the Japanese reviewed various reforms instituted during the Occupation, and through this process they made the constitution their own.

The conception of the emperor as a symbol had already gained popular currency by 1952. A poll conducted by the *Yomiuri shinbun* newspaper that year showed that the majority supported maintaining the emperor's constitutional position as a symbol.[89] It would be misleading, however, to view this interpretation of the monarchy as the orthodox position at this time. Most of the right was not yet comfortable with the symbolic monarchy. As Japan's independence approached in 1952, opponents and defenders of the symbolic monarchy mobilized to contest the legitimacy of the Occupation reforms.

In 1951, Minister of Education Amano Teiyū (1884–1980), a prewar liberal, sparked a major debate when he proclaimed that the "emperor was the moral center" (*tennō wa dōtokuteki chūshin*) of the nation, a concept that he outlined in his *Kokumin jissen yōryō* (Guidelines for popular practical morality). A proponent of "quiet patriotism" (*shizuka naru aikokushin*), Amano was by no means in favor of reestablishing the Meiji political system:

> The special feature of the Japanese nation is the symbolic essence of the emperor; saying that the emperor is a symbol is not to be understood as making the emperor into a god. It will not do to think of the emperor in religious terms. The emperor must not be the center of religious worship. Emperor worship along those lines must be rejected. Moreover, it will not do for the emperor to have sovereignty. It will not do for the emperor to be the center of power. We reject such a conception of the emperor as power-holder. The emperor has no power, but he has authority.[90]

Amano did not specify what he meant by "authority," but evidently he had some sense of the influence that the emperor could exert through symbolic acts. Amano went on to explain that to respect the emperor was to respect Japan. As minister of Education, he tried to reintroduce respect for the emperor and moral education into the curriculum of public schools. This was part of the Yoshida Cabinet's emphasis on reviving patriotism, which began in 1950.

Historian Inoue Kiyoshi (1913–2001) spoke for many on the left in interpreting what he called "Amano's Rescript on Education," a biting reference to the defunct Imperial Rescript on Education. Inoue saw this as part of a government program to strengthen "emperorism" (*tennōshugi*), part of an overall plan to remilitarize Japan, an accusation that individuals on the left regularly leveled against their political opponents.[91] Some leftist critics of Amano's platform agreed with certain of the minister's points, however. Philosopher Kuno Osamu (1910–99), for example, found a few areas of common ground: "First, I agree with Minister Amano's point denying the divine nature of the emperor. Second, I agree with his point emphasizing that the emperor is not the possessor of political power."[92] In the end, Kuno questioned Amano's proposal: "In light of [Japan's] past experience, doesn't moral education that makes the emperor the symbol of patriotism offer an extremely one-sided, inflexible morality?"[93]

Still, at the time of Japan's independence, Kuno, another leftist who had spent time in prison under the old system, and Amano, a government minister, found themselves in agreement on the need to keep the emperor out of politics. The far right disagreed with that part of Amano's program. It supported Amano's call for a nationalism centered on the throne but continued to propose the reestablishment of a political role for the emperor. Popular opposition eventually forced Amano to withdraw his proposal from inclusion in the curriculum.

In the 1950s, Koizumi Shinzō (1888–1966) emerged as a prominent supporter of the symbolic monarchy. The firmly anti-Marxist Koizumi was another member of the school of "prewar liberals" that included Amano, Minobe, and Tsuda. From 1933 until 1944, Koizumi served as president of Keio University, which had been founded by Fukuzawa Yukichi. In 1949, Koizumi was appointed advisor to Crown Prince Akihito and soon thereafter became director of the prince's education. In this position, Koizumi was one of the most influential palace officials during the 1950s and early 1960s. Koizumi turned to Fukuzawa for a model for the symbolic monarchy.

During the postwar era, Fukuzawa was canonized as one of the greatest liberal thinkers of modern Japan. Fukuzawa's celebrated statement "Heaven never created a man above or below another man" has been featured so prominently in postwar education that, in an informal but very tangible sense, it can be said to have replaced the Imperial Rescript on Education. In 1981, Fukuzawa was elevated to a select pantheon when the Ministry of Finance decided to put his image on the ¥10,000 bill. Not all Japanese saw in Fukuzawa a distinguished liberal thinker, however. In a 1885 article, Fukuzawa had recommended that his country "get out of Asia and join the [civilized] West." Sinologist Takeuchi Yoshimi (1910–77) interpreted Fukuzawa's recommendation as having served as a justification for Japan's brutal colonization of its less "civilized" Asian neighbors.[94]

Koizumi turned to Fukuzawa's two tracts on the monarchy for guidance (see chapter 1). After the war, many historians pinpointed the 1880s as the crucial decade when Japan's modern history might have taken a more liberal route. During this decade, there were movements for liberty and popular rights in many areas before the Imperial Constitution settled the nature of the polity by creating an oligarchic monarchy instead of an imperial system that would have provided for greater popular political participation and civil rights. Koizumi was not the first intellectual in the postwar period to champion Fukuzawa's model of the monarchy, but as a result of his position as director of the crown prince's education, he was the most visible proponent of Fukuzawa and, in the case of the prince himself, the most influential.

On New Year's day in 1952, Koizumi published a short piece titled "Fukuzawa Yukichi on the Imperial Family" in the newspaper *Jiji shinpō*.[95] What, Koizumi asked, had Fukuzawa intended seventy years earlier when he wrote about the "principle of esteeming the emperor?"[96] According to Koizumi, Fukuzawa had meant that the imperial house should not "be troubled with politics." The duty (*goninmu*) of the imperial house was to serve as the "center soothing the hearts of the Japanese people." Koizumi supported Fukuzawa's stance that the imperial house should dispense honors and promote the arts. Koizumi found in Fukuzawa's writings an earlier, "domestic" model for the postwar symbolic monarchy. Indeed, the claim of native origins was true in the sense that although Fukuzawa borrowed from writings on the British monarchy, he also invoked the long history of the imperial house to justify his interpretation of the throne's proper role.[97]

Historian Tsuda Sōkichi also rose in defense of the symbolic monarchy.[98] In a July 1952 essay, he criticized the mass media for mouthing the incorrect conception that the emperor's role had always been that of a "political powerholder" (*seijiteki kenryokusha*). Tsuda's argument broadly followed that of his earlier essay that had so shocked the intellectual world in 1946. "Almost without exception the historic emperors have been fond of scholarship and the arts. . . . This is the tradition of the imperial house."[99] Tsuda sought to blunt the reactionary challenge to Chapter I of the Postwar Constitution by winning over his countrymen to the interpretation that the symbolic monarchy was anchored firmly in Japan's tradition. The fact that Tsuda, Koizumi, and Amano—distinguished prewar liberals who found themselves nearer the center of the political spectrum in the postwar political environment—vigorously championed the symbolic monarchy served to undermine the revisionist cause.

The constitutional revision movement was by no means limited to political parties. Numerous civil groups with significant constituencies such as the Association of Shinto Shrines called for an independent constitution. Founded in 1946 after Occupation authorities ordered state support for Shinto abolished, the Association of Shinto Shrines enjoys the legal status of a religious corporation (*shūkyō hōjin*). Former Home Ministry bureaucrats with connections to shrines played a critical role in its establishment. The goal of the association, in simple terms, was to reverse the Occupation reforms that damaged the prestige and the economic basis of the shrines. A 1954 book based on a conference sponsored by individuals affiliated with the Association of Shinto Shrines called for reestablishing imperial sovereignty: "There is an inseparable relationship between the fact that the emperor was revered as the sovereign ever since the origin of the Japanese nation and the fact that the emperor was the symbol of the Japanese nation. The Constitution of Japan ignores this inseparability."[100] In calling for the reestablishment of imperial sovereignty, the Association of Shinto Shrines found itself on the far right.

Whatever the Japanese felt about the foreign origins of their constitution, by the early 1950s there was little support even among the political right for a wholesale return to the Meiji system. And by 1954, at the very moment when constitutional revision stood its greatest chance of success, the right found itself divided on the issue of the emperor, as well as on other constitutional questions. The two major conservative parties—the Progressive and the Liberal parties—agreed that the emperor should be head of state but differed over the details of what that should mean in practice. The Progressive Party's proposal did not recommend a change in the emperor's ceremonial position, although it did call for a slight increase in the number of ceremonial acts.[101] The party included politicians such as Ashida Hitoshi, who sought fundamental revision of certain articles in the constitution, notably the no-war clause. Its constitutional committee was not, however, inclined to alter the emperor's position in any significant way. The ruling Liberal Party proposed greater revisions. Some of its politicians were inclined to support a thorough revision of the constitution. These included Kishi Nobusuke (1896–1989), who chaired his party's constitutional committee. In preparing the party's proposal to revise the emperor's position, the constitutional committee called four experts in imperial history and constitutional law to testify. Three of the four, constitutional scholar Mitsuma Shingo (1916–) and historians Hiraizumi Kiyoshi (1895-1984) and Fujii Jintarō (1883–1958), held reactionary views about the proper legal position of the emperor.

Mitsuma, a young professor at Meiji University, argued that one of the problems with the Postwar Constitution was that it had omitted an article specifying that Japan was headed by a "line of emperors unbroken for ages eternal" (*bansei ikkei*). This meant that the emperor's position was determined in essence by a "majority vote of the people."[102] Mitsuma found reprehensible what many supporters of the Postwar Constitution delighted in stressing: the monarchy's existence was dependent on the will of the people.

Hiraizumi also criticized the "MacArthur Constitution." Hiraizumi became a professor of Japanese history at Tokyo University in 1923. During the 1930s, he emerged as one of the leading scholars of official imperial history (*kōkokushi*) and served on governmental committees including the one charged with authenticating the "vestiges" of Emperor Jimmu's eastward expedition. Imperial history, or the study of the monarchy's centrality in Japanese history, was a sacrosanct field in Imperial Japan. After the war, however, the study of imperial history was discredited thoroughly and was considered no more than an exercise in propaganda. Hiraizumi resigned his post and retired to his home prefecture of

Fukui. In 1954, the peak year of the reactionary right's movement to revise the constitution, Hiraizumi made a special trip to the capital to testify before the Liberal Party's constitutional committee about the monarchy. His testimony can be summarized as an unqualified plea for a return to the system of direct imperial rule. The Liberal Party's willingness to give someone like Hiraizumi a hearing could not help but increase the left's suspicions about the government's intentions.

"It is clear," Hiraizumi argued, "that it is correct for our country to have direct rule by the emperor (*tennō no shinsei*)."[103] He stressed that imperial rule should not be confused with despotism: "Our country is not a democracy (*minshu no kuni*) but a monarchy to the utmost; however, a very important point is that the monarch's aim is 'politics for the people' (*minpon no seiji*)."[104] Hiraizumi decried the MacArthur Constitution as a humiliation that Japanese should "wash from their faces." Toward the end of his testimony, Hiraizumi belittled the postwar polity:

> In this world it seems more and more that there are people who argue that even in adopting the MacArthur Constitution the national polity (*kokutai*) has not changed. I think that this probably arises from loyal feelings of anxiety about the imperial house. . . . I do not doubt the loyal feelings of such people. However, as someone who is a scholar, if I were to address the facts straight on without fear . . . the truth is that if the MacArthur Constitution is practiced as is, then the national polity inevitably has changed. . . . The Emperor has become merely the symbol of the country. History is forgotten, and the family system denied. . . . The virtually limitless rights of the people are stressed, but there is no concept of service to the throne (*hōshi*). . . . Things like loyalty and filial piety are discarded like worn-out sandals. . . . Under such conditions, it is impossible to say that the national polity has not changed. . . . The history and textbooks constructed under this constitution, even though they undergo inspection by the Ministry of Education, basically employ communist historical theory; the Japanese themselves disgrace the history of their fatherland. . . . Among the vulgar books in circulation, there are many that slander and disgrace the imperial house.[105]

Hiraizumi proceeded to argue, in language reminiscent of the jingoistic 1930s, that it was necessary to "clarify the national polity" (*kokutai o meikaku ni suru*) to correct the spiritual confusion that reigned in Japan.

For Hiraizumi, destruction of the so-called MacArthur Constitution had to be the first step in cleansing Japan of spiritual pollution. The second was reestablishing the constitution authorized by Emperor Meiji:

> If this takes place, then Japan will become independent of its subordination to the United States, the dignity (*igen*) of the Emperor will be restored, and people will continue to shout "Long Live His Majesty the Emperor!" (*Tennō heika banzai*). When people happily devote themselves in service to the eternal life of the fatherland, then Japan again will stand as one of the great nations of the world and win the respect of other nations.[106]

Even a decade after Japan's defeat in a war fought in the name of the emperor, Hiraizumi argued that revering the emperor and serving the state along prewar lines would be the best course. With conservative witnesses such as Mitsuma and Hiraizumi and a chair as reactionary as Kishi, the Liberal Party's constitutional committee was viewed with intense skepticism by defenders of the postwar order.

The most significant change in the emperor's position proposed by the Liberal Party was to remove the requirement that the Cabinet had to give prior approval for acts in matters of state performed by the emperor. The party's proposal—"The emperor, with the advice of the Cabinet, performs the acts provided for in the constitution"—suggested that the emperor would have a voice in acts that, under the Postwar Constitution, he carried out only ceremonially. Another salient feature of the proposal was a provision to give the emperor, with the advice of the Cabinet, the legal authority to declare a state of emergency. To representatives of the left, this modification conjured up bitter memories of the prewar government's use of imperial rescripts to constrict the civil liberties of the people to protect the state from "dangerous" thoughts and movements. The Liberal Party was the sponsor of the Subversive Activities Prevention Law (1952), the first major law to pass the Diet after Japan regained independence. The left, which viewed the Subversive Activities Prevention Law as a threat to civil liberties, had reason to be suspicious of attempts by the Liberal Party to provide the state with further powers that might then be used to stifle all forms of dissent.

The Liberal Party's draft also featured one progressive article: it allowed women to occupy the throne.[107] This change did not require revision of the constitution, simply a modification of the Imperial House Law by a majority vote in the Diet. Altogether, the Liberal Party's proposal for modifying the emperor's position was considerably more reactionary than that of the Progressive Party, but still closer to the Postwar Constitution than to the Meiji Constitution. It did not even begin to provide the emperor with the sort of powers afforded him under the Meiji Constitution, nor did it seek to infringe on popular sovereignty.

The details of the Progressive and Liberal parties' proposals were largely eclipsed by their use of the term *genshu*, which suggested a return to the Meiji system. The JSP, the main opposition party, rose to protect the constitution, as did private associations such as the Citizens' Federation for the Defense of the Constitution (Kenpō yōgo kokumin rengō). Although the left was divided over various articles in the Postwar Constitution, in the face of the revisionist challenge from the right, the left unified to mount a spirited defense of the postwar system. Representatives of the left linked proposals to make the emperor head of state with what they saw as an overall program championed by the right to restore the prewar emperor system. In a piece that appeared in the left-wing journal *Kaizō* in 1955, one commentator helped readers grasp what the change from "symbol" to "head of state" would entail for Japan: "Since [this is not a change] understood conceptually, let us transform it into something that one can feel. Political power is attached to the head of state. A military established through remilitarization and conscription would protect the head of state, and make no mistake that emperor worship would be re-established."[108] This commentator invoked an apocalyptic scenario to cast the conservative proposals in an especially frightful manner.

Surveys by the mass media after the Liberal and Progressive parties released their drafts showed public support for the emperor's position as a symbol and widespread distrust of plans to make him head of state. When Fukuda Shōjirō, a twenty-seven-year-old worker from Akita prefecture, was asked by reporters from the general magazine *Bungei shunjū* in 1954 whether he thought the emperor's constitutional position should be changed from symbol to head of state, he replied, "To make the emperor head of state under this terrible government is like giving a weapon to a robber."[109] That same year, the *Tōkyō shinbun* asked 1,000 residents of the metropolis: "Should the emperor be made into the head of state (*genshu*), or is his present position as a symbol acceptable?" The results were as follows:

Symbol	*Genshu*	Don't Understand
62%	22%	16%[110]

The rejection of the term *genshu* contrasts with the results of other polls that found pluralities of respondents favoring general plans to revise the constitution.[111] Popular support for the symbolic monarchy was the most important factor in the survival of the constitutional chapter on the emperor. Within a decade of the constitution's promulgation, a decided majority of the Japanese had become backers of the symbolic monarchy. Polls consistently showed that the majority favored retention of the emperor's position as a symbol. Elected representatives who wished to remain in office could not ignore the stance of their constituency on this often emotional issue.

Official Legitimation

The symbolic monarchy won the popular stamp of approval within a decade of its establishment; official legitimation required another decade. The constitutional revision movement continued into the early 1960s. Because a two-thirds majority in both houses of the Diet is required to revise the constitution, in practical terms, the battle over the constitution revolved around winning seats in the parliament. In February 1955, the antirevisionists succeeded in preventing revision-minded conservative parties from achieving a two-thirds majority in the elections for the House of Representatives. Nor have the conservatives yet achieved a two-thirds majority in both houses.

In November 1955, conservative parties, partly in reaction to the fact that earlier that year socialist factions had cast aside their differences over the U.S.-Japan Security Treaty to form a unified socialist party, joined together to establish the Liberal Democratic Party (LDP). Constitutional revision was at the heart of the new party's platform. Led by Prime Minister Hatoyama, the LDP set up an intraparty committee to suggest constitutional revisions. It immediately bogged down as a result of intraparty divisions and produced no concrete proposals. A report issued by the committee in April 1956 revealed the caution that had overtaken the LDP. A short section on the emperor began with a notable statement expressing the committee's unwavering support of popular sovereignty. The report pointed out that use of the term "symbol" to describe the emperor's position had created confusion and rather hesitantly noted that "there were opinions that it was necessary to change this term" and that the issue was "under serious study." "Related to this," the report continued, "is the problem of whether an unambiguous provision indicating that the emperor is head of state should be established; this point demands especially serious reflection."[112] The committee seemed to be bending over backward to avoid being labeled dogmatic and reactionary.

On 11 June 1956, the LDP secured passage of a bill to establish the Commission on the Constitution (Kenpō chōsakai). Although the law establishing the commission did not mention revision, many proponents and opponents of revision perceived the commission as a political tool to help the LDP engineer constitutional changes. But the very act of establishing the commission exhibited the LDP's unwillingness to address the issue directly. Although the commission was meant to be bipartisan, the JSP, and many prominent academicians refused to participate. Before leaving office in December 1956, Prime Minister Hatoyama offered the chairmanship to liberal constitutional scholar Miyazawa Toshiyoshi. Miyazawa turned it down because he interpreted the commission as a mechanism for revision along reactionary lines.

As eventually constituted, the commission consisted of approximately forty members (the number fluctuated over its seven years of operation). Most of them were generally in favor of revision, although they were by no means unified about how to do so. Most were born in the Meiji era, and their average age in 1957 was fifty-nine. The most junior member, Nakasone Yasuhiro (1918–), was a generation younger than the average member.

The commission began its work in a polemical environment. The left insisted that the commission was illegal for technical reasons and that it provided a mechanism for the LDP's plan to revise the constitution, but there were attacks on the commission from the right as well. In a 1957 essay, constitutional scholar Mitsuma Shingo, at age forty-one no octogenarian relic of Imperial Japan, insisted that the circumstances surrounding the drafting of the constitution rendered it void. The corollary of this reasoning was that the Meiji Constitution was still in effect. "If the Commission on the Constitution really wants to become an official government body," Mitsuma argued, " it should first obtain the consent of the emperor; from the perspective of the essential principle (*hongi*) of our national polity (*kokutai*), and from the perspective of the relation between the emperor and the Constitution of Japan, this is absolutely necessary."[113] Mitsuma interpreted the commission as illegal because it had not received permission from the emperor to begin its work, as would have been required under the Meiji Constitution.[114]

Although individuals like Mitsuma who clung to the Meiji system still held positions of respect, by 1957 popular sovereignty had come to be widely accepted by both the left and the right as the principle that legitimated political decisions. Use of the imperial will to justify political decisions was no longer considered acceptable, and reaction against those who invoked it was swift and severe. Even when the Postwar Constitution's legitimacy was under attack, anyone who dared to invoke the emperor for political ends risked a public skewering. A drama involving Governor Kuwahara Mikine (1895–1991) of Aichi prefecture that occurred just as the commission began its work exemplifies this.

Governor Kuwahara had selected the Maruei Hotel to lodge the emperor and empress during a visit to the prefecture for the annual Arbor Day Festival. At a session of the Aichi Prefectural Assembly on 6 March 1957, Suwara Shoji, a JSP representative, began to probe Governor Kuwahara's reasons for choosing this particular hotel. Suwara concluded his interpellation by suggesting that since Governor Kuwahara was a director of the hotel, perhaps this was a case of conflict of interest. In response, Kuwahara claimed that the hotel had been selected according to the "emperor's will" (*tennō no goishi*). Kuwahara also called Representative Suwara a twelve-year-old for asking such a question.[115]

Suwara's reaction was scathing. He compared Kuwahara's use of the imperial will for his own personal profit to prewar militarists' use of the emperor's name to drag Japan into war.[116] He promptly traveled to Tokyo to meet with JSP representatives in the Diet and with Usami Takeshi, director of the Imperial Household Agency. "Decisions regarding lodging are delegated to the prefecture," Usami told Suwara. "It is not the case that the emperor or the Imperial Household Agency selects a particular hotel. Regarding the matter in question, because Governor Kuwahara said that the Maruei Hotel had been selected, we approved it."[117] Governor Kuwahara had claimed to speak for the emperor when this simply was not the case. Suwara's analogy to the military's occasional use of the imperial will to justify its actions after the fact rang true, although the consequences were very different.

JSP representatives made Governor Kuwahara's use of the emperor an issue in the Diet. As soon as the 14 March meeting of the House of Councillors Budget Committee opened, Representative Kuriyama Yoshio began questioning Prime Minister Kishi Nobusuke about the planning of regional visits by the imperial couple. At one point, Kuriyama quoted Governor Kuwahara's comment about the "emperor's will." Prime Minister Kishi, although a proponent of constitutional revision, expressed strong disapproval of Kuwahara's claims: "Although I do not know the details of the matter in question, if such a matter has taken place, then it is extremely regrettable." Kishi further suggested that it should be made clear to the governor how unfortunate his comment was.[118] Representing the Imperial Household Agency, Usami explained in the Diet that the Maruei Hotel had been selected on Kuwahara's recommendation.

In a special meeting of the Aichi Prefectural Assembly on 22 March, Kuwahara apologized for the "insufficient and improper" words that he had used in responding to Suwara's questions.[119] People close to Kuwahara commented that he had been surprised about the controversy surrounding his gaffe. Not only was it constitutionally insupportable to invoke the imperial will, but a widespread and virulent allergy had developed against a principle that had been so fundamental to the Meiji constitutional system. This was true even though many Japanese still did not consider the postwar constitutional system to be legitimate.

In the early years of the Commission on the Constitution's deliberations, polls showed growing public unease with proposals to revise the constitution. The Japanese were beginning to enjoy the fruits of a period of sustained economic growth that began in 1955 and later was labeled "miraculous." The constitution, it seemed to many Japanese, was the best protection against a repeat of the Pacific War. Many Japanese equated democracy with peace, perhaps taking refuge in the comforting but false assumption that democracies do not wage wars of aggression, especially not against other democracies. Pacifism has featured prominently in one definition of democracy popular in postwar Japan. The Japanese also linked the constitution to the emerging prosperity that was bringing everything from televisions to refrigerators into their homes.

The Japanese had particularly strong reservations with plans to define the emperor explicitly as head of state. In 1959, the *Tōkyō shinbun* repeated its 1954 poll, again asking 1,000 residents of the metropolis: "Should the emperor be made into the head of state (*genshu*), or is his present position as a symbol acceptable?" The results were as follows:

Symbol	Genshu	Don't Know
76%	11%	13%[120]

Saitō Dōichi, who studied twenty years of polls about the emperor, has argued that these figures indicate a rejection of the prewar "absolutist emperor system" with which the term *genshu* was associated.[121] In contrast, in response to the question whether the emperor, even though he had no political power, should be allowed to represent Japan vis-à-vis foreign countries, a slight plurality was in favor of allowing him to do so.[122]

The Commission on the Constitution was shaped to a great extent by its chair, Takayanagi Kenzō (1887–1967), after his election by fellow members in 1957. Takayanagi and one of the two vice-chairs, Yabe Teiji (1902–1967), were inclined against revision. They also sought to guard the commission's impartiality. Shortly after the commission began its work, Takayanagi and other cautious members overcame the opposition of hard-core revisionists in adopting a policy that effectively served to limit the commission's political power: "In the absence of unanimity after due deliberation, the commission was not to resort to majority rule. In such a case, the opinions of all members were to be fairly reported with a full statement of their reasons."[123] The commission thus immediately rendered itself into something along the lines of a study group rather than a policymaking organ. In retrospect, the prospects for success for the revisionists, especially regarding the status of the emperor, were all but null by 1957.

At the time, however, many Japanese did not consider the issue of constitutional revision resolved. The commission was the subject of intense attention throughout its seven-year life. Between 1957 and 1961, the commission, divided into four committees, focused on gathering information about how the constitution had been written and how it was interpreted in practice. This exercise served to clarify and validate certain interpretations, including a reading of Article 9, the no-war clause, that justified the maintenance of a defensive force.

The political climate evolved rapidly during the commission's seven-year life. In 1960, protests over renewal of the U.S.-Japan Security Treaty rocked Japan. At the center of political conflict between the left and the right, the Security Treaty was renewed, in revised form, by the Kishi Cabinet in January 1960. Fearful of rearmament and of being dragged into a U.S. military conflict, many Japanese were against renewal. The opposition parties resorted to nonparliamentary means to delay ratification; in response, the government ordered police to enter the Diet. Enraged, opposition parties boycotted Diet proceedings. Unions, the JSP, and students led hundreds of thousands of Japanese into the streets in protest. There were some violent clashes with police. As soon as the Security Treaty was formally ratified, Kishi resigned, and this eventually resolved the crisis. But parties across the political spectrum were shaken by the mass demonstrations in the streets and the turmoil in the Diet. The LDP's rank and file turned away from the divisive issue of constitutional revision, although conservatives have not abandoned the issue.

The year after the Security Treaty crisis, the commission issued comprehensive reports about its first stage of investigations. The Third Committee's report on the emperor affirmed the interpretation that there were valid public acts by the emperor in addition to acts in matters of state: "In actual practice, acts in matters of state are limited to those specified in Articles [4], 6, and 7. However, it is not the case that the emperor has no other public acts outside these acts in matters of state, but rather that public acts by the emperor . . . are limited in that they must not be functions related to government."[124] The Third Committee's report also indicated that in practice the emperor was Japan's head of state vis-à-vis the outside world: "According to officials from the Foreign Ministry . . . every foreign country without exception treats the emperor as head of state (*genshu*)."[125]

Takayanagi used these findings in his landmark 1962 essay, "The Emperor: A Symbolic Head of State."[126] Takayanagi stressed that the drafters had followed MacArthur's orders to make the emperor head of state: "There is clearly no problem in saying that the emperor's position under the new constitution is [that of] symbolic head of state (*shōchōteki genshu*). This was the intention of the officials of the Government Section who produced the draft. According to them, Japan under its new constitution is a constitutional monarchy along the lines of Britain, and its head is the emperor."[127] Takayanagi argued that there was no need to revise the constitution to specify that the emperor is the head of state since he already served that role in practice. In arguing that the emperor was a "symbolic head of state," Takayanagi used the precise term that General Fellers had used in a memorandum about the future of the monarchy submitted to MacArthur on 2 October 1945.[128]

Takayanagi emphasized that theories viewing Japan as a republic and the emperor as no more than an accessory served, in fact, to increase support for the constitutional revision movement:

> Even people who do not desire the revival of the emperor system of the Meiji Constitution "turn their necks" and wonder about a new constitution that provides for such a thing, and the reaction, instead of being against the interpretation, is against the new constitution itself. This has increased the number of people who think that the constitution must be revised to indicate clearly that Japan is a constitutional monarchy and that the emperor is head of state. Since I think that this type of interpretation makes an unfair charge against the constitution, I have told these people that under the new constitution the emperor is a symbolic head of state . . . and [when they understand that,] they come to think that there is no need for revision.[129]

Takayanagi's argument that the emperor was a symbolic head of state was persuasive.

Here it is informative to compare Takayanagi's interpretation of the nature of the Japanese polity with that of Miyazawa, who argued that Japan was a republic. Relevant to this comparison is Bagehot's description of Britain in the nineteenth century. Bagehot argued that the limited monarchy simply served to disguise the fact that Britain was a republic: "It has not been sufficiently remarked that a change has taken place in the structure of our society exactly analogous to the change in our polity. A Republic has insinuated itself beneath the folds of a Monarchy."[130] Bagehot underestimated Queen Victoria's political influence, but his observation aptly applies to twentieth-century Britain.

Bagehot's observation also applies to Japan under the Postwar Constitution. The monarchy served to mask the political revolution that took place as a result of the Occupation reforms. The Postwar Constitution centered decisionmaking in the Diet, which represents the sovereign people. In this sense, Japan is a republic, as Miyazawa argued.

Preserving the monarchy maintained an illusion of continuity that made the sweeping reforms, from equality under the law (Article 14) to universal adult suffrage (Article 15) to freedom of assembly and association (Article 21) to "the right of workers to organize and to bargain and act collectively" (Article 28), appear less radical and soothed the psyche of conservatives. Miyazawa sought to protect the constitution, particularly on the question of sovereignty, from misinterpretation by conservatives. Takayanagi, for his part, sought to protect the constitution from revision by reassuring conservatives that Japan remained a constitutional monarchy. Eventually conservatives would find even more comfort in the interpretation that the symbolic monarchy was in fact a return to domestic tradition.

From 1961 to 1964, the commission examined if and how the constitution should be changed. During these years, reactionary proposals regarding the emperor continued to come from time to time from individuals outside the commission, such as far right scholar Satomi Kishio (1897–1974). Satomi, who held a doctorate in law and had published various tracts on the imperial house before the war, issued a draft constitution in 1962 that called for sovereignty to be shared by the people and the emperor. Satomi's reactionary nature was exemplified by one article in his draft: "All speech, expression, and action seeking to abolish the emperor [system] or to revolutionize the national polity will be punished as a crime of overturning the national polity (*kokutai kakumei-zai*)."[131] Satomi, like many on the right, regularly invoked the communist threat to justify his proposals. But one had to move far to the right on the political continuum to find support for revising Article 21 of the constitution that protects "all . . . forms of expression."

Records of the commission show that the majority of its members overwhelmingly supported the principle of popular sovereignty. Once they understood how the emperor's position and role were interpreted in practice, the majority did not favor revising Chapter I.[132] In 1964, the commission duly submitted its final report to the prime minister; ironically, there were no recommendations by the commission as a whole concerning revision. After seven years of deliberation, the commission had found no faults with the constitution that could not be corrected through interpretation. The postwar system was legitimized officially, nearly two decades after its creation.

The "Constitutional Symbolic Monarchy under Popular Sovereignty"

Of all the views on the emperor propounded by the members of the Commission on the Constitution, those of the youngest member merit particular attention. In searching for a model for the monarchy, Nakasone Yasuhiro reached far back in Japan's history. During a general meeting of the commission on 13 March 1963, Nakasone criticized the Meiji system of imperial sovereignty as an aberration in the long history of the imperial house:

> Seen from 2,000 years of Japanese history, the conception of the emperor under the Meiji Constitution . . . was a special conception of that particular period and does not accord with ancient traditions. I think that to get rid of the provisions, the way of doing things, and the historical character of the Meiji Constitution regarding the emperor would further enlarge and enrich the conception of the emperor.[133]

Nakasone emphasized that for most of Japanese history, the emperor had held neither military nor political power. Nakasone was an outspoken conservative and nationalist throughout his career (he was first elected to the Diet in 1947). As a young maverick in 1963, he rattled some of his elders not only by his wholesale rejection of the Meiji system of imperial sovereignty but also by his proposal to reduce the emperor's already limited ceremonial acts to one. Nakasone suggested that the emperor be freed from all state duties other than ceremonially appointing the prime minister, and that the "emperor's ability, with the advice and approval of the Cabinet, to work positively for peace, foster culture and the arts, and promote scholarship and international friendship should be increased."[134]

Nakasone was a transwar conservative instead of a prewar one. Although right of center, he was not attached to Imperial Japan. Although Nakasone never wavered from his position that U.S. authorities had imposed the constitution on Japan and that it should be revised as an exercise in autonomy, in the mid-1950s he became one of the political right's earliest advocates of the symbolic monarchy.[135] It is useful to trace Nakasone's views on the emperor because, as prime minister between 1982 and 1987, he was interpreted, correctly, as a fervent nationalist. An important point that is often overlooked, however, is that he was not a nationalist along prewar lines.

With the postwar system legitimized by the early 1960s, the imperial decoration system resurfaced as an issue. In 1963, without drawing much protest from the main opposition party, the JSP, Prime Minister Ikeda Hayato (1899–1965) simply overturned the Cabinet decree of 1946 and reestablished the prewar system, with the exception of decorations specifically designed for the military or aristocracy.[136] The Ikeda Cabinet argued that whereas the prewar system had been directed toward honoring military men and bureaucrats, the postwar system would recognize the achievements of "private citizens" (*minkanjin*) of all classes.

At a ceremony in spring 1964, Emperor Hirohito bestowed the tremendously prestigious Grand Cordon of the Supreme Order of the Chrysanthemum on former prime minister Yoshida Shigeru. Yoshida became the first Japanese in the postwar era to receive an imperial decoration (*seizonsha jokun*). At that time, no individual better symbolized postwar Japan, including its links to Imperial Japan, than Yoshida. In this sense it was appropriate that he was the first to receive an imperial decoration since the war. On the same day that Yoshida was honored, 196 other people received decorations. In the fall of that same year, an additional 534 people were honored. Thereafter, the biannual awarding of imperial decorations was ritualized.[137]

After a decade of debate that served to validate the symbolic monarchy, the emperor finally began to perform one of the fundamental functions reserved to him under the Constitution of Japan—the ritual attestation of honors. The monarchy began to function fully in accord with the terms intended by the Occupation reforms. Was the postwar symbolic monarchy new, or was it a return to tradition? Nakasone's view represented the interpretation that the symbolic monarchy was a return to premodern tradition. Whereas the emperor system created during the Meiji era had lasted less than a century, conferring honors had been an essential function of the monarchy for more than 1,000 years. But did the stripping away of the Meiji politico-legal system result in exposing the "traditional" monarchy?

The bestowal of honors and the performance of religious rituals (particularly those carried out to ensure a bountiful rice crop) have been two of the most enduring imperial house functions. However, the interpretation that the postwar symbolic monarchy represents a return to premodern tradition, although not outlandish in broad terms, is nonetheless problematic for several reasons. First, the postwar monarchy represents a reformed version of the constitutional monarchy established during the Meiji era. In important areas, the postwar monarchy continues to be shaped far more by practices instituted under the Meiji Constitution than by ancient traditions, as we shall see in chapter 3.

Second, the imperial house's position as a symbol had never before been based on the sovereign will of the people. Even while agreeing that in a broad sense the emperor's postwar position as a symbol accorded with tradition, legal scholar Ishii Ryōsuke was careful to highlight the significant discontinuity introduced into the monarchy by the concept of popular sovereignty. An appropriate label for the postwar version of the imperial house is "constitutional symbolic monarchy under popular sovereignty," a description that hardly applies to the institution's premodern ancestor.

The third and most overlooked reason that it is simplistic to regard the postwar symbolic monarchy as a return to tradition is that not only as a politico-legal institution but also as a cultural institution, the present monarchy is distinctly modern and by no means purely Japanese. The historian Takagi Hiroshi has shown that precisely those Shinto imperial rituals seen as most traditional are by and large a product of the Meiji era. One such example is the Great Food Offering (Daijōsai) performed by the emperor during the accession ceremonies.[138] The Meiji Constitution was based on European models, but so was much of the cultural side of Japan's modern monarchy, as Takagi, Takashi Fujitani, and other scholars have shown. Many of the cultural adaptations imported from abroad, such as the pageantry at imperial weddings to create a sense of shared national community, did not disappear with the "return" of the emperor to the position of symbol after the war.

Watsuji Tetsurō wrote of a cultural community of Japanese united by their reverence for the throne as though such a community was timeless, but in fact the national community defined by a shared allegiance to the emperor was a modern invention. Although it began during the Tokugawa period, the making of the modern nation-state was not completed until the Meiji era, when peasants were made into Japanese. How can one speak of a "traditional" symbol of the nation when the sense of nationhood is so recent?

CHAPTER 3

Ministerial Briefings and Emperor Hirohito in Politics

The Postwar Constitution reformed the emperor's public role, but what became of the emperor's private role, as an individual, in politics behind closed doors? Throughout his reign, from 1926 to 1989, Emperor Hirohito saw himself as a monarch whose political opinions were important. Not only under the Meiji Constitution but also under the Postwar Constitution, Emperor Hirohito engaged in politics. This contradicts the widely repeated description of the emperor's postwar role, a description that is often accepted literally in Japan: the emperor is "merely no more than a symbol" (*tan ni shōchō ni suginai*). This phrase appears to date from constitutional scholar Yokota Kisaburō's landmark 1949 study of the emperor system. Although constitutional reform thoroughly discredited the imperial prerogative, its effect on the emperor's individual political role was less sweeping.

Long after his constitutional position was redefined, Emperor Hirohito continued to send messages to his ministers expressing, for example, the need for anticommunist measures. Hirohito had spent two decades on the throne before becoming the "symbol emperor" in 1947. Constitutions may change overnight, but imperial practices and habits do not necessarily transform so quickly. Indeed, by chronicling Hirohito's political role under the Postwar Constitution, this chapter further undermines claims that his political role under the Meiji Constitution was minimal. After all, if he was still engaged in politics under the Postwar Constitution, can one believe that, with a few exceptions, he had no significant political role under the Meiji Constitution, which gave him comprehensive authority?

Prewar and wartime politics revolved around the palace, as David Titus has shown.[1] This is not to say that the emperor was the most significant political actor; rather, politics were legitimized through the emperor. Still, the emperor was an active and important agent in the political process. The emperor was kept informed of political and military affairs by the imperial household minister, the grand chamberlain, the chief aide-de-camp, and the lord keeper of the privy seal. It is not always possible to ascertain to what extent the emperor exercised his authority, however. Since governmental decisions required the emperor's sanction (*saika*), ministers briefed the emperor almost on a daily basis, especially during crises. Briefings were such an important feature of politics under the Meiji Constitution that one prewar dictionary of the imperial house listed more than thirty terms to describe the act of briefing the emperor and members of the imperial family.[2] In many cases, ministers had to fathom the emperor's will during briefings by interpreting subtle mannerisms. Okada Keisuke (1868–1952), prime minister from 1934 to 1936, recounted in his memoirs how the emperor indicated his opinion: "On occasions when the emperor was briefed by the Cabinet, he would respond unequivocally, 'That's right,' to positions that corresponded to his own will; when he did not agree, he would remain silent."[3] Ministers, to a greater or lesser extent depending on the individual, were conditioned to respond to the emperor's will, however subtly it might be expressed.

The question of ministerial response is a crucial one. In the case of relations between King George VI (r. 1936–52) and Prime Minister Winston Churchill during World War II, historians have concluded that although Churchill would gladly have died for the throne if necessary, there was not a "single instance in which [he] changed his views or his course of action on any important question in accordance with his perceptions of the wishes of the monarch."[4] This was true even though the king occasionally expressed reservations, in a forthright manner, about Churchill's policies. In itself the fact that a monarch regularly expresses an opinion does not necessarily indicate that he or she is politically influential. One must determine whether the monarch's will is then transformed into policy.

Titus's excellent study of the monarchy in prewar Japan, published in 1974, downplayed the emperor's influence as an individual agent in the political process, although it does emphasize that the emperor was not a robot. The view that the emperor, before and during the war, was little more than a figurehead who simply ratified his ministers' decisions was the orthodox interpretation, at least until recently.[5] This interpretation allows for a few exceptions, but its proponents generally highlight only those cases of imperial intervention that can be interpreted as having had positive results. Historians who sought to question this interpretation were hampered by a paucity of sources. Under the Meiji system, the emperor's conversations in chambers with his ministers and other officials were tightly guarded secrets. Only after the war, especially after Hirohito's death in 1989, was this secrecy surrounding the emperor's presurrender role breached to some extent.

Many documents pertaining to Hirohito have become available in recent years. The debate over his presurrender role nonetheless remains polemical. In the English-language literature, there are no recent wholehearted champions of the orthodox interpretation. However, in his 1990 biography of Emperor Hirohito, Stephen Large, who has served as an apologist for Hirohito in the English-speaking world, downplayed the significance of the emperor's overall political influence. Although acknowledging the emperor's engagement in politics and his ability at times to influence appointments to high office, Large stressed the disjunction between the emperor's personal opinions and the "imperial will," the collective product presented to the public as the official line.[6]

Large reached his conclusions even after examining Hirohito's "Monologue." The Monologue is a record of the emperor's comments about his role in prewar and wartime politics. When Hirohito faced the possibility of being tried as a war criminal in 1946, five aides asked him questions that SCAP wanted answered. One of the aides, Terasaki Hidenari (1900–1951), wrote notes about the conversations; these remained in his family's possession until his daughter made them public in 1990.[7] The Monologue's appearance created a sensation in Japan, for it undermined the image of the passive, figurehead emperor held by many Japanese.

There were instances in prewar and wartime Japan when Emperor Hirohito did exercise his authority and when his personal will was decisive. The most famous example was his intervention in August 1945 that broke the deadlock among the six ministers on the Supreme War Council that was delaying Japan's surrender. Two of Japan's major cities just had been destroyed by atomic bombs, the Soviet Union had joined the conflict against Japan, and the War Council was still deadlocked over the issue of whether to surrender. In a choreographed move, Prime Minister Suzuki Kantarō (1868–1948) then asked the emperor's opinion, and Hirohito called for surrender.

There were earlier instances of the emperor's exercising influence. In 1929, the emperor forthrightly expressed his anger with Prime Minister Tanaka Giichi (1863–1929) during a briefing. Tanaka had contradicted himself in his reports to the throne about the Japanese military's role in the murder of the Manchurian warlord Chang Tso-lin the year before. After the emperor angrily pointed out this contradiction, Tanaka resigned. Large interprets the emperor's reaction to this incident as follows:

> In short, the legacy of his confrontation with Tanaka in 1929 was a lasting determination, bred of his constitutional scruples, to maintain a strict neutrality in dealing with the prime minister and his Cabinet. Thereafter, his concern not to exceed what he felt were the proper limits of his influence would prevent him, with several notable exceptions, from exerting influence as forcefully as he had in 1929, when reprimanding Tanaka.[8]

An important and often overlooked point about the Tanaka Incident, however, is that every subsequent prime minister knew that Emperor Hirohito had once forced a prime minister to resign. The fact that he could do so again might have weighed on the minds of Tanaka's successors.

Another famous example of the emperor exercising his authority was his role in suppressing the coup d'état attempt of young officers in February 1936. The emperor's forceful intervention preserved the government. Large stresses the exceptional nature of this and other cases when the emperor's influence was important: "This sensitivity, to having acted beyond the proper authority of a constitutional monarch, ultimately would govern his conduct in the aftermath of the rebellion."[9]

In contrast to Large, Irokawa Daikichi (1925–), Awaya Kentarō, and Herbert Bix have interpreted the new documents that provide information on the secret political maneuvering behind the palace gates as showing that it was not exceptional for the emperor to exert his authority on a variety of fronts, large and small.[10] Irokawa shows that Hirohito had strong opinions in such areas as diplomacy, war strategy, and personnel and exerted influence on several occasions. In August 1939, the emperor expressly designated two candidates, Umezu Yoshijirō (1882–1949) and

Hata Shunroku (1879–1962), for the office of war minister in the Cabinet of Abe Nobuyuki (1875–1953), and Hata was selected.[11] Irokawa wrote: "The emperor . . . was actively involved in the crucial affairs of state; he certainly was not the passive constitutional monarch that the official scholars (and Hirohito himself, in postwar years) have so convincingly portrayed."[12] Bix drew similar conclusions from his study of Hirohito's Monologue.

One of the most surprising revelations of the Monologue was its portrayal of the emperor's active involvement in war strategy. The emperor recalled that toward the end of the war, when an early surrender would have prevented the atomic bombing of Hiroshima and Nagasaki:

> I was worried that Okinawa should really be defended with three divisions, but [General] Umezu initially thought two divisions would suffice. Later when he felt there were not enough troops and wanted to send another division to reinforce them, it was too late: there was no way to transport them there. . . .
>
> After being defeated on Okinawa, we could not devise any plans for a naval battle. Thinking that our last ray of hope was that we might be able to inflict considerable damage on Britain and the United States if we attacked Yunnan in concert with the Burma campaign, I told this to Umezu but he disagreed, saying we could no longer continue supplying the troops.[13]

The emperor's own account of his involvement even in the fine details of war strategy amazed many Japanese who had accepted the post-war portrayal of the emperor as the unwilling tool of the military establishment.

The extent of the emperor's role in prewar and wartime politics remains a divisive issue among historians. The ground covered by Awaya, Bix, Irokawa, Large, and others need not be reexamined here. An increasing number of "exceptions" that reveal the emperor's political predominance in Imperial Japan have come to light, however, and it is more appropriate to stress Hirohito's active engagement in politics and his ongoing and significant (if by no means decisive) influence in the tremendously complex political processes that characterized prewar and wartime Japan.

The goal of this chapter is to investigate what became of the emperor's political role under the Postwar Constitution. The emperor as an individual, not as a tool used for political legitimation, is the focus here. In response to a question comparing his prewar and postwar roles, the emperor commented in 1975, "I feel I have always acted in strict observance of the constitution."[14] The comment, however, tells us little about how the emperor behaved in practice under the prewar and postwar constitutions.

The Postwar Constitution was designed to remove the emperor from politics. It limited the emperor to the performance of ceremonial acts. However, the Constitution of Japan does not explicitly forbid ministerial briefings of the emperor or political statements by the emperor. These gray areas became sources of contention. During the four decades from 1947 until his death in 1989, the emperor continued to be briefed on political matters on a regular basis by government ministers, although at least one prime minister had reservations about the constitutionality of this practice. In the end, however, the strength of custom won out over strict interpretations of the constitution: the briefings continued. Under the Occupation, the emperor's engagement with politics extended to secret communications with U.S. officials, a topic also addressed in this chapter.

Briefings under the New Constitution and the Occupation, 1947–52

The political situation in Japan remained fluid after the new constitution went into effect on 3 May 1947. In legal terms, SCAP had assumed sovereignty over Japan with that nation's unconditional surrender on 15 August 1945 and maintained it until Japan regained independence in April 1952. SCAP retained this extraconstitutional authority even under the new constitution. During the Occupation, the emperor enjoyed privileged access to the highest political figures on both the Japanese and the U.S. sides. In a 6 May 1947 meeting with Douglas MacArthur, the emperor raised the issue of the no-war clause. This was the emperor's fourth meeting with MacArthur, but his first under the new constitution. At the time, there was confusion about whether Article 9 could be interpreted to permit Japan to maintain the military means for self-defense. Article 9 reads:

> Aspiring sincerely to an international peace based on justice and order, the Japanese people forever renounce war as a sovereign right of the nation and the threat or use of force as means of settling international disputes.
>
> In order to accomplish the aim of the preceding paragraph, land, sea, and air forces, as well as other war potential, will never be maintained. The right of belligerency of the state will not be recognized.

Emperor Hirohito was anxious about his country's future security and expressed his concerns to MacArthur. MacArthur reportedly pledged, "The basic principle of the United States is to guarantee Japan's security."[15]

Someone on the Japanese side told reporters the details of the meeting, apparently on the assumption that they understood he was speaking off the record, but Associated Press reporters in Tokyo made the story public.[16] MacArthur promptly denied that he and the emperor had discussed security issues.[17] Shortly thereafter, Okumura Katsuzō (1903–75), who had served as translator, took a leave of absence from his position at the Japanese Foreign Ministry to accept responsibility for the leak. This action strongly suggested that the published accounts had been accurate.[18]

Three decades later, as Okumura was near death, the emperor told Irie Sukemasa (1905–85), his longtime chamberlain, that the culprit was in fact Shirasu Jirō (1902–85) and that Okumura had done nothing wrong. The emperor in no way indicated to Irie that the leak had been false.[19] Irie's diary was not published until after the death of the emperor, and it now serves as crucial evidence that ministers often briefed the emperor on political matters.

It is difficult to determine whether the emperor exercised any influence over MacArthur. One of the defining characteristics of the Occupation was MacArthur's use of the emperor to legitimize SCAP's reforms. Once SCAP had decided on a policy, the emperor was asked to affirm it or even take responsibility for initiating it. Through the use of private channels, the policy was made to look as if it had originated on the Japanese side. SCAP portrayed the emperor as backing the Postwar Constitution, the most important reform of the Occupation.

The location of the meetings between the emperor and MacArthur symbolized the structure of authority during the Occupation. Whereas Japanese politicians briefed the emperor at the palace before and after

Japan's surrender, MacArthur never set foot in the palace. Instead he hosted the emperor at his headquarters for their meetings. This territorialization of authority made it clear who was the dominant figure. There were eight such meetings under the Postwar Constitution (of which one, on the occasion of MacArthur's recall in 1951, likely had little significance).

Accounts of the 6 May 1947 meeting are important because they suggest that the emperor was forthrightly expressing his political concerns from the earliest days of the new constitutional system. The emperor did not interpret the new constitution as making himself a passive symbol, like a flag or a puppet. One of the most telling postwar examples of Hirohito's influence was his eventual refusal to abdicate, something the emperor considered in the months after the surrender. In the end, Hirohito insisted on remaining on the throne despite calls, before and after the new constitution went into effect, from all sides for his abdication, including some from close advisors. In contrast, MacArthur and other influential leaders of the Occupation worked behind the scenes to ensure that Hirohito did not abdicate.[20] They found him too useful for legitimizing reforms.

The first prime minister under the new constitution was Katayama Tetsu (1887–1978), head of the JSP. In the April 1947 House of Representatives elections, the JSP won a plurality of seats. It joined with the centrist Democratic Party headed by Ashida Hitoshi to form the government. The right wing of the JSP and the Democratic Party each held seven Cabinet posts; the JSP's left wing was excluded from the Cabinet. The conservative Liberal Party headed by Yoshida Shigeru found itself in the opposition.

When Matsuoka Komakichi (1888–1958), speaker of the House of Representatives, rushed to the palace on 24 May 1947 to tell the emperor that Katayama had been selected prime minister, the emperor commented: "Katayama seems weak to me."[21] In September 1947, Emperor Hirohito had a chamberlain deliver to Katayama a long memo of advice on the art of being prime minister (the memo became public in 1990).[22] The emperor warned Katayama not to move too fast with reforms: "There is a natural tempo to reform. If one gently pushes the pendulum, the result is that it swings smoothly. If one forcefully pushes the pendulum, it never fails to swing wildly. The principle of the pendulum is something that I always keep in mind. It would be a problem if there were reaction to the reforms."[23] He particularly urged Katayama to remember the pendulum principle with regard to changes in palace personnel.

In his memo, Emperor Hirohito also instructed Katayama to place the public (welfare) before the private. Hirohito even cited the example of Nintoku, the emperor who is said to have lowered taxes after seeing little smoke rising from the cottages of the people (Nintoku, regarded as legendary by many scholars, is said to have reigned during the first half of the fifth century). Finally, he suggested that there was much to be learned from the British royal house. It is evident from this memo that the emperor, even after the new constitution went into effect, continued to think that it was his job to nurture and supervise prime ministers. It is not known how Katayama reacted to this memo. In fact, very little is known about relations between Prime Minister Katayama and the emperor.

Prewar organs of government that had advised the emperor on political and military matters, such as the Office of Lord Privy Seal, Office of Chief Aide-de-camp, and the Privy Council, were abolished either before the new constitution went into effect or as it went into effect. Several of the emperor's customary sources of information thus disappeared. During the Katayama Cabinet, the emperor turned to Foreign Minister Ashida Hitoshi, a moderate conservative, for information.

The Ashida diary, published in 1986, has proved valuable for understanding the emperor's political activities during the Occupation. The entry for 22 July 1947 shows the emperor particularly eager for political news:

> I heard from the vice foreign minister that the vice grand chamberlain had told him that His Majesty is very interested in foreign affairs. His Majesty is said to have asked why the foreign minister does not come to brief him. The deputy grand chamberlain said that if the foreign minister would brief the Emperor, even Saturday would be fine.
>
> Under the new constitution, to give the impression that the Emperor is being overly involved in domestic or foreign affairs is not a good thing for the imperial house or for Japan as a whole. For this reason I don't go [to the palace] and conduct briefings. However, I decided that if it was the Emperor's desire, I must go. I sent news of my decision to visit the palace next Monday.

> [During the briefing,] the Emperor said, "Japan must cooperate with the United States, after all, and it is difficult for us to cooperate with Russia, I think."
>
> When the Emperor said [as I was leaving], "Please come again from time to time," I replied, "Yes."[24]

This entry demonstrates the tension that Ashida felt in trying to govern according to the new constitution while respecting the wishes of the emperor. The emperor remained a figure of commanding authority in spite of the change in his constitutional position, and he wanted the briefings to continue.

Under the new constitution, the validity of imperial briefings was open to question. Three terms continued to be used to describe briefings in the postwar, especially the early postwar, era. The terms are unfamiliar even to most Japanese: (1) *jōsō*: "briefing to obtain imperial sanction (*saika*)"; (2) *sōjō*: "briefing the emperor"; and (3) *naisō*: "briefing the emperor in advance" (with the nuance of "in advance of a decision").[25] *Naisō* became the dominant term. Although it strongly implies secrecy, linguistically it avoids suggesting that the emperor sanctioned or otherwise influenced decisions.

In a diary entry for 24 September 1947, Ashida recorded that the emperor was intensely interested in national security: "On the 19th I briefed the emperor on foreign affairs. The main topics were preparations for the peace treaty and the problem of Japan's future security. . . . Regarding security issues, the emperor listened with all his strength."[26] The conditions under which Japan would regain its independence became the crucial political issue after the initial reforms of the Occupation were completed. U.S. and Japanese officials were discussing this topic by the summer of 1947. There were divisions in Japan and among the American authorities negotiating the treaty regarding the proper course for Japan. The sticking point was whether Japan should be neutral or align itself with the United States.

After the war, the emperor became pro-American and favored placing Japan's security in the hands of the United States. One reason for this was that he did not have much choice in the matter. He was beholden to MacArthur and the U.S. government for protecting the throne and for rebuilding, not punishing, Japan. But there was another reason. Emperor Hirohito found an anticommunist ally in the United States.

U.S. documents revealed in Japan in 1979 by Shindō Eiichi, a scholar of international politics, generated widespread interest. According to these documents, soon after being briefed by Foreign Minister Ashida about the ongoing negotiations for a peace treaty, the emperor had chamberlain Terasaki Hidenari tell William J. Sebald, political advisor to SCAP, of his views regarding Okinawa, and Sebald forwarded the message to the State Department:

> According to Terasaki, the emperor hopes that the United States will continue its military occupation of Okinawa and the Ryūkyū Islands. In the emperor's opinion this will be beneficial to the United States and it will also ensure Japan's defense. The people of Japan fear the threat from Russia, and its intervention in Japan's domestic affairs. So this policy will have broad support. . . . According to the emperor, the military occupation of Okinawa should be instituted under the legal fiction that a long-term lease (25 to 50 years) has been extended to the United States by Japan, which retains its sovereignty over the islands.[27]

The publishing of this message in the April 1979 issue of *Sekai* created quite a stir in Japan, especially in Okinawa. Questions were raised about the authenticity of the message, which portrayed the emperor as sacrificing Okinawa for the good of the mainland. Irie recorded in his diary (published in 1989) that he asked the emperor about the message on 19 April 1979. The emperor's reply substantiated the message: "If the United States had not occupied and protected Japan, who knows what would have become of not only Okinawa but also of the main islands."[28]

Had Japan not been under foreign occupation—in other words, if Japan had been operating fully under the constitution instead of the amorphous conditions that characterized the Occupation—the emperor's message would seem to have been a constitutional violation. In 1983, a few years after the U.S. records of the emperor's message became public, Yokota Kōichi (1939–), a constitutional scholar who tended to interpret the emperor's role narrowly, wrote: "If it is authentic, then it was a clear constitutional violation."[29] Whereas the Meiji Constitution acknowledged the emperor's extensive foreign policy powers, Article 73 of the Postwar Constitution states that the "Cabinet . . . shall . . . manage foreign affairs."

Constitutional violation or not, the emperor's message regarding Okinawa was one of the most controversial examples of his attempts to influence policy under the new system. The emperor's motivations remain open to interpretation, however. Historian Robert Eldridge has suggested that Emperor Hirohito, in the face of U.S. officials' unwillingness to fulfill the hopes that Okinawa would be returned according to the peace treaty restoring mainland Japan's sovereignty, may have prevented Okinawa from being separated permanently from Japan by cleverly suggesting an alternative scenario that guaranteed residual Japanese sovereignty over the islands.[30] This interpretation of the emperor's role is plausible. It is also open to use by apologists for Emperor Hirohito who insist that on those rare occasions when he intervened in politics, the end result was always for the good of the nation.

The Katayama Cabinet collapsed in March 1948 after having accomplished little. On 10 March 1948, Ashida Hitoshi became prime minister. Ashida had misgivings about the practice of briefings; nonetheless, on the day that he took office he met with the emperor to discuss the political situation. Ashida recorded in his diary that the emperor expressed concern about the growing strength of the JCP. He also wanted to know what effect the "entry of the left" into the Cabinet—this referred to Ashida's selection of two ministers from the left wing of the JSP—would have:

> I was asked, "Aren't some measures against the Communist Party necessary?"
>
> Next . . . I was asked about the effect of the entry of the left into the Cabinet, and I said that so long as it was only to the extent of Katō [Kanjū; 1887–1974] and Nomizo [Masaru; 1898–1978],[31] who were not pro-communist, it would not have much effect, and on the contrary the left's inclusion [in the government] would perhaps serve to quiet the left.[32]

As the second prime minister under the Postwar Constitution assumed office, the emperor continued to question the prime minister's choice of ministers and to suggest political measures, in this case against the Communists. The emperor not only was concerned with the communist threat domestically but also watched anxiously as the Chinese Communist Party fought for dominance in China and in 1949 gained control of that country.[33]

When Ashida became prime minister, he, as Katayama had before him, came under pressure from SCAP to replace the emperor's top two advisors. Between 1946 and 1949, a series of reforms brought the palace into line with SCAP's vision of a symbolic monarchy, and the replacements were part of these efforts to democratize the palace. The once autonomous Imperial Household Ministry was reduced first to an office and then to an agency under the supervision of the prime minister. The agency's duties no longer included such tasks as managing the aristocracy. By 1947, the number of officials working in the Imperial Household Agency had dropped from 6,200 to 1,500.[34]

The monarchy was also divested of its fortune. Shortly after the surrender, SCAP ordered the Japanese government to submit an account of the imperial house's wealth. The Imperial Household Ministry concluded that the total was over ¥1.5 billion, an astonishing sum.[35] U.S. officials viewed the monarchy, with its diverse sources of wealth, as a financial clique (*zaibatsu*) along the lines of Mitsui, Mitsubishi, Sumitomo, and Yasuda. "The Imperial House possesses many characteristics of the several 'Honsha'[36] which are in the process of liquidation," wrote Colonel R. C. Kramer of SCAP's Economic and Finance Section in a memorandum to his superiors.[37] SCAP proposed the following article for the constitution: "All property of the Imperial Household shall belong to the State. All expenses of the Imperial Household shall be appropriated by the Diet in the budget" (now Article 88 of the constitution).

SCAP's plan initially met with resistance from Japanese officials, but SCAP insisted that all of the imperial house's wealth be transferred to the state. The Imperial House Economy Law (Kōshitsu keizaihō), which went into effect with the new constitution, provides for the annual allocation of funds for the emperor and members of his family in their private status.[38] This arrangement makes the Japanese royal house particularly dependent on public funds.

The financial dependence of the Japanese monarchy contrasts with the case of the British throne. Once the Japanese imperial house became almost entirely dependent on the Diet for funds, it lost the financial autonomy still enjoyed by the British royal house, which is independently wealthy. Most of the expenses incurred by British royal family members in their private status (for example, the costs of their vacations) are paid for out of the royal family's personal fortune.[39] The crown also uses its personal wealth to make sizable donations to charities. In contrast, even the vacations taken by Japanese imperial family members are paid for with funds annually allotted by the Diet. Journalist Takahashi Hiroshi (1941–2011) calculated that if one divided the imperial household's budget by the number of Japanese citizens (121 million), each individual paid ¥130 (less than $1 according to exchange rates at that time) to support the imperial house in 1986.[40] This budget supported a lifestyle that was obviously privileged but not luxurious, at least in comparison to households, royal or otherwise, that enjoyed tremendous wealth.

Until the Occupation reforms, the monarchy was not only financially independent but also legally autonomous. The prewar Imperial House Law (Kōshitsu tenpan), enacted concurrently with the Meiji Constitution, reserved to the emperor legal authority over the affairs of the imperial house. The Imperial House Law was, in the words of its author Itō Hirobumi, "the family law of the Imperial House."[41] Unlike other laws, it lay outside the purview of the Diet. Article 74 of the Meiji Constitution specified that "no modification of the Imperial House Law shall be required to be submitted to the deliberation of the Imperial Diet." The Imperial House Law could be amended only by the Imperial Family Council and Privy Council, two bodies beyond the supervision of the Diet.[42]

U.S. officials wanted the monarchy to be under the legal supervision of the Diet to establish the parliament as the highest decision-making body. Many articles in the constitutional draft that the Government Section presented to the Japanese government in February 1946 roiled the Japanese authorities, and what eventually became Article 2 of the Constitution of Japan was no exception: "The Imperial Throne shall be dynastic and succeeded to in accordance with the Imperial House Law *passed by the Diet*" (emphasis added).

On 4 March, Minister of State Matsumoto Jōji, who led the Japanese delegation in the negotiations with SCAP about constitutional revision, met with General Courtney Whitney (1897–1969), chief of the Government Section, and Colonel Charles Kades (1906–96), the principal drafter. Matsumoto brought with him a Japanese translation of the draft. During a thirty-hour marathon session, U.S. officials translated Matsumoto's version back into English to check whether it maintained the basic principles of the Government Section's draft. The U.S. officials soon noticed that the clause "passed by the Diet" had been omitted from the Japanese version. According to SCAP records, the following exchange ensued between Matsumoto and Whitney:

> Matsumoto: "Is it essential that the Imperial House Law be enacted by the Diet? Under the present Japanese constitution the Imperial House Law is made by members of the Imperial House. The Imperial House has autonomy."
>
> Whitney: "Unless the Imperial House Law is made subject to approval by the representatives of the people, we pay only lip service to the supremacy of the people."[43]

Ashida, then minister of Welfare, recorded in his diary that Matsumoto and Prime Minister Shidehara Kijūrō entered the Cabinet meeting that next day with "serious looks on their faces."[44] In noting Matsumoto's report of how the U.S. officials had quickly noticed that the clause "passed by the Diet" was missing in the translation, Ashida entered this phrase into his diary in the original English.

According to Ashida's diary, the emperor asked the prime minister if it were possible for him "to maintain the right to propose revisions of the Imperial House Law."[45] Article 62 of the prewar Imperial House Law read: "When in the future it shall become necessary either to amend or make additions to the present Law, the matter shall be decided by the Emperor, with the advice of the Imperial Family Council and with that of the Privy Council."[46] Ashida's diary suggests that the emperor, rather than being the wholehearted champion of the Occupation reforms that he is sometimes portrayed as being, sought to maintain some of his prerogatives, including his authority over the imperial house. In the end, however, the emperor and the Japanese government reluctantly acquiesced to SCAP's demands that the imperial house be brought fully under the supervision of the Diet.[47]

In 1948, Prime Minister Ashida faced telling the emperor, who already had seen his authority in various areas sharply curtailed, that his top two advisors, the grand chamberlain and the director of the Imperial Household Office, would have to be replaced. Although the emperor could not stop the overall reform of the palace, he at least wanted to retain his leading advisors. He had urged Katayama the year before to remember the pendulum principle when changing palace personnel.

On 6 April 1948, Ashida informed the emperor that the personnel changes could not be avoided. Ashida recorded in his diary that the emperor, who tended to express his displeasure in subtle ways, outspokenly opposed the changes: "It is 'not funny' (*omoshiroku nai*) that every time the government changes, the director of the Imperial Household Office will switch." The emperor continued, "The present director and grand chamberlain suit me fine so . . . ."[48] In late May, the emperor voiced his displeasure over the proposed personnel changes to Ashida in such a strong manner that Ashida thought about resigning: "From 10:15 for about one hour and twenty minutes [I listened to] the emperor express various complaints about the replacement of the grand chamberlain and the plan to reform the Imperial Household Ministry. It was to the point that I thought for a moment about dissolving the government."[49] Irie's diary corroborated that the emperor was upset about the personnel changes: "[Today] was Prime Minister Ashida's audience . . . it appears that the worst conditions have arisen."[50] In the end, the personnel changes were carried out because SCAP insisted on them. This represented a drastic change from prewar practices. Although the emperor had expressed his opposition in a forceful manner, the prime minister (with SCAP pushing him) made the changes in palace personnel.

Earlier in May, Ashida recorded in his diary that he had explained to the emperor that the number of ministerial briefings would have to be decreased under the new constitution: "I explained that since, according to the new constitution, the extent [of the emperor's role] in state affairs had been restricted, it would not be possible for each minister to brief the emperor on political affairs as before, but the sentiments of the ministers toward His Majesty had in no way changed."[51] On 3 June, however, Prime Minister Ashida himself briefed the emperor at the palace at the request of one of the emperor's chamberlains. At the end of their conversation, Emperor Hirohito asked Ashida "to visit the palace from time to time to report on the food situation and economic conditions."[52] The emperor, who did not want to be weaned from politics, was resisting the prime minister's attempt to decrease the number of briefings.

The Ashida Cabinet fell in October 1948, and the JSP would not participate in another government for over four decades. Yoshida Shigeru, head of the conservative Liberal Party, began his six-year reign as prime minister that same month. When the emperor saw Yoshida's proposed Cabinet members, he is said to have pointed to Satō Eisaku's (1901–75) name and said, "Is this all right?"[53] The emperor was no less shy about questioning Yoshida's choice of ministers than he had been those of Ashida. The emperor apparently was concerned that Satō was tainted because his older brother, Kishi Nobusuke, had been arrested as a war criminal and was in Sugamo Prison at that time. Both Kishi and Satō later served as prime minister.

Yoshida's first Cabinet enjoyed only tenuous power, but the left found itself in the opposition for the first time under the new constitution. Yoshida's return to power in 1948 marked the beginning of more than four decades of conservative predominance in Japan. In 1949 the Liberal Party won a comprehensive victory in the House of Representatives elections. Not until 1993 would the left again participate in the government. Excluded from power, left-wing parties assumed a watchdog role on a variety of fronts, including the question of the emperor. Yoshida had been in office only a few months, for example, when opposition parties demanded an explanation for the emperor's message to U.S. President Harry Truman.

In spite of pressure from the opposition parties to exclude the emperor from politics, Yoshida reformalized the practice of political briefings. One only can speculate what would have become of such briefings if Ashida had remained in office or if someone who had an even stricter interpretation of the emperor's role under the constitution had succeeded Ashida. What is apparent, however, is that Yoshida, a conservative, was far more inclined than his predecessor to look favorably on the practice. Yoshida not only personally briefed the emperor often, he also recommended that other ministers regularly brief the emperor as well.[54] The emperor, as we have seen, wanted to be briefed, and Yoshida strove to please the emperor. It was Yoshida, after all, who referred to himself as a "servant" of the emperor on the occasion of Akihito's investiture as crown prince in 1952.

Few contemporary articles in the mass media questioned Yoshida's reestablishment of secret briefings. One of the exceptions, which appeared in the *Shūkan asahi* in September 1953, described how, at Prime Minister Yoshida's directions, one minister after another briefed the emperor in August of that year: 1 August: minister of Agriculture and Forestry; 10 August: minister of State; 11 August: Foreign minister; 12 August: prime minister; 19 August: minister of Finance; 24 August: Foreign minister. The article criticized these briefings for making it seem as though government ministers continued to be servants of the emperor when in fact they were servants of the sovereign people.[55]

During his prime ministership, Yoshida, following prewar custom, prohibited ministers from publicly discussing details of the briefings, especially the emperor's comments and questions.[56] With one important exception, this secrecy was not breached until Hirohito's death. Thus, one of the key mechanisms by which the emperor intersected with politics in the postwar era was "privatized." Yoshida's purpose in making the briefings private was to maintain a constitutionally murky practice that kept the emperor informed about and, to some extent, involved in politics by drawing as little attention to it as possible. By keeping the emperor's comments secret, he maintained the public neutrality of the emperor and thus avoided the charge that the government was deploying the emperor for political ends.

Since no official records of the briefings are available, one has to reconstruct their significance through diaries and memoirs, which provide only secondhand snippets of the emperor's comments. Mitani Takanobu, the emperor's chamberlain when the Korean War began, recounted a memorable briefing that he conducted on the day hostilities commenced on the Korean Peninsula. On 25 June 1950, Mitani was at home listening to a baseball game on the radio when he learned through a special announcement that war had broken out in Korea. Mitani immediately realized that he would have to prepare himself to brief the emperor that day.

A former diplomat who had served as ambassador to France during the war, Mitani telephoned friends in the Foreign Ministry to learn what the war meant for Japan. In his briefing, Mitani stressed that the war, for Japan, was only a "nearby fire" (*chikabi*). The emperor, however, considered the Korean War to be a "fire already approaching the front gate" (*hi wa sude ni monzen ni sematte iru*).[57] Emperor Hirohito's education had included extensive training in military affairs, and he was undoubtedly aware of the view that Korea was, in strategic terms, a dagger pointed at Japan. The potential communization of the Korean Peninsula, part of Japan's colonial empire for four decades before the surrender, was a threat that Emperor Hirohito could not dismiss lightly.

U.S. documents that became available in the 1970s showed that the emperor continued to reach out to American officials late into the

Occupation. The emperor sent a message of gratitude to U.S. Secretary of State Dean Acheson in July 1950 for the U.S. military intervention in Korea.[58] Other American documents suggest that earlier that year the emperor had sent John Foster Dulles, the special ambassador to the peace treaty negotiations, a message asking for an easing of the purge of politicians and officials tainted by the war.[59] The emperor sent these messages three years after he had been stripped of all constitutional authority to direct foreign affairs and two years after he had sent the controversial message to President Truman. It is not known whether these were interpreted as "private" or "official" communications.

In February 1951, Dulles met with the emperor on one of his visits to Japan. It was a rough trip for Dulles. Politicians from the JSP presented him with opinion papers proposing an unarmed, nonaligned Japan. Dulles explained to the emperor that negotiations were under way for an agreement for the United States to station troops in Japan on a provisional basis until Japan gained the strength to defend itself. He wondered aloud whether the emperor's support for the peace treaty then being negotiated would make the Japanese people more likely to accept the treaty. The emperor apparently replied that he totally agreed with Dulles's line of thinking. According to the message that Dulles sent to Washington, the emperor wanted to express his wish to President Truman that Japan and the United States would march forward hand in hand.[60]

Historian Toyoshita Narahiko has confirmed that during the San Francisco Peace Treaty negotiations, Prime Minister Yoshida regularly briefed the emperor on developments. In fact, Yoshida would arrive at the palace with special "briefing documents" prepared by the Treaty Bureau to turn over to the emperor.[61] The emperor, who favored an alliance with the United States, apparently was keenly interested in the conditions under which Japan would regain its independence.

After MacArthur was recalled by President Truman in 1951, General Matthew Ridgway assumed the position of Supreme Commander for the Allied Powers, and he met with the emperor occasionally during the last months of the Occupation. At the time of their first meeting, in May 1951, Ridgway had also been put in command of the war in Korea:

> As the talk progressed the Emperor asked questions freely, and seemed to have a very sound grasp of what I was presenting. He was deeply pleased, he

> said, at my assurance that the war in Korea could, and would, be brought to a satisfactory close, and expressed the hope that relationships between Japan and the Republic of Korea could be worked out satisfactorily.
>
> He expressed his pleasure also at my decision to allow a review of existing directives, imposed by us, which barred certain Japanese from political office who had been active in the war government of Japan. He also said he was pleased at my actions in supporting the Japanese government in opposing the May Day meeting on the Imperial Plaza.
>
> He said he was delighted that the U.S. had seen fit to send troops to protect northern Hokkaido. I told him that we considered the security of Japan intimately related to our own, and that future co-operation between Japan and America was fundamental in our national policy.[62]

Northern Hokkaido was only a short distance from the Soviet Union. Emperor Hirohito considered the Soviet Union, long one of Japan's competitors for hegemony in East Asia, to be a dangerous military threat. The emperor's concern with Japan's security and the left, especially anything to do with political subversion and social unrest, were recurring themes in his comments.

The peace treaty was signed in 1951, as was the U.S.–Japan Security Treaty. Japan's sovereignty was restored, with the exception of Okinawa, which remained under the direct rule of the U.S. military, although there was an understanding on both sides that residual sovereignty over the territory lay with Japan. In April 1952, the Occupation came to an end.

As a result of the Occupation reforms, politics no longer revolved around the palace. Since decisions were no longer legitimized through the principle of imperial prerogative, the scope of political activity at the palace greatly declined. The palace was pushed to the periphery as the political process came to be centered in the Diet. Under the Postwar Constitution, Emperor Hirohito had no decisionmaking authority, and there were no examples after May 1947 of Hirohito exercising authority as he had in earlier times to force a prime minister to resign or have a rebellion suppressed.

It was with Japan's independence, ironically, that the emperor lost yet another of his channels to the political process. Not only did his privileged access to U.S. officials decrease, but this channel's significance was greatly curtailed when Japan regained its sovereignty. The U.S.-written Constitution of Japan was intended to make the emperor's role in the political process ceremonial. Yet throughout the Occupation, the emperor reached out to and was received by U.S. officials, although it is virtually impossible to measure whether he influenced them. There was, for example, already strong support in various quarters in the United States for retaining Okinawa for security reasons before the emperor sent his message to that effect.

In the face of constitutional reform, the emperor fought to maintain contact with Japanese politicians. The emperor's insistence that briefings continue is the best example of his struggle to keep involved. Opposition parties and others worked to push the emperor away from politics, and they encountered resistance from the palace, including from the emperor himself. In addition, Yoshida's role in maintaining briefings was critical, although it drew little popular attention. Briefings did not become much of a public issue in the period immediately after May 1947. The Japanese had more fundamental changes to their legal system to address.

Measuring the emperor's political influence over Japanese politicians under the new constitution is almost as difficult as fathoming his influence over U.S. officials. One important factor remained: the emperor had lost his constitutional authority, but he remained a figure of awe for many Japanese. As we have seen, even Ashida, who worked to distance the emperor from the political process, was so shaken by the emperor's anger during one briefing that he thought of dissolving his Cabinet. Yoshida Shigeru, Shigemitsu Mamoru (1887–1957), Satō Eisaku, and other leading postwar politicians had been bureaucrats in service to the emperor in the prewar era and thus may have continued to be particularly susceptible to his influence. Constitutions can do only so much to overcome such feelings of loyalty.

It is apparent that the emperor continued to voice his political opinions. He wondered aloud about the desirability of anticommunist measures. He questioned the prime minister's choice of personnel. He did not want his advisors changed. He wanted his country aligned with the United States. The emperor's prewar engagement in politics continued into the postwar period.

The Post-Occupation Period

In 1956, Tanaka Minoru, one of a select group of journalists affiliated with the Imperial House Press Club (membership is limited to representatives of mainstream organs of the mass media, such as the national newspapers),[63] published a short article about the emperor in *Bungei shunjū* titled "A Day in the Life of the Emperor." Tanaka wrote: "Following his longstanding custom, the emperor awakes at 7:30. He reads the newspaper first thing, noting the important topics of the day. Since the emperor, as a symbol, is in no way involved in politics, the so-called political briefings are being dispensed with. Thus, newspapers are the emperor's only window into current affairs."[64]

The emperor was, it is true, an avid reader of newspapers, but the briefings were never discontinued, although they decreased somewhat in number. It is inconceivable that Tanaka, who would have been intimately familiar with the visits of politicians to the palace, did not know that the emperor continued to receive regular briefings on political matters and that there were no plans to discontinue these briefings.[65] Journalist Takahashi Hiroshi, who served in the Imperial House Press Club in the 1970s, commented that in deemphasizing briefings, Tanaka was probably "responding to the wishes of the Imperial Household Agency."[66] The Imperial Household Agency's campaign to make it appear that the emperor was no longer involved in politics was the principal reason for the significant gap between public expectations of the emperor in his symbolic role and his actual political role.

The Imperial Household Agency serves as the gatekeeper to the throne. Journalists disagree on the extent to which the agency is able to shape coverage of the monarchy today, but two points are evident. First, the agency's authority over the mass media has declined steadily throughout the postwar era. Second, journalists who belong to the Imperial House Press Club carefully weigh the costs and benefits of publishing stories that, by antagonizing the agency, might jeopardize the steady flow of information and photographs they receive through their privileged membership in the club. After all, stories about the imperial family, particularly those that include visual images, are a major revenue source for the mass media, especially for women's magazines.

It is well known that on several occasions supra-organizations that represent a broad segment of the Japanese media have signed agreements with the Imperial Household Agency to limit coverage of certain topics to respect the privacy of imperial family members. Examples include pacts reached to regulate coverage of Akihito's search for a bride in the

1950s and of Naruhito's more extended courting process in the 1980s and early 1990s.[67] It is true that the Imperial Household Agency maintains some ability, even today, to influence mainstream mass media coverage of the imperial house. However, the agency by no means has the power to choreograph coverage of the throne (a power that, to a considerable extent, it did possess in the prewar era), especially in light of the plurality of Japan's media today and the constitutional protection they enjoy. Since the British mass media's sensationalistic coverage of the British throne is often invoked to suggest the compliance of the Japanese mass media in covering all imperial matters, it is worth recalling that in Britain from 1945 until the late 1950s the crown, linked to the victorious war, enjoyed largely uncritical press coverage.[68]

Although the Imperial Household Agency sought to draw attention away from briefings, and the press generally avoided the topic (in part because there was little to report), ironically one of the chief spokesmen for the symbolic monarchy hinted that the emperor's role was more than just symbolic. Koizumi Shinzō remained the central commentator on the imperial house throughout the 1950s. For the crown prince's education, Koizumi drew on Fukuzawa's model of the imperial house and on the British model. Koizumi and the crown prince read Fukuzawa's "Teishitsuron" together. Akihito thus learned of the famous Meiji thinker's interpretation of the monarchy, which was a mixture of the British model and Fukuzawa's particular views. Koizumi also had Akihito read aloud Harold Nicolson's biography of King George V (r. 1910–36) in the original English. This took years, since Nicolson's study of the public life of the king is 530 pages long.[69] Koizumi and Akihito finished reading it one week before the crown prince's marriage in 1959.

In 1955, at the height of the constitutional revision movement, Koizumi published three short essays on George V. These essays were drawn from Nicolson's book and may have been the same sections he had emphasized to the crown prince. Koizumi chronicled George V's struggle to maintain his strict impartiality (*fuhen futōsei*) in the face of political crises during his reign. For example, George V presided over the formation of the first Labour government in England. Koizumi, relying on Nicolson's account, described the king's role in 1924 as follows: "At that time there were elements that feared the appearance of a Labour Cabinet and they employed various measures to try to block it, but the king made it clear that because the Conservatives had lost the vote in the House of Commons, he intended to order the head of the Labour Party to form a Cabinet without stipulations."[70]

Although stressing the necessity of the throne's neutrality (especially in public), Koizumi nonetheless noted in detail the close contact between the prime minister and the monarch in Britain. On more than one occasion, Koizumi paraphrased Bagehot's description of the king's rights: "According to the 'British Constitution,' the king has the right to be advised by the government, to encourage the government, and to warn the government."[71] Koizumi's essays, like Nicolson's book, made it clear that the British monarch, even King George V who strove to maintain his neutrality, was nonetheless on occasion more than a passive entity in political affairs.

Yoshida was succeeded as prime minister by Hatoyama Ichirō in December 1954, who, according to longtime Imperial House Press Club journalist Togashi Junji (1897–1985), "avoided meeting the emperor with all his might."[72] The reasons for Hatoyama's reluctance are not known. Anecdotal evidence that became available after the death of the emperor revealed that Konō Ichirō (1898–1965), minister of Agriculture and Forestry in the first Hatoyama Cabinet, also refused to conduct briefings after an unpleasant first meeting with the emperor. During Konō's first briefing, which covered the topic of commercial tree production in Japan, the emperor, who had extensive knowledge of the natural sciences, asked Konō about the production of deciduous trees. Nervous and confused, Konō responded that deciduous trees, too, were being planted. When Konō returned to ministry headquarters, he learned that not one deciduous tree, which are not suitable to commercial production in Japan because of the climate, had been planted. The emperor was known for playing such jokes to tweak his ministers. Although Konō served frequently as a minister in LDP Cabinets in the 1950s and 1960s, he never again briefed the emperor.[73]

Since decisions no longer constitutionally required the emperor's sanction, ministers were not obligated to brief him. Hatoyama and Konō appear to have been exceptions, however. Most ministers dutifully briefed the emperor, and some, such as Satō Eisaku, seemed to relish the practice. During Hatoyama's prime ministership, Hirohito turned to Shigemitsu Mamoru, Foreign minister in all three of Hatoyama's Cabinets and long a devoted servant of the emperor, for information.

Hatoyama favored the restoration of diplomatic relations with the Soviet Union, a task he completed in 1956. During Hatoyama's tenure as prime minister, there were loud calls from his supporters for Japan to develop a defense capability independent of the United States. The opposition parties were hostile to both domestic defense buildups and the Security Treaty. The emperor was profoundly interested in the complex political situation.

Entries in Shigemitsu's diary (published in 1988) showed that he often briefed the emperor as Foreign Minister; there were, for example, no fewer than five such briefings in April 1955. One entry in Shigemitsu's diary reveals the emperor's anticommunist, pro-American line. After briefing the emperor on 20 August 1955, Shigemitsu recorded in his diary that the emperor "directed" him that "Japanese-American cooperation, and 'anti-communism,' are necessary; the withdrawal of [American] troops is not an option."[74] Just a few days later, Shigemitsu was in Washington with Kishi Nobusuke to discuss the question of Japan's defense with U.S. officials. Shigemitsu made no mention of whether he was influenced by the emperor's comments; all that can be said is that he considered them significant enough to record in his diary.

Little is known about the briefings that took place under the Ishibashi Tanzan (1956–57), Kishi (1957–60), and Ikeda Hayato (1960–64) Cabinets.[75] Kishi, who briefed the emperor as a minister under both the prewar and postwar constitutions, did make one telling remark in his memoirs. Comparing the practice of briefings under the two constitutions, he said that "the emperor's attitude had not changed particularly."[76]

In January 1960, Koizumi provided another hint about the monarchy's political role in an essay about Fukuzawa's "Teishitsuron" in *Bungei shunjū*.[77] By 1960, Koizumi faced the necessity of explaining to those Japanese accustomed to the emperor as a symbol why Fukuzawa's 1882 proposal for a monarchy outside the formal decisionmaking process was so prescient:

> Today, looking back [from the perspective] of the present constitution, it seems to be extremely natural, not unusual in the least; however, when you think that Fukuzawa wrote . . . seventy-odd years ago, before the old Imperial Constitution even was established, indeed before the Japanese people had a thing called a constitution . . . one must think that Fukuzawa's views were ahead of the times.[78]

Koizumi proceeded to explain the same tenets of Fukuzawa's "Teishitsuron" discussed above, but in far more detail than he had in his short 1952 article.

Toward the end of his essay, Koizumi drew on his knowledge of the British monarchy, especially of George V, to supplement Fukuzawa's interpretation of the monarch's proper role. Koizumi stressed Bagehot's point that in "the course of a long reign a sagacious king would acquire an experience with which few ministers could contend." Koizumi claimed that in comparison with politicians monarchs tend to give the nation precedence over other concerns. Thus, they could play a valuable role in the country's politics:

> It goes without saying that in a constitutional monarchy, the prime minister, who enjoys the support of the parliament, must shoulder all political responsibility. But politicians, who change frequently, . . . sometimes forget tomorrow for the sake of today; politicians themselves sufficiently understand that there is a concern that they will forget the country for the party. . . . If there are many opportunities for politicians to hear the opinions of a monarch who embraces a special consciousness and viewpoint regarding the interests of the country and countrymen, it is of great value to them and others.
>
> In this way, a constitutional monarch can play the role of one who morally encourages and of one who warns. This is an "enlargement" (*fuen sareru koto*) of Fukuzawa's "Teishitsuron."[79]

In calling for a monarch who exercises a moderating influence on the political process, Koizumi was influenced far more by Bagehot's model of the monarchy than Fukuzawa had been. In light of the practice of briefings, Koizumi's supplement to Fukuzawa's model was necessary to justify the emperor's actual role. Indeed, Koizumi demonstrated that a symbolic monarch's role was more than symbolic.

Satō Eisaku, who became prime minister in 1964, worked hard to keep the emperor updated on political matters. Satō's diary (first published in 1997), which covers the eight years that he was prime minister, includes numerous references to briefings on topics ranging from the 1968 Tet Offensive in Vietnam to the Osaka International Exposition of 1970.[80] Satō recorded more than once that briefings ran long because the emperor asked so many questions.

Satō's diary indicated that he always sought the emperor's sanction (*saika*) before finalizing the list of individuals selected to receive imperial decorations.[81] Emperor Hirohito apparently was aware of the potential for cronyism to seep into the selection process. Indeed, other sources indicate that Hirohito, after the fact, expressed his dissatisfaction with the Satō Cabinet's decision to present the Order of Culture to Akagi Masao (1887–1972) in 1971. Akagi, who had served in the prewar Home Ministry, is famous in Japan for his erosion control projects. During the awards ceremony in 1971, however, Emperor Hirohito asked Chamberlain Irie if it were not the case that the Order of Culture had originally been reserved for "individuals who, in spite of coming from a poor family and in spite of not having had enough research support, devoted themselves to making scientific and cultural contributions." Irie responded that His Majesty's memory correctly served him. Not only did Akagi come from a privileged background, but as an elite civil servant he also would have had access to the resources of the state. The emperor's question later led Irie to put a stop to behind-the-scene efforts by Satō, after he left office, to have the Order of Culture awarded to an industrialist friend.[82]

Satō's diary reveals that Crown Prince Akihito sat in on briefings from time to time and on rare occasions received individual briefings as well. In August 1970, when Japanese officials were secretly discussing the possibility of the emperor's making a trip to Europe, Satō asked the crown prince's opinion on this difficult issue.[83] On another occasion, Satō personally apologized to the crown prince for an unpleasant incident involving Crown Princess Michiko in early 1972.[84] On 6 January of that year, a young man unsuccessfully attempted to throw himself on the crown princess at the Nikko Station.

Satō's attempts to curry imperial favor were as legendary as those of his mentor, Yoshida Shigeru. In several places in his diary he wrote of being profoundly moved (*kangeki*) upon receiving gifts from the imperial couple, such as sake from the emperor and cakes from the empress. Irie recorded in his diary, however, that the prime minister annoyed the emperor by trying to reciprocate. Once when Satō was trying to convince Usami Takeshi, director of the Imperial Household Agency, over the phone to allow him and Mrs. Satō to give the empress a length of silk cloth, he blurted out, "Have you seen the empress's kimono? It's awful (*hidoi*)."[85] Usami hung up. Before long, however, a deliveryman appeared at the gate with a present for the empress. Usami had the imperial house guards refuse it. When Usami briefed the emperor on this matter, the emperor said, "What is Satō thinking? Hasn't he read the law?"[86]

The emperor was well aware that Article 8 of the Constitution of Japan forbids giving property to the imperial house without the authorization of the Diet. Satō continued to try to give the emperor and empress expensive gifts such as bonsai trees; these were always returned by officials of the Imperial Household Agency.[87] According to Irie's diary, on the day that Satō's successor, Tanaka Kakuei (1918–93), became prime minister, the emperor personally warned Tanaka not to give him lavish presents such as bonsai trees. This suggested the trouble that he had had with Satō.[88]

One of Satō's most significant accomplishments as prime minister was negotiating the reversion of Okinawa to Japanese sovereignty. The negotiations between Japan and the United States continued over several years. Satō's biographer wrote that the prime minister would rush to the palace to report new developments in the negotiations. During a visit to the United States in 1966 during which he received a concrete commitment from President Lyndon Johnson to return Okinawa, Satō happily told a staff member, "*Now* I can brief His Majesty."[89]

The day after returning to Japan, Satō briefed the emperor at length. According to Irie's diary, during the eight months between the opening of the "Okinawa Diet" on 18 October 1971 and the ceremony on 15 May 1972 commemorating the reversion to Japan, Satō met with the emperor eight times to discuss Okinawa's return.[90] At the ceremony celebrating Okinawa's return, Prime Minister Satō, who like his mentor sometimes referred to himself as a "servant" of the emperor, concluded his statement with the prewar-style exclamation, "Long Live His Majesty the Emperor!"

Reporters knew that imperial briefings continued, but ministers were unwilling to provide details. Hence, there was little to report. It was not until the prime ministership of Tanaka Kakuei that briefings became a public issue. On 26 May 1973, Masuhara Keikichi (1903–85), chief of the Defense Agency, emerged from the palace after briefing the emperor. At this time, nearly thirty years after the end of the war, the emperor was widely seen as being entirely out of politics, as required by the Constitution. In particular, the link between the emperor and the military was thought to have been severed. In a formal sense it was, but Hirohito never lost his interest in security issues.

Masuhara apparently had been profoundly moved by his meeting with the emperor.[91] Following their usual routine, reporters asked him for a comment, and, to their astonishment, Masuhara reported what the emperor had said: "The press says the Fourth Defense Buildup Plan is very large, whereas it seems rather small compared with those of some neighboring countries. Why has it become such a problem in the Diet? The defense of the country is important. Why not adopt the good points of the old army while leaving out the bad?" Masuhara's blunder did not end there. He suggested that he had been influenced by the emperor's comments. "It gave me the courage to go on with the deliberations on the two defense laws," Masuhara told reporters.[92] The press called Masuhara a "Meiji man," apparently to stress his prewar consciousness,[93] but it was by no means permissible under the prewar system for ministers to publicize the emperor's comments in chambers.

The Masuhara Statement immediately created a political firestorm. First, the leak of the emperor's comments during a briefing in the post-Occupation era showed the symbol emperor, who had been recast as a pacifist after the war, supporting, of all things, a military buildup. At the time, the Japanese were divided over the need for a defense buildup. Both the JSP and JCP adamantly opposed it. The briefings almost surely would not have become such an issue if the first leak had involved a minister reporting that the emperor thought that pesticides were being overused. Second, Masuhara not only leaked the emperor's comments, which had the potential to influence the public, but also suggested that he, a government official, had been influenced by them. Finally, at the very time Masuhara made his injudicious statement, Prime Minister Tanaka was embroiled in a controversy over the use of the emperor for political ends. Just a few weeks before Masuhara leaked the emperor's comments, Anesaki Kisaburō, an elderly farmer in Niigata prefecture's third electoral district, Tanaka's home district, was stunned to receive an invitation to the spring garden party hosted by the emperor and the empress. Anesaki then remembered that he had supported Prime Minister Tanaka from the time Tanaka had been no more than a poor lawyer trying to win his first election to the Diet in 1947.

It turned out that eight longtime members of Tanaka's support group, the Etsuzankai, had received invitations to the garden party to be held at the palace on 17 May. It was customary at that time for the prime minister to recommend 31 of the approximately 2,000 people invited to imperial garden parties. It was not uncommon for prime ministers to have friends and acquaintances invited, but the invitations were generally extended to people who had made some concrete contribution to society. Tanaka sought to recognize individuals who "had contributed to society at the grassroots level" by inviting Anesaki and seven other average citizens from his electoral district. The problem was that the only apparent social contribution several of the individuals had made was to advance Tanaka's career.[94] When questioned about this issue by reporters, one of Tanaka's secretaries lied to protect his boss. The secretary claimed that in Niigata members of Tanaka's support group were so numerous that it was no more than a coincidence that all the grassroots individuals invited to the garden party were members of the Etsuzankai.[95] Tanaka's use of invitations to the garden party to reward supporters became a public issue at the very time Masuhara leaked the emperor's comments; it was an especially inopportune moment for the Tanaka Cabinet.

The reaction to Masuhara's blunder was swift, and criticism was by no means limited to members of opposition parties. Many LDP politicians were furious with Masuhara for making such a mistake, especially when the Tanaka Cabinet's popularity was already in a downward spiral. Masuhara was criticized by one wing of the LDP for his "old constitution consciousness" and condemned just as bitterly by the more conservative wing of the party for his "disloyalty [to the emperor]" for having revealed the emperor's comments.[96] Demands for Masuhara's resignation quickly emanated from inside and outside the LDP.

JSP representatives lambasted Masuhara for using the emperor politically (*seiji riyō*). Although one JSP member of the Diet used the occasion to call for the emperor's abdication because of his responsibility for the war, other members admitted off the record that what really annoyed them about the practice of briefings was that *they*, as members of an opposition party that had not participated in the government since 1948, never got a chance to meet the emperor.[97] In many areas, the JSP's views on the monarchy were closer to those of the LDP than of the JCP. The JCP focused as much on the emperor's statement as on Masuhara's alleged use of the emperor. It stressed that it could not approve of the emperor's comment not only from a constitutional position but also from the historical perspective of Japan's wars of aggression. Unlike the JSP, the JCP argued that briefings were unconstitutional.

At a meeting of the House of Councillors Budget Committee on 28 June, Prime Minister Tanaka explained that the purpose of briefings was simply to allow the emperor "to learn the general conditions of the country and to extend [his] knowledge."[98] Nonetheless, Masuhara was forced to resign on 29 May. He apologized for having "troubled His Majesty the Emperor" (*tennō heika ni gomeiwaku o okakeshita*).

The *Asahi shinbun* published an editorial welcoming Masuhara's resignation, as did all other national newspapers:

> The fact that a leading politician can become indifferent to the importance of observing the constitution constitutes a danger to the political system itself. Masuhara Keikichi, former chief of the Defense Agency, disclosed at a recent press conference the contents of his discussions with the emperor during his briefing on Japan's defense policy. . . . The problem is that Masuhara revealed the emperor's remarks to reporters as if the emperor supported LDP defense policy. Public opinion is divided over the necessity of Japan's Fourth Defense Buildup Plan. . . . We contend that Masuhara tried to manipulate the emperor's statement in support of LDP policies. The emperor should not be involved in politics since the constitution prescribes that he shall have no powers related to government. No politician should be allowed to ignore the constitutional principle that sovereignty rests with the people.[99]

The *Asahi shinbun* emphasized the difference between the Meiji Constitution and the Postwar Constitution. The *Mainichi shinbun* also noted the impropriety of Masuhara's actions: "To seemingly involve the emperor in defense policy invites misunderstanding. To drag the emperor into politics is forbidden under the constitution."[100]

In spite of Masuhara's resignation, the opposition parties demanded a formal explanation by the government in the Diet. In a meeting of the House of Representatives Cabinet Committee on 7 June, Prime Minister Tanaka, who was said to have spent hours studying the legal issues involved under the tutelage of the director of the Cabinet Legislation Bureau, faced two hours and thirty-seven minutes of parliamentary interpellation. Tanaka made the specious argument that briefings fell within the category of public acts by the emperor in his position as a symbol.

This third category of the emperor's acts was first put forth by the government in 1952 to justify official foreign trips by imperial family members, but only in 1973 was it used to justify political briefings.

The first questioner, a JSP Diet member, asked the prime minister to confirm whether the emperor in fact had made the comments leaked by Masuhara. Tanaka evaded the question. One representative raised the issue of Tanaka having invited supporters to the palace garden party to suggest a pattern of LDP use of the imperial house for political ends. The prime minister continued to dance around difficult questions and never confirmed whether the emperor had made the statement in question. At one point Tanaka stressed, "In light of custom, there is no reason to believe that the emperor made the statement. I, too, brief the emperor, but there never has been an instance of the emperor's making a statement for or against, or a statement to influence, national policy. He is an extremely fair and impartial man."[101]

It is doubtful that many Diet members, especially JCP representatives, believed Tanaka on that point, but it should be remembered that the details of all briefings up until Masuhara's had remained secret. One wonders how Diet representatives would have reacted to Tanaka's justification of briefings in 1973 if they had known that the prime minister, according to one of his ministers interviewed after Tanaka resigned as prime minister, "would be late for a general meeting of the Diet in order to complete the briefing of the emperor."[102] According to the constitution, the Diet, the highest decisionmaking organ of the sovereign people, takes precedence over the emperor.

Constitutional scholars were asked to give opinions on the legitimacy of briefings. It was the first time that most scholars had given serious thought to the constitutionality of this practice. Kobayashi Naoki (1921–), professor of constitutional law at Tokyo University, voiced his interpretation that briefings were legal as "acts by the emperor [in his position] as symbol," but he also stressed the danger that briefings could exceed constitutional boundaries because of (1) the subject matter of the briefings; (2) the secrecy that surrounds them; and (3) the degree to which the emperor actively asks questions and voices his impressions.[103] Kobayashi's concern with the secrecy surrounding briefings is puzzling; if briefings are to take place at all, it is their very confidentiality that protects the emperor's public neutrality.

Irie's diary seems to confirm that the emperor did indeed make the controversial statement about the Fourth Defense Buildup Plan. On 29 May 1973, Irie recorded that the emperor, upon hearing of the stir caused by Masuhara's comments, said, "So I am to be no more than a 'papier-maché stage prop' (*haribote*)?"[104] No other comment that has become public better demonstrates Hirohito's chafing at the notion that he had become no more than a passive symbol solely subject to manipulation by others. The emperor, in response to the political troubles his comments had caused, regretfully promised Prime Minister Tanaka to "crack the whip" on himself.[105] Irie's diary also indicated that the emperor asked his longtime chamberlain, "In Britain doesn't the prime minister brief the Queen weekly?"[106]

The answer is yes. In her memoirs, Margaret Thatcher (1925–2013; prime minister, 1979–90) touched on the audiences, as they are called in Britain, that the prime minister regularly has with the monarch:

> All audiences with the Queen take place in strict confidence—a confidentiality which is vital to the working of both government and constitution. I was to have such audiences with Her Majesty once a week, usually on a Tuesday, which was in London and sometimes elsewhere when the royal family were at Windsor or Balmoral.
>
> Perhaps it is permissible to make just two points about these meetings. Anyone who imagines that they are a mere formality or confined to social niceties is quite wrong; they are quietly businesslike and Her Majesty brings to bear a formidable grasp of current issues and breadth of experience.[107]

According to Thatcher's interpretation of audiences, confidentiality, and not the practice of the audiences itself, is the crucial issue. Queen Elizabeth II (b. 1926; r. 1952–) viewed some of Thatcher's policies with disfavor, and so the former prime minister had particularly strong reasons for insisting on the confidentiality of the queen's political views. Moreover, maintaining the confidentiality of briefings had been a long-standing practice in Britain.

In Japan, too, one interpretation of briefings is that they are permissible so long as the public neutrality of the emperor is not compromised. But in Japan, the government's hurried justification of briefings in 1973 rested on the interpretation that they were public acts by the emperor in his position as symbol. In contrast to the emperor's domestic tours and other acts included in this category, however, there was customarily nothing *public* about the briefings. Many scholars did not accept the inclusion of briefings in this category.[108]

The chapter on the emperor in the Postwar Constitution was modeled on British practices, and in this sense briefings were not necessarily out of line with the drafters' intentions. But there was one significant gap between the British practice of audiences and the Japanese practice of briefings. In Britain it is customary for only the prime minister to brief the monarch, whereas in Japan, in spite of Ashida's efforts to curtail the practice in 1948, other Cabinet ministers continued to brief the emperor on a regular basis.

This represents a continuity with Imperial Japan. According to the Meiji Constitution, the prime minister's position was not necessarily superior to that of other ministers. All ministers served the emperor, and thus all regularly briefed him. Article 55 of the Meiji Constitution reads: "The respective Ministers of State shall give their advice to the Emperor and be responsible for it." The Postwar Constitution, in contrast, expressly made the prime minister the head (*shuchō*) of the Cabinet; all other ministers now answer to the prime minister, not the emperor. In spite of this change, peculiarities still existed. It is odd, for example, that the emperor was briefed more often by a foreign minister (Shigemitsu) than by a prime minister (Hatoyama).

In other areas, in contrast, the emperor's political role seemed limited in comparison with that of the British monarch. Whereas the emperor's prerogatives were terminated by the Postwar Constitution, the British crown's prerogatives survived, in certain areas, decades into the postwar era. As recently as 1963, Queen Elizabeth II played a decisive role in choosing between two candidates to succeed Prime Minister Harold Macmillan by indicating her preference to the outgoing prime minister.[109] At the time, the Tory Party had no clear-cut mechanism for choosing a party leader. Since the Tories remedied this situation in 1965, there have been no more examples of the queen selecting the prime minister.

The Constitution of Japan leaves no doubt about the mechanism for selecting prime ministers: "The prime minister shall be designated from among the members of the Diet by a resolution of the Diet." Although Emperor Hirohito was not reticent about expressing his views on personnel when the prime minister briefed him, there are no known examples of him influencing who was selected for the Cabinet, not to mention the prime minister himself, after the new constitution went into effect.

The emperor's behavior during briefings was not out of line with the practices of the British monarch, nor those of the Spanish king. In fact, after ascending to the throne in 1975, King Juan Carlos (1938– ; r. 1975–2014) played an active political role. Juan Carlos is widely credited for his role in the democratization of his country. During the transition period from the death of Franco in 1975 to the promulgation of the Spanish constitution in 1978, King Juan Carlos was involved intricately in politics, as was his right. In 1976, he dismissed a prime minister whom he believed to be holding back the democratization process. During the consolidation period after the new constitution, which provided for a limited monarchy, went into effect, Juan Carlos continued to play an important political role. This was demonstrated most dramatically in 1981 when his resolute condemnation, during a stirring television address, of a military coup attempt carried out in his name served to protect the nascent democratic system.[110] The Constitution of Spain defines the king as a "symbol," but also provides him with the vague right to "arbitrate and moderate" the activities of the state. Throughout his reign King Juan Carlos held "daily private *audiencias* with politicians, businessmen, journalists, academics and military officers at his residence. . . . The [audiences] provide him with an occasion to dispense discreet advice and get his opinions across."[111]

The monarchs of Denmark and Sweden are thoroughly distanced from the formal decisionmaking process but continue to be informed of the political situation by government ministers. The Swedish king is briefed three times a year by the entire Cabinet. Since these briefings typically last about one hour, there is little time for discussion.[112] In the case of Denmark, on every other Wednesday the prime minister and minister of Foreign Affairs brief the queen, but it is unthinkable that she would in any way indicate her displeasure with governmental policy. Interestingly, on every second Monday the queen also holds public audiences for any Danish citizen with a plausible reason to speak with her. Queen Margrethe II (r. 1972–) has used her New Year's speech to express her opinion on certain issues, however, and on one occasion she called on her countrymen to show more sympathy for immigrants.[113]

In Japan's case, Emperor Hirohito was monarch during his country's disastrous attempt to dominate Asia through military means, and after 1945 the palace undertook a campaign to disassociate the emperor from the decisionmaking process that had embroiled Japan in war. This made any suggestion that he continued to be involved in politics particularly controversial. Furthermore, whatever the intentions of the drafters, the constitution defines the emperor's position narrowly. Masuhara's leak raised questions not only about the emperor's role under the Postwar Constitution but also about his engagement with politics in Imperial Japan. If the so-called symbol emperor was still engaged in politics under the Postwar Constitution, clearly it was difficult to deny his political role in Imperial Japan.

In spite of the controversy that followed Masuhara's leak, the briefings continued. Masuhara's unfortunate experience reminded ministers never to publicize comments made by the emperor. Public interest in briefings receded, only to resurface again when documents relating to the practice were released in the late 1980s and early 1990s. After Shigemitsu's diary was published in 1988, briefings again became an issue in the Diet. Hashimoto Atsushi, a JCP representative in the House of Councillors, raised the issue. Referring to an entry in which the emperor expressed to Shigemitsu his support of American–Japanese cooperation and "anticommunism," Hashimoto pointed out that the emperor had made an irrefutably political statement and demanded to know what purpose briefings served. Prime Minister Takeshita Noboru (1924–2000) denied that the emperor exerted any influence on the political process and explained that briefings served only "to raise the general knowledge of His Majesty the Emperor" (*tennō heika ga ippanteki chishiki o takameru tame no mono*).[114]

After Emperor Hirohito's death in 1989, a team of reporters from the *Mainichi* newspaper set out to probe the emperor's relationship to postwar politics by interviewing politicians and bureaucrats who had briefed him.[115] Some individuals were willing to discuss their briefings now that the emperor was dead. The *Mainichi* reporters' book, *Heika no goshitsumon* (His Majesty's questions), which won the Japan Press Club's Award for 1992, stressed that (1) the emperor received frequent briefings on political matters from individuals at the highest levels of the government, including Cabinet ministers, the speakers of both houses of the Diet, and elite bureaucrats throughout his reign (he also annually dined with the chief justice of the Supreme Court); and (2) his demeanor in these briefings was by no means passive or neutral.

Anecdotes recounted by those who had briefed him reveal that the emperor's interest in political matters had been quite comprehensive. For example, he wanted to know whether Soviet submarines could pass undetected through the strait that separates Hokkaido and what the Japanese call the Northern Islands.[116] Japan still disputes the sovereignty of these islands with Russia. In a similar vein, the emperor was interested in the war between Argentina and Britain over the Falkland Islands in 1982. After Argentina seized the Falkland Islands, the emperor asked an official from the Foreign Ministry if Thatcher "would send out the warships."[117] Thatcher, for her part, recounted in her memoirs that after British forces recaptured one of the islands from Argentina, an audience was arranged with the queen. Thatcher "was glad to be able personally to give her the news that one of her islands had been recovered."[118]

According to *Heika no goshitsumon*, at least one postwar prime minister was subjected to the silent treatment by the emperor. In 1979, Ōhira Masayoshi (1910–80) narrowly beat out former prime minister Fukuda Takeo (1905–95) to maintain the prime ministership after a bruising and divisive intraparty struggle. Fukuda was said to be a favorite of the emperor. On the day that Ōhira was reelected prime minister, he briefed the emperor about the political situation. The emperor said not a word during the entire briefing.[119] It was an obvious rebuke.

Nakasone Yasuhiro, who liked to stress his closeness to the throne, told the reporters several stories about the emperor. During a trip to Washington in January 1983, Prime Minister Nakasone, in a comment directed to his hosts and to the Soviet Union, referred to Japan as "an unsinkable aircraft carrier." He emphasized that the United States–Japan alliance was an "inevitable community" stretching across the Pacific. Nakasone's staunch support of the U.S.–Japanese security alliance endeared him to the emperor, who had become a diehard supporter of the alliance soon after Japan's surrender in 1945. In February the emperor privately praised Nakasone for having improved Japanese–American relations.[120]

As part of his policy of "settling postwar accounts," on 15 August 1985, Nakasone became the first prime minister in the postwar era to make an "official visit as prime minister" to Yasukuni Shrine. The relationship between the state and this shrine has been an ideologically divisive issue throughout the post-Occupation period. Conservative groups have waged a seventy-five-year movement to restore Yasukuni's official status, a proposal rejected by the left for constitutional and ideological reasons.

Nakasone's visit led not only to domestic protests but also to condemnations from abroad. The governments of China, South Korea, and other Asian countries protested this symbolic gesture, which seemed to lend legitimacy to Japan's wars of aggression. In response to these protests, Nakasone refrained from repeating the visit in 1986. This, in turn, sparked bitter protests from groups to the right of Nakasone. Someone even placed a political sign critical of the prime minister near the graves of Nakasone's ancestors.

In a special session of the Diet, Nakasone explained his decision not to make another official visit:

> Japan cannot survive as a country without promoting cooperation with neighboring countries. Although Japanese views on death, the feelings of our countrymen, [Japan's] sovereignty and independence, and non-interference in domestic affairs must be respected, on the international stage it is dangerous for us . . . to think only about our way of perceiving matters. If we were to become isolated from Asia, would the spirits of the war heroes (*eirei*) be happy?"[121]

Shortly thereafter, Nakasone received a message, through the director of the Imperial Household Agency, from the emperor. The message congratulated Nakasone on his "extremely appropriate" (*kiwamete tekisetsu*) handling of the Yasukuni Shrine matter.[122] Nakasone's official visit to Yasukuni was in fact designed to lay the groundwork for Emperor Hirohito to resume periodic visits to Yasukuni Shrine, which the emperor had discontinued after the head priest there enshrined Class A war criminals. But Emperor Hirohito never visited Yasukuni Shrine again.

Hashimoto Hiroshi, an elite civil servant in the Foreign Ministry who had often briefed the emperor, was another one of the individuals interviewed by the *Mainichi* reporters.[123] He made a carefully worded comment about the emperor's demeanor during briefings: "About the China question, or the Soviet Union, or about other matters, there were many extremely important comments [made by the emperor]. However, even off the record, let alone for a newspaper article, I must not speak about it. What I can say is, regarding domestic matters, regarding foreign affairs, the emperor certainly had a clear opinion on each point."[124] Hashimoto's observation of the well-informed emperor bears comparison to Thatcher's description of her audiences with Queen Elizabeth II. Hirohito's outspoken interest in politics, behind closed doors, was not necessarily greater than that of the British monarch, but the efforts by certain authorities to portray him as a passive symbol were intense. This was a legacy of Japan's defeat in the war, for Hirohito's handlers considered it necessary to disassociate the emperor thoroughly from the politics that had led Japan into war.

The Constitution of Japan specifies that the emperor, with the advice and approval of the Cabinet, promulgates laws, Cabinet orders, and treaties. This means that the emperor has to stamp large numbers of official documents with his official seal. It would be strange if he were expected simply to stamp these documents without receiving an explanation of their meaning and purpose. Briefings keep the emperor informed on political affairs.

The symbol of Japan is simultaneously a person. It is thus difficult to imagine the symbol emperor operating only as an automaton. Moreover, the practice of briefings is not out of line with British customs or the practices of other symbolic monarchies, for that matter. Bagehot wrote that a constitutional monarch has "three rights—the right to be consulted, the right to encourage, the right to warn,"[125] and he went on to suggest that the monarch could play a valuable role, especially as his years on the throne increased:

> The king could say: "Have you referred to the transactions which happened during such and such an administration, I think about fourteen years ago? They afford an instructive example of the bad results which are sure to attend the policy which you propose. You did not at that time take so prominent a part in public life as you now do, and it is possible you do not fully remember all the events. I should recommend you to recur to them, and to discuss them with your older colleagues who took part in them. It is unwise to recommence a policy which so lately worked so ill."[126]

Accounts of Emperor Hirohito suggest that both before and after constitutional reform, he insisted on being consulted by government ministers and encouraged and even warned them on occasion. In light of the emperor's frequent contact with government ministers, it is thus somewhat misleading to say that he was nothing more than a symbol. At the same time, the emperor's role in postwar politics did evolve along the lines of the British monarch, with the emperor enjoying, and only by custom, something like the three rights defined by Bagehot.

Although comparisons with the British constitutional system are valuable, British practices evolved over a long period within a particular political culture. Under the Meiji Constitution, Japan's monarchical system differed from the British system. Japan also had its own political culture, which is very different from Britain's. Irokawa Daikichi wrote of Emperor Hirohito's authority over government officials before the war:

> It is said . . . that he never allowed generals and marshals, old enough to be his father, to sit in a chair in his presence. When addressing his subjects, he dropped all honorifics. In speaking to the army chief of staff, General Sugiyama, he once said, "Say, Sugiyama, when you were war minister you said this, didn't you? (As "you," the emperor used the term *omae*, which is a form of address used toward an "inferior.")[127]

Unlike the British monarch in the twentieth century, the emperor exercised his legal authority under the Meiji Constitution to topple Cabinets and repress rebellions. Even if such instances of the emperor dramatically exercising his authority were exceptions—and there is debate on this point—they nonetheless stand in contrast with the more limited roles played by King George V and King George VI, who were Emperor Hirohito's contemporaries during the first two decades of his reign.

After Japan's surrender, the Japanese constitutional system was reformed by Americans—from outside—to function along the lines of the British monarchy. Overnight, the emperor's constitutional position was changed from sovereign to symbol. Unsurprisingly, there was a period of confusion, a period of settlement. Some Japanese interpreted a "symbol emperor" to be a passive entity, like a flag. This led to the question of whether political briefings were permissible, or if they did take place, whether the emperor should be permitted to make comments and to ask questions. The fact that the same emperor's reign spanned the reform of the constitution was no small issue, for Hirohito had a customary way of doing things, and many Japanese politicians who had grown up under the prewar system were conditioned to respond to the emperor's will.

It appears from the available evidence that all the prime ministers from 1956 to the present have briefed the emperor on a regular basis, and it can be said that the practice was stabilized as a custom in the late 1950s. Since there are no examples after 1947 of Japanese politicians' admitting that they were influenced by the emperor (with the possible exception of Masuhara), one conclusion would be that as the Meiji system grew distant and politicians attached to it gradually faded from the scene, any special influence that Hirohito might have exercised declined. However, it is also possible that he continued to exert subtle influence until late in life.

Among the opposition parties, the JCP has denied the constitutional legitimacy of briefings, and the JSP has expressed concern with the manner in which they are carried out. In 1989, Emperor Akihito ascended the throne, and he, too, was briefed regularly by government ministers.[128] It is said that Emperor Akihito was no less active in making comments and asking questions during his briefings.[129] Even Murayama Tomiichi (1924–), who in 1994 became Japan's first JSP prime minister since 1948, briefed the emperor periodically.

The 1995 version of the *Kunaichō yōran*, the official guidebook to the imperial house published by the Imperial Household Agency, includes no reference to the practice of briefing, however. Unlike in Britain, where audiences are simply accepted as part of the constitutional tradition, in Japan the government remains unable to provide any firm justification for the briefings based on the text of the constitution. Furthermore, there is a considerable gap between the public's expectation that the emperor is separated strictly from politics and the reality of the emperor's close contact with ministers. For these reasons, briefings remain controversial.

CHAPTER 4

Imperial War Responsibility and Apologies

Nearly seventy-five years have passed since fifteen years of war came to an end for the Japanese. The war has remained an "ever-present past" in Japan, however.[1] The death of Emperor Hirohito in 1989, rather than ending the postwar era, was one of several factors that sparked a reexamination of the war during the 1990s. Hirohito's postwar reconstruction as a pacifist symbolized the myth that those responsible for the war were an indefinite but conspicuously limited number of "militarists" who victimized the people and the emperor by dragging Japan into conflict with Great Britain and the United States. The death of the central symbol of this self-pitying, inward-looking memory helped ignite a national crisis of conscience over how to remember the wartime past.

After ascending the throne, the new emperor, Akihito, promptly addressed troubling questions of national responsibility for the war by apologizing to neighboring countries. The fact that responsibility for the war was deflected from Hirohito immediately after the surrender was an important reason that the task of making amends for Japan's wartime behavior was left to Akihito, but it was not the only one. Why did the symbolic monarchy become involved in what can be called the "politics of apologies"? By the 1980s, in neighboring Asian countries, the primary victims of Japan's wartime aggression, citizens and political leaders alike had become increasingly vocal in demanding official statements of contrition, but why was it necessary that these apologies come from the emperor (especially from Emperor Akihito, who was not even twelve when the war ended)? The answer lies partially in the importance that "imperial house diplomacy" (*kōshitsu gaikō*) assumed in the 1970s. During that decade, Hirohito made two trips abroad and hosted numerous official visitors to Japan, and these acts solidified the emperor's role as Japan's external representative.

The debates over the constitutionality of imperial apologies produced strange political bedfellows. The most right-wing faction of the LDP, the same part of the political spectrum that had opposed the Occupation-era reform of the monarchy and then supported a broad interpretation of the emperor's role under the Postwar Constitution, found itself allied with the left, long the proponent of keeping the emperor out of politics, in opposing imperial apologies as unconstitutional. Overnight, it seemed, many conservatives came to espouse a purely symbolic monarchy simply through their resistance to apologies. Although their antagonism to imperial apologies was politically motivated, the right's support for a symbolic monarchy predated the 1990s. By the 1970s, most of the right had already come to accept the symbolic monarchy, indeed to view it as a return to Japanese tradition.

Emperor Hirohito's New Clothes

In what way did Emperor Hirohito bear war responsibility? As David Cohen has shown, neither the Nuremberg nor the Tokyo war crimes trials established an authoritative definition of "war responsibility." Although Cohen argues that lesser-known trials in the immediate aftermath of World War II resulted in far more rigorous definitions of this concept, there is no agreement on the meaning of this term.[2] This was even more true as World War II drew to a close. The Potsdam Declaration of July 1945, like earlier proclamations from the Allies, stressed that "stern justice shall be meted out to all war criminals," but was vague on details.[3] A clause about the mistreatment of prisoners was the only specific indication of what constituted a "war crime" in the declaration concerning Japan's surrender.

If "war responsibility" means participating in the policymaking process that led to the commencement and prosecution of an "aggressive" war (for many Japanese, the key issue was the responsibility for defeat, not complicity in an aggressive war), then there is growing evidence that Emperor Hirohito played a considerable role in this area. Thanks to Herbert Bix's biography of Hirohito, much of this evidence is now available to the English-language reader. Even if one believes the official account that exculpates Hirohito from political responsibility by insisting that he was used by the militarists, there is the question of his moral responsibility for letting himself be used in such a positive manner as a symbol of Japan's righteous wars. Whatever misgivings Hirohito may have expressed to his close advisors and governmental ministers about the policies that resulted in conflicts between Japan and other countries, between 1931 and the surrender in 1945 he never once publicly indicated anything but support for the war. Finally, the issue of Hirohito's war responsibility would be less significant had there not been the remarkable campaign after the surrender to remake him into a man of peace. This campaign was central to efforts by a segment of the political elite to concentrate responsibility for the war on as narrow a group of individuals as possible or to diffuse responsibility so widely and equally that individual accountability was blurred.

The retailoring of Hirohito into a man of peace began with the imperial rescript announcing the end of the war, which included astonishing understatements and exaggerations:

> We declared war on America and Britain out of sincere desire to ensure Japan's self-preservation and the stabilization of East Asia, it being far from our thought either to infringe upon the sovereignty of other nations or to embark upon territorial aggrandizement.
>
> But now the war has lasted for nearly four years. Despite the best that has been done by everyone—the gallant fighting of the military and naval forces, the diligence and assiduity of our servants of the state and the devoted service of our 100 million people—the war situation has developed not necessarily to Japan's advantage. . . .
>
> Moreover, the enemy has begun to employ a new and most cruel bomb, the power of which to do damage is, indeed, incalculable, taking the toll of many innocent lives. Should we continue to fight, it would not only result in the ultimate collapse and obliteration of the Japanese nation, but also it would lead to the total extinction of human civilization. . . .
>
> We are keenly aware of the inmost feelings of all you, our subjects. However, it is according to the dictates of time and fate that we have resolved to pave the way for a grand peace for all the generations to come by enduring the unendurable and suffering what is insufferable.[4]

Immediately after the emperor's announcement, Prime Minister Suzuki Kantarō (1868–1948) explained in a radio address to the nation why the emperor had ended the war: "His Majesty made the sacred decision to end the war in order to save the people and contribute to the welfare and peace of mankind. . . . The nation sincerely apologizes to His Majesty [for the way the war ended]."[5] The viciousness of the atomic bombs provided Japan's leaders with the opportunity to recast the emperor as the savior of the country (and even of "human civilization"). In his interpretation, Suzuki even blamed the people for the defeat.

In August 1945, many Japanese were susceptible to a glorification of the emperor's role in the complicated process leading to the government's decision to surrender for two reasons. First, by the time of the surrender, most of Japan's civilian population had been socialized for a final, suicidal battle against the invading armies. Many Japanese did have a sense of having narrowly escaped death as a result of the imperial rescript announcing Japan's acceptance of the Potsdam Declaration. Second, throughout the war, the emperor, through official announcements, had expressed concern for the people's suffering,[6] suggesting that responsibility for their misery lay elsewhere.

In his opening address to the Diet on 5 September 1945, Prince Higashikuni Naruhiko (1897–1990), Suzuki's successor as prime minister, gave an even loftier interpretation of how the emperor had ended the war and employed Confucian terminology to remind the people to obey their leader:

> The Imperial Proclamation [terminating the war] has been issued. As His Majesty's subjects, our duty lies in absolute obedience to the Imperial Will. We must conform to the proclamation in letter and spirit, and follow the Imperial instructions, not departing an inch therefrom. The entire nation, as one family under perfect order and discipline, must face the new situation, and strive to keep strictly to the way of rectitude.
>
> The termination of the war has been brought about solely through the benevolence of our Sovereign. It was His Majesty Himself, who, apologizing to the spirits of the Ancestors, decided to save the millions of His subjects from privation and misery, and to pave the way for an era of grand peace for generations to come. Never before have we been moved so profoundly as by this act of boundless benevolence. With tears of overwhelming gratitude, we can only offer our humble apologies for having troubled so much the August Mind of our Sovereign.[7]

According to Higashikuni, the people were indebted to the emperor for stopping the war. Buried by the establishment was the question of the emperor's role in Japan's aggression abroad from 1931 to 1945.

Higashikuni went on to stress, in what was surprising news to most Japanese, the reservations Emperor Hirohito had had regarding the decision to go to war with the "Anglo-Saxon countries." The prime minister proceeded to spread responsibility in both a broad and egalitarian manner, while noting that in any case it was not an appropriate moment to render judgment on who was accountable for the defeat:

> Notwithstanding the wisdom of His Majesty, we have brought our country face to face with the tragic situation of today for which I do not know how we might atone ourselves. All we can do is appeal to His Imperial magnanimity to pardon our unpardonable stupidity and incompetence.
>
> As for the causes of our defeat, there are certainly more than one, and they may well be left to the historians of after-days for unbiased study and criticism. There is little use in going back to the past trying to put the blame upon one person or another. We should rather reflect calmly upon our own conduct, each and every one of us, whether on the front or at home, whether in or out of the government. A general repentance is demanded of the whole nation.[8]

Higashikuni's suggestion that the Japanese accept collective responsibility could have been a useful step, but it also allowed him to brush over the fact that it was possible for the Japanese to assign different degrees of responsibility to figures of authority, including the emperor. Higashikuni completely exonerated the emperor. The Cabinet of Prime Minister Shidehara, Higashikuni's successor, upheld the interpretation that Hirohito bore no responsibility for the war and formalized it through an official report.[9] Before long, blame for the entire debacle was shifted to the "militarists," thus distancing the rest of the people, like the emperor, from responsibility.

Whereas the other Axis countries changed their national symbols after the war, Japanese leaders (with the cooperation of SCAP) sought to reinvent the national symbol. The case of Spain in the aftermath of the Franco dictatorship bears some similarities to that of Japan after the war. After Franco's death in 1975, King Juan Carlos was faced with disengaging longtime symbols of the monarchy from their association with the Franco regime, which had appropriated them. The greatest difference is that King Juan Carlos's personal association with the Franco regime was much less than Hirohito's association with the authoritarian and militaristic Japan of the first twenty years of his reign (1926–45). New clothes were tailored for Emperor Hirohito after the surrender. A suit and tie replaced the emperor's military outfit. Hirohito never again wore a uniform. He distanced himself from the war, from the defeat. Virtually overnight, the emperor's close link with the military was severed, to the disillusionment of many soldiers who had fought so diligently on his behalf. Even seventy years after the conclusion of the war, the imperial house maintains only a carefully measured relationship with the Self Defense Forces (SDF), as Japan's reconstituted military, under the command of the prime minister and required by the constitution to be only defensive in nature, is called. This contrasts with the British royal family's close links with the armed forces.

In November 1945, the Imperial Household Ministry recalled from schools and offices throughout the country copies of the official prewar portraits of the emperor and empress (*goshin'ei*), which pictured Hirohito as a generalissimo. Deluged by school principals for guidance, the Imperial Household Ministry also candidly announced through the newspapers that until a new official portrait could be issued, any portrait of the emperor could be displayed so long as it did not show him in military clothes.[10] No official portrait was ever distributed in the postwar era, however. In fact, today in Japan one rarely sees formal photographs of the emperor on display in public spaces.

Journalists with the closest access to the throne, such as Togashi Junji, played a particularly important role in remaking Hirohito to suit the New Japan. A *Mainichi shinbun* reporter, Togashi had been a member of the Imperial House Press Club since 1920. Like all other Japanese journalists, however, he had never met the emperor before the end of the war. He nonetheless became one of the most prominent chroniclers of the "real" emperor after August 1945.

In 1946, Togashi published an account of the imperial house intended for a popular audience that praised Hirohito as a longtime, wholehearted pacifist. The book included a photograph of the extended imperial family, with the emperor dressed in civilian clothes. Togashi stressed in his book's opening pages that until the end of the war, the military and the bureaucracy had kept the emperor from the people. "I deeply believe that this was not the will of His Majesty," Togashi wrote.[11]

Togashi depicted a selfless emperor whose decision to end the war had prevented the very extinction of the Japanese race:

> It is difficult for me to forget the impression [I have] of the emperor, when Japan stood on the edge of survival or death, singlehandedly saving the people from extinction by ordering the acceptance of the Potsdam Declaration. One step before the complete destruction of the homeland, 100 million [Japanese] were saved from pulverization according to the emperor's decision, and the extinction of the race was prevented. At that time His Majesty thought not of protecting the national polity, or of the emperor's position, but only of protecting the country.[12]

Togashi thus became one of many commentators to glorify the emperor's role in ending the war while burying troubling questions about all that had transpired during fifteen years of war. He penned a chapter about the emperor titled "Inexhaustible Examples of Love of Peace." Togashi described how the emperor had opposed all the conflicts in which Japan had been involved, from the Manchurian Incident of 1931 through the end of the war.

It is neither fair nor historically correct to make Hirohito a scapegoat for the war, for the emperor was far from being a powerful leader along the lines of Hitler. Nonetheless, Hirohito's responsibility for the war was immense in comparison to that of the average Japanese. Togashi's portrayal of a resolutely pacifist emperor appears laughable when read in tandem with accounts of Hirohito's deep interest in matters of war. On those occasions when Emperor Hirohito expressed reservations about Japan's entering into a conflict with other nations, his foremost concern was whether Japan could win. Furthermore, Hirohito's primary concern in the process leading to Japan's surrender was the preservation of the *kokutai*, or unbroken imperial line,[13] not concluding the war as quickly as possible to prevent further suffering.

Togashi's panegyric was written from the supposedly authoritative position of member of the Imperial House Press Club, but he simply based his account on information provided by palace officials, who were gravely concerned with reconstructing the emperor's image. Togashi's book was not exceptional among commentaries by Imperial House Press Club journalists of the time. In 1947, Ono Noboru (1910–) of the *Asahi shinbun* also published an encomium about the staunchly pacifistic emperor.[14] Several elegant picture albums published in the years after the war stressed the pacifistic character of the emperor as well.[15] Takahashi Hiroshi, a journalist who served in the Imperial House Press Club with Togashi in the 1970s, has argued that Togashi, Ono, and other club journalists active immediately after the surrender simply wrote what palace officials told them to write.[16] Indeed, this is what Imperial House Press Club journalists had done for years. According to Takahashi, their writings immediately after the war influenced a broad audience.

Takahashi was nonetheless on good personal terms with Togashi. He claimed that before dying in 1985, Togashi admitted that the secretary of Imperial Household Minister Ishiwatari Sōtarō (1891–1950) had him write his 1946 book and even provided publishing expenses.[17] Although unverifiable, this account is by no means implausible. In any case, Togashi's uncritical book cooperated with the palace's campaign to distance the emperor from the war. For his service to the nation, Togashi was the recipient of an imperial decoration (*kunshō*) in 1974; he remained in the Imperial House Press Club for eleven years thereafter.

Another of the emperor's many defenders was Nagai Tadashi (1908–51). Nagai achieved literary fame with the publication of *The Bells of Nagasaki* (1949), a reflection on the meaning of the atomic bombings. One elegy to Nagai, who was Catholic, suggested that the doctor-turned-author believed that in the aftermath of the atomic destruction of the two cities, God had inspired Emperor Hirohito to issue the "sacred proclamation that ended the war."[18] This curious interpretation of the process leading to Japan's surrender linked the high priest of Shinto with the Christian God. In 1949, Emperor Hirohito made a bedside visit to Nagai, who was suffering from the radiation sickness that soon claimed his life.

The effort to disassociate Hirohito and the monarchy from the war met with dissent, indeed scorn, from some Japanese. In a famous essay about the origins of emperor worship, Takakura Teru indicted the political system: "The recent war occurred because Japan had the emperor system."[19] Takakura reinterpreted the prewar nationalistic concept of "a national polity without parallel in the world" (*sekai muhi no kokutai*) negatively. For him, its uniqueness lay in the fact that it was a barbaric and extremely absolutist despotic political form found nowhere else in the world.

Between September 1945 and April 1946, the ex-serviceman Watanabe Kiyoshi (1925–) privately wrote of his rage against the emperor who accepted no responsibility for the war. Watanabe wondered if such an example of negligence would corrupt the Japanese people as a whole: "Even the emperor gets away without taking responsibility, so there is no need for us to take responsibility, no matter what we did."[20] Watanabe wrote at a time when the Japanese were publicly debating the emperor's responsibility for the war, which, by ending in defeat, had brought so much harm to the homeland. Less frequently discussed among the Japanese was the emperor's responsibility, indeed, the nation's responsibility, for the dreadful suffering that Japan had inflicted on other peoples, especially its neighbors in Asia. Japan's aggression resulted in the deaths of as many as twenty million Chinese and Koreans, the majority of whom were civilians.

In a formal sense, the question of the emperor's war responsibility was settled when the U.S.-orchestrated International Military Tribunal for the Far East (Tokyo War Crimes Trial, 1946–48) declined to indict him. Historian John Dower has documented the substantial and decisive efforts of U.S. authorities to shield the emperor.[21] As a result of the tribunal's verdict, seven of the emperor's former advisors were sentenced to death for their "crimes against humanity" and "crimes against peace," whereas Hirohito remained on the throne until 1989. In a symbolic sense, however, the Americans apparently did have the throne in mind at the conclusion of the tribunal. The death sentences were carried out on 23 December 1948, Crown Prince Akihito's fifteenth birthday. For many Japanese, these executions of "militarists" settled the question of who was responsible for the war.

As the distance from the war increased, a taboo against public discussion of Emperor Hirohito's responsibility gradually took hold. In Hans Christian Andersen's fairy tale "The Emperor's New Clothes," an innocent child announces that the emperor "hasn't got anything on!" This impolitic observation awakens the mostly adult audience, which until then had played along with the charade of the emperor's fabulous "new clothes." In fact, the emperor was marching around entirely naked.[22]

Many Japanese probably never accepted the myth of the pacifist emperor even if they publicly observed the taboo. There are no studies showing that the official history of the war in Japan, whether of Hirohito's wartime role or otherwise, has definitively shaped popular memories of the war over the past seventy-five years. Diverse personal memories of the emperor's wartime role surely coexisted alongside the official line, and the greater willingness of the Japanese, after Hirohito's death, to speak of the late emperor's war responsibility in part reflects the survival of these alternative memories.

After the taboo had been established but long before Hirohito's death, there were also Japanese who, like the child in Andersen's tale, were so brash as to speak publicly of the emperor's culpability. JCP representatives repeatedly cited the emperor's war responsibility, Kurihara Sadako (1913–2005) pointed an accusing finger at the emperor in several biting poems,[23] and Okuzaki Kenzō (1920–2005), arguably the most active of the emperor's critics, indicted Hirohito by shooting pachinko balls (metal balls the size of small marbles) at him with a slingshot in 1969.[24] It was not only individuals on the left who broached this subject, however, as a memorable exchange that took place in the Diet in the year that Japan regained independence reminds us.

In 1952, speculation resurfaced as to whether Hirohito would abdicate. Immediately after the surrender and again after the conclusion of the Tokyo War Crimes Trial, there had been widespread public discussion about whether the emperor would—or should—abdicate. Hirohito wanted to stay on the throne, and SCAP was adamant that he remain emperor. However, by 1952 Crown Prince Akihito had come of age, and not all Japanese could brush over the emperor's role in a war that had brought humiliation and devastation on their country. During a Diet committee meeting in January of that year, a young nationalistic Diet member who had served as a junior officer in the navy raised the question of the emperor's moral responsibility for the war. Nakasone Yasuhiro proceeded carefully in his interpellation of Prime Minister Yoshida. After making the by-then obligatory reference to the emperor's pacifistic nature, Nakasone subtly asked the government's opinion about a possible abdication that would serve to renew the monarchy and console the victims of the war. An enraged Yoshida responded that anyone who proposed the abdication of the beloved emperor was a traitor (*hikokumin*).[25]

This led Nakasone to comment outside the Diet that "it is regrettable that leading politicians suffer from arteriosclerosis of the brain."[26] But there was to be no abdication by the emperor, who ended such talk by publicly indicating his intention to stay on the throne a few days after Japan formally regained sovereignty on 28 April. Nakasone apparently considered Akihito a more viable symbol for postwar Japan, but Akihito would remain crown prince for thirty-seven more years.

Although this was not known publicly at the time, only a few months before Nakasone's subtle call for the emperor's abdication, one of Hirohito's closest former advisors had sent the emperor a private message bluntly urging him to step down for reasons similar to those outlined by Nakasone. In October 1951, Kido Kōichi (1899–1977), who, as lord keeper of the privy seal from 1940 until the office was abolished after the war, served as Hirohito's closest confidant, strongly advised the emperor that the appropriate moment had arrived for him to accept responsibility for losing the war.[27] Hirohito's insistence on remaining on the throne would haunt the monarchy and Japan for decades. In spite of the spin doctors' best efforts, he never transcended his association with the war.

Emperor Hirohito and General Charles de Gaulle: Referents for Sanitized Memories of the War in Japan and France

In a short essay published in 1959, renowned film reviewer Satō Tadao (1930–) observed that Hirohito's evasion of responsibility in fact was useful for many Japanese: "Why didn't the Japanese people try to pursue the emperor's war responsibility? I think that the reason is that, for the vast majority of the people, the easiest way to exonerate themselves of war responsibility was to exonerate the emperor."[28] After all, if the spiritual leader of the nation declines to accept responsibility for his role in a war fought in his name, then why should the average person trouble himself with unpleasant questions about his own actions during the war? The myth of the pacifist emperor who agonized in mute opposition to the war found believers among many Japanese because they found it useful in shaping their own soothing memories of the war years. It was easier for many Japanese to see themselves in the emperor than to reflect seriously on the responsibility of not just the "militarists" but of the people for fifteen years of war.

Although elements of the American mass media periodically overstate the extent to which the Japanese have conveniently forgotten aspects of the wartime past, it is nonetheless true that Emperor Hirohito, the symbol of the nation, embodied a popular feeling of victimization. Many Japanese saw themselves in the emperor: like he, they had been deceived—victimized—by the military establishment, with whom lay all responsibility for the disastrous war. Forgotten was the widespread popular enthusiasm that had greeted Japanese victories before the war brought suffering to the homeland itself. However troubling the tendency among some Japanese to ignore the fact that support at all levels of society was required to wage fifteen years of war, it is true that information about the decisionmaking process and the war itself was tightly controlled. The Japanese people were often deceived by misleading war reports spread by a complicit mass media. In contrast, Emperor Hirohito enjoyed privileged access to the most intimate details regarding the conduct of the war.

Japan was not the only country whose political elite constructed an edifying account of the immediate past at the conclusion of World War II. The fact that in Japan much of the political elite rallied to protect the emperor was specific to that country, but mythmaking knows no national boundaries. France provides an interesting comparison because in that country, too, one man came to embody a sanitized official memory of the war. France was not on the losing side at the end of World War II, but at the same time it was hardly a major player on the winning side. General Charles de Gaulle (1890–1970) nonetheless provided his country with an immediate and glorious interpretation of the painful Vichy era (1940–44) when France was under German occupation: only a few traitorous misfits had collaborated with the Nazis; the majority of citizens had resisted and eventually joined together to drive the German armies from France.

Historian Henry Rousso has traced the origin of postwar France's foundational myth to a speech de Gaulle delivered on 25 August 1944. At the time, France stood on the verge of civil war as the French were settling old domestic political scores with assassinations. General de Gaulle sought to reunite his country with an emotional speech proclaiming the liberation of Paris: "Paris! Paris Humiliated! Paris Broken! Paris Martyrized! But Paris Liberated! Liberated by itself, by its own people with the help of the armies of France, with the support and aid of France as a whole, of fighting France, of the only France, of the true France, of eternal France."[29] In seeking to resurrect the "glory of France," de Gaulle not only exaggerated the French people's role in the liberation of their country but, more important, also deliberately ignored widespread French collaboration with the Nazis in deporting Jews and other unsavory details of the Vichy era. The general's leading role in the Resistance was no fantasy, but for decades he also personally symbolized the official emphasis on the Resistance as the proper memory of the period. Rousso's monograph is primarily a study of the construction, and eventual collapse, of the official memory of the Vichy era. Alternative French memories of the Vichy era coexisted with the official memory, just as alternative memories of the emperor's wartime role coexisted with the official line in Japan.

Nonetheless, in official and polite circles in France during the 1950s and 1960s, etiquette required avoiding the issue of collaboration. The French political elite, from left to right on the political spectrum, supported the myth for various reasons. The communists, for example, gained political capital from the emphasis on the Resistance, in which their central role was widely acknowledged. The Gaullists, for their part, simply considered any mention of the collaboration to be unpatriotic. In May 1968, however, widespread demonstrations challenged the political order headed by President de Gaulle, including its vision of the past. Students found it both delightful and politically useful to call into question the "invented honor" of their parents' generation. The demonstrations broke the taboo inhibiting discussion of unsavory details of the Occupation. The protests also drove de Gaulle from power in 1969, and by 1970 the general was dead.

Rousso interprets the importance of de Gaulle's death as follows: "Having first exorcised the memory of Vichy, de Gaulle had gone on to concoct a sacred and edifying history of the Resistance. For a time his charisma had forestalled all agonizing or provocative questions. After his death, however, the public suddenly found itself confronted with a confused image of the past, 'unable to find the thread of its history and anxious about not living up to its heroic dream.'"[30] The death of de Gaulle was only one factor in undermining the self-satisfied national conscience about the Vichy era. There were other, more important factors at work, from the challenge of the generation of 1968 to the refusal of Jewish survivors to continue to keep a low profile about their suffering, as they did in the years immediately after the war. Marcel Ophuls's 1971 documentary, *The Sorrow and the Pity*, and then Robert Paxton's *Vichy France* provided stunning empirical evidence of widespread French initiative in various anti-Jewish measures.[31] Yet the fact that such revised accounts of the Vichy era enjoyed the reception they did was facilitated by de Gaulle's departure from the scene. Along the same lines, Hirohito's demise would be a factor in the creation of a social climate in Japan hospitable to a reappraisal of the war.

The Right's Endorsement of the Symbolic Monarchy

Hirohito's lengthy reign is intriguing precisely because he ascended to the throne as the national sovereign and the supreme commander of the military and died more than six decades later as a pacifist (at least publicly) and, constitutionally, a symbol. How did the reconstituted monarchy gain widespread acceptance? In broad terms, individuals on the left either continued to favor the abolition of the monarchy or quickly came to support, with varying degrees of enthusiasm, the symbolic monarchy. What was equally if not more important, however, was that support for the emperor's new constitutional position also developed among an increasing number of figures on the right, especially members of the younger generation, as distance from the Meiji system increased. Drawing (sometimes unconsciously) on the scholarship of Tsuda Sōkichi, Watsuji Tetsurō, Ishii Ryōsuke, and others, most of the right eventually came to endorse the interpretation that the traditional and proper role of the emperor was that of a cultural symbol outside politics and that this had been the case, with only limited exceptions, throughout Japanese history.

Although occasionally comparing the Japanese royal house to monarchies around the world, this interpretation stresses the distinctiveness of Japan's imperial line. Proponents of this interpretation now maintain that it is precisely the emperor's longtime symbolic role that makes the imperial house's "2,000-year" history unique (conservatives round up when speaking of the monarchy's age). This interpretation contrasts with the prewar notion of the *kokutai* characterized by imperial sovereignty, a principle the reactionary right continued to champion even after the promulgation of the Postwar Constitution.

Support for the symbolic monarchy could be found in surprising quarters by the 1970s. Right-wing broker Kodama Yoshio (1911–84), a fixture on the extreme nationalistic right from before the war, was asked by a reporter in 1971 if any changes in the emperor's position were necessary. Kodama replied, "The present symbol emperor system is good."[32] He went on to criticize the Meiji system and describe the postwar system as a return to tradition. Kodama elaborated on this view in a 1975 interview: "The Japanese emperor was not a conqueror or powerholder along the lines of European or other countries' monarchs; therefore, there was usually no friction between the people and the emperor of Japan because the emperor existed at the center of the people, or in other words as the spiritual center (*seishinteki chūshin*)."[33] Kodama stressed that Japan "has a form of monarchy that exists nowhere else in the world." He argued that the Meiji system was a mistake and thus at the time of Japan's defeat, "It was necessary to return to the original [conception of the] throne in order that the emperor continue for all eternity as the spiritual center of the Japanese race."[34]

Among politicians, Nakasone became a leading spokesman for the "symbolic monarchy equals Japanese tradition" interpretation. His views appeared in a popular forum with an essay published in the weekly *Sandē mainichi* in 1973.[35] Nakasone was in the news because of a statement regarding the monarchy that he had made in the Diet that same month. In a meeting of the House of Councillors Cabinet Committee on 5 June, Nakasone innocently repeated a comment he had made to the Iranian prime minister during a visit to Iran. One of the common points shared by the two countries, remarked Nakasone, was that they were both monarchies. Nakasone was trying on behalf of an oil-hungry Japan to reach out to Iran. At that time Iran remained under the authoritarian rule of the Shah.

Nakasone's statement inflamed the opposition parties, who demanded a formal explanation. In a general meeting of the House of Councillors on 13 June, Nakasone expressed regret for his remark. He argued that the comment came from his desire to find common ground and use a term which was "easy for foreigners to understand." In addition, Nakasone emphasized that "along with popular sovereignty," he "was fully conscious of the character of [Japan's] unique system of the symbol emperor."[36]

The article in the *Sandē mainichi* drew heavily on a speech about the monarchy Nakasone gave in Osaka on 2 June 1973. Nakasone blended his support of the symbolic emperor with references to imperial mythology. While avoiding the term *kokutai*, he nonetheless made ambiguous reference to Jimmu as though this mythical emperor might have been an actual historical figure. Such references to imperial mythology made it difficult for opponents of the prewar emperor system to see anything new about Nakasone's affirmation of the emperor's position as symbol, but his interpretation, as had been the case with the views he expressed as a member of the Commission on the Constitution, represented a significant departure from the reactionary right:

> I think that the essential character (*honshitsuteki seikaku*) of the Japanese emperor from time past until today was like the symbol emperor. The reason the emperor was supported for 2,000 years of history was that he in reality did not have political power and did not enter into the fray of political disputes. . . .
>
> [The so-called symbol emperor] had no power, but was an emperor with a spiritual, centripetal force. I think that this symbol emperor was changed mistakenly by the Meiji Constitution. . . .
>
> Japan lost the war, the new constitution was drafted, and I think that the emperor was returned to the original Japanese form (*Nihon honrai no sugata*).[37]

In 1973, Nakasone still favored revision of the U.S.-authored Constitution of Japan. But he argued, as had Tsuda, that the constitution served to return the emperor to his premodern, traditional position as a cultural symbol.

On 14 July 1973, more than one hundred promonarchy scholars came together for a symposium. Support for the symbolic monarchy was prevalent.[38] The organizer, Aihara Ryōichi, a professor of the theory of the state at Tokyo Fisheries University, stressed that the JCP's electoral success the previous year had been the catalyst that propelled him to organize the meeting. Aihara admitted that he had a feeling of crisis about the national polity (*kokutai*), by which he meant the survival of the monarchy itself and not the Meiji system. Aihara indicated that of the individuals in attendance, only a minority hoped to restore elements of the Meiji system.

Kinoshita Hiroyasu, a professor of political science at Sōka University who presented a paper at the symposium, affirmed the postwar symbolic monarchy. What was unique about Japan's monarchy, he stressed, was that unlike other monarchies, the emperor traditionally had not been despotic. According to Kinoshita, throughout most of Japanese history, emperors held neither political nor military power.[39] The postwar symbolic monarchy thus represented a return to, not a departure from, Japanese tradition.

Ishihara Shintarō (1932–), who emerged on the international scene as an outspoken representative of Japan's right with the 1989 publication of *The Japan That Can Say No*,[40] was also a firm supporter of the symbol emperor by the 1970s. Ishihara, an LDP representative in the House of Representatives (and later governor of Tokyo), voiced his support in a 1978 essay about the reign-name system. Ishihara criticized opposition parties for linking the reign-name system to the political conception of the emperor: "The emperor system, even if it was for a very short time directly linked to politics, is a unique cultural tradition of Japan that from the beginning was linked only indirectly to politics."[41] Ishihara went on to claim that in the free world, countries with monarchies were the most stable politically (a claim frequently made by supporters of monarchy that appears to lack any empirical basis). He pitied the United States: "After the uproar of the 'Watergate' Nixon, the fact that an incompetent, 'dangerous' president like Carter would emerge can hardly be called political stability."[42] As seen from Ishihara's bellowing, the symbolic monarchy, while differing from the prewar conception of the emperor, could still serve as a powerful focus for nationalism.

By the 1980s, the LDP had no intention of changing the emperor's constitutional position. In 1983, during the time that Nakasone was prime minister, the LDP's constitutional committee issued a report on revision. The opening statement of the section on the emperor summed up the predominant view within the LDP: "The symbol emperor is at present widely liked among the Japanese people, and there is no need to change the basic spirit of the present [chapter on the emperor]."[43] Nakasone often held up the imperial line as a unique feature of Japan to be honored by various rites and practices. An example is the 1986 staging of a prominent ceremony to mark the sixtieth year on the throne of the pacifist emperor (according to Nakasone's interpretation as prime minister).[44] His invocation of the monarchy did not extend to support for the Meiji emperor system, however.

By the 1980s, the interpretation that the symbolic monarchy represented a return to domestic tradition had become the orthodox view, and proponents of the prewar *kokutai* interpretation of the throne were rare indeed. The conservative scholars Ueyama Shunpei (1921–2012), Umehara Takeshi (1925–2019), and Yano Tōru (1936–), in a roundtable discussion about "The Emperor in Japanese History," agreed that the original and proper role of the emperor was ceremonial and outside politics.[45] The three also concurred that a political conception of the emperor was not true to Japanese tradition.

The details of these scholars' theories of the emperor system did not always accord with the earlier works of Tsuda, Watsuji, and Ishii. Yano differed from Watsuji in that he conflated the conception of the state (*kokka gainen*) and the emperor in a manner suggesting an organic relationship: "So long as Japan continues, the emperor system will continue."[46] In contrast, Watsuji had drawn a distinction between the conception of the emperor and of the state. But Yano agreed with Watsuji that the position of the emperor as symbol corresponded with ancient tradition. This interpretation provided conservatives with a face-saving way to endorse the Occupation-era reform of the emperor's position enthusiastically, rather than simply accept it grudgingly. To maintain the appearance of continuity, the right could claim that the symbolic monarchy was traditional, indeed, in its long history, unique to Japan. The symbolic monarchy whose existence is based on the will of the people was new, of course, but by invoking the long tradition of the monarchy as a symbol, conservatives could conveniently deflect attention from developments that undermined the underlying theme of continuity. The significance of the interpretation that the emperor as a symbol equals tradition was that it allowed the political right to accept the postwar democratic system and continue to champion the monarchy as distinctly Japanese.

Imperial Apologies and the Constitution

One might have thought that the widespread acceptance of the symbolic monarchy would have calmed controversy surrounding the emperor, but this was not the case. The emperor's assumption of a greater role on the international stage in the 1970s would create new constitutional questions that eventually would see the far right become the most vocal champion of the publicly neutral emperor. In the fall of 1971, Emperor Hirohito and Empress Nagako toured seven European countries. Part of the trip retraced ground covered by Crown Prince Hirohito during his 1921 travels in Europe. Although postwar trips abroad by Crown Prince Akihito had established a legal precedent for the emperor's trip, Hirohito traveling abroad nonetheless represented a new stage in imperial house diplomacy.

Twenty-six years had passed since Japan's humiliating defeat, and Japan's international stature had been redeemed greatly. Japan was now a valued member of the free world and had also joined the first tier of industrialized nations. The West German newspaper *Süddeutsche Zeitung* published a cartoon showing Hirohito being trailed by a contingent of car salesmen to indicate Japan's return to being an economic competitor with Europe. This cartoon was off the mark in the sense that although the British monarch often does advocate for British business, such a role is typically not played by Japan's emperor.[47]

The imperial couple's stay in Europe began well enough with stops in Denmark, Belgium, and France. The *Asahi shinbun*'s midpoint summary of the trip reported that Europeans' image of the emperor was changing from that of a "militarist" to a "kind," "sincere" "scientist."[48] Emperor Hirohito had a lifelong interest in marine biology, with several scholarly publications to his credit. The *Yomiuri shinbun* reported in its 2 October edition that the emperor was impressing Belgians as a "kind," "grandfatherly" man.

The imperial couple traveled from France to Britain and then on to the Netherlands, two countries whose people had bitter memories of Hirohito's role as a wartime leader. The Japanese government miscalculated the extent to which Emperor Hirohito's visit would stir memories of the war in Britain and the Netherlands. British tabloids deplored Hirohito's visit, calling him a "war criminal" as "despicable" as Hitler. The newspapers commented on the hush that greeted him: "It was a silence all the way for Emperor Hirohito. A powerful eloquent silence. A silence that spoke for Britain," the *Daily Mirror* wrote.[49]

At the official reception at Buckingham Palace, Queen Elizabeth II reminded everyone present that relations between the two countries had not always been so cordial. In contrast, Emperor Hirohito made no reference to the past in his statement at the official banquet. The most common criticism voiced by British commentators was that it would have been easier to accept the visit by Hirohito, as well as forgive the past, if an apology had been forthcoming from the "silent emperor."

If the welcome in Britain was cold, the reception in the Netherlands was icy. Dutch politicians emphasized to their constituents that Hirohito's visit was unofficial and was not the result of an invitation by the Dutch government. Dressed in suits, Dutch businessmen burned the Japanese flag and held up signs reading, "Hirohitler, Go." Many households flew the Dutch flag at half-mast. One representative in the Dutch legislature sent a letter to the Amsterdam public prosecutor demanding that Hirohito be arrested and tried for the deaths of 19,000 Dutch citizens in Japanese prisoner-of-war camps in the Dutch East Indies during World War II. An article in the *Asahi shinbun* pointed out that Dutch protesters were demonstrating specifically against the "war criminal Hirohito" and did not harbor anti-Japanese feelings.[50]

Although not ignoring the protests, all the major national newspapers in Japan editorialized after the imperial couple's return that the trip had been a success. The *Mainichi shinbun*'s editorial took refuge in a simplistic cultural interpretation of Europeans to explain the protests:

> In Denmark, Belgium, France, England, the Netherlands, Switzerland, and West Germany . . . the Imperial Couple was welcomed warmly. Their majesties carried out an important duty in improving international goodwill. . . .
>
> It is regrettable that the imperial trip was marred by some unpleasant developments. In Britain and the Netherlands there were some protests. . . . A tree that the Emperor expressly (*sekkaku*) planted in London was uprooted, and in the Netherlands there was the unfortunate incident [of a thermos being thrown at the emperor's car].
>
> These protests reflected smoldering anti-Japanese feelings in these countries. The Japanese people are quick to become excited, but they are also quick to discard unpleasant memories. Europeans do not forget

> the past. This is a difference in national traits. . . . The Japanese people must keep this harsh fact in mind in maintaining friendly relations with European countries.[51]

In an interview with reporters, the director of the Imperial Household Agency, Usami Takeshi, dismissed the protests—which he called the work of young radicals—as having had nothing to do with the war.[52] In spite of the government's best efforts to make Hirohito's association with the war magically vanish, the imperial couple's trip served to show precisely how much the war remained attached to the monarchy so long as Hirohito reigned. The *Asahi shinbun*, in its editorial about the trip, suggested that the question of the emperor's making some reference to the past should be considered.[53]

It was not only foreigners whose memories of Hirohito's wartime role clashed with the official line. In early 1972, an astonishing drama unfolded in Japan that showed how much the monarchy had changed since 1945 and provided further evidence of the problems Hirohito's continuing occupancy of the throne created. On 24 January, a Japanese soldier, Yokoi Shōichi (1915–97), emerged from the jungles of Guam, where he had continued to carry out his duties as a soldier of the emperor for twenty-seven years after the official end of the war. Yokoi had been afraid to surrender, an act forbidden—and punished by execution—under the military code he learned after being conscripted in 1941. To understand what a curious spectacle the return of this loyal soldier presented to most Japanese, one should bear in mind the low social prestige of the SDF in 1972. Three decades after the war, the status of the SDF remained pitifully low, and it remained muted until late in the twentieth century. Thereafter, largely as the result of the SDF's critical role in responding to a series of natural disasters that caused large-scale casualties and damage, the status of the SDF began to improve.

A special medical team was dispatched to Guam to care for Yokoi, and reporters flocked there. Ever loyal, Yokoi promptly told journalists that his hope after returning to Japan was to visit the Imperial Palace and Yasukuni Shrine. Virtually the entire nation watched television broadcasts of Yokoi's arrival by special plane at Haneda Airport in Tokyo on 2 February. Yokoi's statement on returning to Japan for the first time in twenty-eight years was, "Embarrassing as it is, I have returned alive. I brought back the rifle that I received from the Emperor."[54] The embarrassment referred to having survived, not to having remained unknowingly in Guam for decades after the end of the war. The mass media termed Yokoi the "emperor's last soldier." As it turned out, he was not the last. Onoda Hiroo (1922–2014) emerged from the jungle in the Philippines two years later. Then Nakamura Teruo (1919–79), a soldier of Taiwanese descent in the Japanese army, was rescued from a remote Indonesian island in December 1974. Nakamura, it appears, was the last.

Commentators labeled Yokoi a "time capsule," among other things. It might be better to call him a "personal memory capsule." After twenty-eight years of living entirely out of contact with Japan, Yokoi was a member of a rare group: he was one of an extremely small number of Japanese nationals who in no way had been exposed to the official memory—including that of the emperor's wartime role—of Imperial Japan constructed after Japan's surrender.

Yokoi's unswerving allegiance to the emperor presented a public relations problem for the palace. Virtually every subsequent comment he made linked the emperor to the war in some way. At a press conference in Guam, Yokoi stated that he would like "to worship from afar the Emperor" if the "Supreme Commander Emperor" were still alive. Reporters quoted Yokoi as saying that he "wanted to report that he had continued to live for His Majesty, to believe in His Majesty."[55] Composer Mayuzumi Toshirō (1929–97), a fervent champion of the throne long active in nationalistic causes, expressed his appreciation of Yokoi's loyalty and called him living proof of how profoundly the Japanese had revered the emperor before the postwar reforms.[56]

The emperor issued no public statement in reference to Yokoi, although palace officials informed reporters that the emperor was following Yokoi's return closely. Weeklies printed comments of citizens criticizing the emperor for saying nothing when Yokoi was first discovered and then chastised him for not meeting Yokoi at the airport. The Imperial Household Agency was said to have been flooded with letters asking the emperor to receive his "last soldier." Various public figures, from Nakasone Yasuhiro to the virulent nationalist and extreme right leader Akao Bin, called for a meeting. Some people worried, however, that if Yokoi met the "suit-and-tie" emperor instead of the "supreme commander" emperor he was expecting, he might die of a heart attack.[57] In the end, the two never met.

At a press conference held at a hospital in Tokyo five days after his return, Yokoi was asked when he planned to visit the Imperial Palace and Yasukuni Shrine. "I would like to go as soon as possible to give thanks and return my rifle. And I would like to make an offering to the war heroes," Yokoi replied. The next question referred to the emperor, and Yokoi expressed his disgust with mass media coverage of "His Majesty": "I would like to know who gave permission for His Majesty to be treated like a toy in magazines, movies, etc."[58]

Ten months after returning home, Yokoi wrote an article telling his story firsthand. He had visited the Imperial Palace and Yasukuni Shrine and was newly married. "I no longer see Guam in my dreams," he wrote. "I think that is because I brought back the spirits of my war buddies from Guam and enshrined them at Yasukuni Shrine."[59] He defended the emperor: "Regarding the twenty-seven years that I spent in Guam and [the issue] of war responsibility, I do not hate the Emperor. I will not even criticize him."[60]

Yokoi's view of the emperor was to change within a few years, however. In 1975, Emperor Hirohito, during an interview with an U.S. journalist before his trip to the United States, distanced himself from the decision to start the war (against the United States and other Allied nations). While taking credit for personally bringing the war to an end, the emperor insisted that he could not override (*kutsugaesu*) the 1941 decision to commence hostilities. Questioned about the emperor's comments, Yokoi could not hide his feelings of betrayal: "The Emperor really said something unexpected. I believed from the bottom of my heart that I went to war as a child of the Emperor according to the Emperor's orders. Now the Emperor says, 'The war was started by the militarists who used me. I could not say "No."' . . . Frankly, I am disappointed."[61] Yokoi's disillusionment with the emperor was shared by many veterans who were told after Japan's surrender that the emperor was a pacifist who never had supported the war.[62] It was often loyal soldiers and individuals closest to the throne who felt the most betrayed by the emperor's disassociation of himself from the war.

It was for the emperor's visit to the United States in 1975 that the Japanese government composed the first of what would be a series of vague public statements about the past for Hirohito to read at international receptions. At a White House banquet hosted by President Gerald

FIGURE 12. Emperor Hirohito signs the guest register at Disneyland in 1975. Empress Nagako is to the right. Although many Americans were willing to accept the reconstructed image of the emperor as a pacifistic opponent of the Pacific War, the question of war responsibility would plague Hirohito until his death in 1989. (Photograph courtesy Kyodo Photo Service.)

Ford, Emperor Hirohito referred to the "most unfortunate war which I deeply deplore." The emperor's statement left the issue of responsibility unclear, however. This was followed by similarly ambiguous statements about the past to visiting heads of states from neighboring countries. In constitutional terms, the government justified these statements as public acts of the emperor in his position as a symbol. The wording of the emperor's statements always taxed the imagination of Japanese officials. Precisely because they were not clear-cut apologies, however, these statements did not become significant political or constitutional issues. But this process, once begun, eventually led to the creation of the "emperor as apologizer," a role played less ambiguously by Akihito after his ascension to the throne.

On the day that Hirohito died, Prime Minister Takeshita Noboru promptly repeated the long-standing official interpretation of Hirohito's historical role: "He resolutely brought to an end the war that had broken out in spite of his wishes, out of a determination to prevent further suffering of the people, regardless of the consequences to his own person."[63]

The wording had changed little since Prime Minister Suzuki, on the day of the surrender, stressed the emperor's heroic role in ending hostilities. The official line, repeated over and over in the five decades since 1945, had come to enjoy tangible popular support. Sumikura Masako, a forty-two-year-old housewife interviewed after visiting the imperial palace at the end of 1988 to pray for the stricken emperor, voiced her opinion that Emperor Hirohito was the "savior" of Japan and even credited him with responsibility for the nation's prosperity.[64] Within months after the emperor's death, the government declared 29 April, Hirohito's birthday, a new national holiday: Greenery Day (*midori no hi*).[65] Transformed into a pacifist after the war, Hirohito was commemorated officially after his death as a symbol of environmentalism. At the same time, however, there were signs that the myth of the pacifist emperor was crumbling. The clearest indication of this was the Motoshima Incident, discussed in the introduction.

For his statement in December 1988 (when Hirohito was on his deathbed) that "the emperor bears war responsibility," Nagasaki Mayor Motoshima Hitoshi was hounded by right-wing protesters. In response, however, thousands of Japanese citizens rose to defend the mayor with letters of support and public demonstrations. Many of the letters agreed with Motoshima's carefully worded interpretation of the emperor's accountability.[66] Public opinion polls taken in the aftermath of Hirohito's death showed that the people were losing their hesitancy to indict the former emperor as at least partially responsible for the war. Twenty-five percent of people polled by the *Asahi shinbun* shortly after Hirohito's death indicated that the emperor bore responsibility for the war.[67]

The fiftieth anniversary of the war's conclusion in 1995 sparked further public debate about the emperor's wartime role. During a discussion about the nature of historical remembrance that took place in a class on Japanese history I taught at Hokkaido University that year, a twenty-three-year-old student stressed, "At the dinner table in my home . . . the emperor always was [spoken of as] a war criminal." On another occasion in 1995, a taxi driver who appeared to be in his late fifties or early sixties, overhearing a discussion between two Japanese scholars and me, offered his opinion that the late emperor was no less responsible for the war than

Asahara Shōkō, leader of the Supreme Truth Cult (Aum shinrikyō), was culpable for the deadly Tokyo subway gas attack in March of that year that so horrified the Japanese.[68] With taboos weakening, the Japanese began to voice opinions about the late emperor that, in some cases, had been maintained quietly for decades. It is impossible to know for sure whether the student expressed a long-held family opinion and the taxi driver a long-standing personal view, for personal memories tend to be reconstituted to suit changing social conditions.[69] It became more acceptable to speak not only of Hirohito's personal responsibility but also of Japan's war responsibility after the emperor's death.[70]

The passing of Emperor Hirohito from the scene was one of several factors that sparked a crisis in the national conscience regarding how to remember the war. Hirohito's death opened the door to public debate about topics such as the emperor's and people's wartime roles as participants rather than mere victims of the military establishment. Even more important in reopening the debate over World War II was the late 1980s collapse of the Soviet Union; silence about the unpleasant past could no longer be justified by the need to meet the Cold War threat. Indeed, not only in Japan but around the world the Cold War's conclusion created an environment hospitable for heads of state to address past wrongs. In 1993, President Bill Clinton apologized for the illegal overthrow of the Hawaiian monarchy 100 years earlier. This followed the decision in 1988 to pay reparations to Japanese Americans who had been relocated to internment centers after the attack on Pearl Harbor in gross violation of their constitutional rights. Queen Elizabeth II, during a visit to New Zealand in 1995, apologized to Maoris for the confiscation of Maori land in the 1860s. And in France, in 1995 Jacques Chirac (b. 1932; president, 1995–2007) became the first French president to apologize for his nation's role in the deportations of thousands of Jews during World War II.

In Japan, the new willingness of victims, such as some of the "comfort women" forced to serve as prostitutes for Japanese soldiers, not only to speak out about their experiences but also to sue the Japanese government to redress the past also proved to be a key factor in encouraging a reexamination of the war.[71] Victims of the comfort women system received support from women's rights groups throughout Asia, and the fact that the victims' testimony resonated strongly in Japan was partly a result of a heightened social sensitivity about the mistreatment of women that Japanese feminists had fostered for years. The colonial subjugation of Korea from 1910 to 1945 reached its nadir during the course of the Fifteen-Year War when Japan forcibly mobilized large numbers of Koreans as soldiers, laborers, and, in the case of women, sexual slaves (comfort women) in support of the war effort. Although women from throughout Asia were forced to service Japanese military men, the majority who were victimized were Korean. Historians in Japan, who have labored for decades to chronicle Japanese brutality during the war, played an important role in pushing their leaders to apologize by providing documentary evidence of the extent of Japanese war crimes, including the state's role in the comfort women system.

Most of all, it was pressure from foreign governments that drove the "politics of apology" that enveloped Japan, including the throne, in the 1990s. The phenomenon of "foreign pressure" (*gaiatsu*) in Japanese politics is typically described in terms of the hegemonic United States pushing Japan into action, usually to address economic issues. In the 1990s, however, Japanese leaders proved susceptible to pressure from weaker neighbors to concede the impropriety of Japan's wartime behavior. In fact, the susceptibility of Japanese leaders to neighboring countries' demands for contrition may be explained partially by a desire to reapproach Asia to decrease Japan's long-standing dependence on the United States.

In 1990, the South Korean government put the Japanese government in a political and constitutional bind by requesting an outright apology from the new emperor on the occasion of President Roh Tae Woo's (b. 1932; president, 1988–93) visit to Japan. The South Korean media called for a statement that clarified the respective identities of the aggressor and the victim.[72] Unlike the situation in the years after the surrender, when some Japanese looked to Emperor Hirohito for an apology for his role in a war with the United States and Britain that had ended in disaster for their country, the South Korean government wanted Emperor Akihito to represent Japan in acknowledging its brutal treatment of a weaker neighbor.

The Japanese government originally planned to respond to South Korea's demand by having Akihito make a statement similar to Emperor Hirohito's vague remarks to President Chun Doo Hwan in 1984[73] and then have Prime Minister Kaifu Toshiki (1931–) follow with an explicit apology. The South Korean government was adamant that the apology should come from the emperor. Throughout the postwar era, the Japanese government had maintained, after all, that the emperor was Japan's head of state vis-à-vis the outside world. Furthermore, the emperor is Japan's most potent national symbol, and an apology from him would have particular resonance. The South Korean government's demand reopened old constitutional questions: Was the emperor head of state (more specifically, what sort of head of state was he)? What public acts by the emperor were permissible?

As the Japanese government wrestled with the wording of the emperor's public statement to be made at the banquet hosting President Roh, a noisy domestic political debate emerged about both the necessity of the apologies and the constitutional legality of such statements from the emperor. The JSP and the JCP had long played the role of gadflies and insisted that the emperor be kept out of politics. In 1990, both parties held to their longtime positions. The JSP stressed that diplomatic problems were the responsibility of the government and called for a Diet resolution acknowledging Japan's war responsibility. Doi Takako (1928–2014), chair of the JSP and a constitutional scholar herself, stressed: "We do not recognize that acts in matters of state provided for by Article 7 of the constitution extend to . . . political statements. Article 4 specifies that the emperor shall not have powers related to government."[74]

What was especially interesting about the political reaction to the question of apologies was that the most right-wing LDP representatives staged what the journalist Takahashi Hiroshi called "a campaign to prevent political use of the symbol emperor."[75] The campaign was directed against the LDP leadership itself, for the LDP was in power at this point. During a meeting of the House of Representatives Budget Committee, LDP representative Noda Takeshi, referring to the upcoming public statement by the emperor, reminded Prime Minister Kaifu that "involving the imperial house in diplomatic problems must be avoided."[76] Chief Secretary of the Cabinet Sakamoto Misoji acknowledged that "there are extremely strict limits on the symbol emperor."[77]

Academics joined the fracas. Ashibe Nobuyoshi (1923–99), a professor emeritus at Tokyo University and a leading interpreter of the constitution, argued that it was unconstitutional for the emperor to apologize on behalf of the state. Ashibe stressed that the "principle of the constitution was to try to separate the emperor from the world of politics."[78] But Inoki Masamichi (1914–2012), former president of Japan's Defense College, called for consistency on the part of the government. He pointed out that if one stood by the interpretation that the emperor was head of state, then "it is natural that the emperor should apologize to a foreign head of state."[79]

At the banquet the emperor hosted for President Roh, Akihito, looking directly at South Korea's president, said:

> While looking back upon the history of long, fruitful exchanges between the Korean Peninsula and Japan, I recall what was stated by the late Emperor Shōwa: "It is indeed regrettable that there was an unfortunate past between us for a period in this century and I believe that it should not be repeated again."
>
> I think of the sufferings your people underwent during this unfortunate period, which was brought about by my country, and cannot but feel the deepest regret.[80]

The emperor's statement acknowledged Japan's responsibility, distinguishing it from earlier imperial statements of regret. President Roh accepted Emperor Akihito's statement as an apology, whereas reaction among the Korean people was diverse. The multiple complexities of such politics of apology further deepened when Roh along with Chun (who had accepted the statement of regret from Hirohito) were later tried and convicted (1996) of treason, mutiny, and corruption for their roles in the 1979 coup, their roles in the 1980 Gwangju Massacre, and for having lined their pockets while in office. In retrospect, in light of their own roles in domestic repression and corruption, Chun and Roh hardly seem worthy of accepting Japan's contrition on behalf of the people of Korea, but such is sometimes the nature of nation-state to nation-state diplomacy.

According to the Cabinet, the emperor's apology, in constitutional terms, was made in his public capacity as a symbol but was not an act in matters of state.[81] In 1952, the Yoshida Cabinet, rejecting strict constitutional interpretations, broadened the emperor's public role by devising the category of public acts carried out by the emperor in his position as symbol. Policies, once instituted, often have unintended consequences. In 1990, the broadened interpretation of the emperor's public role was

FIGURE 13. At a state banquet in honor of South Korean President Roh Tae Woo in 1990, Emperor Akihito apologizes for Japan's mistreatment of Korea during the first half of the twentieth century: "I think of the sufferings your people underwent during this unfortunate period, which was brought about by my country, and cannot but feel the deepest regret." (Photograph courtesy Imperial Household Agency.)

used in a manner that surely could not have been imagined by anyone in the Yoshida Cabinet—to justify imperial apologies.

Emperor Akihito's apology to Korea was followed two years later by a statement of contrition to China during his visit there. This was the first visit to China ever by a reigning emperor. Chinese officials made it known that they expected no less of an apology than that offered to South Korea. Japanese atrocities during fifteen years of war in China ranged from systematic scorched earth campaigns in the north and northeast to the notorious Rape of Nanjing to the gruesome germ warfare and human experimentation conducted by Unit 731. On 23 September 1992, during a speech covering the entire history of exchanges between China and Japan, the emperor said, "In the long history of the relationship between our two countries, there was an unfortunate period in which my country inflicted great sufferings on the people of China. I deeply deplore this." Emperor Akihito is said to have strengthened the final wording of the apology.[82] Symbolic though his constitutional position was, Akhito nonetheless committed himself to a campaign to bring an end to the postwar era.

Are apologies merely symbolic? By making statements of remorse that, at a broad level, clarified Japan's responsibility, Akihito called into

FIGURE 14. As part of his policy of "disposing of the postwar," Emperor Akihito, at the palace spring garden party in 1991, acknowledged Yokoi Shōichi for his service to the nation. Yokoi emerged from the jungle in Guam in 1972 after having continued to fight for the emperor for twenty-seven years after the formal end of the war. Emperor Hirohito never met Yokoi, whom the mass media labeled the "emperor's last soldier." (Photograph courtesy Imperial Household Agency.)

question conservative interpretations that reject the notion that Japan bears special culpability for the war. Whether Emperor Akihito's statements went far enough is open to interpretation. Individuals who deny their significance should bear in mind the following, however. Emperor Akihito's emergence as a symbol for a revised imperial memory of the war that acknowledges Japan's responsibility was a most unwelcome development for the emperorists on the far right and the extreme right. A 1995 position paper issued by the Shinto Political Association (Shintō seiji renmei), a political arm of the Association of Shinto Shrines, severely criticized the government for involving the emperor in politics through diplomacy. The Association of Shinto Shrines, it should be recalled, was an important agent in the movement that sought to restore the Meiji political and constitutional system.

The Shinto Political Association's 1995 paper reminded people that the emperor's position under the Constitution of Japan was that of a "symbol" who "performed only acts in matters of state" and had no "powers related to government." The paper went on to stress that diplomacy involving the imperial house, the most important example being the trip to China, raised grave constitutional questions.[83] Although the Association of Shinto Shrines' apparent support of the symbolic monarchy, a reversal of its earlier position, was notable, the association rejected imperial apologies for reasons other than the constitutional problems they raised. A vocal nationalistic group, it opposes all official statements of remorse about the war, and it has been a key player in the conservative movement to undermine the fragile national consensus (at least something of a consensus) regarding Japan's culpability that seemed to be taking shape in the mid-1990s. Public memory is central to nationalism, and in the mid- and late 1990s Japanese nationalists reacted sharply against what they interpreted as malicious attacks on national pride. A "civil war over memory" resulted.[84] This contest over historical memory is integral to debates about Japan's identity in the post–Cold War era.[85]

The LDP was divided not only about the constitutionality of imperial apologies, but about whether Japan should apologize. Ishihara Shintarō, one of the most prominent politicians in Japan by the 1990s, opposed imperial apologies. Ishihara represented the same spectrum of the political continuum that in the 1950s supported strengthening the emperor's political role through constitutional revision. In the 1990s, however, Ishihara and the rest of the right wing of the LDP demanded that the symbol emperor be kept out of politics. Ishihara opposed the emperor's trip to China:

> The emperor's public acts are specified by Article 7, and there are some other public acts, too, such as the emperor's attending the National Athletic Meet and traveling abroad. However, in those cases, there are no past examples of so many Japanese people holding doubts about them. I never have heard of opposition even from the JCP to the emperor's attending the National Athletic Meet.
>
> If the purpose of the emperor's trip to China is, as the Foreign Ministry says, to use Japan's "ace card" to put Sino-Japanese relations in order and to open a new era, then this is clearly a matter of diplomacy—the work of the government—not something that is outside politics in other words; how is one to think that entrusting this to the emperor is not a deviation from the criterion of the constitutionally defined position of the emperor as "symbol"?[86]

The far right, once the most vocal defenders of the Meiji system that placed the monarchy at the center of the political process, had reversed course regarding the monarchy. In interpreting the constitution, Ishihara found himself in agreement—for very different reasons—with those on the opposite end of the political spectrum, the JSP and even the JCP, that the emperor should be kept out of politics. The chair of the JSP, Doi Takako, argued that Japan should apologize for its imperialistic past; Ishihara's opposition to imperial apologies went beyond constitutional issues. He insists that although Japan behaved aggressively toward its Asian neighbors, this aggression transpired in the context of the fight against European imperialism in Asia. LDP representatives to the right of Ishihara opposed apologies (whether by the emperor or by other government officials) altogether, while more moderate representatives than Ishihara supported unqualified statements of contrition for Japan's wartime aggression.

Ishihara might have found a sympathetic ear among British conservatives regarding the necessity of a politically neutral throne. After becoming monarch in 1952, Queen Elizabeth II maintained a studious public neutrality regarding the government's domestic policies for thirty-four years. In 1986, at the height of Thatcherism, this changed. Michael Shea, the queen's press secretary, "leaked" accounts of Queen Elizabeth II's displeasure with the Thatcher Cabinet's policies. Palace observers in Britain interpreted this as inconceivable without the complicity of the queen. The queen was portrayed, by impeccable sources, as being angered by Thatcher's unbending position opposing sanctions against South Africa, which was threatening to tear apart the Commonwealth. The Commonwealth, a voluntary organization composed of many of Britain's former colonies, including several African states, is headed by the queen. The queen also was quoted, in reference to Thatcher's attacks on the welfare state, as criticizing the prime minister's approach as "uncaring, confrontational and socially divisive."[87] The crown long had been seen by conservatives as a bulwark against the radicalism of Labour governments, but now it stood in opposition to the welfare bashing of the conservatives. Hardline British conservatives, unwilling to criticize the queen publicly for fear of a political backlash, found themselves gritting their teeth and silently cursing her lack of neutrality.[88]

Editorials in the left-wing *Guardian* expressed reservations about the queen's breach of neutrality, even against the objectionable Thatcher Cabinet. The *Guardian*'s stance paralleled the position later taken by the JSP and JCP regarding Emperor Akihito's apology to Korea. The left in Japan proposed that the state recognize its war responsibility, but it opposed involving the emperor in such a matter. Nationalistic groups and the most right-wing faction of the LDP, home to some of the most outspoken champions of the throne, avoided personal criticism of the monarch as had their British counterparts, but they loudly indicted the government for violating the constitution.

In Japan, the emperor lies at the center of symbolic politics, which at times are no less important than the politics of drafting the budget. For decades Japan had an emperor who simply refused to accept any responsibility for the war publicly and played along with the official account that blamed the militarists. So long as the symbol of the nation chose to do so, it was easier for the Japanese to evade the question of how an indeterminate but still narrowly defined group of militarists could be fully responsible for fifteen years of war that resulted in so much suffering in Asia and, in the end, brought disaster to Japan. In contrast to his father's evasiveness, Emperor Akihito has acknowledged publicly that Japan, for example, "inflicted great sufferings on the people of China." The cacophony of conservative protests against imperial apologies suggests the symbolic importance of the throne, in this case, in contributing to a more contrite national narrative of the war.[89] Imperial apologies represent a step in the direction of coming to terms with Japan's responsibility for the war. In light of imperial apologies, one must avoid interpretations that continue to portray the throne as a tool used only for conservative ends, for this often has not been the case under Akihito. For constitutional reasons, the JCP and JSP opposed imperial apologies, but they had long been calling for a more contrite official history of the war along the lines of that offered by Akihito. No doubt the battle over defining the emperor's public acts will continue, however; the term "symbol" is inherently vague.

CHAPTER 5

Nationalistic Movements to Restore Cultural Symbols of the Monarchy

> There is no relationship between Foundation Day and Emperor Jimmu. Under the present constitution, His Highness is a symbol emperor, and it is difficult to celebrate . . . Emperor Jimmu at a ceremony attended by the prime minister.
>
> —Nakayama Masaki, representing Prime Minister Nakasone Yasuhiro in 1984 in negotiations with far-right groups regarding arrangements for a Foundation Day celebration that the prime minister could attend

> At the governmental ceremony, they don't have [a reading] of Emperor Jimmu's imperial rescript on the founding of the nation, they don't [say] 'Long Live His Majesty the Emperor!' (*Tennō heika banzai*), and they don't worship from afar the Kashihara Shrine. Just which nation's founding is [being celebrated]?
>
> —The far-right leader Nakamura Takehiko in 1992, commenting on the quasi-official Foundation Day celebration established under Prime Minister Nakasone

As prospects for constitutional revision dimmed in the late 1950s, individuals and groups active in the revision effort redirected their energy into other movements, especially those concerning symbolic issues. Far right lobbies spearheaded successful movements to reestablish both National Foundation Day (*Kenkoku kinen no hi*; *Kigensetsu* in the prewar era) as a national holiday (accomplished in 1966) and the legal basis for the reign-name (*gengō*) system for counting years. The Reign-Name Law (*Gengōhō*), in effect since 1979, stipulates that reign names are Japan's official system for year dates.

Critics accused the ruling LDP of attempting to reestablish the prewar emperor system "from above" with these measures. This was not the case. The Diet reestablished Foundation Day and enacted the Reign-Name Law only after national movements demonstrating grassroots support for these two measures pushed or enabled a hesitant LDP to take action. The Japanese left has tended to define democracy as "contestatory or participatory social behavior"[1] in reference to its own protests against the establishment, but elements of the right have also challenged the status quo through social movements. The goal of this chapter is not to redeem the far right,[2] but to improve our understanding of right-wing movements in postwar Japan.

To pressure the Diet to take action on these measures, far right lobbies employed a variety of grassroots techniques often associated only with left-wing movements. These far right organizations form part of Japan's diverse "public sphere" or "civil society,"[3] and their political influence must be taken into account. The simplistic dichotomy of a supposedly liberal civil society on the one hand and a conservative state on the other should be laid to rest once and for all. Even with regard to issues concerning the emperor system, it misleads far more than it informs. Many aspects of the postwar monarchy irksome to leftist critics of the throne have been propelled by widespread popular support.

The movement to reestablish Foundation Day (1951–66) deserves special attention because it was the first movement led by far-right groups that succeeded in both attracting considerable numbers of supporters and achieving its basic political goal. Continuities between the Foundation Day movement and the reign-name legalization movement (1968–79) are striking in terms of the actors involved and the methods of political lobbying employed. Over the years, the far right learned how to mount a successful campaign in the democratic political order.

Although this chapter focuses on two practices that were abolished during the Occupation only to be reestablished later, it also shows that support among the Japanese for the prewar emperor system as a whole withered as the postwar era progressed. Foundation Day and the reign-name system enjoyed popular backing, but only in the context of the postwar system defined by the new constitution. Many nationalism*s* were articulated in postwar Japan, but no nationalism opposed to democracy has garnered popular support. Although the throne has remained a central nationalistic symbol, prewar-style *kokutai* myths have proved unappealing to the majority of Japanese citizens. Indeed, questions about how the reestablished Foundation Day should be celebrated generated stark divisions within the political right.

The Foundation Day Reestablishment Movement

Although public opinion polls indicate that the "passive majority" consistently favored reestablishment of Foundation Day, the contest over this holiday's fate was contentious because it featured two bitterly opposed factions.[4] For leftist historians, schoolteachers, and others committed to preventing reestablishment of the holiday, Foundation Day symbolized the feudal, irrational, unscientific, undemocratic, and militaristic old regime, vestiges of which had to be eradicated. Scientific rationality was not featured explicitly in the Postwar Constitution, but liberals, among others, elevated it into a positive principle in the postwar era. Critics of Foundation Day held the government responsible for having mobilized the citizenry to support the war by inventing and expanding a spurious ideology centered on the emperor, and they saw the reestablishment movement as part of a larger effort to reverse course and attack the postwar democratic system.

Historians stress that there is no scientific evidence for the existence of Emperor Jimmu, not to mention the fanciful notion that he founded the Empire of Japan on 11 February 660 BCE. They argued that it was improper for the state once again to lend legitimacy to such mythology.[5] In the Diet, the anti–11 February Foundation Day forces enjoyed the support of the JCP and JSP. The JSP proposed that 3 May, the day the Constitution of Japan went into effect in 1947, be celebrated as National Foundation Day. Many individuals on the left believed that the only "Japan" whose foundation was worth celebrating was that of postwar, democratic Japan. Although unsuccessful in preventing the reestablishment of Foundation Day as a national holiday on 11 February, the opposition was successful in restricting the manner in which it would be celebrated.

In contrast, the most committed members of the reestablishment faction positively evaluated the old regime and Japanese traditions in general. They interpreted the Occupation as a national shame. Although their own feelings toward democracy might have been lukewarm or even hostile, they emphasized that SCAP had undemocratically abolished

Foundation Day in spite of the popular backing the holiday enjoyed. Foundation Day supporters emphasized the spiritual emptiness—the dearth of patriotism—among the Japanese under the postwar system established by the army of occupation, which had not only reformed Japan's political system but also trampled Japanese cultural traditions. Foundation Day was a mechanism to encourage the Japanese to love their country. Supporters stressed that the unique feature of Japan was the unbroken imperial line dating back to Emperor Jimmu, and they saw Foundation Day as a means of reinforcing the imperial house's importance in Japanese society. They sought not only the reestablishment of Foundation Day as a national holiday but also widespread government-sponsored celebrations along prewar lines.

The Association of Shinto Shrines was the most prominent agent in the reestablishment coalition. In many ways, the association differs little from thousands of private organizations throughout Japan. Each weekday morning, several hundred conservatively dressed employees, many of them college educated, arrive for work at the organization's headquarters next to the Meiji Shrine in downtown Tokyo. They are no less interested in the size of their annual bonuses than salaried employees throughout the archipelago, but their work focuses on articulating and furthering the interests of the "shrine world" (*jinjakai*). This imprecise term applies to individuals such as priests who make their living from Shinto and to people simply interested in Shinto issues.

In the decades after Japan regained independence, the Association of Shinto Shrines strongly supported measures to reestablish elements of the Meiji polity and ideology.[6] Rejecting the postwar system symbolized by the U.S.-written constitution, the association's chief aims during the postwar era have been (1) abolishing, or establishing a new interpretation of, Article 20 of the 1946 Constitution, which requires the strict separation of church and state; and (2) increasing reverence for the imperial house.[7] Through its branches in Japan's forty-seven prefectures, the association coordinates action among more than 80,000 shrines.[8] The association also sponsors several affiliates, including the National Shinto Youth Council (Shintō seinen zenkoku kyōgikai) and the National Women's Piety Federation (Zenkoku keishin fujin rengōkai),[9] which played important roles in the Foundation Day reestablishment movement and later political campaigns. In looking back at the Foundation Day reestablishment movement, Shinto scholar Tanaka Takashi (1923–2018), an active participant in the movement, emphasized that the shrine world was not necessarily unified in its desire to reestablish this national holiday.[10] Nonetheless, the most intense support came from the shrine world.

The Association of Shinto Shrines brought together numerous organizations that worked in coalition to champion Foundation Day. In 1955, it was the main agent behind the organization of the Foundation Day Celebration People's Steering Committee (Kigensetsu hōshuku kokumin taikai un'ei iinkai). This committee represented more than eighty diverse groups advocating the reestablishment of this prewar holiday.[11] It came to include several mass-membership organizations, such as the Japan Veterans Friendship League (Nihon gōyū renmei),[12] the Japan Society of War-Bereaved Families (Nihon izokukai), and the religious group Seichō no ie (House of growth).[13] Youth and women's groups affiliated with these organizations played important roles in the movement as well.

Usually, the beginning of the reestablishment movement is dated to Prime Minister Yoshida Shigeru's request on 9 March 1951 that the holiday be reinstituted. Asked during a Diet committee meeting how the government intended to strengthen patriotic feelings, Yoshida responded that he "would like to re-establish Foundation Day after independence." He continued, "It is acceptable to re-establish Foundation Day based on the power that arises from the general will of the people."[14] Earlier that year, the Association of Shinto Shrines had begun planning how to convince the Diet to reinstate Foundation Day as a holiday. Shortly after the signing of the San Francisco Peace Treaty, the Association of Shinto Shrines announced its intention to inaugurate a movement to reinstate Foundation Day.[15] In 1952, the National Shinto Youth Council began to collect signatures in support of reestablishing Foundation Day from people visiting shrines during the New Year's holiday.[16] Petition drives were the first of many democratic methods used by the reestablishment coalition in its fifteen-year movement.

The political environment in the early 1950s seemed to favor reestablishment. Yoshida's Liberal Party, which backed the holiday, was in power. Public opinion favored it as well. But an intense minority led by historians, such as Wakamori Tarō (1915–77), who sought to discredit national myths mounted a vigorous opposition campaign. The contest over Foundation Day symbolized the broad ideological battle between the left and the right regarding the legitimacy of various Occupation-era reforms.

In 1954, an *Asahi shinbun* journalist wrote of the resiliency of Foundation Day supporters: "The people who fervently wish for the re-establishment of Foundation Day are like a well-rooted weed; no matter how much they are stepped on, they keep putting out sprouts."[17] This journalist expressed skepticism about the policy statement of the newly formed Foundation Day Establishment Promotion Association (Kenkoku kinenbi [Kigensetsu] seitei sokushinkai). He was suspicious that this association's announced intent of fostering grassroots democratic movements in support of reestablishing Foundation Day was simply camouflage to avoid the charge that it sought to reimpose the emperor system from above.[18] His critical attitude toward Foundation Day was representative of the postwar mainstream mass media's rejection of the holiday, a significant change from the prewar era.

The reestablishment coalition used annual celebrations staged on 11 February as its main mechanism to demonstrate public support for Foundation Day. In 1954, the Association of Shinto Shrines directed all shrines to celebrate Foundation Day. That year, the coalition began staging an annual grand celebration of Foundation Day in Tokyo. This rally drew a few thousand participants each year and brought together leaders of the various groups participating in the coalition to discuss strategy and coordination of their lobbying activities. Foundation Day ceremonies included patriotic speeches, songs, dances, and conspicuous flag-waving. The celebrations concluded with the adoption of a resolution in favor of reestablishing Foundation Day, which then was forwarded to government representatives.

Participation levels in Foundation Day celebrations varied regionally, especially during the early stage of the movement. Local celebrations of Foundation Day often were sponsored jointly by branches of several groups participating in the reestablishment movement or by organizations only loosely aligned. Nowhere did the movement become as much of a spectacle as it did in Kashihara City.

Elevated to the apex of the imperial landscape by 1940, the area of Kashihara was a loser in terms of money and prestige after the surrender. The Kashihara Shrine, along with Foundation Day, was discredited as supporting pernicious myths. The number of tourists visiting the area greatly declined. In 1956, Yoshikawa Saburō, a former army officer, was elected the first mayor of the newly incorporated Kashihara City. Thirty-eight at the time of his election, Yoshikawa staked his political life on the reestablishment of Foundation Day.[19] He was swept into office with the support of local notables, especially merchants who hoped to make Kashihara an obligatory destination on the national tourist landscape once again.[20] Mayor Yoshikawa served four full terms (1956–72), and during his tenure Kashihara City's population doubled from 39,000 to 78,000.

In the fall of 1956, the mayor, who kept a bronze statue of Emperor Jimmu in his office, won the approval of the city assembly to use municipal funds to stage an annual parade on Foundation Day. Mayor Yoshikawa suggested that such a parade not only would encourage Kashihara City's development but would also promote the reestablishment of Foundation Day as a national holiday.[21] Yoshikawa was so eager to base his city's identity and development on the Jimmu-related sites in Kashihara that in the 1960s he supported plans for the construction of a major highway that would pass through Kashihara and in the process cut directly through what many archeologists and historians believed to be the site of the ancient capital of Fujiwara.[22] The highway was never built, and archeologists proceeded to excavate astonishing vestiges of this ancient capital, including the Fujiwara Palace (694–710) itself, within the city of Kashihara. This contrasts with the complete lack of empirical evidence to support the authenticity of Emperor Jimmu's mausoleum and the Kashihara Shrine.

Yoshikawa's brainstorm, the Ancient Yamato Procession (*Yamato kodai gyōretsu*), or simply the Yamato Parade (fig. 15), first took place in 1957.[23] The parade soon attracted participants from all over Japan. The governor of Nara prefecture, in which Kashihara is located, often attended, as did Diet members, especially those representing the prefecture. The main roles in the Yamato Parade were reserved for local notables. As mayor, Yoshikawa assumed the role of Emperor Jimmu. Dressed in ancient costume, he led the procession on a white horse. Next came the chair of the city assembly playing the legendary hero Yamato Takeru no Mikoto.[24] He was followed by the chair of the municipal local rule association as Prince Shōtoku, who in the early seventh century gave Japan its first set of basic laws. Next came the head of the local chamber

FIGURE 15. Mayor Yoshikawa Saburō of Kashihara City (on the white horse) playing the role of Emperor Jimmu in his city's Yamato Parade. By means of the Yamato Parade, Yoshikawa sought not only to attract tourists to Kashihara, where the Kashihara Shrine and Emperor Jimmu's mausoleum are located, but to encourage the reestablishment of Foundation Day as a national holiday. (Photograph courtesy of the City of Kashihara.)

of commerce, playing the part of Emperor Tenji (626–72), one of the most powerful sovereigns in Japanese history. He was followed by the city's fairest young lady, that year's Miss Foundation Day (*Misu kigensetsu*). She was followed by approximately 2,000 young women performing the Foundation Day Dance (*Kigensetsu odori*).[25]

The appearance of a Miss Foundation Day at a ceremony in Imperial Japan would have been considered as irreverent as the presence of a bikini-clad Miss Garden of Eden in a Catholic Church ceremony.[26] In 2000, decades after the last Miss Foundation Day was crowned, one priest at the Kashihara Shrine, Nishino Keiichi, criticized Yoshikawa's use of such gimmicks.[27] The practice of naming a Miss Such-and-Such was in fact a cultural borrowing from the United States, yet the Yamato Parade's organizers, whose motivations extended beyond nationalism, apparently saw no irony in including Miss Foundation Day in the festivities. Miss Foundation Day symbolized the changing meaning and tone of this celebration. Eventually other localities began to crown a Miss Foundation Day as well, but no national contest to choose the fairest Miss Foundation

Day was ever staged. A skeptic might have argued that the appearance of more than one Miss Foundation Day in any given year raised troubling questions about the legitimacy of the Miss Foundation Day lineage, just as historical episodes such as the appearance of the Northern and Southern dynasties in the fourteenth century raised questions about claims of an unbroken imperial line.

Miss Foundation Day and the Foundation Day Dance were sometimes referred to as Misu kenkoku and the Kenkoku odori. Depending on the context, there can be an important difference between the terms *Kigensetsu* and *Kenkoku kinen no hi*, both translated into English as "Foundation Day." *Kigensetsu* was the name of the prewar holiday, and sometimes it was used consciously by those who had in mind the reestablishment of the prewar-style Foundation Day. On the other hand, *Kenkoku kinen no hi* was used expressly by those who wished to differentiate the postwar Foundation Day from the prewar one. Complicating the situation further was the fact that these terms often were used interchangeably by both proponents and opponents of Foundation Day.

The Yamato Parade in Kashihara annually drew several thousand spectators, making it the largest celebration of Foundation Day anywhere in Japan. Miyazaki prefecture in Kyushu also had reaped economic benefits from prewar celebrations of Foundation Day, and support for reestablishment there was second in intensity only to Nara prefecture. According to imperial mythology, Emperor Jimmu began his journey, which eventually concluded with his founding of the Empire of Japan, from Takachiho Palace in what is now Miyazaki prefecture.

Residents of Miyazaki prefecture were proud that their prefecture was the home of Jimmu and hoped to profit from this distinction. During the late 1960s, Japan was enveloped in a "native place boom," as the Japanese, who lived more and more in urban areas, sought to rediscover in idealized form their roots in rural villages. At the same time, as metropolitan culture spread throughout the archipelago, localities sought to clarify their distinct identities. These trends were evident not only in Mayor Yoshikawa's efforts to portray Kashihara as the heartland of Japan but also in a comment made by a representative of the Miyazaki Prefectural Tourism Bureau shortly after Foundation Day was reestablished: "Mister Jimmu left from here to go to Yamato. The native place (*furusato*) of Mister Jimmu is here." The reporter who interviewed this representative explained that people in Miyazaki affectionately refer to their hometown son as Mister Jimmu (*Jimmu-san*) and not as the more formal Emperor Jimmu (*Jimmu tennō*).[28] From the mid-1950s until the holiday was reestablished, celebrations of Foundation Day in Miyazaki City attracted a few thousand participants annually. The well-attended celebrations in Miyazaki and Kashihara, as well as in Tokyo, dated from the earliest stage of the movement, a time when celebrations were few and in most cases poorly attended.

Certain individuals became known for their commitment to Foundation Day's reestablishment. As early as 1949, Mizobuchi Tadahiro, the thirty-year-old principal of the Shigeto Elementary School in Yamada-chō, Tosa (Kōchi prefecture), recommenced annual schoolwide celebrations of Foundation Day. Mizobuchi became known as the Foundation Day Principal for his tireless efforts to win reestablishment.[29]

Mizobuchi even had students and staff sing the Foundation Day Song together. When the *Asahi shinbun* reported Mizobuchi's sponsorship of a schoolwide Foundation Day celebration in 1956, the principal's actions became an issue in the Diet.[30] JSP representative Nohara Osamu used the occasion to ask Minister of Education Kiyose Ichirō (1884–1967) about the government's stance on schools sponsoring emperor-centered ceremonies.[31] Kiyose said that the government's position was that although the Ministry of Education refrained from recommending that schools celebrate Foundation Day, it would permit individual schools to hold ceremonies if they obtained permission from the local board of education. This ruling served as a catalyst for a limited number of schools to recommence celebrations. In 1957, the Aichi Prefectural Board of Education suggested that elementary and junior high schools in that prefecture celebrate Foundation Day every year.

Just as some school principals continued to sponsor celebrations of Foundation Day, there were chairmen of private corporations committed to commemorating Japan's origin. Misu Takeo, a 1934 graduate of the Faculty of Law, Tokyo Imperial University, and chair of Nihon shokuryō sōko (a foodstuffs warehousing company), was a resolute supporter of the holiday. Beginning in 1954, he annually placed an advertisement in major newspapers championing the celebration.[32] Misu later recalled that on the first occasion, a representative from one of the newspapers called to ask if he really wanted to make such a right-wing gesture.[33]

Misu had his company celebrate 11 February as a holiday. Employees participated in Foundation Day activities. The main office in Tokyo sent a delegation to the Meiji Shrine, and company branches in the Kansai area (western and southern Japan) sent delegations to the Kashihara Shrine. When interviewed in 1960, Misu stressed, "It does not make sense that just because Japan lost the war, the nation's origin (*kigen*) suddenly changes. For this reason, we at Nihon shokuryō sōko have celebrated Foundation Day throughout the postwar period. I have a little experience abroad, and as far as I know, there is no country that does not celebrate its origin."[34]

More forceful in his support of the holiday was Dekura Ichitarō, chair of Sankyō kikai seisakujo, a machinery company that recommenced the celebration of Foundation Day in 1950: "Foundation Day is absolutely necessary. It is natural that the Japanese should celebrate 11 February as the day the nation was founded." In 1960, Dekura was upset with Japanese attitudes regarding Foundation Day: "It would be good if there were politicians and scholars who exerted themselves to re-establish Foundation Day, but there are so few it is embarrassing."[35] Sankyō's annual celebration of Foundation Day began before the workday started. Employees gathered in front of a huge Japanese flag flying from the company's factory in Tokyo. In honor of the occasion, male workers received two bottles of sake and five bags of dried cuttlefish; women employees received the same portion of cuttlefish but were given cakes instead of sake.

Although individual corporations played an energetic role in the reestablishment of Foundation Day, the "business world," as represented by business federations, was not a particularly active player in the movement. This contrasts with the business world's role in the later reign-name legalization movement. Members of the People's Committee to Achieve Legalization of the Reign Name (Gengō hōseika jitsugen kokumin kaigi), the coalition behind the movement to perpetuate the reign-name system, included the chairmen of major business organizations such as the Federation of Economic Organizations (Keidanren). In contrast, only the chair of Nihon shokuryō sōko was listed as a member of the national committee behind the coalition urging the reestablishment of Foundation Day.[36]

Six years after the reestablishment movement began, it was still able to trumpet public opinion polls, which consistently showed about

70 percent support for reestablishment. In addition, there were active demonstrations in favor of Foundation Day. In 1957, an LDP representative introduced into the Diet a bill to amend the National Holiday Law to reestablish Foundation Day (Kenkoku kinen no hi; no bill ever was introduced to reestablish Kigensetsu by its prewar name). This was the first time that a bill to reinstate the holiday was introduced into the Diet, and the reestablishment coalition was confident of victory. After passing the House of Representatives, however, the bill was killed easily by the JSP chair of the House of Councillors Culture and Education Committee, who simply delayed discussion of it. Once the Diet session ended in May, it became necessary for the bill to be reintroduced to the Diet if it were to be reconsidered.

At the time, the reestablishment coalition was shocked at the ease with which the JSP quashed the bill, and it railed against the socialists for blocking the will of the people. This is one example of the JSP's ability to impede legislation in Diet committees, even if it was unable to enact its own programs. What also was to become apparent by the late 1950s, however, was the lack of support, or only lukewarm support, for the bill among many LDP representatives. By 1957, the LDP already was moving away from revising the constitution. Popular demonstrations of support for the Postwar Constitution had made many LDP representatives hesitant to associate themselves with measures that smacked of the prewar system.

The general trend of the movement can be characterized as increasing efforts by the reestablishment coalition to foster broader and more active demonstrations of grassroots support to push the LDP to take decisive action in the face of fervent opposition from the JSP. In the early days of the movement, coalition members had sent a series of deferential petitions to the prime minister requesting the holiday's reestablishment. As the movement progressed, they began to use more and more conspicuous methods to increase awareness and support. In 1957, the Foundation Day Celebration Association (Kigensetsu hōshukukai),[37] as the coalition had renamed itself, staged a contest to select the music for the Foundation Day Dance. The contest was underwritten by the Japan Victor Corporation and several other companies. The winner was chosen from over 1,200 submissions.[38] On 11 February 1960, the association distributed thousands of commemorative Foundation Day kites to children.[39] In 1962, several young men participating in the reestablishment movement transported by car, over several days, a sacred flame lit in the Kashihara Shrine to the main Tokyo celebration of Foundation Day. They visited important shrines along the way. Such stunts garnered welcome media attention.[40]

The opposition movement, led largely by university professors, responded with vigor. Not all professors were against Foundation Day, however. In 1958, thirty-five professors from Hitotsubashi, Tōyō, and Nihon universities (among other schools) issued a joint statement in favor of Foundation Day.[41] This broke a taboo in the scholarly world. In the following months and years, more professors announced their support of the holiday. Later in 1958, a collection of essays written by scholars strongly in favor of Foundation Day was published.[42]

At the end of 1958, debates over Foundation Day became all the more interesting when Prince Mikasa Takahito (1915–2016), younger brother of Emperor Hirohito and lecturer in Japanese history at Tokyo Women's University, formally expressed his opposition to Foundation Day with an essay in *Bungei shunjū*.[43] Although worried about the implications of an imperial family member taking a public stance on a political issue, left-wing critics of Foundation Day could not help but welcome Prince Mikasa's opposition.[44] Advocates of reestablishment found themselves in the delicate position of criticizing a member of the imperial family. Right-wing groups staged noisy protests in front of Prince Mikasa's home all the same.

LDP Diet members committed to reestablishment continued to introduce bills to revise the National Holiday Law at each new session of the Diet. The JSP then used internal Diet mechanisms to derail these bills. The 1960 protests against the renewal of the U.S.-Japan Security Treaty that roiled Japan, especially the Diet, increased the LDP leadership's reluctance to support such an ideologically charged issue. They wanted to wait for the right opportunity. Between 1958 and 1964, bills without government sponsorship were introduced six times, only to be halted by the JSP. The reestablishment coalition began to suspect that this was a ritual orchestrated by the JSP and LDP leaderships. It began to focus its criticism on the LDP.

Some members of the LDP remained committed to reestablishment. One of them, Konō Ichirō, assumed the chairmanship of an LDP commission (*chōsakai*) established in 1960 to study the issue of national holidays. There had long been plans to increase the number of national holidays, a proposal that few Japanese citizens, whatever their political inclinations, opposed. Aikawa Katsuroku, a LDP Dietman in the House of Representatives representing Miyazaki prefecture, stressed his support of Foundation Day in a two-part editorial in the *Miyazaki konnichi* daily newspaper in 1963.[45] LDP representative Nakasone Yasuhiro, known for his nationalistic views, was also a supporter. This future prime minister attended, as Konō's representative, the 1963 Tokyo celebration of Foundation Day sponsored by the Foundation Day Celebration Association.

In the early 1960s, coalition members began to focus on fostering widespread local demonstrations of grassroots support for Foundation Day. In 1961, celebrations took place in 350 locations throughout Japan.[46] That same year, Taniguchi Teijirō and others formed a preparatory committee to work toward the establishment of a Foundation Day celebration council in Nara prefecture.[47] This committee then brought together reestablishment proponents from the nineteen prefectures west of and including Shizuoka prefecture to form the Western Japan Foundation Day Re-establishment Council (Kigensetsu fukkō nishi Nihon kyōgikai),[48] an organization that pooled information and coordinated lobbying activities in this large region of Japan.

In 1963, disagreements over Foundation Day led to violence in the Diet. Some LDP members were disgusted with their party's hesitancy to use its majority position to enact legislation such as the revised National Holiday Law. On 20 June, LDP representative Nagayama Tadanori, chair of the House of Representatives Cabinet Committee, pushed a bill through his committee by majority vote that would have reestablished Foundation Day. He did so in the face of bitter JSP opposition. JSP members physically attacked Nagayama, and he had to be hospitalized.

It is telling that the speaker of the House of Representatives, Kiyose Ichirō, ruled that consideration of the bill had been insufficient. He returned it to the Cabinet Committee for further study. Similar bills already had been under study in the Diet for six years. Nonetheless, the LDP leadership remained reluctant to use its majority to enact legislation distasteful to the JSP. This attitude was an important legacy of the chaos that had followed Prime Minister Kishi's decision to ram through the bill renewing a revised version of the U.S.-Japan Security Treaty.

Reestablishment coalition members promptly petitioned Kiyose to express their outrage.[49] In retrospect, the official history of the Foundation Day Celebration Association noted that in 1963 "it already had become evident that the LDP was the biggest barrier to the movement to legalize Foundation Day."[50] This dissatisfaction referred not to the LDP's opposition, but to its passivity. After Kiyose's decision to send the bill back to committee in 1963, the reestablishment coalition began to lobby each LDP member individually.[51]

In 1964, the movement was bolstered by a show of support at the prefectural level. That year, the Okayama Prefectural Assembly became the first public body to pass a resolution calling for the reestablishment of Foundation Day. This led the coalition to ponder whether resolutions by local assemblies might not give the movement a needed boost.[52] Other city, town, and village assemblies passed similar resolutions. Such resolutions were always forwarded to the prime minister and the Diet.

The Olympic Games were held in Tokyo in the summer of 1964. That year a bill to reestablish Foundation Day was once again introduced into the Diet. This time it died without even being discussed. The Olympics served to heighten national pride, however, and it was in this context that the movement entered its decisive stage. The movement received a helpful push at the beginning of 1965. In a New Year's message to prefectural employees, Kanagawa Governor Uchiyama Iwatarō, then seventy-four, announced, "From this year on, Foundation Day will be re-established in Kanagawa prefecture."[53] Uchiyama's announcement had a ripple effect throughout the country. Foundation Day regained legitimacy.

Questioned by reporters, Uchiyama, a veteran diplomat with considerable experience abroad, voiced various reasons for his decision. He mentioned that 1965 was both the fortieth anniversary of Emperor Hirohito's enthronement and the 2,625th anniversary of the empire's foundation. Uchiyama's logic resonated with popular opinion and left room for interpreting Foundation Day's meaning. The governor stressed that "individuals have birthdays, and it is therefore strange for nations not to have them. Only Japan is such a country [without a birthday]."[54] The birthday argument had long been a feature of the debates about Foundation Day, but Uchiyama's announcement made this reasoning famous. This line of thought lay behind much of the burgeoning of support for Foundation Day in 1965.

Uchiyama's decision sparked a flurry of public debate, and the birthday argument appeared repeatedly. The weekly magazine *Asahi jānaru* was popular among the younger generation, and after Uchiyama's announcement, the magazine received more than forty letters from secondary and college students about Foundation Day. Tamura Kazuhiko, age eighteen, interpreted Uchiyama's decision as follows: "America has Independence Day, France has Bastille Day, and the Soviet Union has a holiday to commemorate the Revolution. Each has a day when countrymen gather and celebrate the birthday of the nation; there is a feeling that Japan, too, should have such a day."[55] Support for the holiday's reestablishment extended beyond nostalgic members of the older generation.

By 1965, however, there was no unity among the Japanese about the broader meaning of Foundation Day. Even those who favored reestablishment did not agree. Many supporters specifically rejected the imperial mythology or at least acknowledged its lack of historical basis. Nothing provides better evidence of this lack of unity than the disagreements over when Foundation Day should be celebrated. Years of protests by historians had called into question the validity of 11 February. Public opinion polls revealed a complicated picture. On one hand, they indicated around 70 percent support for reestablishment. On the other hand, they found declining support for celebrating Foundation Day on 11 February. This was true even though in the years leading up to the bill's passage in 1966, reports by newspapers, even those opposed to the holiday such as the *Asahi shinbun*, indicated an upward trend in the number of participants in the annual celebrations of Foundation Day, as well as a significant increase in the number of areas in which demonstrations took place.

As participation increased, the publicity organs of groups involved in but not at the center of the movement, such as Seichō no ie, joined the bandwagon and urged their readers to celebrate Foundation Day.[56] In 1965, Foundation Day celebrations took place in 598 locations across Japan, nearly twice the number that had occurred in 1961.[57] Consider the case of sparsely populated Kumamoto prefecture. In 1965, the *Kumamoto nichinichi shinbun* daily newspaper reported that 1,900 individuals had participated in celebrations in thirty-one locations in the prefecture. The newspaper noted that the growing support from year to year in the prefecture for reestablishment of Foundation Day as a national holiday reflected countrywide trends.[58]

On 3 February 1965, Prime Minister Satō Eisaku, in response to a question by Governor Uchiyama at the annual meeting of the National Conference of Governors, pledged to introduce a bill to reestablish Foundation Day with government sponsorship. Even with government sponsorship, however, the bill to revise the National Holiday Law did not pass the Diet in 1965. The LDP, worried about more important legislation, decided not to risk disruption of the Diet by insisting on the bill's passage. It was the eighth time the bill had failed in the Diet.

On 11 February 1966, Miyazaki City and Kashihara City, longtime supporters of Foundation Day, signed an agreement to become sister cities. Mayor Yoshikawa of Kashihara expressed his happiness that these "two hometowns of the Yamato spirit (*yamato damashii*) had been joined."[59] The *Jinja shinpō*, newspaper of the shrine world, reported in 1966 that Foundation Day celebrations had taken place throughout Japan, from Hokkaido to Kagoshima, as well as in Okinawa, which remained under U.S. military occupation at the time.

The meaning of imperial symbols in postwar Okinawa is an especially complex topic. In the case of the Japanese flag, for example, one Japanese professor born in 1945, Takami Katsutoshi, recounted the following anecdote. As a high school student in Hyōgo prefecture in the early 1960s, he participated in debates with delegations of high school students from Okinawa. A common subject of debate was whether the Rising Sun should be retained as the de facto national flag. Takami remembers how he opposed retention of this symbol of Japanese militarism, whereas students from Okinawa supported the flag as a symbol of protest against the ongoing U.S. military occupation of their prefecture.[60] Once Okinawa reverted to Japan in 1972, however, latent opposition to the Rising Sun flag surfaced in that prefecture to express protest against mainland mistreatment of Okinawa.

In 1966, the *Jinja shinpō* noted the attendance of a few individuals at Foundation Day celebrations in Naha City in Okinawa, of 1,300 people in Tochigi, and of 5,000 people in Mie.[61] The reestablishment coalition, as well as LDP representatives committed to reestablishment, could thus point to widespread and growing demonstrations of support. The Foundation Day bill nonetheless bogged down again in the fifty-first session of the Diet in 1966. It was passed only through a compromise involving the LDP, JSP, and the Democratic Socialist Party (DSP; this party, founded in 1960, can be placed between the LDP and JSP on the Japanese political spectrum) engineered by Yamaguchi Kikuichirō (1897–1981), speaker of the House of Representatives. Yamaguchi was able to convince the JSP and DSP, which had already foiled the constitutional revision movement, to end their opposition to a revised version of the bill by arranging for a commission to be established by the prime minister to investigate on which day the Japanese preferred to celebrate this holiday.

The LDP continued to support 11 February as the appropriate day, but apparently the party leadership considered the issue too volatile to be addressed in the Diet. The reestablishment coalition vehemently opposed this revision of the bill.[62] The coalition's unflagging pressure had kept the question of Foundation Day in the political arena for years, and not winning reestablishment of the holiday on 11 February would have represented a demoralizing defeat. Nonetheless, the revised version passed the Diet on 26 June. Foundation Day was reestablished as a holiday "to commemorate the foundation of and foster love for the nation." Attention shifted to the commission that would set its date of celebration.

Over a period of five months beginning in July 1966, the ten-member Foundation Day Commission (Kenkoku kinenbi shingikai) called in expert witnesses and asked citizens to express their opinions in public hearings held in four regional locations. The records of the public hearings illustrate the diversity of opinions regarding Foundation Day and scant support for a holiday that legitimized imperial mythology. They record word for word statements made by approximately fifty citizens advocating a day for Foundation Day. This is a revealing record of popular historical consciousness. One person who testified, Nangō Midori, age thirty-seven, summed up the nature of the debate at the beginning of her statement to the Foundation Day Commission: "I cannot avoid addressing Japanese history when speaking about Foundation Day."[63]

Individuals opposed to 11 February repeated key words and themes that strongly validated the postwar system and rejected the Meiji system. They often began their statements by stressing their support of a holiday to celebrate the nation, but they opposed doing so on 11 February. Although this may have been a result of the hearings' narrow focus, none of the citizens who testified called for a holiday that went beyond honoring the nation-state by celebrating, for example, the United Nations.

Iizaka Hiromi, age twenty, worried about the lack of patriotism among the Japanese but wanted a holiday that celebrated a peaceful, democratic, and independent Japan.[64] Iizaka suggested 28 April, the day on which Japan regained its independence in 1952. Igarashi Noboru, thirty-two, wanted a holiday that commemorated the founding of the "New Japan" and suggested 15 August, the day the war ended.[65] Itō Takefumi, twenty-seven, interpreted the prewar Foundation Day as integral to an ideology that served as the backbone of militarism.[66] He spoke of the duty of teachers like himself to base education on scientific rationalism and argued that the old Foundation Day had absolutely no scientific basis. Itō suggested 3 May, the day the Postwar Constitution went into effect, as the best day. Both Igarashi and Itō proposed what might be called "New Japan nationalism," a celebration of Postwar Japan through Foundation Day, provided that the holiday was celebrated on some day other than 11 February. There were many nationalisms articulated during the discussions of Foundation Day in 1966, and few Japanese supported a holiday that contradicted the postwar democratic system.

In expressing his opposition to 11 February, Komuro Hiroshi, nineteen, recited—in a negative sense—virtually every idiom associated with or used to describe the prewar emperor system: "Eight corners of the earth under one roof" (*hakkō ichiu*), "absolutely despotic emperor politics" (*tennō zettai sensei seiji*), and so on. "It is common knowledge," he confidently reminded the commission at one point, "that the root of prewar militarism was State Shinto." Before announcing his support for 28 April, Komuro denounced as undemocratic (*himinshuteki*) the reestablishment movement as well as the commission.[67]

Kaneko Hajime, a professor of economics, argued that Foundation Day should be celebrated on 3 May. Kaneko, thirty-three, emphasized that 11 February was the worst of all options: "For citizens 11 February is a shameful day that should commemorate how we were driven into a war of aggression against China and countries in Southeast Asia." For some Japanese, Foundation Day was as noxious a symbol as the Confederate flag is to African Americans. Kaneko remembered how the people were nothing more than subjects (*shinmin*) of the emperor under the Meiji system. He spoke with distaste about the fanatical (*kyōshinteki*) 2,600th anniversary celebrations staged in 1940 and the prewar witch hunts against scholars such as historian Tsuda Sōkichi who questioned the imperial mythology. It was not at all unusual for statements like Kaneko's to become personal at points. He recounted with displeasure how, as a child, he "was taught that the emperor was a deity in human form, and to shout 'Long Live His Majesty the Emperor!' before dying [in battle]."[68]

Okada Toku, a housewife, also strongly opposed 11 February. She favored 3 May and spoke especially frankly about her experiences in China during the war years. She remembered Foundation Day as part of an ideology that encouraged the Japanese to think of themselves as a superior race: "When I think back now, the thing about which I am most ashamed . . . is that I treated the Chinese as though they were lower than myself and was unable to question the war of invasion against that country."[69]

Many citizens testified in favor of 11 February, but none of them categorically rejected the postwar system. They tended to stress the good points of Japan's long history and were sometimes critical of elements of postwar history, especially the Occupation. The reactionary platform advocated by the Association of Shinto Shrines was present, but it existed only fragmentarily and blended with overall support of the postwar polity. Individuals in favor of 11 February stressed that Foundation Day was compatible with the postwar system and often pointed out that in a democracy the principle of the majority vote must be respected.

Some individuals who supported 11 February were sympathetic toward 3 May but worried that if Foundation Day celebrated the Postwar Constitution, people would think that Japan was a country with a short history. Tradition—the fact that Foundation Day had been celebrated on 11 February since the early Meiji era—weighed heavily in favor of the pro–11 February faction even though opponents repeatedly pointed out, and some supporters conceded, that the Meiji government simply had manufactured that day. Some supporters were baffled or bored by the intense debates over holding the holiday on 11 February. Chiba Shigeru, forty, claimed, "The majority of the people do not care whether it has historical or scientific basis."[70] Honda Kōzō, also forty, stressed that it was impossible to prove (*risshō suru*) when Japan originated, but he supported 11 February because his ancestors had celebrated the holiday on that day.[71] Uetsugi Kiyoji, sixty, explained why he was in favor of 11 February:

> I was born during the Meiji era. For more than thirty years after the time that I became conscious of matters, 11 February was celebrated as Foundation Day. Now I hear opinions that 11 February is not correct, but it is difficult for me suddenly to submit to such opinions. Theoretically, I can agree with what the opposition faction is saying. However, I think that it will not do to ignore the feelings (*kanjō*) of so many countrymen.[72]

Uetsugi then cited polls showing public support for 11 February.

Questions of war and peace lay at the center of this debate. Uetsugi used the birthday metaphor both to reject the war and to support 11 February: "Even if a person experiences difficulties in the middle of his life, his birthday does not change. This is the same with a country's birthday."[73] Katō Kinuko, fifty-three, was one of many to argue that Foundation Day, although used by the militarists, was not the cause of prewar militarism.[74]

There were still a few individuals who literally accepted that Emperor Jimmu had founded the empire on 11 February 660 BCE. Sasaki Fuminori, a university professor, began by stressing that the *Nihon shoki* was Japan's oldest "authentic history" (*seishi*). Sasaki, forty, reminded the commission that Foundation Day had been abolished during the Occupation under the sword of the U.S. military. In response to his own question about whether there was another country in the world with a monarchy as old as Japan's, Sasaki concluded that there was not. Sasaki was one of the most right-wing of those who testified, but even he stressed the democratic principle of majority vote.[75]

Murozaki Kiyohira, sixty-one, framed his statement about Foundation Day around his interpretation of the spirit of the Meiji Restoration, which he called a "miracle in world history." He extolled the achievements of the Meiji era, accomplishments that, according to him, had been possible because the Japanese race came together under "the banner of the imperial house." He interpreted the Restoration as the second founding of Japan and suggested that this miracle could not have been possible without the earlier achievements of Emperor Jimmu. Murozaki even quoted a poem by Emperor Meiji praising Jimmu to show how the men of Meiji had been inspired by the first emperor. Toward the end of his speech, however, Murozaki suddenly shifted to the present. He argued that there was a close and positive connection between the legends and myths of the Japanese race and the values of the Postwar Constitution.[76]

The commission determined through public opinion polls that slightly over 47 percent of the Japanese favored 11 February. If those opposed to celebrating Foundation Day on 11 February had been able to unify around one alternative, they might have prevented the holiday's reestablishment on that day. But the Foundation Day Commission's poll indicated that the second most favored day, 3 May, found support among only a little over 10 percent of those polled.[77] Other possible days, such as 28 April, drew even less support. Although supporters of 11 February did not agree on why Foundation Day should be celebrated on that day, 11 February was nearly five times more popular than the next alternative. The commission voted to celebrate the holiday on that day. Historians often portray the 1960s as a decade when ideological battles cooled as Japan experienced stunning economic growth, but they had hardly disappeared, as exemplified by the case of Foundation Day.

The reestablishment of Foundation Day soothed the pride of participants in the unsuccessful movement to overturn the Occupation-era constitution. In 1967, Foundation Day was celebrated as a national holiday for the first time in two decades. On 11 February, the "Foundation Day Principal," Mizobuchi Tadahiro, recalled the eighteen years of persecution (*hōnan*) he had suffered in working to reestablish the holiday. In voicing his relief that Foundation Day would now be celebrated on 11 February, Mizobuchi spoke for the devout reestablishment faction: "If 11 February had not been chosen, everything that I had taught the children until now would be a lie."[78] At a cost of ¥800,000 (a little more than US$2,000 at the time), the local Board of Education had a large bronze statue of Mizobuchi built on school grounds. The statue commemorated his long and initially lonely mission to win reestablishment of the holiday.

Some members of the reestablishment faction overinterpreted the meaning of their victory in projecting the future course of Japan. Nakamura Tadashi, chair of the Miyazaki branch of the Japan Veterans Friendship League, rejoiced on 11 February 1967: "I am ecstatic that Foundation Day (*Kigensetsu*) was re-established. The next goal . . . is re-establishment of the Imperial Rescript on Education. Then constitutional revision—what is this business of having one's country defended by foreign troops?"[79]

The devout reestablishment faction, in joy, and the opposition, in mourning, concluded that Kigensetsu had been reinstated. However, the holiday is officially called Kenkoku kinen no hi, and differences from the prewar holiday were more than semantic. Much to the disappointment of steadfast members of the reestablishment coalition, the government refrained from sponsoring an official celebration of Foundation Day, even after it became a national holiday.[80] This difference from the prewar era devalued the meaning of Foundation Day in the eyes of proponents and represented a victory for the opposition.

The eleventh of February became a national holiday, and some committed supporters and opponents continued to publicize their respective platforms on that day. Every year, groups led by historians who had fought reestablishment sponsored annual meetings throughout Japan in nonrecognition of Foundation Day. For its part, the Foundation Day Celebration Steering Committee, which consists of representatives of the numerous groups that had worked to win reestablishment, continues to hold annual celebrations of Foundation Day in Tokyo while lobbying for government sponsorship of an official celebration. Little changed for a decade after reestablishment. No popular movements to hold official celebrations of Foundation Day or to abolish the holiday emerged, and the LDP and the government maintained the status quo.

In 1976 the *Asahi jānaru* polled Diet representatives about their feelings toward the imperial house and the emperor system. One question inquired whether representatives supported changing the name of the holiday from Kenkoku kinen no hi to Kigensetsu or abolishing the holiday altogether. The majority of respondents from the LDP and DSP supported the status quo, whereas representatives from the JSP, JCP, and Kōmeitō (the political wing of the Buddhist organization Sōka gakkai) wanted the holiday abolished.[81] A holiday sometimes compared by its supporters to Independence Day in the United States, Foundation Day was not promoting unity among the Japanese and was perhaps even a barrier to unity.

In 1978, a government link with Foundation Day celebrations was established when the Office of the Prime Minister provided support (*kōen*) for the annual ceremony sponsored by the Foundation Day Celebration Steering Committee. Support from the Ministry of Education followed in 1981, the Ministry of Home Affairs in 1983, and the Foreign Ministry in 1985. When Nakasone Yasuhiro became prime minister in 1982, he began to plan how to become the first post-Occupation prime minister to attend a celebration of Foundation Day. He concluded that the ceremony sponsored by the Foundation Day Celebration Steering Committee, composed of what might be called the "purist faction" led by the Association of Shinto Shrines, was too reactionary. Nakasone asked Nakayama Masaki, chair of the LDP's Citizens' Movements Bureau, to negotiate with the purist faction to try to devise a ceremony that Nakasone could attend as prime minister.

Nakasone wanted a new organization to sponsor the ceremony as well as changes in the content of the ceremony itself. During negotiations that began in November 1984, Nakayama explained to members of the Foundation Day Celebration Steering Committee that all political and religious coloring would have to be excluded from the ceremony.[82] Nakayama stressed that participants could not "worship from afar" the mausoleum of Emperor Jimmu, or shout "Long Live His Majesty the Emperor!"[83] The purist faction initially rejected Nakayama's conditions, but later asked him to come to the Association of Shinto Shrines on 4 December for another meeting. At the meeting Nakayama denied any "relationship between Foundation Day and Emperor Jimmu" (see the epigraphs to this chapter). The purist faction refused to accept a diluted Foundation Day celebration.

In December 1984, Gojima Noboru, a member of Nakasone's brain trust or informal advisory network, formed the Association to Celebrate Foundation Day (Kenkoku kinen no hi o iwau kai) to sponsor a celebration in 1985 that the prime minister could attend.[84] At the last minute, a compromise was arranged that convinced members of the purist faction to attend this celebration. As a result of the agreement, at the beginning of the ceremony reference was made to Emperor Jimmu, and the ceremony concluded with three shouts of *banzai* wishing for the long life of the emperor (*Tennō heika no gochōju o inori, banzai!*), which is not quite the prewar "Long Live His Majesty the Emperor!"[85] The ceremony, attended by most members of the Cabinet, had an official air to it. Nakasone later stressed in the Diet, however, that he had no plans to hold a ceremony with government sponsorship (*seifu shusai*).[86]

After the celebration of Foundation Day in 1986, the Association to Celebrate Foundation Day—Nakasone's organization—changed its name to the Association to Celebrate the People's Holidays (Kokumin no shukujitsu o iwau kai). This dilution of the association's stress on Foundation Day, coupled with ongoing disagreements over the content of the ceremony, led the purist faction to break with Nakasone and return to sponsoring its own celebration.[87] LDP prime ministers have continued to attend the celebration sponsored by the Association to Celebrate the People's Holidays, while the purist faction stages it own celebration under the sponsorship of the Foundation Day Celebration Steering Committee. Transcripts of the speeches given at these competing ceremonies in 1988, published by the journal *Sokoku to seinen*, allow for easy comparison.[88]

At the ceremony sponsored by the purist faction, held to commemorate the 2,648th anniversary of the founding of the empire, Shinto scholar Sakurai Katsunoshin (1909–2005) immediately invoked Emperor Jimmu in his short opening greeting. Mayuzumi Toshirō, long a leading figure in movements to reestablish imperial ideology, gave the keynote address. Mayuzumi stressed how, according to the *Nihon shoki*, Japan's oldest "authentic history," Emperor Jimmu had founded the empire 2,648 years earlier. Mayuzumi extolled the spirit of Jimmu and the imperial line, using such phrases as "Eight corners of the world under one roof," "family-state," and "unbroken imperial line." Mayuzumi criticized Nakasone for establishing a ceremony "far removed from the essential principle of the true founding of the nation." Journalist and scholar Shimizu Ikutarō (1907–88), who offered the concluding statement, made reference to Jimmu's establishment of the empire before leading the participants in three shouts of the prewar-style "Long Live His Majesty the Emperor!"

At the ceremony attended by Prime Minister Takeshita Noboru, the opening speaker made no reference to Emperor Jimmu in his words of greeting. Ōtsuki Bunpei (1903–1992), who delivered the main speech, addressed the question of imperial mythology and Emperor Jimmu in a somewhat muted manner. He even admitted that there were many opinions regarding "this 11 February Foundation Day based on the *Nihon shoki* and *Kojiki*." Ōtsuki, the former chair of the Federation of Economic Organizations, seemed more interested in lauding Japan's economic achievements than in touting imperial mythology: "Japan, a country without natural resources, has become the second largest economic power in the world today, and the country with the biggest trade surplus." To judge from Ōtsuki's address, self-assured economic nationalism had been superimposed on Foundation Day at the official celebration of the holiday. Prime Minister Takeshita made no reference to Emperor Jimmu in his address. The Panamanian ambassador spoke for the diplomatic community, and Nakagawa Sunao (1919–2010), a leading television personality, concluded the ceremony by leading participants in three shouts of *banzai* to the emperor's longevity, among other things.

Both ceremonies were nationalistic, of course, but what exactly does that tell us? There are many patriots in Japan, on the left and right. Nakasone, for example, has long been known for his nationalistic views. Throughout his career, he has been a fervent supporter of the monarchy. During his prime ministership, however, many individuals on the far right came to think of him as a traitor. By diluting the imperial rhetoric favored by the far right, Nakasone attempted to craft a Foundation Day celebration that would attract popular support.

There is little doubt that Nakasone was moving in the direction of establishing official sponsorship of a Foundation Day celebration, as critics charged. Still, he had no intention of lending official legitimacy to a celebration carried out along prewar lines. As prime minister he was, to begin with, sensitive about terminology and did not want to hear prewar catchwords associated with the emperor system bandied about at the ceremony. His successors also displayed an aversion to official representations of Jimmu, a major break in practice from Imperial Japan. During the November 1990 enthronement ceremony for Akihito, the banners with motifs symbolizing Jimmu's eastward expedition, which had been used in Hirohito's enthronement ceremony in 1928, were replaced with ones displaying a chrysanthemum motif.[89]

It is in the area of imperial "tradition" that discord has arisen between the Imperial Household Agency and stalwart supporters of the throne, such as the Association of Shinto Shrines. The association stubbornly insists that imperial rituals cannot be changed and argues that their invariancy lends them authority. In contrast, on occasion representatives of the Imperial Household Agency have discreetly accused the Association of Shinto Shrines of trying to use the emperor to enhance its own status rather than thinking of what is best for the monarchy. Still, the palace has never interrupted its practice of sending an envoy of the emperor to the Kashihara Shrine on 11 February, even in 1946. The Imperial Household Agency also continues to maintain the tombs of all emperors, including that of Jimmu,[90] a practice that suggests official recognition of their authenticity.

In 1992, the far right leader Nakamura Takehiko (1912–2005), after listing various defects in what he interpreted as the governmental Foundation Day celebration established during Nakasone's prime ministership (quoted in the epigraphs to this chapter), asked, "Just which nation's founding is [being celebrated]?"[91] What Nakamura called the governmental ceremony cannot be interpreted simplistically as an attempt by the LDP to reestablish the prewar emperor system. Today, proponents of the prewar emperor system invoke prewar-style *kokutai* nationalism in protest against the state. In the same year Nakamura belittled the "official" observance of Foundation Day, groups led by historians celebrated the twenty-fifth anniversary of their "anti-, nonrecognition of Foundation Day movement" in protest against the state's staging any celebration of Foundation Day.[92]

Nakasone's cautious attempt to mold a Foundation Day celebration whose significance might have popular resonance showed how unsuccessful the reestablishment of this holiday has been in furthering the unity of the Japanese. Prewar emperor system rhetoric is distasteful to most Japanese citizens, who would feel uncomfortable at anything approaching a purist celebration of Foundation Day. At the same time, those Japanese interested in using their day off from work to attend a celebration of Foundation Day are largely those with far right leanings. Thus, Nakasone was attacked by the far right for blasphemy and by representatives of the left for attempting to reimpose the prewar emperor system. A consensus on the meaning of the holiday remains elusive.

The Movement to Perpetuate the Reign-Name System

Broader than the Foundation Day reestablishment movement, the effort to perpetuate the reign-name system was one of the most extensive social movements in postwar Japan. Before the Diet passed the Reign-Name Bill in 1979, forty-six of the forty-seven regional assemblies (*todōfuken gikai*) and more than half—nearly 1,600—of all village, town, and city assemblies in Japan had passed resolutions (*ketsugi*) urging the Diet to take action on this matter.[93] Many of the same groups that had worked to win reestablishment of Foundation Day organized this swell of resolutions.

There was considerable overlap between the actors involved in the Foundation Day and the reign-name system movements—both for and against. The intense minorities on both sides of the issue involved many of the same groups and people, or same types of groups and people. The shrine world championed legalization, and historians such as Irokawa Daikichi who felt distaste at nationalistic practices worked to prevent it.

Debates about the reign-name system flared periodically in postwar Japan before passage of the Reign-Name Bill. The alternative to the reign-name system is to count years according to the Christian era, the system used by much of the world and by all of the countries that have been models for Japan's development. In Japanese, the first character in *seireki* simply means "West" or "Western" and does not necessarily convey the fact that according to this system, years are counted according to the Christian era. For many Japanese, *seireki* has a connotation of universality. Use of the reign-name system, in contrast, emphasizes Japan's distinctiveness. The debate about the reign-name system was shaped by a simple problem: should Japan adopt so-called universal practices or maintain its own cultural practices? The use of reign names encourages the Japanese to think of time in terms of imperial reigns.

In 1950, among the nations not counting years according to the Christian era was Israel. The Republic of China, relocated to Taiwan as a result of the Chinese Communist Party's victory on the mainland, continued to date years according to the time elapsed since the foundation of the Chinese Republic in 1912. The nascent Republic of Korea also was experimenting with the use of a nationalistic way of counting years. As part of an effort spearheaded by Minister of Education An Hosang to restore Korean pride after four decades of Japanese rule, in 1949 the National Assembly decided that years would be counted according to the Tan'gi dating system. Years were to be numbered from the accession to the throne of Tan'gun, the supposed progenitor of the Korean race and founder of the first Korean state in 2333 BCE. The National Assembly declared the Tan'gi year of 4281 to be the first year of the republic and established 3 October as a national holiday to commemorate Tan'gun. The Republic of Korea abandoned the Tan'gi system in 1961, but 3 October remains a national holiday.[94]

In February 1950, the House of Councillors Education Committee, chaired by Tanaka Kotarō (1890–1974), undertook a one-month investigation of the reign-name system.[95] The central question was whether the system should be abolished formally in advance of Japan's independence. This question reflected Tanaka's concerns. The investigation's stated goals included determining whether the reign-name system was appropriate to the spirit of the new constitution and whether Japan should adopt the dating system used by the "civilized nations" (*bunmei shokoku*) of the world.[96]

The Education Committee headed by Tanaka called twenty-six prominent men to testify. Sixteen of these men recommended abolition, and only seven favored retention. Most of the individuals who favored abolishing the reign-name system stressed the convenience of counting years according to the Christian era. Many individuals who argued for the Western calendar reasoned that Japan needed to adopt universal values and practices to become a cooperative member of international society. Kameyama Naoto (1890–1963), chair of the Science Council of Japan, testified that in an increasingly international and interconnected world it was better to discard the reign-name system and adopt the Western calendar: "It would be extremely strange spiritually for only Japan to become an isolated island. I think that it is appropriate for Japan to live among the cultured nations (*bunka kokka*) of the world."[97] Among critics of the reign-name system, constitutional scholar Miyazawa Toshiyoshi was representative of those who viewed the system as a vestige of the repressive prewar emperor system that had to be obliterated from Japanese society.

In contrast, proponents of the system pointed out that many Japanese were accustomed to the reign-name system and in fact found it convenient. A representative from the Association of Shinto Shrines, Takatsukasa Nobusuke, stressed that the reign-name system had been a Japanese cultural tradition for more than 1,300 years. He insisted that the system did not necessarily have any relation to power structures such as imperial sovereignty provided for by the Meiji Constitution.[98] Sakamoto Tarō (1901–87), professor of Japanese history at Tokyo University, argued that the reign-name system should be retained as a "symbol of an independent country."[99]

In the end, the Education Committee made no recommendations regarding the reign-name system, in part because during the middle of the investigation, Tanaka resigned from the Diet and a representative more favorably inclined toward the reign-name system assumed the chair of the committee. The debate about the system nonetheless continued outside the Diet. The shrine world, through its publicity organ *Jinja shinpō*, initiated a movement to demonstrate the extent of support for the system.

The National Shinto Youth Council gathered signatures in favor of retaining the system, which were presented to the Education Committee of each house of the Diet on 10 March 1950. The shrine world also mounted a letter-writing campaign directed at all governmental figures, especially Diet representatives.[100] Polls showed support for joint use of the reign-name system along with the Western calendar. A poll in the *Tōkyō shinbun* found 27 percent of respondents favoring adoption of the Western calendar and 54 percent in favor of joint use of both systems.[101]

Academic figures on both sides of the debate publicized their positions. One essay that seems prescient from today's perspective was that of historian Tsuda Sōkichi. Tsuda defended the reign-name system in an essay in *Chūō kōron*.[102] He began by stressing that the so-called Western calendar counted years according to the Christian era and then traced the lengthy history of the reign-name system. He warned readers against the tendency, popular at the time, of discarding all old customs in the name of reformation.

Tsuda's key interpretation was that because the reign-name system was symbolic, its symbolic meaning could and would change, much as it had at other times in Japanese history. He reminded readers that the meaning, the spirit, of the system was different before and after the Meiji Restoration. Tsuda also emphasized that the reign-name system would evolve to suit the postwar polity: "If we countrymen use the reign name as something with a new significance, then it will not in the least go against democratic politics or contradict the new constitution."[103] In short, he argued that it was possible to support both the reign-name system and the postwar system. Nothing, he held, about the reign-name system contradicts the text of the constitution.

The debate about the reign-name system sparked by the Diet committee in 1950 cooled even before Japan regained independence. After all, nothing prevented the Japanese from continuing to count years by the emperor's reign name, Shōwa, and the emperor was not approaching old age. Not until the late 1960s would the reign-name system again become a political issue. In 1961, the issue was raised briefly in the Diet. It did not go unnoticed by the shrine world that the government spokesman stated that the reign-name system no longer had a basis in law. At the time, however, the Association of Shinto Shrines and other far-right groups were devoting their energies to reestablishing Foundation Day and other issues such as the Yasukuni Shrine.

The case of the Yasukuni Shrine and the issue of lèse-majesté provide an interesting contrast to those of Foundation Day and the reign-name system. This chapter is meant as a corrective to historiography that understates or ignores the political influence that far-right groups on occasion have exerted through legitimate channels, but readers nonetheless should bear in mind that precisely because groups such as the Association of Shinto Shrines stood to the right of the mainstream, many of their campaigns failed. This was especially true of the attempt to reestablish lèse-majesté as a crime.

In reaction to the publication in the fall of 1959 of a scandalous short story about the imperial house by Fukazawa Shichirō (1914–87), the Association of Shinto Shrines and other groups attempted to drum up support for reestablishing lèse-majesté as a crime.[104] Although polls showed that 59 percent of those Japanese who had read Fukazawa's fictional story "Fūryū mutan" found it distasteful,[105] popular support for criminalizing lèse-majesté never developed. The LDP certainly never adopted the issue as a party.

Even when far-right groups succeeded in demonstrating mass support for a cause, they were not always successful in achieving their political goals. Such was the case with the movement to reestablish state administration of the Yasukuni Shrine. From the immediate post-Occupation period through to the present, the Japan Society of War-Bereaved Families has led a movement to reinstate the Yasukuni Shrine as the official, government-supported shrine to the war dead.[106] Polls reveal considerable popular backing for this,[107] and one source suggests that by 1970 the number of signatures collected nationally in support of such a measure had risen to twelve million.[108] Beginning in 1969, the LDP introduced bills to restore the link between the state and the Yasukuni Shrine several times, only to see each one fail. One crucial reason that the movement failed was that it proved impossible for conservatives committed to this cause to wiggle around the constitutional requirement that church and state remain separate (Articles 20 and 89). Movements in favor of reestablishing Foundation Day and the reign name succeeded in large part because they did not present constitutional problems.

The year 1968 marks the beginning of the organized movement to perpetuate the reign-name system. On 23 October of that year, the government staged the official centennial celebration of the Meiji Restoration. The shrine world and other champions of the imperial institution recognized the symbolism of this date, chosen in 1966 by the government committee organizing the centennial celebration. On that day in 1868, the Japanese government selected Meiji as the new reign name and instituted the modern reign-name system.[109] The Association of Shinto Shrines' official history of the reign-name legalization movement credited the centennial with serving as a wake-up call about the importance of the system.[110]

Three points about the centennial celebration are worth noting. First, like many of the issues studied in this book, the centennial celebration was ideologically divisive. The LDP emphasized that the centennial's purpose was to recover lost values such as patriotism through a celebration of 100 years of development (in 1968, Japan surpassed West Germany to become the second largest economy in the free world), but historians critical of Imperial Japan refused to sanction a ceremony glorifying Japan's modern history.[111] Second, the essential impetus for celebrating the centennial of the Meiji Restoration came from the government, that is, from above. Third, although 1968 was dotted with government-sponsored ceremonies, numerous functions sponsored by private organizations also were held.[112] The centennial served to energize the far right.

The shrine world threw itself behind the cause of pushing the Diet to establish a legal mechanism to ensure the continuation of the reign-name system by carrying out publicity and signature campaigns across the country. The Shinto Political Association (Shintō seiji renmei), founded in 1969, made winning legalization of the reign-name system its top priority. The association sponsored politicians, including its own chair, Nishimura Shōji, an LDP representative in the House of Councillors. (It is common in Japan for representatives to occupy leadership positions in private interest groups even as they serve in the Diet.)[113] Nishimura played a crucial role in shepherding the Reign-Name Bill through the Diet.

In 1970 the LDP's Policy Affairs Research Council (PARC) turned its attention to the reign-name system, and in 1972 a special PARC division chaired by Nishimura was formed. By 1974, this division had approved the bill that became the Reign-Name Law in 1979. Polls conducted by the government in the 1970s showed support for "primary use of the reign-name [system]" hovering around 80 percent.[114] However, the LDP moved cautiously and did not introduce the bill until after demonstrations of its popular support had taken place.

The centennial celebrations of the Meiji Restoration had served as a catalyst for the reign-name legalization movement, and the fiftieth anniversary of the emperor's reign in 1975 provided the movement with a decisive push. Private groups such as the far-right Association to Protect Japan (Nihon o mamoru kai) initiated celebrations of Emperor Hirohito's fiftieth year on the throne, and in early 1975 the ruling LDP began to plan an official celebration. It was staged in mid-1976, but throughout 1975, private groups sponsored various events celebrating the golden anniversary of the emperor's reign.[115]

In May 1975, the Association of Shinto Shrines sponsored a celebration at the Meiji Shrine that drew 500 participants. Similar celebrations were held at shrines across the land. The shrine world adopted resolutions in support of legalizing the reign-name system at these ceremonies and forwarded them to the prime minister. The shrine world vigorously pushed its signature campaign in 1975 to honor the emperor's fifty years on the throne.[116] By the end of the year, the association claimed to have collected nearly one million signatures calling for perpetuation of the reign-name system.[117]

The main governmental celebration, held on 10 November 1976, served further to heighten consciousness about imperial practices.[118] In 1975 and 1976, *Risō sekai* and other far right journals began to devote considerable coverage to the reign-name system. There was much grassroots interest in ceremonies commemorating the emperor's fifty years on the throne, and this served to focus attention on the system. This interest was not limited to the surviving members of the prewar generation. Teenage members of Seichō no ie wrote poems praising Japan after attending such ceremonies.[119]

There were direct continuities between the reign-name legalization movement and the Foundation Day reestablishment movement. At no fewer than twenty celebrations of Foundation Day held throughout Japan on 11 February 1977, various groups jointly passed resolutions pledging to work to win legalization of the reign-name system.[120] In May of that year, fifty-seven groups joined to hold the People's Rally Calling for the Legalization of the Reign Name (Gengō hōseika yokyū kokumin taikai) in Tokyo. This rally, chaired by Professor Uno Seiichi (1910–2008) of Tokyo University, featured many of the groups active in the Foundation Day reestablishment movement, including the Foundation Day Celebration Association itself. Among the sponsors were the Association of Shinto Shrines, Seichō no ie, the Japan Veterans Friendship League, the Association to Protect Japan, and the National Congress for the Establishment of an Autonomous Constitution (Jishu kenpō seitei kokumin kaigi). As had been the case with the Foundation Day movement, women's and youth groups were also active.

The Japan Youth Council (Nihon seinen kyōgikai) played a particularly important role.[121] The council had been founded in 1970 by university students to counter what it called the "revolutionary," or left-wing, student movement. The political right was no doubt disturbed by the student protests of the late 1960s against the Vietnam War and the 1970 renewal of the U.S.-Japan Security Treaty (the radical left in fact had limited adherents among the protesters but was quite active and in some cases violent), but it was the success in the late 1960s and early 1970s of progressive but hardly radical citizens' antipollution movements in gaining control of many local governments that served as a model to the right about how to influence the national political agenda through popular action at the local level. Individuals in their twenties affiliated with branches throughout Japan formed the core of the Japan Youth Council.[122] In 1977, the council proposed the following strategy to win legalization of the reign-name system at a time of political stalemate between the left and the right:

> In order to achieve legalization, a large force that can push the Diet and the government is by all means necessary. To this end, we must go to every nook and cranny in the country and plead for the necessity of legalizing the reign name, and locally work to foster groups that will adopt the reign name as their concern. Through these groups, we will ask regional assemblies as well as local assemblies to pass resolutions, and harnessing this power we will win legalization by the government.[123]

The Japan Youth Council's plan of action to overcome the status quo was, in fact, precisely what took place over the next two years. In August 1977, the Japan Youth Council, with the joint sponsorship of the Association of Shinto Shrines and National Congress for the Establishment of an Autonomous Constitution, dispatched a caravan to western Japan to energize local forces. This trip, which lasted twenty-two days and covered 5,000 kilometers, proved a phenomenal success.

Everywhere the caravan visited, its participants sponsored lectures and films to educate people about the reign-name system. It linked up not only with local branches of its three sponsors but also with representatives of other far-right groups, whom it encouraged to form grassroots coalitions that could lobby assemblies for resolutions. On 17 August, in a public hall in Kumamoto prefecture, the caravan gathered together more than 200 representatives of seventeen nationalistic groups to form the Kumamoto Prefecture Reign-Name System Legalization Promotion Council.[124] The caravan provided sample petitions calling for the legalization of the reign-name system, and local groups used these samples as models for their own petitions, which were then submitted to local assemblies.

Members of the caravan also experienced considerable success in securing promises to pass resolutions calling for legalization of the reign-name system directly from prefectural and local politicians. After meeting with representatives of the caravan, the chair of the Nagasaki Prefectural Assembly asked them to submit a petition to the assembly. He promised to exert himself to the utmost to pass a resolution. On 22 September 1977, the assembly of Imari, a city in Saga prefecture visited by the caravan, became the first local assembly to pass a resolution calling for legalization of the reign-name system. A reporter for the Japan Youth Council chronicled the history leading up to the passage of this important first resolution (the following is an abridged version).

Local Report: The Path to the Imari City Resolution

At 3:50 p.m. on 22 September, a wave of applause arose from individuals seated in the spectators' section of the Imari City Assembly. This was the instant that the assembly passed a resolution calling for the legalization of the reign-name system. Beginning with Chair Kataoka Takafusa, almost all the members of the Imari branch of the Youth and Fatherland Association [Sokoku to seinen; part of the Japan Youth Council] had taken the afternoon off to attend the assembly.

The twelve members of the Imari branch all have local roots. The oldest is Yoshitake [no first name provided] at thirty-two, and the youngest is Eguchi Fusao at twenty-five. The average age of members is twenty-eight, the same as the national average for members of the Youth and Fatherland Association.

Kataoka graduated from the Kyushu College of Industry in Shōwa 46 [1971], and took over the family rice shop. From that time on, he was involved in activities with an Imari youth group chaired by Yoshitake. Yoshitake joined the Youth and Fatherland Association after last year's activities to celebrate the emperor's fiftieth year on the throne. The vice-chair is Mitsue [no first name provided], who since Shōwa 49 [1974] has been Kataoka's right-hand man in building up the Youth and Fatherland Association [in Imari]. He runs a *sake* shop, and a cottage that he oversees is convenient for group meetings. Maeda Hideyuki, who works for a trucking company, handles the group's accounting.

Maeda Kiyofusa runs a barber shop in Kataoka's neighborhood. His father also was very involved in the signature movement [calling for a resolution in support of the reign-name system]. He kept petitions in his shop and used to talk to customers about the importance of the reign-name system while cutting their hair. Without fail, they signed on the way home.

And then there is the farmer Yoshino Yōsuke, who even signed up his one-year-old son as a member of the group. He, too, joined at the time of the celebrations [of the emperor's fiftieth year on the throne]. Another farmer, Nonaka Yoshiyori, has, along with Yoshitake, a long history of involvement with local youth groups. It is for this reason that these groups cooperated with us this time. Eguchi Fumiaki is also a farmer and onetime chair of a local youth organization. Eguchi Fusao is our organization's representative from the salaryman world. Harada Hiroshi is a plasterer. The membership of Kajiyama Kazuyasu, who has ties to the LDP, was influential in moving the Imari political world. The final member, Matsuo Nobuyuji, is a white-collar man who joined this July.

The movement to win passage of the Reign-Name Resolution proceeded as follows. It began with Eguchi Fusao attending the People's Rally Calling for the Legalization of the Reign Name in Tokyo this past May. Based on Eguchi's report from this meeting, our group, along with shrine-based groups, religious groups, seniors clubs, and the Veterans' Pension League (Gunjin onkyū renmei) decided to undertake a signature movement. At the same time, we also planned to lobby city assembly representatives.

The Imari City Assembly has thirty representatives (one seat is presently vacant), of which twenty-six are unaffiliated but conservative, and three are

> members of the JSP. Moreover, each section of Imari City is divided into ten to fifteen wards, and it is said that the person who ignores ward chairmen fails in city politics.
>
> In June the Imari branch confirmed [with its allies] that it would carry out a signature movement, and it was at this time that the revolutionary circular petition method (*kairanban hōshiki*) was born.[125] [In Japan, information circulars issued by government offices such as the local city hall have long been passed from house to house to disseminate information about practical matters such as fire prevention,] but to use this method to gather signatures for a national matter such as the reign-name system became the talk of every household. Through the cooperation of ward chairmen, almost total penetration of petitions was achieved. It was a vivid demonstration of a grassroots movement (*kusa no ne undō*).
>
> The visit of the caravan served as a catalyst for the formation of the Imari Citizens Reign-Name System Legalization Promotion Society on 16 August. With this association and several thousand signatures behind us, we opened our formal attack on the city assembly.
>
> On 5 September, we submitted petitions [calling for a resolution]. Three days later we presented more than 6,400 signatures [supporting this demand] from heads of households, more than half the households in Imari,[126] to the city assembly. The next day the city assembly chair announced that a vote on the resolution would be taken on 22 September.[127]

The circular petition method was coercive. The fact that neighbors saw whether the family next door had signed raises serious questions about just how democratic this method was, but the lobbying techniques used by the far right in other areas were typical of grassroots movements in democracies everywhere.

The case of Imari—local groups exerting pressure on local assemblies to pass resolutions calling for the legalization of the reign-name system—was by no means unique. It was repeated throughout Japan between 1977 and the passage of the Reign-Name Bill in 1979. Assemblies in the area where the caravan had undertaken organizing activities in August 1977, such as the Nagasaki Prefectural Assembly, followed Imari with their own resolutions in September and October 1977.

It was no coincidence that the texts of these resolutions were largely identical, for each assembly drew on model resolutions provided by the Japan Youth Council and other far-right groups. A typical resolution reads:

22 September, Shōwa 52 [1977]
Prime Minister Fukuda Takeo:
A Resolution Concerning Legalization of the Reign-Name System
As a result of the new Imperial House Law, the legal basis of our reign-name system of Meiji, Taishō, and Shōwa was made vague, and this situation has continued until today. The reign-name system, which has continued without interruption for 1,300 years since [the] Taika [reforms], is a tradition of the independent country of Japan symbolized by the emperor and is an important pillar of the unity of the people (*kokumin tōgō*). We strongly request the timely legalization of the reign-name system.
Imari City Assembly
Kamura Kaneo, Chair[128]

Before the Reign-Name Bill passed, the Office of the Prime Minister received more than 1,600 such resolutions from assemblies throughout Japan.

The rapidity with which the wave of resolutions advanced was striking. Just eight months after passage of the first resolution, more than 342 assemblies, including 36 prefectural assemblies, had followed suit.[129] A critical factor in producing this swell of resolutions was the organizing hand of the Japan Youth Council, the Association of Shinto Shrines, and other far-right groups with national networks. Between 1977 and 1979, the offices of the Association of Shinto Shrines resembled a war room. Highlighted maps showed the locations of assemblies that had passed resolutions as well as those being targeted. The Japan Youth Council was able to provide interested parties with strategy sheets such as "Method for Achieving a Local Assembly Resolution," prepared in cooperation with the Association of Shinto Shrines and Seichō no ie. This sheet recommended that people seeking to pressure local assemblies form "coalitions with as many groups as possible. Not only religious groups, but also senior groups, veteran groups, the Bereaved Society, the Chamber of Commerce and Industry, and others. [It is best to have] twenty to fifty groups. It is necessary to have many pressure groups when it comes to the LDP."[130] The sheet went on to explain that the LDP was especially receptive to lobbying from (monied) interest groups, such as the Japan Doctors' Association (Nihon ishikai).

Although national organizations played a critical role, without the type of local, grassroots organizing exhibited in Imari City, local assemblies would not have responded with resolutions. Behind every resolution passed by a local assembly were individuals, often working through groups such as the Kumamoto Prefecture Reign-Name System Legalization Promotion Council, who canvassed door to door and then delivered signatures and petitions to their local assembly. Numerous women's groups led by the National Women's Piety Federation were active in the reign-name legalization movement as well.[131]

By 1978, far-right groups had succeeded in raising to a fever pitch all activities relating to the Reign-Name Bill. In May, after more than 400 local assemblies had passed resolutions, the Association of Shinto Shrines, the Shinto Political Association, the Japan Youth Council, and 120 other groups sponsored another rally calling for legalization of the reign-name system.[132] This rally was attended by more than 2,000 individuals, including representatives from the LDP, the New Liberal Club (NLC; a party formed in 1976 when a small faction withdrew from the LDP), and the DSP. Nishioka Takeo (1936–2011), chair of the NLC, publicly promised to form an interparty association of Diet representatives committed to passing a bill to legalize the reign-name system.[133]

In June, the Reign-Name Legalization Promotion League of Diet Representatives was formed with Nishimura Shōji as its chair. This league comprised 428 representatives from the LDP, NLC, and DSP. In July the Association of Shinto Shrines, to better coordinate the movement, organized the People's Committee to Achieve Legalization of the Reign Name. Sponsored by numerous large civil organizations and chaired by a former chief justice of Japan, Ishida Kazuto (1903–79), it consisted of prominent individuals, including many of Japan's business leaders such as Sakurada Takeshi (1904–85), chair of the Federation of Economic Organizations. The chairmen of the Japan Chamber of Commerce and Industry, the Junior Executive Council, and the General Federation of Small & Medium Enterprise Associations were also members.[134]

The People's Committee to Achieve Legalization of the Reign Name seems to have had ample financial resources at its disposal. It carried out various publicity activities. It underwrote large ads in newspapers showing, with the help of highlighted maps, how many of the prefectural assemblies had passed resolutions calling for legalization of the reign-name system.[135] It also published its own newspaper, appropriately named the *Reign-Name Newspaper* (*Gengō shinbun*).

The Reign-Name Legalization Promotion League of Diet Representatives and the People's Committee to Achieve Legalization of the Reign Name were in contact with each other on almost a daily basis until their political objective was achieved. In mid-1978, the Fukuda Cabinet was already moving in the direction of sponsoring a bill that would legalize the reign-name system. To keep the political heat on the government, the People's Committee to Achieve Legalization of the Reign Name sponsored a national caravan along the lines of the earlier caravan carried out by members of the Japan Youth Council.[136] By the time this caravan returned to Tokyo, prefectural citizens' councils (*kenmin kaigi*) had been formed in each of the forty-seven prefectures of Japan. Their purpose was to lobby prefectural and local assemblies to pass resolutions in support of the system.[137]

The tidal wave of resolutions continued. By August 1978, the number of prefectural assemblies that had passed resolutions reached 45 and the number of local assemblies nearly 700. At that point, of the forty-seven regional assemblies, only those of Hokkaido and Okinawa—the northern and southern peripheries of Japan—had not yet passed resolutions. Before the bill was introduced into the Diet in 1979, Hokkaido, after a tumultuous debate in the assembly, fell into line and passed a resolution. This left Okinawa—Japan's renegade prefecture regarding emperor-system issues—as the only prefecture whose assembly did not support establishing a legal mechanism to perpetuate the reign-name system.

On 17 August 1978, Prime Minister Fukuda responded to the resolution movement. He publicly stated his support for ensuring the continuation of the reign-name system, commenting, "I, too, am surprised that this many local assemblies have passed resolutions."[138] The People's Committee to Achieve Legalization of the Reign Name maintained the political pressure. On 3 October, it sponsored a rally in Tokyo calling for passage of the Reign-Name Bill during a special session of the Diet. The rally drew more than 20,000 people from throughout Japan. A total of 318 Diet representatives were present, including major figures from the LDP, NLC, DSP, and Kōmeitō. A message from Fukuda read at the rally promised that the government would soon take measures regarding the reign-name system.[139]

At the time of the rally, Fukuda was in a fierce contest with Ōhira Masayoshi over who would be the next president of the LDP and thus the next prime minister. On 17 October, Fukuda and Ōhira issued a joint statement promising that whoever became the next prime minister, the LDP would introduce the Reign-Name Bill into the next regular session of the Diet. Thus, with the LDP publicly committed to the Reign-Name Bill, a decade of lobbying by the Association of Shinto Shrines, the Japan Youth Council, and other groups was about to bear fruit. The technique of lobbying local assemblies to pass resolutions had played the decisive role in convincing the LDP to sponsor a bill.

Once the Reign-Name Bill was introduced into the Diet on 2 February 1979, there was not much question that it would pass. The bill enjoyed the support of the LDP, DSP, Kōmeitō, and NLC; only the JSP and JCP were opposed. A NHK poll released on 9 February showed that over 59 percent of respondents favored legalizing the system, and only 19 percent opposed this measure.[140] The Reign-Name Bill was only a few lines long. It provided for the selection of a new reign name by Cabinet ordinance on the accession of a new emperor. Nonetheless, the debate in the Diet about the bill was lengthy.[141]

Numerous representatives voiced their opinions, and ten witnesses, five for each house of the Diet, were called to give testimony about the reign-name system. The Diet records of this debate, which often drifted off into a general discussion of the emperor system, run to several hundred pages. The debate about the reign-name system in 1979 invites comparison to the debate about the same issue that had taken place in the House of Councillors Education Committee nearly three decades earlier.

The investigation in 1950 had addressed whether the reign-name system should be abolished, whereas the 1979 debate centered on the necessity of providing a legal mechanism to ensure the continued use of reign names. Much of the debate in 1979 nonetheless echoed that of 1950. The key differences were that opponents of the system now found themselves in the minority. Not only were proponents in the majority, they also felt far more confident in defending the system as a symbol of Japan's culture. There was almost no talk, even from opponents of the system, of the need for Japan to adopt the Western calendar to join the "civilized nations" of the world. In his study of discourse about Japanese culture during the postwar era, anthropologist Aoki Tamotsu identified the late 1970s and early 1980s as a period when the Japanese held particularly positive views about the distinctiveness of their culture.[142] The debates over the reign-name system reflected this self-assurance.

The parameters of the debate were established on the first day the bill was discussed in the Diet, 16 March. As it would throughout the debate, the government, whether represented by Prime Minister Ōhira or other ministers, stressed that the bill's purpose was simply to answer to popular demands for stabilization of the reign-name system. The government sought to avoid ideological debates about the measure even if individual LDP, and also DSP and NLC, representatives, as well as witnesses, used the occasion to beat nationalistic drums. In his opening remarks about the reign-name system in the Diet, Ōhira emphasized, "The real intention of introducing the Reign-Name Bill . . . [is that] the vast majority of citizens desire the reign-name system's continuation. Moreover, forty-six prefectural assemblies, and more than 1,000 city, town, and village assemblies have passed resolutions calling for its legalization."[143]

JSP representative Ueda Takumi was the first to question the government. Ueda promptly introduced most of the common criticisms of the reign-name system. He asked the government to address whether the modern system, developed as part of the Meiji polity that was characterized by imperial sovereignty, was compatible with the Postwar Constitution, which was designed expressly to provide for popular sovereignty.[144] Many Diet representatives who questioned the government about the bill asked for an assurance that passage of the bill did not represent a return to the Meiji system. Government representatives repeated their interpretation that providing a legal basis for the reign-name system in no way would contravene the Postwar Constitution.

Ueda pointed out that the modern system was not very traditional. It was, after all, only about a century old. He also stressed the system's inconvenience and questioned why Japan, during a time of unprecedented internationalization, would want to block itself off from the rest of the world by adopting a system understood only domestically. Ueda concluded by indicting the reign-name system as part of a "structure of thought control:"

> In addressing legalization of the reign-name system, one cannot forget its function in thought control. The reign-name system, like [the ideology of the] unbroken imperial line, the Imperial Rescript on Education, the so-called national anthem (*Kimigayo*), State Shinto, standardization of education, and regulation of thought and speech, was established as one of the gears in the equipment of hegemonic control over the thoughts of the people.[145]

In response to this charge, Minister of State Mihara Asao stressed that the bill was being debated freely in the Diet, Japan's highest decisionmaking body.[146]

Kōmeitō representative Arai Yoshiyuki reminded everyone that the vast majority of citizens desired the system's continuation. He also made it understood that his party's support of the system was in the context of the postwar system: "As something that is entirely different from the reign-name system established according to the emperor's supreme power under the old Imperial Constitution, as something that is established according to the people's sovereignty, the Kōmeitō supports the continuation of the reign-name system."[147] Arai stressed that his party supported both the system and the Postwar Constitution.

The Diet member who came across as the most nationalistic during the first day of interpellation was Nakano Kansei, a representative of the DSP, the proponent of socialism with a national instead of an entirely working-class basis.[148] The DSP, it should be remembered, had opposed the bill to reestablish Foundation Day. Nakano spoke of his pride in Japan's recent prosperity and in its magnificent tradition. He called the reign-name system a "symbol of independent Japan" and a "'novel' (*roman*) of the glorious Japanese race." He also suggested that the reason counting years according to the Christian era enjoyed such widespread use was that Christian countries had colonized much of the world. He stressed that the Japan Federation of Labor (Dōmei), his party's main constituency, was a sponsor of the People's Committee to Achieve Legalization of the Reign Name. Nakano was thus a strong supporter of the bill.[149]

The final representative to speak on 16 March was Shibata Mutsuo of the JCP. Shibata immediately launched a denunciation: "It is common knowledge that the modern reign-name system played a role in supporting the despotic rule of the absolutist emperor system." Shibata interpreted the Reign-Name Bill as one of a long line of reactionary measures supported by the LDP. He also questioned the validity of the resolutions passed by regional and local assemblies: "They are passed forcibly by majority vote, thus breaking the custom of unanimous votes. They do not reflect the opinion of local residents."[150] In response to Shibata's devaluation of the resolutions, Minister of State Mihara emphasized, "When forty-six regional assemblies and more than 1,500 local assemblies pass resolutions, I think that this must be regarded as an important trend."[151] Repeatedly, the government used the wave of resolutions as its trump card. After ten more weeks of debate, the bill passed. It became law on 12 June 1979.

According to the Reign-Name Law, government officials (with the exception of those preparing diplomatic documents) are required to date years according to the reigns of emperors, but citizens are only asked to use the Japanese-style calendar. After the Reign-Name Law went into effect, some Japanese citizens made a point of using the Christian way of counting years to protest the government's invocation of the reign-name system to foster nationalism. Tomino Kiichirō (1944–), mayor of Zushi City from 1984 to 1992, had city bureaucrats devise application forms special to his city that gave citizens the option of using whatever calendar they desired, since this was their right under the law.[152] As was earlier the case with Foundation Day, stubborn opposition to the reign-name system continued after the Diet restored its official status. But the system was far less divisive than was Foundation Day, and it is precisely through seemingly banal practices such as dating forms according to the reign-name system that nationalism is nurtured at the popular level.

What do the Foundation Day and reign-name system movements tell us about postwar Japan? First, they show the diversity of associations engaged in politics and the far right's skillful use of lobbying techniques. I do not interpret the postwar Japanese state to be neutral—it tended to lean to the right. Nonetheless, the far-right Association of Shinto Shrines is an organization that existed, as did many citizens groups on the left, in tension with the postwar government. This association's views often contrasted with those of the LDP, not to mention the left-wing parties. Like the far-right Christian Coalition in the United States, the Association of Shinto Shrines occupies a place in civil society between the individual citizen and the state. And similarly to the Christian Coalition in the late 1980s and 1990s, the Association of Shinto Shrines has shown itself capable of manufacturing popular support for some of its programs.[153]

Indeed, ignoring the political influence of groups such as the Association of Shinto Shrines leads to a distorted picture of Japanese politics. Interest groups have played a crucial role in shaping social policy in postwar Japan. The role of religious groups in particular needs to be underscored. It is highly unlikely that Foundation Day would have been reestablished if the coalition headed by the Association of Shinto Shrines had not fostered grassroots movements and lobbied the LDP for years. Still, although many LDP politicians courted the support of groups such as the Association of Shinto Shrines, which could deliver votes and contributions, only fragments of the association's platform ever found their way into law. Foundation Day and the reign-name system were two such fragments.

Although it is possible to speak of transwar support for features of the emperor system, this piecemeal support should by no means be interpreted as reactionary backing for the entire prewar emperor system. Little of the ideology associated with the prewar-style Foundation Day exemplified by the 2,600th anniversary celebrations in 1940—the type of ideology still glorified by the Association of Shinto Shrines—is accepted by the Japanese today. Only a very few Japanese celebrate the holiday along prewar lines. If the public mobilizes on Foundation Day at all, it is to get to the ski slopes to capitalize on this winter holiday.[154] It goes without saying that most LDP politicians work to promote nationalism, which in Japan is often associated with the imperial house. But one must not assume simplistically that this nationalism, while perhaps distasteful, is in opposition to Japan's democratic system, for today that is generally not the case.

This study stresses the importance of symbols and the difficulties in drawing strict boundaries between the symbolic and the political, which tend to be mutually reinforcing. However, it is worth considering the relative importance of Foundation Day and the reign-name system to postwar Japan. Powerful though symbols may be, are the reestablishment of Foundation Day and the legalization of the reign-name system as significant as the failure of the effort to revise the constitution, which defines the basic democratic political structure? One need not privilege structures over symbols in all cases, but in postwar Japan the constitution, however much conservatives may have tried to manipulate it, not only has served to redefine fundamentally the rules by which politics are carried out but also has exercised a profound social influence in numerous areas. In contrast, Foundation Day remains divisive, and although the reign-name system is one of several mechanisms that reinforce the monarchy's importance in Japanese society, it operates only within the postwar system defined by the constitution and in no way undermines that system.

2019 Addendum

Before I published the earlier version of this book in 2001, when I was still at the stage of presenting parts of my manuscript at scholarly conferences and asking peers to provide feedback on individual chapters, it was already becoming clear that the most controversial chapter, at least for left-wing scholars, was this one. My argument was that whatever one thought of movements such as those to reestablish National Foundation Day and stabilize the legal basis of the reign-name system, it was simply not correct to claim that the ruling LDP had passed these measures "from above" with disregard for how the people truly felt. This argument rubbed some scholars the wrong way. How could grassroots movements from the right be democratic? But the evidence overwhelmingly suggested that the agents behind these movements had skillfully used grassroots lobbying techniques that until then were typically associated only with progressive movements to demonstrate considerable (if ambiguous when it came to certain fine details, such as how to celebrate Foundation Day) support for reestablishing Foundation Day and for stabilizing the reign-name system.

There was some shock (and a few incidents of anger) directed at me before and after publication of the original book by scholars on both sides of the Pacific for claiming that the far right was behaving in a democratic manner, that the far right had learned to play the game of democracy to advance its agenda. Some scholars refused to believe that a grassroots movement might be anything other than progressive. Although I was a junior scholar at the time, I found this stance puzzling for one simple reason: the history of fascist movements worldwide before 1945.

Some of the criticism directed my way seemed to go beyond scholarly debate to hint that perhaps I was in fact secretly sympathetic toward the far right. Why else would I be writing about these movements? Time has proven such criticism nonsensical. If one fast-forwards to the present, would anyone deny that one must analyze the influence of the far right (e.g., the Nihon kaigi or Japan Conference) to understand Japan? Obviously in the interim the rise of populism in Europe and the Americas has put to rest (for the meantime) the question of whether grassroots movements can originate on the right. Should we refrain from studying such populism because we dislike it? I would argue that the exact opposite should be the case.

My claim at the time the original book was published was that to truly understand Japan, it was necessary to take seriously the movement to reestablish Foundation Day—as seriously as one did the antipollution movements around the same time. I stand by this assertion. I am flattered that in recent years thoughtful journalists and scholars such as Aoki Osamu, Yamazaki Masahiro, Uesugi Satoshi, and Sugano Tamotsu, who have published studies of the Nihon kaigi, have kindly gone out of their way to identify me as the first scholar to pinpoint the significance of the Foundation Day reestablishment movement and the reign-name legalization movement, grassroots movements from the right earlier in the postwar period.[155] Aoki argues convincingly that later organizations (e.g, the Nihon kaigi) likely studied these earlier, successful far-right movements carefully. They drew lessons from them as they plotted strategy, for example, to mobilize Japanese against changing the Imperial House Law to permit female *tennō*, or to nurture support in favor of measures such as reforming the Basic Law on Education to include provisions for cultivating patriotism.

I personally do not agree with Japan's far right on issues ranging from how one should interpret the national history, especially the history of Imperial Japan, to whether the country should permit female *tennō*. Nonetheless, one must recognize that at times the far right does rally popular opinion behind its proposals (and thus when the government takes action regarding these proposals the situation is not one of the ruling coalition ramming policies down the throats of the people whether they like them or not). Often when one examines the fine details of, say, a law that was passed by the government in comparison to what the far right really wanted, one learns that the far right got less than it hoped for. But they do have some influence, and to ignore their role is to put forth a distorted analysis of Japan.

CHAPTER 6

The "Monarchy of the Masses"

In an analysis of the postwar development of the monarchy published at the time of Crown Prince Akihito's engagement in 1958, political scientist Matsushita Keiichi (1929–2015) used the term "emperor system of the masses" (*taishū tennōsei*; or simply the "monarchy of the masses") to describe the imperial house's active efforts to reach out to the people, to win, not command, the hearts of the Japanese.[1] This change in the monarchy's operational style was associated first and foremost with Akihito, although it matured under Hirohito. The effort to remake Emperor Hirohito, symbol of wartime Japan, into a symbol of postwar Japan was never as successful as the grooming of Akihito to suit the "New Japan." So long as Emperor Hirohito remained on the throne, the monarchy of the masses was constrained.

One of the greatest changes faced by the monarchy under the Postwar Constitution was that the throne became fair game for unfettered press coverage. The palace endeavors to transmit a certain image of the imperial house, and the media play a key role in presenting that image to the people. Virtually every public act by a member of the imperial family is choreographed, and the media are instrumental in disseminating information about the emperor and other imperial family members. At the same time, the imperial house uses the media to gauge the public's evaluation of its performance; public opinion of the throne flows upward through the media to the keenly interested imperial family members and their handlers.[2] In addition to being a transmission belt for information to and from the palace, the mass media are themselves independent actors in shaping the imperial house's image.

The severe criticism that intellectuals publicly leveled at the monarchy, or the emperor system as distinguished from the monarchy itself, in the immediate postwar years was indicative of the changed environment. In a

February 1946 essay, JCP leader Miyamoto Kenji forcefully called for the abolition of the emperor system, which he attacked from a variety of angles:

> The perspective of separating the militarists, a central element in the structure of the emperor system, from the emperor system and making them solely responsible for the aggression not only is a fallacy but . . . has left room for the beautification of the emperor system. Yesterday's pure militarists and aggressors say things today such as Japan's emperor system is basically democratic in nature, that the imperial house is the embodiment of democracy . . . things about which one cannot stop laughing.[3]

After the war, Marxists were by no means alone in criticizing the monarchy and its societal role. The liberal Maruyama Masao (1914–95) and other "modernists" diagnosed the Japanese people, in part because of their mentality toward the throne, as underdeveloped.[4]

Yokota Kisaburō, who became chief justice of Japan in 1960, adopted a "modernist" line in a 1949 monograph about the emperor system:

> The reason that until now the Japanese made themselves passive and served the emperor was that they were inured to feudalism and despotism under the emperor system and did not have a consciousness of individuality or an awareness of self or understand the value of liberty or the significance of equality. Westerners discovered individuality and became aware of the self as a result of the Renaissance. Based on the enlightened ideas of the eighteenth century, they learned the value of liberty and discerned the significance of equality. As a result, they rejected despotic monarchism and established democracy. In Japan, since there was no Renaissance or enlightened ideas, the value and significance of individuality, self, liberty, and equality were not understood. [The people] were taught, under extreme statism and feudal ideas, only loyalty to the emperor and service to the state. The reason there was no opposition between the people and the emperor . . . was because of the ignorance of the Japanese people. . . . Once liberated from feudal ideas and the despotic system, the Japanese will discover as a matter of course the self, discern individuality, realize the value of liberty, and learn the principle of equality.[5]

Yokota saw the people's loyalty to the throne as a sign of their backwardness and championed the Enlightenment values featured in the Postwar Constitution. British critics of the royal house had long been insisting that as Britain modernized, the monarchy would lose its role.[6] Yet as modern and as democratic as Britain became, the monarchy nonetheless survived and retained the loyalty of the people, to some degree and in changed form. This also was the case with Japan in the postwar era because of the remaking of the imperial house into a symbol of the new polity. Industrialized democracies require myths and symbols, too.

Hirohito, Emperor of the People?

The palace never created a master plan for remaking the monarchy. Instead, the imperial family and the palace staff attempted to respond to rapidly changing conditions as best they could. Although Japanese authorities began to remake Hirohito into a man of peace on the day of the surrender, they nonetheless sought to retain his inviolability. Just weeks into the Occupation, however, the emperor's preeminence was struck a devastating blow when SCAP insisted that Japanese newspapers publish a photograph of the first meeting between MacArthur and Hirohito. Newspapers printed the photograph on 29 September. In the picture, MacArthur, dressed in casual clothes, towers over Hirohito, who appears in full morning dress. The image left no question as to who was the dominant figure and which was the winning side. Even decades later, far-right defenders of imperial dignity were still complaining that MacArthur at least could have worn a necktie. Yet it is also true that the image was useful not only to MacArthur but also to Hirohito. It provided MacArthur with imperial legitimation, but it also indicated SCAP's intention to work with the emperor.

On 1 January 1946, the Imperial Household Ministry issued an imperial rescript in which the emperor denied his divinity: "The ties between Us and Our people have always stood upon mutual trust and affection. They do not depend upon mere legends and myths. They are not predicated on the false conception that the Emperor is divine and that the Japanese people are superior to other races and fated to rule the world."[7] Hirohito was careful not to deny his descent from Amaterasu, however. The Japanese came to call this the "Declaration of Humanity" (*Ningen sengen*), although the official title was "Rescript to Promote the National Destiny." Although this imperial performance was staged to a great extent for the Americans, it nonetheless proved for the Japanese to be one of several defrockings of the once-sacrosanct emperor.

FIGURE 16. General Douglas MacArthur, informally dressed, towers over Emperor Hirohito, dressed in a morning coat, in this famous photograph of their first meeting on 27 September 1945. The Japanese government attempted to suppress publication of this photograph, but U.S. Occupation authorities ordered that it be published widely. (Photograph courtesy Kyodo Photo Service.)

Traditionally the monarchy had been described as being "above the clouds." In the postwar era, the palace worked hard to bring it, if not to ground level, then at least to an altitude where it could be seen from the ground. The media played a critical role in transmitting the imperial house's new image to the people. On 1 January 1946, to coincide with the Declaration of Humanity, major newspapers carried a picture of the emperor, dressed in a suit and tie, walking with one of his daughters in a garden. Thereafter newspapers and magazines inundated the Japanese with palace-approved photographs of the imperial family. It is not that the imperial family had not been perceived as a family in prewar Japan, but that the stress on the familial side of the imperial house increased dramatically after 1945. Previously, photographs of the emperor typically showed the supreme commander in solemn situations, such as reviewing his troops. Published photographs of Empress Nagako indicated her

FIGURE 17. Beginning in 1946, the mass media deluged the Japanese with numerous images of the "happy imperial family." Here Emperor Hirohito and Empress Nagako walk on the beach in Hayama with four of their children, April 1946. (Photograph courtesy Kyodo Photo Service.)

secondary role to the emperor, although in both the pre- and postwar eras she was an important symbol of a loyal wife and mother.

This flood of visual images was accompanied by accounts of the imperial family's daily life, little of which had been known to Japanese. Beginning in 1946, countless books and articles told the "inside story" of the imperial family. Imperial House Press Club journalists such as Togashi Junji played important roles in remaking the emperor into a democratic man of the people, just as they helped construct Hirohito the man of peace. As suggested by the title of his 1946 book, *His Majesty's Declaration of "Humanity,"* Togashi credited the emperor with the idea of publicly denying his divinity—the official line at the time—although a wealth of evidence released later shows that SCAP had demanded the gesture.

Togashi quoted palace officials as taking responsibility for allowing a distorted image of the emperor to be publicized. Okane Masujirō, vice-director of the Imperial Household Ministry, corrected Togashi's impression that the emperor had been democratized only recently: "From the beginning, His Majesty was a democratic, common (*heiminteki*) fellow. The fact that he was seen as divine until recently was because we [palace officials] were bad; I apologize."[8] Someone had to take responsibility for this widespread misunderstanding.

The subtitle of the tenth chapter of Togashi's inside account of the imperial family was "A Normal Family Life in Every Way." Togashi, using quotation marks, explained the average person's reaction to seeing pictures of the imperial family for the first time: "It's just like our family, isn't it?"[9] The emperor was portrayed as a loving but firm father. Togashi recounted that the emperor had asked his eldest son what he wanted for his graduation from Gakushūin Elementary School in the spring of 1946. Crown Prince Akihito responded that he wanted a camera. Togashi represented palace officials as scrambling to find a marvelous camera for the crown prince until the emperor intervened to insist that his son be given a secondhand one: "To give him lavish things is not good for his future."[10]

Togashi's account of the imperial house was sanitized in various ways. In one anecdote, he characterized the emperor as unusually impartial. A young laborer who had come to the capital from the Tōhoku region in the spring of 1946 to help repair war damage to the palace grounds sponsored a roundtable discussion (*zadankai*) one evening and invited a palace official to join the group. At the discussion, one young participant asked the official, "How does His Majesty feel about the [Japan] Communist Party?" The official replied, "I have never heard anything specific from the emperor regarding the Communist Party, but because he has a very just character and because the party members are themselves Japanese citizens, I think that he probably bears them no ill feelings whatsoever."[11] In the same year that Togashi's book was published, Prime Minister Ashida recorded in his diary the emperor's expression of grave concern about the JCP's growing influence.

There were nonetheless elements of truth to the journalist's portrayal of Hirohito. Close associates of Hirohito described him as feeling like a caged bird who had been freed during his trip to Europe in 1921, especially when he visited with the British royal family.[12] He probably would have liked to mix more freely with people; after the war, he seemed to enjoy many of the occasions that brought him into contact with his countrymen. By many accounts, the imperial family lived (for a royal family anyhow) a frugal personal life in the postwar period. Togashi stressed the emperor's research in marine biology, which according to many sources was one of his true passions.

While the mass media provided accounts of the "real" emperor and imperial house, the emperor personally reached out to the people with a series of tours. Even harsh critics of the emperor system agree that the popular welcome that greeted the emperor on these tours was overwhelmingly positive, at least on the surface.[13] This was true even though the emperor's attempts to mingle with the people, at least in the eyes of foreign observers, came across as comically awkward. In the miserable aftermath of the defeat, the imperial house was one of the few sources of national pride still available to the Japanese.

The tours, which between 1946 and 1954 brought the emperor to every prefecture except Okinawa, were the first step in the making of the monarchy of the masses. They took the emperor not only to urban areas but also to the countryside (at the time, almost half of all workers were employed in agriculture). Imperial tours were not a postwar innovation, nor were attempts by the imperial house to reach out to the people. Before and during the war, the imperial family periodically carried out acts of benevolence, such as making charitable donations to assist people in areas hit by natural disasters. Before 1945, however, tours were a mechanism for the emperor to inspect his subjects. The emperor did not try to be one of the people; indeed, the stress was on his differences from the people and his position at the pinnacle of the social and political order. In contrast, the emperor's handlers choreographed postwar tours so that the emperor walked among his countrymen, to make him seem, to some extent, like "everyman."

The first imperial performance devised to allow the emperor to mix with the people took place on 19 February 1946. That morning, escorted by U.S. soldiers, the emperor and his entourage of palace officials traveled by car to nearby Kawasaki City to visit a factory that had been the first since the end of the war to produce the fertilizer desperately needed to increase food production. Specially placed microphones captured the emperor's questions and responses by the factory manager and city mayor. The emperor also engaged in "free conversation" with workers. Three days later, a recording of the emperor's visit was broadcast on the national radio station, NHK, the only network at the time.[14] Radio had been used since the 1920s to link the Japanese in listening to live descrip-

FIGURE 18. During a tour of Tochigi prefecture in September 1947, Emperor Hirohito, hat removed, greets his countrymen. Emperor Hirohito's countrywide tours between 1946 and 1954 played a critical role in remaking the imperial house into what political scientist Matsushita Keiichi called the "monarchy of the masses." (Photography courtesy Kyodo Photo Service.)

tions of imperial events. Emperor Hirohito's enthronement in 1928, for example, was broadcast on radio. Only beginning with the postwar tours, however, was radio employed to transmit into millions of Japanese homes the emperor conversing with his countrymen.

Throughout the numerous regional tours, which concluded with a visit to Hokkaido in 1954, the emperor not only encouraged workers to increase production but also comforted those who had been injured or had lost loved ones in the war. He consoled those whose homes had been destroyed in the air raids and reached out to the people in other ways. The emperor's tours were not triumphal, nor were they draped in pageantry. There was nothing elegantly anachronistic about the emperor's automobile and train rides. Much of Japan was in ruins, and the emperor encouraged his hungry and psychologically devastated countrymen to rebuild.

Naturally, the emperor's mixing with the people provided unprecedented photo ops for cameramen. Countless images of him were later published in newspapers and magazines, or shown in theaters as short

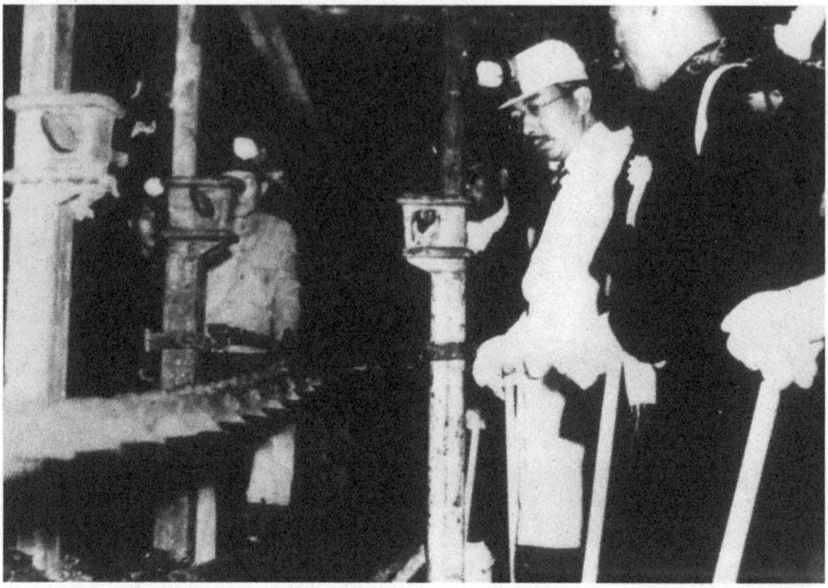

FIGURE 19. Emperor Hirohito visiting the Miike Coal Mine in Fukuoka prefecture, May 1949. Everywhere he went Emperor Hirohito exhorted his countrymen to work for Japan's recovery. The production of coal was critical to Japan's economic rehabilitation. (Photograph courtesy Kyodo News Service.)

newsreels: the emperor wearing a miner's hard hat while visiting workers inside a mine; the emperor in the rice fields with farmers; Empress Nagako affectionately brushing the emperor's hair into place. Every available technology transmitted the emperor's new image to his countrymen.

Other important steps in the development of the monarchy of the masses included the ritualization of opening the palace to the people on specific holidays. In 1948, the practice of allowing congratulatory visits by the public (*ippan sanga*) on 2 January to celebrate the New Year commenced. That same year, the palace was opened for the emperor's birthday on 29 April, a practice that continued on that day until Hirohito's death. Beginning in 1951, the emperor and empress greeted their countrymen from a special balcony. Typically, several tens of thousands of Japanese citizens take advantage of these opportunities to pay their respects to the imperial family. The campaign to remake the imperial house to suit the postwar polity culminated with Crown Prince Akihito's wedding in 1959.[15]

FIGURE 20. Emperor Hirohito and Empress Nagako (center), Crown Prince Akihito and Crown Princess Michiko (to each side of the emperor and empress), and other members of the imperial family greet countrymen making a congratulatory visit to the palace on Hirohito's birthday (29 April) in 1986. The practice of *ippan sanga* takes place twice annually, to celebrate the New Year (2 January) and the emperor's birthday. (Photograph courtesy of the Imperial Household Agency.)

The Emergence of Crown Prince Akihito

It was not until the end of the Occupation that Crown Prince Akihito fully emerged on the public stage. Throughout the Occupation, Akihito, still a teenager, was kept somewhat out of the limelight. The fact that he was being tutored by a U.S. Quaker, Elizabeth Vining (1902–99), was a central theme in the restrained coverage of the adolescent heir to the throne. Whereas his father's education had included military training from leading generals and admirals, Akihito's education included tutoring in English (as well as in etiquette and democratic principles) by a resolutely pacifistic American woman. Mass media portrayals of the crown prince also stressed his ordinariness. For example, one report described a spill he took when learning to ski. Hirohito remained to skeptics a symbol of militaristic Imperial Japan, but few could doubt that Akihito, as a result of his education, was different from his father in certain ways.

Like his father before him, Akihito lived separately from his parents for most of his childhood. In fact, it was only as a result of his father's stubborn insistence in the face of resistance from conservative courtiers that Akihito was kept under the care of his parents for the first three years of his life. In the period immediately after the war, however, the crown prince had far more casual social contacts than his father had as a teenager. After graduating from Gakushūin Elementary School, he was allowed to continue as a regular student at Gakushūin until his college years. After Hirohito graduated from elementary school, a special institute was established for his education; he attended classes with a few companions, who were expected to show him utmost deference at all times. This also had been the case with Emperor Taishō. In contrast, Akihito spent his middle school years living in a dormitory, where he not only had an older roommate but also shared with his classmates the spartan conditions found throughout Japan in the years immediately following the surrender. These experiences made Akihito far more at ease with his countrymen in informal situations than his father had ever been.

In 1952, Crown Prince Akihito became an overnight star in the mass media. On 10 November of that year, coincidentally the same year Japan regained its independence, the government staged his investiture ceremony. In 1953, the government and the palace sent Crown Prince Akihito on a world tour, his first foreign trip. The prince's six-month tour, from

FIGURE 21. Elizabeth Vining, an American Quaker, instructing Crown Prince Akihito (in the middle, looking toward his left) and his classmates in English at Gakushūin Middle School in 1947. Vining always credited Emperor Hirohito with the decision to provide the crown prince with an American tutor, but in fact it was SCAP that first proposed and pushed the idea. (Photograph courtesy Kyodo News Service.)

31 March until 12 October, centered around his attendance at Queen Elizabeth II's coronation on 2 June. The trip not only was a rite of passage for the crown prince but also was interpreted at the time as bearing tremendous meaning for Japan's reentry into the international community. In advance of the crown prince's trip, the Imperial Household Agency established a Preparatory Committee for His Imperial Highness the Crown Prince's Trip to Britain, chaired by chamberlain Mitani Takanobu. The purpose of the committee was to study local conditions and customs of every place the crown prince would visit and prepare him so that he could make the best possible impression.[16]

On 1 January 1953, a photograph of the crown prince, emperor, and empress examining a globe appeared in the *Asahi shinbun* and other major newspapers. Below this picture appeared a map of the route Akihito was to follow. Japan appeared not at the map's center but on the left side, an unusual arrangement for a Japanese map. The United States conspicuously occupied the center of the map, with Britain, an important model for the imperial house at the time, on the right. Asia barely appeared on the map at all. This was the worldview of many Japanese in 1953, and in that sense the map was appropriate. Journalist and scholar Shimizu Ikutarō, who at that time was still critical of the emperor system (political apostate Shimizu later participated in purist celebrations of Foundation Day), wrote that the map—and the crown prince's tour—gave the impression that Japan "did not need . . . the various countries of Asia." For Shimizu, Japan's true peers were precisely its Asian neighbors.[17] The crown prince's trip seemed to be a postwar version of "Get-out-of-Asia-and-join-the-West" thinking by Japan's leaders.

Crown Prince Akihito visited the United States, Canada, and twelve European countries, five of which were monarchies; he did not stop in Asia. His longest stay in any country, forty days, was in Britain; the second longest was in the United States. As indicated by the widely published map, these two countries were the key destinations on the crown prince's trip. The tour was the subject of considerable media coverage, particularly in the popular weeklies, an important form of mass publication. At the time of the crown prince's trip, the combined circulation of the top four weeklies was approaching 2.6 million (Japan's population was then approaching 90 million).[18] Twenty-four reporters and cameramen from thirteen news organizations accompanied the crown prince. They carefully investigated local reactions to the crown prince's visit, especially in Britain and the United States. In 1953, when Japan's economy had not yet recovered to prewar levels, a trip to Europe or the United States remained unthinkable for all but an extremely limited number of Japanese citizens. Most people could experience foreign travel only vicariously through the crown prince's trip.

Expectations for Akihito's tour could not have been clearer. The trip was regular news in the popular weeklies. An article in the *Sandē mainichi* described the crown prince's trip as an opportunity for him "to show pacifist Japan's true form to the world" (*heiwa Nihon no shin no sugata o sekai ni oshimeshi ni naru*).[19] This wording seemed to suggest that the wars of aggression between 1931 and 1945 were an aberration that had masked the traditionally pacifistic nature of the Japanese. Widespread pacifism is, it is true, a distinctive feature of postwar Japan, but this represents a postwar development rather than the reemergence of a traditional Japanese value. Many commentators stressed that the crown prince "was being groomed to become a new type of emperor appropriate to democratic Japan."[20] There was a consensus that Akihito should take a good look "at how the British royal house does things."[21] The popular weekly *Shūkan sankei* printed a forum titled "What Are Your Hopes for the Crown Prince's Trip to Britain?" Commentator Shimazu Tadashige wrote:

> At present, it is no exaggeration to say that in the world only Britain has a national polity (*kokutai*) and a royal house similar to our country's; moreover, in Europe it often is said that Britain is the most advanced democracy. Therefore on this occasion I wish from my heart that the crown prince will study everything about [Britain's] royal house.[22]

In the same forum, Horii Michiko, a college student, referred to Britain as Japan's *senpai*, or senior, in reference to the workings of the monarchy.[23]

Commentators proposed that the imperial house should reach out to the people just as members of the British royal house did. Three points are worth noting about this proposal, which was often made by Japanese observers of the imperial house. First, the effort by the British crown to identify with the people, so admired by Japanese commentators, was a product of the twentieth century, particularly of King George V's reign from 1910 to 1936. Political scientist Frank Prochaska has traced the British royal house's active campaign toward the end of World War I to stem the growth of republican sentiments by expanding the throne's social and charitable activities. Prochaska has documented that King George V "kept a chart in Buckingham Palace which chronicled his family's public work, complete with little flags showing locations. Labour strongholds were very well flagged."[24]

In his 1938 study of British parliamentary government, Harold Laski chronicled the changes that the monarchy had undergone since the Victorian age:

> No one who looks at the direction of royal interests in [the early twentieth century] and compares them with those of the Victorian epoch can, I think, doubt that a conscious effort has been made, again remarkably intensified by adroit propaganda, to associate the royal family with solicitude for those objects upon which working-class interest is bound to concentrate. One prince is specialized to housing; another devotes his attention to industrial

> welfare; hospitals, the boy scouts, homes for aged miners, the retraining of the unemployed, the value of the settlement movement, all receive their due meed of attention. And since every item of royal activity is blazoned forth by every device that modern publicity can utilize, there is an awareness of this activity different in quality from anything the Victorians knew. *The monarchy, to put it bluntly, has been sold to the democracy as the symbol of itself.* [Emphasis added][25]

Laski's account of the gradual transformation of the British crown around the turn of the century could apply to the Japanese monarchy, with the more radical disruption of the surrender, after August 1945. Crown Prince Akihito would learn of King George V's strategy for identifying with ordinary people through reading, under Koizumi's stewardship, Nicolson's biography of the king.

Second, whereas in Japan the war years had resulted in further elevation of the emperor "above the clouds," in Britain the war pushed the British royal family further toward the people. Throughout the German Blitz, King George VI and Queen Elizabeth left the relative safety of Buckingham Palace to inspect the damage caused by the relentless German bombings. They also regularly toured the country to encourage their countrymen to carry on the fight until total victory was achieved. These sorties brought the king and queen into close personal contact with the people on an especially regular basis; this had not been the norm before the war.[26]

Third, in spite of the remarkable unity forged between the British royal house and the people as a result of the victorious war, the monarchy retained quite an aristocratic flavor. It was only in 1957, for example, that the queen, under public criticism, discontinued the practice of hosting debutante presentation balls. These parties, which had served to initiate young upper-class women into society, were replaced with garden parties to which people broadly representative of British society were invited.[27]

Japanese commentators' expectations of the extent to which Crown Prince Akihito would become a man of the people were somewhat restrained. An article in the 5 May 1953 *Asahi shinbun*, referring to rumors that the crown prince would become engaged after his return, noted that "it was commonly thought" that a marriage partner would be selected from among the former aristocracy. After all, Elizabeth II had married a prince, Philip of Greece, in 1947. The British royal family long had been part of a transnational royalty that intermarried, however, and Philip's foreign origins were no impediment. In contrast, the Japanese royal house did not have a history of intermarriage with continental royal houses, and there was never much chance that Akihito would marry someone who was not Japanese.

The welcome that Crown Prince Akihito received at both the popular and the official levels during his stops in the United States on the way to and from Europe reassured the Japanese. Friendly crowds greeted the crown prince wherever he went, and President Dwight Eisenhower hosted him at the White House. The crown prince enjoyed an overnight stay at the home of his former tutor, Elizabeth Vining, as well as a week riding horses in Wyoming with Harry Brenn and Bruce Brenn, two brothers to whom he had been introduced by Vining in 1950.[28] Vining believed that contact with Western teenagers living in Japan would help prepare the crown prince for his future role on the international stage.

There were advance signs that his welcome in Britain would not be so warm. Some protests spearheaded by groups of former prisoners of war took place. Journalist Shimada Tatsumi, citing an unnamed British source, myopically suggested that anti-Japanese feelings among the British people resulted from a particular feature of British culture: "Unlike Americans, the British character does not allow them easily to let bygones be bygones."[29] Two public statements by British leaders effectively ended the protests against the crown prince's visit before Akihito's arrival. Prime Minister Winston Churchill, who later hosted Akihito for a private meeting, reminded his countrymen that the crown prince had been only a boy when the war ended. Then, even more important, Queen Elizabeth II let it be known that she, too, intended to meet with Crown Prince Akihito in private, separate from the coronation ceremony. After the queen's statement, public protest ended.

Coverage of the crown prince's trip in the Japanese mass media included remarks about Japan's status in the world, a concern of Japanese commentators throughout the modern era. One article called Japan a "fourth-class country,"[30] suggesting that the Japanese had made little progress since General MacArthur gave the subjugated nation this label just days after the surrender. The contrast with the Britain on display at Queen Elizabeth II's coronation could not have been greater. Historian

David Cannadine described Elizabeth II's 1953 coronation as Britain's last great imperial event linking the monarchy and the empire:

> The last great ceremony in this sequence, successfully conflating monarchy and empire, stressing stability in an age of change, and celebrating the continuity of Britain as a great power, was the coronation of Elizabeth II in 1953. For it was still avowedly an imperial occasion, with the queen's dress containing embroidered emblems of the dominions, with regiments of Commonwealth and colonial troops marching in procession, with the prime ministers of the Dominions and India present in the Abbey, and an assortment of heads of state from various exotic colonial protectorates. At the time, it seemed as though the threats and challenges of the war and austerity period had been surmounted: the empire was still largely intact; the problem of Indian independence and republican status within the Commonwealth had been triumphantly resolved; Churchill was back at 10 Downing Street; Britain had once more asserted her place as a great power; there was a new Elizabethan age around the corner. All this was not only implicit, but was self-consciously articulated at the time of the coronation.[31]

Britain's empire would soon fall apart, but memories of imperial glory continued to soothe the national psyche for decades.

In contrast, virtually overnight the Japanese had to adjust to the fact that their country was no longer a great power and had little hope of becoming one soon. It took the British far longer to bring themselves to this unpleasant conclusion. Whereas in the postwar era the Japanese imperial house distanced itself from Japan's former colonies, whose people still harbored bitter memories of colonial brutalities, the British monarchy clung to the splendor of the empire. As a result of the cataclysmic nature of Japan's defeat, nothing like the Commonwealth, which links Britain's former colonies under the leadership of the queen, could have developed in Japan. The terms of the surrender limited Japan's territory to the home islands, which were themselves occupied until 1952. Japan's international stature withered to its lowest point in the modern era of nation-state competition. The reporters who accompanied Crown Prince Akihito were pleasantly surprised that European views of Japan were not necessarily as bad as the Japanese feared: "Wherever we went, we did not in the least experience that humiliating feeling of viewing ourselves as fifth-class people that we had experienced immediately after the defeat. Since gaining independence, the position and power of Japan is on the mend."[32]

As is the case with many imperial performances, Crown Prince Akihito made few public statements during his trip. This made his comment to reporters after he emerged from the United Nations in New York City all the more prominent:

> My visit to the United Nations was one of the most important events in my entire trip. When I saw the inside of the United Nations, it made a deep impression; at the same time, as an individual Japanese, I felt a strong desire well up in my heart for the day that my homeland of Japan will join this symbol of world peace, the United Nations, to come as soon as possible.[33]

Crown Prince Akihito made this mildly political statement, which was almost surely a performance staged by his advisors, at one of his last stops. It linked him and Japan to the United Nations, which was an important symbol of peace for the Japanese. (After re-establishing diplomatic relations with the Soviet Union in 1956, Japan gained entry to the United Nations.)

Most of the Japanese—at least if one is to believe the impressions conveyed in the mass media—felt relief and joy at the crown prince's success in representing a New Japan to the world. Even so, a professor at Gakushūin University, Shimizu Ikutarō, who had already criticized the "Get out of Asia" nature of the crown prince's trip, sought to make a point about how Akihito should be treated at home in democratic Japan. On 7 July, while the crown prince was still abroad, Shimizu raised a question in a faculty meeting of the Department of Economics and Politics. Should the crown prince, a student in the department, be allowed to advance with his classmates, since he had missed so many classes as a result of his trip? This incident continued to be a sensitive issue at Gakushūin University when I probed it a half-century later, but apparently enough professors agreed with Shimizu's concerns that the president of the university, Abe Yoshishige (1883–1966), was forced to intervene. After a lengthy process of internal review and negotiation with the palace, university officials decided that the crown prince, instead of repeating a year, would advance with his class but only as an auditor.

Therefore he would not receive a university diploma. In fact, Akihito never officially graduated from Gakushūin University.

This incident is largely unknown in Japan. For reasons that are still unclear, the national newspapers published only the most minimal and vague coverage of this story. The weeklies ignored it. It is possible that the Imperial Household Agency successfully applied informal pressure on the mainstream mass media to tread gently on the issue. One possible explanation for the paucity of coverage was that the mass media either considered it ungentlemanly to dramatize the controversy at Gakushūin or did not see it as the sort of event that would interest readers in the way that the crown prince's engagement to a commoner later did. In any case, the crown prince's encounter with equality in the university never was interpreted widely for its symbolic meaning in the context of the new, democratic Japan. It did serve to make self-appointed defenders of the throne's dignity, such as Mayuzumi Toshirō (1929–97) and Fujishima Taisuke (1937–97), a secondary school classmate of Akihito, suspicious of Shimizu, who would later became a resolute supporter of the throne. In a roundtable discussion two decades after the incident, Mayuzumi and Fujishima castigated Shimizu for his role in having caused trouble for the crown prince when Akihito was a college student.[34]

Another spokesman for the far right, Satomi Kishio (1897–1974), was appalled by such democratic treatment of imperial family members. Satomi held a doctorate in law and was the head of his own research center, appropriately named the Satomi Research Institute. In his 1954 *Nihon no minshushugi* (Japan's democracy), Satomi noted, with annoyance, that "democracy has become the national polity (*kokutai*) of before."[35] Satomi meant that democracy was the new sacrosanct civic religion, and its legitimacy was not open to question, just as the cult of the emperor had been beyond question in Imperial Japan.

Satomi expressed disgust with the "rough language" used by the Japanese in referring to the imperial house in the postwar era. Citing the term "human emperor" (*ningen tennō*), he criticized the tendency of some Japanese to "treat the emperor like a friend." Such people, Satomi pointed out, justified this practice with Fukuzawa Yukichi's celebrated statement: "Heaven never created a man above or below another man."[36] Satomi allowed that it was fine to hold such utopian opinions, but he reminded readers that in the end society was hierarchical, and "the emperor is of superior rank and the people of inferior rank." He noted with distaste that the "crazy" system constructed by MacArthur created the illusion that the emperor was inferior to the people.[37] Satomi's concern for the declining dignity of the throne was shared by many conservatives.

An Imperial "Love Match"

Most Japanese citizens were enthralled with Crown Prince Akihito's engagement to Shōda Michiko (1934–) in 1958. Their love was said to have blossomed on the tennis courts of Karuizawa, the resort where they first met. Under the Meiji system, imperial family members were legally restricted to choosing their marriage partners from the aristocracy. The crown prince's choice of someone from outside the former aristocracy—a "commoner"—was welcomed enthusiastically by the growing middle class, which had benefited from the postwar system provided for by the constitution. The love match served to wed the imperial house to the Postwar Constitution and further wed the people to the imperial house and the postwar polity.

Akihito's choice of a commoner did not come as a total shock. This possibility had been discussed previously. In *Windows for the Crown Prince* (which was read widely in translation in Japan), Elizabeth Vining described how in the early 1950s the crown prince's advisors were already devising broad principles to guide the selection of a crown princess: "The principle was established that character, rather than pedigree, was the primary essential."[38] In a 1955 meeting of the Liberal Party's constitutional committee, Nakasone Yasuhiro made a prescient statement about the qualifications a proper bride for the crown prince should have:

> In the case of the Crown Prince's marriage it is obsolete to think that his wife must be a graduate of the Peer's [S]chool (Gakushūin) or a blood relative of a prince or above. To put it frankly, I think that even a daughter of a country farmer is well qualified to become Crown Princess if she is intelligent and healthy, worthy of respect as a representative Japanese.[39]

Nakasone also suggested that the Imperial House Law should be changed to allow women to occupy the throne. He argued that this would be in accordance with the constitutional principle of equality. Japan's Imperial

House Law, which can be changed by a majority vote in the Diet, continues to restrict the throne to men of patrilineal imperial lineage. In the postwar era, several constitutional monarchies, including Sweden and Denmark, revised their constitutions to allow for queens to reign. Of the ten surviving European monarchies in 2019, two were headed by queens (the number was three until Queen Beatrix abdicated in 2013), and although a king reigns in Sweden, the heir to the throne is the crown princess.

No imperial performance in the decades after the war captured the imagination of the Japanese more than Crown Prince Akihito's wedding to Michiko. Thus it is especially worth stressing that the ceremonies, including the Shinto rites, and pageantry that now characterize imperial weddings in Japan are a distinctly modern construct. Although Emperor Meiji never formally wed in the Western sense (or in the modern Japanese sense) of the term, the government nonetheless staged a silver anniversary celebration for him and the empress in 1894.[40] The occasion was just too good an excuse for a demonstration of imperial pageantry for the government to let it pass uncommemorated. However, as was customary at the time (and throughout premodern Japan), Emperor Meiji made no particular secret of his practice of sleeping with numerous concubines in residence at the court throughout his reign. Indeed, Emperor Taishō was the son of a concubine, a fact that came as a great shock to Hirohito when he learned of it. In 1900, when he was still the crown prince, Emperor Taishō became the first emperor for whom a lavish wedding ceremony was staged.[41] Crown Prince Hirohito's wedding ceremony in 1924, like the one staged two decades earlier for his father, was an international event. Thus Akihito's grand wedding festivities were only the third such ceremony staged by the imperial house and government, and all of them took place in the twentieth century.

It is doubtful that the majority of people living in the Japanese archipelago would have known of an imperial union during, for example, the Tokugawa era, and they certainly would not have had access to the bust and waist sizes of the princess via a weekly magazine bought at a train station, as was possible in 1958. Crown Prince Akihito's engagement was followed by a flood of commentary without precedent in Japanese history, both in volume and in tone. Nor would people in the Tokugawa era, not to mention the prewar era, have been questioned at length about their feelings about the engagement. The practice of regular polling of popular opinion about the monarchy developed only after Japan's surrender in 1945. Polling has proved important to the monarchy in that it creates a discourse about the meaning of the monarchy, or what the monarchy should symbolize, that in turn shapes the monarchy.

Although the basic goal of the 1959 festivities—reaching out to the people—was no different from that of the emperor's tours immediately after the war, the context had changed greatly. The atmosphere in the Japan of 1959 was, in a word, hopeful. In 1956, the government, citing statistics that indicated that the economy had recovered to prewar levels, declared the postwar era over. Between 1955 and 1973, Japan's gross national product grew at a remarkable annual rate in excess of 10 percent, and 1955 is often referenced as the year the dramatic social transformation of Japan commenced. By 1959, many Japanese enjoyed a measure of prosperity; a large "new middle class" of urban white-collar employees of corporations had emerged. The so-called metropolitan culture also was extending rapidly outward to the countryside, and the economic and cultural gap between urban and rural areas would narrow dramatically in the coming decades. Scholars stress that the extension of metropolitan culture throughout the archipelago—the thorough massification of culture—was one of the most profound societal transformations of the postwar era.[42]

In 1959, the Japanese looked forward to a bright future symbolized by the romantic wedding of the young crown prince and his beautiful commoner bride. At 2:30 in the afternoon of 10 April, which had been declared a special national holiday, a very traditional-looking, horse-drawn open carriage transported the newly married Crown Prince Akihito and Crown Princess Michiko along an 8.8-kilometer route through the streets of Tokyo to their new home. Greeting the newlyweds were more than 530,000 spectators. At a time when automobiles and the subway were the reigning modes of transportation in Tokyo, the horse-drawn carriage slowly and majestically wound its way through central Tokyo, as Crown Prince Akihito and Crown Princess Michiko gently waved to the wildly cheering onlookers. According to one commentator, the carriage looked "like a toy."[43]

Nothing symbolized the nature of the wedding festivities better than the parade, which was staged to delight the people. The parade, includ-

FIGURE 22. A horse-drawn carriage transported Crown Prince Akihito and Crown Princess Michiko around downtown Tokyo for the parade celebrating their wedding on 10 April 1959. Both the parade and the horse-drawn carriage were modeled on British practices. (Photograph courtesy Kyodo Photo Service.)

ing the horse-drawn carriage, was modeled on British practices.[44] As English historian David Cannadine points out, the British monarchy's use of anachronistic modes of transportation in the twentieth century has added splendor to royal pageantry and heightened impressions of the royal house as traditional. In Japan the use of a carriage by Akihito and Michiko in 1959 augmented the feeling of the wedding's "traditionality" for some observers while striking others as chicly Western. In any case, the carriage has no precedent in premodern Japan, when a closed palanquin would have been used to transport imperial family members.

To capture Crown Prince Akihito and Crown Princess Michiko's wedding parade for live transmission on television, 108 cameras were positioned along the route. An estimated audience of fifteen million people, many of whom had purchased televisions just to see the celebrations, watched at home. Even many Japanese who lived within easy walking distance of the parade route chose to watch the parade on television, which provided coverage of it from beginning to end.[45] The percentage of Japanese families owning televisions was approaching 50 percent. By means of television, millions of Japanese citizens across the nation experienced a sharpened sense (compared with listening simply on the radio) of "participating" in a grand imperial performance.

Television, although pushing radio aside as the preferred medium for live coverage, did not displace the print media. Togashi Junji's 1958 account of life in the palace, *Chiyodajō* (Chiyoda Palace), became a best-seller as a result of the public interest in the wedding.[46] The weeklies flourished as well, experiencing their greatest success in the years just before the nearly universal extension of television ownership eclipsed some of their attraction. In 1958, the top weekly, *Shūkan asahi*, had a circulation of 1.3 million.[47] The first issue of *Josei jishin* (Women's own), which came to exemplify the weeklies' obsessive coverage of the imperial family, appeared in December 1958, between the engagement and the wedding ceremony. Devoting the majority of its pages to articles about Michiko, *Josei jishin* was an immediate success among young women. The newsworthy arrival of Michiko on the imperial scene makes it impossible to examine the imperial house as first and foremost a male institution and simply to footnote information about the empress or princesses. Unlike her mother-in-law, Crown Princess Michiko was to play a prominent public role, a fact that is sometimes cited as contributing to the reputed tension between Empress Nagako and Michiko.

Articles in *Josei jishin* and other weeklies provided readers with intimate information about Akihito and Michiko. An article titled "Karuizawa no kōtu de" (On the courts of Karuizawa), published in the *Sandē mainichi* in December 1958, is representative. The article began by telling the story of how Akihito and Michiko met on the tennis courts and revealed that Akihito's mixed doubles team had lost to Michiko's on occasion. The article quickly moved into an up close and personal description of Michiko, beginning with her physical features: height: 160 centimeters; weight: 50 kilos; bust: 82 centimeters; waist: 56 centimeters; hips: 92 centimeters; and neck: 37.6 centimeters.[48] Michiko's biography from birth to present was recounted. The article concluded with an interpretation of the forthcoming wedding's significance:

> The crown prince selected a princess from among the people. It appears that there was a movement among one faction in opposition to this. However,

> both of them love and respect each other from their hearts, and if they become Japan's ideal couple and establish a model home life, then for their countrymen there could be no happier thing.
>
> The crown prince and Michiko themselves probably are thinking that they will become the symbol of a Japanese couple. As a result of the crown prince's making a democratic engagement, one can say that Japan's democratization was advanced one step.[49]

The theme of democracy recurs over and over in popular accounts of the marriage. By 1959, a process begun in 1945 to remake the imperial house to suit a New Japan had produced a young imperial couple interpreted as embodying the essential spirit of democratic Japan.

Public fascination with Crown Prince Akihito and Crown Princess Michiko continued long after the wedding. Akihito was determined to establish a home for his children, in contrast to his experience of living apart from his parents. In a press conference soon after the engagement, Akihito stated his plan "to separate public duties from private life in his marriage."[50] Michiko was equally determined to raise their children. The mass media would come to represent the young imperial couple as an ideal nuclear family, but the "nuclearization" of Akihito and Michiko's home followed a different path from that of other families. It resulted more from Akihito and Michiko's insistence on raising their own children than from a decision on their part to live separately from Hirohito and Nagako; there was never much chance that they would share living quarters with the emperor and empress. In contrast to the situation of many married couples in Japan, there was no expectation that the crown prince and princess would have to make space in their own home to care for their aging parents.

The young couple established a family with the birth of Prince Naruhito on 23 February 1960. The birth proved to be another great media event. The weeklies continued to supply tantalizing details about the new couple and "Baby Naru." As would later be the case with Princess Diana and the British royal family, Michiko's greatest impact on the imperial house as crown princess resulted from her authority over her children, two sons and a daughter. She endeavored to provide them with something of a normal childhood, including a home life. Michiko shocked some of the old guard by personally nursing and rearing her chil-

FIGURE 23. Crown Prince Akihito and Crown Princess Michiko with their firstborn, Prince Naruhito (the heir to the throne), in June 1961. Public interest in the young couple was immense, and the mass media supplied countless images of the "ideal family." (Photograph courtesy Kyodo News Service.)

FIGURE 24. Crown Princess Michiko in the kitchen, on her twenty-seventh birthday (16 Oct. 1961). Although such photographs were part of a cleverly orchestrated campaign to make the home of the young crown prince and princess appear to be ordinary, it is true that Akihito and Michiko broke with imperial tradition by insisting on keeping their children in their home to raise them. (Photograph courtesy Kyodo News Service.)

dren, a task that included stints at cooking in the the small family kitchen she had installed in the Tōgū Palace.

In terms of gender roles, Akihito never could be the prototypical salaryman diligently laboring to further his company's interests, or the national interests through those of the enterprise, but he was officially charged with carrying out the important duty of representing Japan in various capacities. Michiko was the deferential wife and full-time homemaker. At the time, the goal for many women who had to work in the field or factory was not to develop an independent career but to become a full-time homemaker, the wife of a middle-class salaryman. The publication of pictures of Michiko wearing an apron in the kitchen drove home the theme, stressed since the end of the war, that the imperial family was just like other families in Japan.

Akihito and Michiko advanced the "family-ization" of the imperial house by establishing a home that came across as middle class. Depending on how the question was phrased, in the 1960s more than 90 percent of the Japanese queried in public opinion polls identified themselves as belonging to the middle class. This compression hardly seemed justified in light of the economic disparities in Japanese society (although inequalities had narrowed significantly in comparison with prewar society), but it did reflect the broad extension of consumer culture, as increasing numbers of people gained the economic power to fulfill more than their basic needs. During the late 1950s and especially the 1960s, a decade when the national income more than doubled, Japan underwent rapid social change.

As a result of the economic growth of the late 1950s, the homes of the average middle-class housewife and the crown princess did share many of the same electrical appliances. Since in the 1960s many Japanese began to define democracy in terms of economic equality, one should not underestimate the symbolic significance of the fact that average housewives could take satisfaction in their access to the same appliances as the crown princess. Equality in electrical appliances perhaps served to dampen class divisions. As Crown Prince Akihito and Crown Princess Michiko saw in their cleverly choreographed and wildly popular visit to a modern public apartment complex (*danchi*) in 1960, not only electric rice cookers and TV sets but also washing machines and even refrigerators were increasingly within reach of the salaryman class. Electric appliances greatly reduced the amount of time and effort required, typically of women, to perform various household tasks such as laundry, one of the many social changes that were to change greatly the lifestyle of the Japanese.[51]

At times, the weeklies were so bold in their coverage as to needle the crown prince. The 5 September 1960 issue of *Shūkan shinchō* carried an article titled "Your Imperial Highness, Your Pants Are Too Large."[52] An expert tailor, called on to judge the crown prince's pants, ruled that they were indeed too large (was the title meant to suggest that the crown prince was getting too big for his britches?). This light treatment of the heir to the throne infuriated self-appointed defenders of the imperial house's dignity. Decades later, far-right commentators continued to cite this article as marking the onset of the decline of the imperial house's dignity.

Crown Prince Akihito's wedding took place almost fifteen years after the end of the war, and it provided a perfect opportunity for commentators to evaluate what was new, and what was traditional, about the postwar monarchy. With the exception of writings from the far right, the use of the term *kokutai* to champion imperial sovereignty was virtually absent from this discourse.

Correctly or incorrectly, many people interpreted Koizumi Shinzō, who had directed the crown prince's education, as having orchestrated Akihito's marriage to a commoner. Koizumi continued to link Fukuzawa and the throne. Interviewed by a popular weekly about the significance of Akihito's engagement to Michiko, Koizumi reminded readers of Fukuzawa's famous saying to which the far-right commentator Satomi so strenuously objected: "Heaven never created a man above or below another man."[53] As incompatible as this adage may seem to be with a hereditary royal house, it nonetheless captured the democratic image that Koizumi and other supporters of the postwar order sought to attach to the monarchy.

Shortly after the crown prince's marriage in 1959, Koizumi, in response to a letter he had received, explained why he had decided to devote so much of his time with Crown Prince Akihito to Nicolson's account of King George V.[54] After mentioning that he selected it in part simply because it was the most recent biography of a constitutional monarch, Koizumi listed several other reasons he had chosen the book.

FIGURE 25. Crown Prince Akihito and Crown Princess Michiko visiting a public apartment complex in September 1960. Note the laundry hanging from balconies in the background. Far more at ease than his father in informal situations that brought him into contact with his countrymen, Akihito also profited from Michiko's astute sense of how to win the people's hearts. (Photograph courtesy Kyodo News Service.)

FIGURE 26. On the day of Crown Prince Akihito's wedding, Koizumi Shinzō, director of the prince's education, and Elizabeth Vining, the prince's English-language tutor from 1946 to 1950, answer questions at a press conference. Not only was Vining a pacifist, but Koizumi's face was burned severely during a wartime air raid. This latter point is worth mentioning because Koizumi's scars likely served as one of numerous reminders to the crown prince of the war's cost to Japan. (Photograph courtesy Kyodo Photo Service.)

The first summed up Koizumi's broad goal, and it is worth quoting in its entirety:

> First, because [George V] was a king faithful to his duty. He was no genius or hero, and during his quarter-century reign there was probably not one example of him doing something brilliant that surprised people. Nonetheless, during the long months and years of his reign, the English people felt secure and peaceful because the king and the royal line were there. The twenty-five years of his reign were twenty-five years of turbulence and change, but nonetheless the English people did not lose the feeling of stability; the king's constant fidelity and conviction played a role in this. I thought that it would be good if the crown prince studied [the example of King George V].[55]

King George V was the first British monarch to have personal contact with the people through regular radio broadcasts. This innovation, dating from 1932, is one of the ways the British monarch continues to reach out to the citizens of Great Britain. It was one of several techniques designed to tighten the bond between the throne and the people that Akihito learned of under the guidance of Koizumi.

Among essays that appeared during the crown prince and princess craze of 1958–60, no other was discussed more widely among intellectuals than Matsushita Keiichi's "The Emperor System of the Masses." At the time, Matsushita was a young professor of European political thought at Hōsei University. He emphasized that whether people reacted to the engagement either positively or negatively, it was impossible to be indifferent to the spectacle. Matsushita argued that "the crown prince has become 'our crown prince'" (*kōtaishi wa "warera no kōtaishi" to natte shimatta*). He interpreted the wedding not as a private affair of the imperial house but as an event central to the postwar political system.

Matsushita noted that the eyes of the nation had focused on the imperial house with the appearance of a commoner (*heimin*) princess who became engaged to the crown prince as result of love (*koi*). Her status as well as the love-match nature of the engagement symbolized equality and liberty, core values of the Postwar Constitution embraced by the growing middle class. In a later essay in which he clarified his theory, Matsushita noted that in rural areas, still home to nearly half of Japan's population, the reaction among the older generation toward the love match was not so positive because elders worried that their own children would want to emulate the crown prince by seeking marriage partners on their own rather than waiting for their parents to arrange introductions to appropriate prospective spouses. Their concern was well founded, for Matsushita also reported that representatives of village youth groups expressed delight with the engagement precisely because it provided support for the right of individuals to select their own marriage partners on the basis of love.[56] One must understand that the concept of marriage based on love was accepted even less in the countryside than in the urban areas, where it was still somewhat novel.

Matsushita sympathized with opponents of the emperor system. The engagement occurred when many Japanese continued to see the monarchy through the lenses of the prewar absolutist emperor system. For example, social critic Murakami Hyōei (1923–2003) was skeptical of the nature of the public's reaction to the crown prince's engagement.[57]

Matsushita quoted Murakami as having written in disbelief about the frenzied popular reaction: "When the whole world has gone crazy, a sane person appears mad." Matsushita would remind readers on several occasions that for many people "the present emperor as an individual remains tied to memories of Shōwa fascism and the Pacific War."[58] In his later essay, Matsushita matter-of-factly remarked that the myth glorifying the emperor's decision to end the war saved Hirohito, as an individual, after Japan's defeat.[59]

In spite of Hirohito's ties to Imperial Japan, Matsushita interpreted the "wedding boom" as marking the final nail in the coffin of the prewar emperor system, not as a sign of its revival: "The princess boom . . . is not, in Murakami's sense, the re-establishment of various old things with new cosmetics; rather, isn't it that, according to the new cosmetics, various old things have suffered a blow? The 'love-match commoner princess' boom surely is premised solely on the new constitution."[60] Matsushita argued that the excitement about the commoner princess marked the maturation of the "monarchy of the masses," a new version of the emperor system or monarchy:

> The monarchy presently reviving of course is not absolutist, nor is it a limited monarchy along the lines that developed in Europe in the nineteenth century and was sought after in Japan during the period of Taishō Democracy [1920s]. While transforming into a monarchy of the masses, the imperial house is absorbing new energy from the cheers of the people.[61]

Matsushita stressed that Japan's postwar monarchy was by no means the only royal house ever to have been "supplied nutrition" from the masses in a democratic society. He cited the cases of various European monarchies, including that of Britain at the end of the nineteenth century and especially in the early twentieth century.

Matsushita, who was himself no champion of the throne, called for critics of the emperor system to recognize the "postwarness" of the monarchy. In the section "From Living God to Star," Matsushita examined the younger generation's overwhelmingly positive reaction to the engagement. One college woman said, "I still have hope since the crown prince's younger brother [Prince Masahito (1935– ; also known as Prince Hitachi)] remains available."[62] Matsushita commented: "This is surely the first time in Japan's modern history that every class could have the consciousness that 'the crown prince's younger brother remains available.'"[63] Matsushita argued that imperial family members had become stars affectionately regarded by the people: "The imperial house is no longer something feared and has become something respected and loved (*keiai sareru*)."[64]

He described the change in the strategy for managing the throne from the prewar era to the postwar period as a movement to make imperial family members objects of popular affection:

> Under the absolutist emperor system until now, the emperor, while occasionally acting benevolently, was, as a living god always to be feared, beyond the clouds. . . . If you imagined the emperor's portrait in the "enclosed altar" (*hōanden*),[65] that was enough. However, the emperor after the surrender has assumed the "suit [and tie] figure." His picture even is taken among his family. The crown prince falls while skiing, and even loses to girls at tennis. Isn't that something to be loved? This change in the atmosphere surrounding the imperial house *is more important than the constitutional change in the emperor's position.* (Emphasis added)[66]

Matsushita stressed that in their new roles, imperial family members were subject to the same close scrutiny that movie stars had to endure. The weeklies published virtually any detail they could learn about the imperial family.

Matsushita interpreted the contests staged by weeklies to find women who looked like Michiko or who shared her birthday as reinforcing the consciousness among young women that "I, too, am Michiko." Under the new constitution, after all, the legitimacy of the monarchy was based on the will of the people. Matsushita pointed out that the engagement was rife with irony: "The crown prince has become a symbol of postwar democracy—of the new constitution. This is ironic, since it contradicts . . . the Kishi Cabinet's policy of constitutional revision. On the other hand, the young generation which until now had been indifferent to the imperial house has been enveloped in the boom."[67] While at several points employing Bagehot's writings on the monarchy in a positive manner, Matsushita called into question Bagehot's assertion that it was the "vacant many" who dwelled on the throne: "The young generation that displays the most enthusiasm for the crown princess is, in the case of Japan, the most rational class."[68]

Matsushita interpreted the engagement as symbolizing a change in the predominant social class: "A commoner princess was the last straw; as a result, the ruin of the old nobility and the maturation of the capitalists as a class was exposed."[69] Michiko was the daughter of Shōda Hidesaburō (1903–99), prosperous founder of the Nisshin Flour Milling Company. A widely repeated remark about the engagement's significance was "The decline of Tokiwa and rise of Seishin." Tokiwa is a club for members of the former aristocracy; Seishin is the short name for Sacred Heart University. Michiko was a graduate of Sacred Heart, a women's college that catered to the daughters of wealthy families. She majored in English literature, an especially appropriate subject for an aspiring housewife at the time. Matsushita concluded that with the crown prince's engagement to the daughter of a wealthy industrialist, "One can say clearly that [this represents] the terminus in the bourgeois revolution."[70] In contrast to the Occupation reforms, "this was not something forced [on Japan] from the outside."[71]

According to Matsushita, the wedding struck a blow not only against the former aristocracy but also against the far right, which disdained Michiko's family for not knowing its proper position in society. In contrast, Matsushita noted that socialists welcomed the wedding. He quoted Suzuki Mosaburō (1893–1970), chair of the JSP, staunch defender of the Postwar Constitution, as saying: "That the crown prince himself would choose through a love-match one of his countrymen [and not someone from the former aristocracy] as his fiancée was extremely appropriate to the new constitution."[72] Matsushita interpreted Suzuki's statement as representative of the feelings of the vast majority of the people, particularly the new middle class. In his later article, Matsushita described the wedding ceremonies as a contemporary carnival geared to the new middle class that also included rituals, such as a visit by the newlyweds to Ise Shrine, meant to draw attention to the imperial house's respect for tradition.[73]

Matsushita pointed out that there were many sides to the imperial house and that these rose and fell in importance over time: "The emperor lost his political and military character and came to have a cultural and familial character."[74] According to Matsushita, this new family character was not to be confused with the prewar notion of an authoritarian, hierarchical family state (*kazoku kokka*) headed by the emperor: "The home of the crown prince is a commoner home (*katei*) based on love."[75] According to Matsushita, nothing had earned the postwar imperial house more popular support and fascination than its image as a "happy family."

Matsushita argued that the mass media, rather than being an agent of the ruling class in dictating popular reaction, was an autonomous political force that shaped the meaning of the engagement. Matsushita remarked that it was impossible to know whether the engagement between Akihito and Michiko had truly resulted from a romantic love-match. However, he stressed that for the media, it was critical that news of the engagement focus on love and the princess's commoner status. In covering the story, "the mass media *made* the imperial house suit the conditions of mass [democratic] society" (emphasis added).[76] Matsushita's stress on the mass media's autonomy stands in stark contrast to oft-repeated claims about the ongoing authority of the Imperial Household Agency to choreograph not only the public lives of imperial family members but also the manner in which events involving the family are reported.

In his later essay, Matsushita, while defending his argument that the mass media was an autonomous political force, was critical of the media for covering the engagement as though "one hundred million hearts were celebrating at once."[77] Unfortunately, in taking the media to task for their lack of diversity of coverage, Matsushita did not define explicitly what he meant by "mass media." Had he excluded the JCP's newspaper, *Akahata*, from his definition? In the United States, where the Communist Party is completely marginalized, such an exclusion would be justified. In Japan's case, however, *Akahata*, generally critical of anything to do with the imperial family, has enjoyed a mass audience throughout the post-Occupation period and has to be considered part of the Japanese mass media. To define the print mass media in Japan as limited to, say, the major national newspapers and weeklies and then to claim that the print mass media lacks diversity is a self-fulfilling manner of analysis, one of the few weak points in Matsushita's framework.

In the conclusion to his initial essay, Matsushita laid down a challenge to interpreters of the emperor system. Many left-wing critics viewed the overwhelming popular enthusiasm for the engagement as abnormal. Matsushita disagreed:

> Theories of the emperor system up until now, as typified by that of Inoue Kiyoshi, cannot address the present emperor system of the masses. The reason that the judgment of the so-called progressive critics was paralyzed as a result of the boom of 27 November was that their theoretical angle was not prepared for this emperor system of the masses. Next . . . will be the birth of a baby [to the crown prince and princess], etc., and the stories will come one after another; the phenomenon of the crown princess boom . . . is not an abnormal reaction limited to this one time.[78]

Even as Matsushita remained critical of the emperor system, he called on scholars to recognize how it had changed from the prewar era. He concluded his follow-up essay with the observation that the emperor's attending a pro baseball game (sports were a central feature of the maturing mass consumer society of the late 1950s)—the emperor together with the people—was "the epitome of the emperor system of the masses."[79] No one would ever make such a similar claim about the prewar emperor system.

Inoue Kiyoshi met Matsushita's challenge with an essay of his own in the next issue of *Chūō kōron*. Inoue argued, "On the occasion of this wedding, the plan of those who order around the mass media seems to have experienced a remarkable success in deepening the intimacy between the people and the imperial house."[80] His interpretation of the mass media's agency differed greatly from that of Matsushita. His detailed accounting of the throne's role in Japan's modern history is negative. A typical sentence reads: "The absolutist emperor system, cleverly 'sucking up' the energy of the people, crushed the People's Rights Revolution [of the 1880s]." But Inoue differed from Matsushita in particular not in his interpretation of the prewar emperor system but in his refusal to see anything new about the postwar version. Inoue's suspicions were not unwarranted, for the palace, still handicapped by the monarchy's association with the war, wanted to identify the throne with the New Japan, even though aspects of the imperial house remained unchanged from the prewar era.

Inoue seemed to downplay the significance of the postwar institutionalization of popular sovereignty. He called into question whether, for example, it was so unusual for the people to refer to "our crown prince." According to Inoue, when Crown Prince Hirohito married in 1924, there was talk of "our crown prince" and "our regent." In fact, for a few years in the 1920s, the imperial handlers had attempted, by relaxing restrictions on press coverage and devising events that brought Crown Prince Hirohito into closer contact with the people, to project a slightly more informal, popular image of the imperial house. Moreover, the concept of the emperor belonging to the people dates back to the Popular Rights Movement of the 1880s. This principle was invoked periodically in the 1930s by right-wing ideologues to justify violent attacks on government officials who putatively stood between the emperor and the people. Inoue was skeptical about claims that the people somehow owned the imperial house: "In reality, isn't it the case that the people belong to the imperial house? What did the so-called imperial house that 'came to belong to the people' actually do for the people?"[81]

Inoue insisted that "there was nothing democratic about this wedding." He pointed out the inferior status of women in the imperial house. Only men could ascend to the throne, after all. Inoue criticized the mass media and Matsushita for putting forth a false image of the imperial house:

> Isn't the way of thinking that "the emperor lost his political and military character, and came to have a cultural and family character" no more than an illusion transmitted to the people by the mass media and Matsushita? With that image transmitted . . . [the LDP and its masters, the monopoly capitalists,] will make the emperor, who is nothing more than a symbol under the present constitution, the head of state and bring to the surface the latent political and military character of the emperor, even if this will not bring about the reappearance of the absolutist emperor system; in short, it is very important and clever preparation for constitutional revision for the worse.[82]

Inoue went on to argue that generating public support for the wedding was part of a plan by the ruling class to change the constitution not only to make the emperor the head of state but also to reestablish conscription, permit nuclear armament, truncate the rights of the people, and reinstitute the paternalistic family system that had been legally abolished during the Occupation. The experience of the war had left Inoue, as it had so many Japanese citizens, acutely suspicious about the intentions of the state, especially when the monarchy was involved. Inoue rejected claims that the "emperor system of the masses" was anything new and painted a sinister picture of the throne, as he interpreted its role throughout most of Japanese history, continuing to serve as the indispensable crown of the ruling class. Toward the end of his essay, Inoue denied that the crown prince's wedding represented a stabilization of the emperor system and predicted that socialism eventually would sweep away the monarchy.

Backlash against the Monarchy of the Masses

Although critics such as Inoue could not accept Matsushita's claim that the monarchy had changed since the end of the war, individuals with conservative leanings were disturbed by the degradation of the throne's dignity since 1945. They cringed at the casual manner in which the throne, on occasion, had come to be treated. The conservative backlash, I think, provides evidence that Matsushita, not Inoue, was correct: the "monarchy of the masses," in certain key ways, was new.

After the war, many conservatives not only found it difficult to conceive of the imperial house as external to the political process but also decried the decline of the imperial house's dignity under the conditions of free speech protected by the constitution. The definition of "dignity" not only depended on the interpreter but also evolved during the seven decades after the war. Some champions of the throne interpreted imperial dignity as the imperial family being different from, above, the people.

In a February 1959 Diet interpellation of Usami Takeshi, director of the Imperial Household Agency, LDP Representative Hirai Giichi expressed his reservations about Crown Prince Akihito's love match to a commoner: "If the crown prince just fell in love on the tennis courts at Karuizawa, well that is no different from this representative's own children." After a neutral response by Usami, Hirai continued: "If it reaches the point of the crown prince's going to the Ginza, wanting a drink with his friends, that absolutely cannot be said to be the 'symbol' of a people. If the emperor is not like Mount Fuji [greater than all other mountains] . . . then the people will not revere him."[83] Hirai further suggested that Koizumi be replaced and the crown prince be given a reeducation. In contrast to the far rightist Hirai, Nakasone, then still somewhat younger than most LDP representatives, welcomed the crown prince's marriage to Michiko.

On several occasions after the crime of lèse-majesté was abolished, members of extreme rightist groups sought to protect the honor of the throne by violently punishing those who, in their opinion, had tarnished it. Such was the case with the Shimanaka Incident of 1960. The December 1959 issue of *Chūō kōron* carried the well-known author Fukazawa Shichirō's (1914–87) fictional short story "Fūryū mutan," or "Humorous Dream Tales." Fukazawa depicted a dream in which members of the imperial family were beheaded during a revolution. Extreme right groups such as the DaiNihon Aikokutō (led by trenchant nationalist Akao Bin) immediately voiced their outrage. Even the Imperial Household Agency threatened a libel suit, but a representative of the Ministry of Justice expressed doubt that there was sufficient basis to file a suit. In response to the threats, Fukazawa went into hiding.

Shimanaka Hōji (1923–97), president of Chūō Kōron Publishing Company, apologized to the Imperial Household Agency for having published the story. Nonetheless, on the evening of 1 February 1960, Komori Kazutaka, age seventeen, who only that morning had resigned his membership in the DaiNihon Aikokutō, broke into Shimanaka's home. Shimanaka was away that night, but Komori fatally stabbed the maid and gravely injured Shimanaka's wife. As this deadly attack showed, authors, editors, publishers, and anyone else accused of irreverent portrayals of the imperial house could face the wrath of the extreme right.

Under the Postwar Constitution, the courts have upheld, without exception, the right of free expression regarding the monarchy. Social taboos, however, have served to regulate media coverage of the imperial house. The threat of violence from the extreme right is only part of the equation that explains imperial taboos in the mass media. Many of the restrictions have been self-enforced by the mass media; it is as though there is a gentleman's agreement regarding coverage of the monarchy. At the same time, the existence, since the 1950s, of so many weeklies has changed the situation dramatically. Many weeklies have ignored the gentleman's agreement and, in the 1990s, some showed their willingness to publish anything, including stories of dubious authenticity, that made a splash and increased circulation.

In the 1960s, famous writer Mishima Yukio (1925–70) launched a challenge against the postwar symbolic monarchy that was different from the reactionary right's effort to restore the emperor's political role.

Mishima first turned his attention to the question of the emperor with his 1961 short story "Yūkoku" (Patriotism), a complex chronicle of one officer's loyalty to the throne. He continued to address the issue in his fiction with the novel *Honba* (Runaway Horses), written shortly before his suicide in 1970. His most detailed nonfiction interpretation of the monarchy is the 1968 essay "Bunka bōeiron" (In defense of culture).[84] Mishima composed his essay in the context of the widespread student protests that swept Japan in the late 1960s as they did the United States and Western European countries.

In "Bunka bōeiron" Mishima, like the politician Nakasone, argued that the true essence of the throne was not political. Although not seeking to restore the Meiji system, Mishima, unlike Nakasone, rejected the symbolic monarchy as it operated in the 1960s. Mishima insisted that the true cultural essence of the imperial house was to be found in the concept of *miyabi*, a term long associated with the imperial house. *Miyabi* is translated variously as "elegant," "graceful," "refined," or "genteel." Mishima interpreted the cultural or aesthetic conception of the emperor—*miyabi*—as (barely) surviving in such imperial practices as poetry (*waka*) festivals sponsored by the emperor. These practices, Mishima claimed, had historically served to link the Japanese cultural community. Mishima's claim may pertain to the elite, but it becomes dubious when applied broadly, since the national community is largely a product of the modern era.

Mishima insisted that as a result of the Occupation reforms, not only had the political conception of the emperor been lost, but *miyabi* had been forgotten. Whereas reactionaries sought only the reestablishment of the political conception of the emperor, no one, according to Mishima, concerned himself with restoring the true, cultural conception of the emperor. Meanwhile, the monarchy had declined to what Mishima derisively called the "emperor system of the weeklies." Mishima's biting criticism of the postwar trivialization of the emperor system particularly influenced his supporters more than did the concept of *miyabi*.

Consider the 1971 roundtable discussion involving representatives of the far right, who often referenced Mishima: literary critic Muramatsu Takeshi (1929–94), Mayuzumi Toshirō, writer Fujishima Taisuke, and Nakamura Kikuo (1919–77, a professor at Keiō University and moderator of the discussion). The conversation between these self-appointed defenders of the throne's dignity took place just a year after Mishima's suicide in the name of the emperor.[85] Muramatsu argued, "Of all the things that America did to Postwar Japan, one of the 'rudest' was to provide the crown prince with the woman tutor Vining."[86] Fujishima recounted how Vining gave the crown prince, as she did the other students she taught at the Gakushūin Middle School, an English name: Jimmy. Fujishima considered this to have been an indignity. Vining explained that one of her motivations in giving the crown prince an English name for use in class was that she "thought it would be a good experience for the Crown Prince for once in his life to be on exactly the same level as the other boys, with no title and no especial treatment at all."[87]

Fujishima suggested that the crown prince, as a result of his distorted education, was afflicted with "fungi." Fujishima perhaps used the term "fungi" to suggest how difficult it would be to eradicate the pernicious influences, including egalitarianism, to which the crown prince had been exposed. In this, Fujishima may have overestimated Vining's influence. However much Vining worked to introduce principles such as equality to the young crown prince, Akihito was well aware of his hereditary status. In one of the more famous passages in *Windows for the Crown Prince*, Vining described how she once asked all the students in her class at Gakushūin Middle School to write down, in English, what they would like to be when they grew up. Crown Prince Akihito wrote, "I shall be Emperor."[88] This simple anecdote serves as another reminder of the contradictions inherent in a hereditary royal family serving as a symbol of democracy and of the constraints in certain areas on the heir to the throne.

The far right found the crown prince's style as a young adult unsatisfactory. Fujishima thought "that the crown prince was trying too hard to be a regular person," a criticism with which Mayuzumi agreed.[89] Mayuzumi did not want the crown prince to act like a mere citizen by gathering shells at the shore with his wife in order to remain popular with the people. The composer wanted the crown prince to become "something like a person beyond comparison" (*saikō muhi mitai na kata*), as he believed Emperor Hirohito to be.[90] Mayuzumi yearned for the unambiguously hierarchical society of Imperial Japan. Fujishima expressed annoyance with Crown Prince Akihito's inability to understand why the publication by the weeklies of a photo of him and Michiko holding hands while ice skating was beneath the dignity of the throne. Although Fujishima did not specify exactly what bothered him about the photograph of Akihito and Michiko showing their affection for each other, there is little doubt that far-right critics of the crown prince believed that the monarchy's value as a symbol that encouraged countrymen to sacrifice for the good of the national community was degraded by lovey-dovey images of the future emperor engrossed in his personal relationship with his wife. Yet it was the very fact that Akihito and Michiko had the means and the leisure time to realize the "my-home" lifestyle with its stress on personal fulfillment that made them such a model couple to many young Japanese.

Nakamura noted that at the time of the imperial marriage in 1959, Mishima had criticized Koizumi. Fujishima, for his part, alleged that at a recent press conference, Michiko had lit a cigarette for a reporter. This story seems implausible, but it did not stop Mayuzumi from comparing her to a "bar hostess." In Japan, to call a woman a "bar hostess" is to label her a prostitute. The far right, in its analysis of the symbiotic relationship between the monarchy and the mass media, interpreted the young imperial couple as lowering itself for the mass media and the mass media as debasing the throne, and it held both parties responsible for the degradation of imperial dignity. Such barbs directed at the "monarchy of the masses" epitomized by the crown prince and princess should be interpreted as attacks on the postwar system itself, as denunciations of the postwar political culture of democracy.

Fujishima, who favored the reestablishment of the aristocracy, expressed dismay that there was no one "to construct the dignity of the imperial house."[91] At times, the participants, especially Mayuzumi and Muramatsu, returned to the longtime constitutional concerns of the right. Muramatsu claimed that the emperor was not legally the head of state and thus, unlike the British monarch, had no moderating right "to warn" the government. Mayuzumi argued that constitutional revision was necessary. But such concerns were secondary to the overwhelming anxiety Muramatsu, Mayuzumi, Fujishima, and Nakamura expressed about maintaining the dignity of the throne. The irony of their position, of course, is that even as they called for a dignified imperial house, these self-appointed imperial patriots reserved for themselves the right to caricature what they interpreted as the vulgarity of the crown prince and princess.

FIGURE 27. This photograph of Crown Prince Akihito and Crown Princess Michiko holding hands while ice skating disgusted some far-right observers of the throne because it made the future emperor seem all too common, hardly the type of symbol that would encourage countrymen to sacrifice for the good of the national community. (Photograph courtesy Kyodo News Service.)

In 1973, the journal *Roman* published a discussion about the emperor system involving Mayuzumi and Fujishima, who repeated many of the concerns they voiced in the 1971 roundtable discussion. Fujishima felt a sense of crisis about the emperor system "symbolized by the lifestyle of the crown prince's family as 'announced' by the weeklies."[92] He stressed: "To borrow Mishima's term, it is not 'the crown prince who is invisible' but rather the 'crown prince who is visible' that is exposed to my eyes too much."[93] Fujishima also expressed his annoyance with people like Koizumi who insisted on comparing the imperial institution to the British monarchy.

Fujishima stressed that the Japanese, in contrast to the British, would never stoop so low as to import a king from a foreign country to continue the royal line. He also found the British royal family to be too commercialized:

> If you visit Britain and go to stores next to Windsor Palace, picture postcards of the royal family are for sale. Among them are images of the queen, [her consort], and their children lined up, with a dog who is sitting, in front of a pond in their garden. They sell those types of postcards! Needless to say, the history and tradition of the British royal house and Japanese imperial house are completely different, and I think that it is better that such things—postcards and postage stamps—not be emulated, and that the unique Japanese emperor be maintained.[94]

Mayuzumi agreed totally. For champions of the imperial house's uniqueness, the British royal house represented an unacceptable model.

Although postcards showing the imperial family were not to be found in stores near the palace, the postal service occasionally did issue stamps to commemorate imperial events. In 1976, the Ministry of Posts and Telecommunications issued stamps marking the emperor's fiftieth year on the throne in conjunction with the governmental celebration of the anniversary. Far right groups had pressured the government to hold a grand celebration. The stamps did not show the emperor or empress lest their images be marred by postmarks, one example of how the definition of imperial dignity differs in Japan (the sovereign is featured on British stamps).[95] This was a minor exception to a process that saw the Japanese imperial house gradually popularized.

The Warm, Fuzzy Heisei Monarchy

Between 1986, when celebrations of the emperor's sixtieth year on the throne sparked controversy, and 1993, the year of Crown Prince Naruhito's wedding, the imperial family seemed to be constantly in the news. These events sparked a flood of writings and television coverage about the monarchy that, in sheer volume, equaled if not exceeded the media coverage of the years immediately after the war. By the 1980s, almost every Japanese home had a color television, a statistical suggestion of its societal importance. Historian Takashi Fujitani uses the phrase "electronic pageantry" to capture television's influence in transmitting and shaping imperial rites. Rites were orchestrated more with the television audience in mind than the live audience, and those who watched important imperial ceremonies at home were offered a full narrative of the day's events spliced with reports of viewer reactions.[96]

Emperor Hirohito's funeral in 1989, characterized by a tortured official effort to maintain the Shinto nature of parts of the ceremony while upholding the constitutional separation of church and state,[97] was attended by representatives from 164 countries—a figure mentioned repeatedly, usually to stress Japan's eminent position in the international hierarchy of nation-states. The message is plain: the task of modernization, begun in 1868, had been completed under Emperor Hirohito. Japan had become a great economic power, and official accounts of the miraculous development sometimes credited the monarchy for the country's prosperity. Absent from the official message were references to the monarchy's role in such unedifying periods of Japanese history as the 1930s, a decade interpreted by some as an aberration in Japan's modern development but by others as a product of modernity itself.

Emperor Akihito's accession and enthronement ceremonies (the latter also raised questions regarding the separation of church and state) continued from 1989 into 1990. Some commentators were surprised by how quickly Emperor Akihito put his personal stamp on the throne. His father had reigned so long, and so many people had come to accept the adage that the emperor was no more than a symbolic automaton, that it came as a shock to some observers to be reminded that individual emperors, while obviously subject to manipulation, can shape the throne in significant ways. Immediately on ascending to the throne, Emperor Akihito made what was interpreted to be a ringing endorsement of the

Postwar Constitution in a formal address delivered, notably, in polite but modern Japanese. He worked to wrap up the postwar by addressing, both domestically and internationally, the thorny legacies of the war. In 1995, to mark the fiftieth anniversary of the war's conclusion, the emperor and empress made symbolic visits to the three areas of Japan most victimized by the war: Nagasaki, Hiroshima, and Okinawa. On these visits as well as on numerous other occasions, Emperor Akihito has stressed repeatedly the need for peace. His apologies to neighboring countries, many of which he visited with the empress, symbolized Japan's effort to reenter Asia as a (partially) repentant and constructive player in regional politics. The emperor and empress also reformed palace practices that they considered outdated. For example, the position of "imperial stool analyzer" was abolished. Thus Emperor Akihito's stool was not subjected to analysis after each bowel movement, as was the case with his father.[98]

In the late 1980s, the Japanese imperial house saw its model, the British royal house, become something of an international laughingstock as a result of the marital infidelities of Prince Charles (1948–) and the late Princess Diana (1961–97). The influence of the British model was particularly great in the decades after the war and continued into the early 1980s. Crown Prince Naruhito was sent to study at Oxford University for two years between 1983 and 1985 as a rite of passage and later published an account of his time in Britain.[99] He was the first Japanese crown prince ever to study at a foreign university. But the scandals of the British royal family in the late 1980s provided ammunition for conservatives who had long rejected the British model. The British monarchy shifted rapidly from the status of being a paradigm to more of a negative example, duplication of which was to be avoided.

Old devaluations of the British royal line were recycled. In a 1987 discussion about the emperor, Kyoto University Professor Ichimura Shin'ichi (1925–) declared that among surviving monarchies, only in Japan did the royal house and the people remain racially inseparable. This racialist interpretation remains surprisingly strong even in the second decade of the twenty-first century. Conservative literary critic Etō Jun (1933–99) agreed with Ichimura and noted that the present British royal line was descended from King George I, a German with little command of the English language.[100] The British throne had long been a nationalistic symbol and stood at the center of British imperialism, which drew distinctions between whites and nonwhites. But it was impossible for British commentators to trumpet the throne as a symbol of British ethnic purity. After all, the German lineage of the royal line was undeniable in spite of the dynasty's adoption, during World War I, of a solidly English name: the House of Windsor. In contrast, Japanese champions of the imperial house often stressed the supposed racial purity of the throne and the Japanese people.

Japanese supporters of the throne cringed at the thought of their imperial family going the way of Prince Charles and Princess Diana. Conservative critic Kase Hideaki (1936–) rejected the validity of the British monarchy as a reference for Japan's imperial house:

> In Japan after the war, there was the opinion centered around Dr. Koizumi Shinzō that the imperial house should henceforth model itself on the British royal house. However, the histories of the British royal house and the Japanese imperial house are completely different, and I think that it is incorrect to make a model of the British royal house.[101]

Kase argued that the outrageous behavior of the British royal family in fact represented a return to this dynasty's essence:

> Recently, the scandals of the British royal house are enveloping the mass media. I think that . . . this is probably nothing more than a return to the original form of the British royal house of the past (*mukashi no honrai no eikoku ōshitsu no sugata*). The motto of the British Royal House is, as is well known, "God and My Right." According to "God and My Right" the British royal house has done selfish things to its own liking and has done so for generations.[102]

According to Kase, the self-indulgent British royal house had been reformed by Queen Victoria during the nineteenth century, but the true nature of the institution had resurfaced again with the scandals of the late 1980s and early 1990s. One could take Kase's facile interpretation of the histories of the British and Japanese monarchies further than Kase did: at roughly the same time after the Meiji Restoration the Japanese emperor's essence as symbol was perverted by his involvement with politics, the "selfish" British monarchy was rectified temporarily by Queen Victoria. By the 1990s, however, both the Japanese and British monarchies had "returned" to their essential nature: the Japanese imperial house's role was again that of a symbol, as it had been throughout most of history, and, at least according to Kase, the traditional selfishness of the British throne again was rearing its head. Since Kase invoked sexual mores to indict the British royal family for selfishness while implicitly trumpeting the moral superiority of the Japanese throne, it is worth recalling that the Japanese imperial house only recently adopted the practice of monogamy from the West.

The backlash against the British monarchy by no means indicated reactionary support for the Meiji system, however. According to public opinion polls, support for the symbolic monarchy has been consistent at around 80 percent since the 1950s. The Japanese simply hoped that their symbolic monarchy would not suffer the degradation undergone by the British throne in the 1980s and 1990s; the desire was for popularization without vulgarization.

While the value of the British model, which was a central element in Emperor Akihito's education, was under sustained attack by conservative commentators, more sophisticated interpreters of the throne found Matsushita's "emperor system of the masses" still to be the most valuable framework for analyzing the monarchy under the new emperor and empress. Emperor Akihito and Empress Michiko worked to project an informal style and reach out to the people in ways that contrasted with those of Hirohito and Nagako. For example, when Emperor Akihito is ready to read his statement at ceremonies such as the opening of the National Athletic Meet, he simply pulls the prepared statement out of his pocket. In his father's time, a courtier formally handed the statement to the emperor at the appropriate moment.

Emperor Akihito and Empress Michiko's efforts to decrease the distance between themselves and the people were especially apparent in their response to the natural disasters that struck Japan in the early years of Heisei. In January 1995, a destructive earthquake in Kobe claimed more than 6,000 lives. When Emperor Akihito and Empress Michiko (who serves as honorary president of the Japan Red Cross Society) visited Kobe, they knelt among survivors at a shelter as they sought to comfort their countrymen. Even during the tours immediately after the war, Emperor Hirohito did not kneel with his countrymen or act in a way that suggested that he truly considered himself on a par with them, a style that

FIGURE 28. After ascending to the throne in 1989, Emperor Akihito and Empress Michiko worked to narrow the distance between themselves and their countrymen. This was particularly apparent during visits by the imperial couple to victims of disasters. This July 1991 image shows Emperor Akihito and Empress Michiko meeting with people displaced by the eruption of the Mount Unzen volcano, which killed more than forty people. As many commentators noted, Emperor Hirohito and Empress Nagako would never have felt comfortable sitting among their countrymen in this manner. (Photograph courtesy Kyodo News Service.)

came easily to Akihito and Michiko. Still, the style of the Japanese imperial house remains closer to the generally reserved British royal house than to the so-called bicycle monarchies of continental Europe. It would have been news indeed if Emperor Akihito had gone for a casual bicycle ride (or stroll) in Tokyo and stopped in at a random café for a cup of coffee with his countrymen. Emperor Akihito is said to admire King Juan Carlos of Spain, but Akihito has never escorted a visiting dignitary on an impromptu visit to a bar, as Juan Carlos did for Vaclav Havel (1936–2011) during his visit to Madrid.

In the satellite age of the 1990s, every movement and gesture of Akihito and Michiko were followed and immediately analyzed. Many people, especially the victims, were moved to tears by the imperial couple's expressions of concern to victims of the Kobe earthquake. For example, Michiko, noticing that the hand of an elderly man in a wheelchair had slipped out from under a blanket, adjusted the blanket to cover

FIGURE 29. In January 1995, a terrible earthquake struck Kobe, Japan, killing more than 6,000 people. During a visit by the imperial couple to Kobe, Empress Michiko hugs a young victim while Emperor Akihito looks on. Such images led commentators to announce the arrival of the symbolic monarchy that "shakes hands and even hugs." (Photograph courtesy Kyodo News Service.)

the hand from the cold. However massified and popularized the imperial house had become under Akihito and Michiko, it was apparent that the symbolic resonance of the imperial couple, at least in their therapeutic role, remained powerful.

The 1990s was also the decade when both imperial princes found wives. Crown Prince Naruhito and Prince Akishino (1965–) were born in the 1960s, a decade characterized by dizzying economic growth rather than the militarism of the 1930s, when their father was born. The two imperial weddings in the 1990s affirmed Matsushita's theory. Following in the footsteps of their father, Akishino and Naruhito chose brides from outside the former nobility. By the 1990s, the fact that a nobility had once existed in Japan was something that most Japanese learned from school textbooks.

The popular response to the weddings was positive. Political scientist Sakamoto Kōjirō (1948–) stressed the importance of imperial weddings: "For the present emperor system, which is the emperor system of the masses, the appearance of a new princess is of course the most important aspect of the contract (*keiyaku*) between the two sides."[103] Sakamoto reminded readers that the throne's existence depended on the will of the people and even suggested that the relationship was contractual.

According to Sakamoto, the people decided whether to renew their "contract" with the monarchy depending on how they judged new princesses. Prince Akishino's selection of Kawashima Kiko (1966–) as his bride was, according to Sakamoto, an unqualified success in reaffirming the "contract between the imperial house and the people." Although a graduate of Gakushūin University, Kiko came from a far more common household than the home from which Michiko entered the imperial family in 1959. Kiko's family lived in an average apartment in Tokyo. Her father was a professor. Most important of all, she gave the impression of being the girl next door. No elements of Japanese society mounted a significant challenge to the commonness of Princess Kiko, who quickly came to play the role of model housewife and mother (to two daughters and one son).

However much conservative Japanese commentators deny similarities between the Japanese and British royal houses, the fact remains that they have much in common. Members of the British royal family have admitted how hard they work to maintain a contract with the people. Prince Philip, Queen Elizabeth II's husband, long has taken the view that "we are fighting an election every day of the week."[104] As he stressed at a press conference in Canada in 1969, "If you don't want us, then let us end it on amicable terms and not have a row about it. The future of the Monarchy depends on the national community, and if at any stage the community decides it is unacceptable then it is up to that community to change it. It is up to the people themselves."[105] Prince Philip's comment was directed to Canadians, but it obviously applied to the British people as well. Although no member of the Japanese imperial family ever has made such a frank observation about the institution's dependence on the goodwill of the people, the royal family labors to maintain its popularity.

One palace official told U.S. journalist Gale Eisenstodt that "Emperor Akihito realizes that the greatest challenge for a monarchy in a democratic society is simply to survive."[106]

The Japanese—at least those who were interested, for many Japanese were, and remain, indifferent to the imperial family—were presented another opportunity to judge the throne on the occasion of Crown Prince Naruhito's marriage to Owada Masako (1963–). Anything but average, Masako was educated at three of the world's most elite universities: Harvard (where she once worked for a professor as a research assistant for $6 an hour),[107] Oxford, and Tokyo. Among other things, she symbolized Japan's meritocracy and education society. Whereas Michiko had come from an economically prosperous family, Masako came from one that might have been upper middle class economically but which had elite cultural and educational resources (her father, Owada Hisashi [1932–], has had an illustrious career as a diplomat). The first woman with a career ever to become crown princess, Masako had earned a position in the Foreign Ministry by passing its demanding entrance examination. Fluent in English as well as German and French, she had spent much of her twenties immersed in complex negotiations over issues such as U.S. companies' access to the semiconductor market in Japan.

Crown Prince Naruhito's marriage to Masako ritualized the practice of princes choosing their brides from among the people, a custom that most of the political right had come to accept. The fact that Naruhito and Masako went on numerous dates (with more formality than most dates, to be sure) before the engagement seemed entirely ordinary to most people in Japan, not only to those living in cities but also to those in the countryside. The economic, social, and cultural divide between urban and rural areas was reduced from the chasm it had been well into the early 1950s to a small gap.

In 1958 many young women had dreamed of being Michiko, but a prolonged discussion among women as to whether Masako had made the right decision in giving up her career as an elite civil servant in the Foreign Ministry greeted her engagement to the crown prince. To young Japanese women, accustomed by the 1990s to using their considerable disposable income to support a lifestyle that included regular trips abroad (with or without their significant other), the notion of becoming a princess under the stifling supervision of the Imperial Household Agency did

FIGURE 30. Naruhito, and Masako in 1999. (Photograph courtesy Imperial Household Agency.)

not necessarily hold much attraction. At their first joint press conference after the engagement was announced, Masako recounted a promise made by the crown prince: "I will protect you for my entire life."[108]

It was a frank admission of the fact that Naruhito had needed to persuade Masako to become his bride. Twenty-nine years old at the time of the engagement, Masako symbolized the tendency of Japanese women of her generation to delay marriage, one of the many factors that has resulted in a fertility crisis in Japan and a population that began to contract in 2011 and is projected to shrink dramatically in the coming decades. The hopes expressed at the time of Masako's engagement that this modern career woman would quickly revolutionize the palace and therefore set a new model for women in Japan were wildly unrealistic in light of the limited power of a crown princess, but it has long been the case that Japanese attach to royals their own hopes.

In the late 1990s, mass media attention devoted to Crown Princess Masako came to focus on her difficulties in getting pregnant, as concern grew about the lack of an heir to the throne. Masako gave birth to Princess Aiko on 1 December 2001. Aiko is the only child of the present emperor and empress, but according to the present Imperial Household Law she is not eligible to succeed her father and in fact will lose her royal status should she marry, topics taken up later in this book.

In one important area, the commoner imperial brides of the 1990s had a crucial ally: Empress Michiko. As the first bridge between the masses and the imperial house, Crown Princess Michiko had faced disdain from Empress Nagako and resentment from the old aristocracy. Commentator Watanabe Midori, a close observer of the imperial house, noted how significant it was that Emperor Akihito and Empress Michiko hosted a dinner for Masako's parents (also present were Kiko's parents) before Masako's marriage to the crown prince: "In Michiko's time, [her parents] did not once eat a meal with the late emperor [and empress]."[109]

Even if most of the political right had learned to live with the practice of princes choosing commoner brides, commentators on the far right still found things to criticize about the monarchy. Many of the same people who had been critical of Akihito's style as crown prince rejected what the mass media called the "open imperial house" (*hikarareta kōshitsu*) under Emperor Akihito and Empress Michiko. A 1995 position paper published by the far-right Shinto Political Association warned of the danger of an "open imperial house" and "mass democracy," which could reduce the imperial house to an "object of curiosity" for "digestion" by the masses. This, the paper argued, would only benefit the rapacious commercial mass media.[110] Frankly, some elements of the Japanese mass media have become predatory. By the 1990s it had become clear that bashing the imperial house was a means for some magazines to increase sales, whether or not the reports were factual. Although the mainstream mass media generally refrained from participating in the episodes of bashing, of course it reported on them. In that sense, bashing initiated by pop weeklies nonetheless periodically shaped overall coverage of the monarchy. The debate over how to balance popularization of the throne with imperial dignity continues in Japan, as it does in Britain and other countries that have constitutional symbolic monarchies.

The imperial house's style under Akihito and Michiko affirmed, thirty years after it was first proposed, the validity of Matsushita's theory of the postwar monarchy that under the Postwar Constitution the imperial house must periodically renew its wedding vows with the people. Matsushita's theory provides a measure of negotiated agreement between the monarchy and the people; the monarchy is certainly more reactive to

FIGURE 31. During a January 2001 visit to a nursery school in Tokyo, Emperor Akihito and Empress Michiko join a dancing game with children. (Photograph courtesy Kyodo News Service.)

popular evaluations, through the agency of the mass media, of its performance than it was before 1945. But then, the monarchy had few choices but to reform its operational style to suit the environment created by the popular-sovereignty constitution and a rapidly evolving society. By selling itself as a symbol of democracy, the postwar Japanese monarchy followed the strategy most likely to ensure its survival.

The "monarchy of the masses" school acknowledges the tremendous symbolic function of the monarchy, but it also interprets the postwar monarchy as a new development in the long history of the imperial institution. As a rule, scholars who use the emperor system of the masses as an explanatory device do not trumpet the monarchy's ancient and unchanging role as a cultural symbol. Matsushita's theory correctly interprets the monarchy as an institution that is changing constantly in spite of the appearance of a timeless tradition.

CHAPTER 7

From the Heisei Era to the Reiwa Era

The reign-name system results in a different concept of time among Japanese, which is what it was designed to do. Today, almost all Japanese are thoroughly familiar with the Christian way of counting years, and in fact many use the Christian system on a daily basis. Nonetheless, the Japanese are regularly reminded of the importance of the monarch, whether by filling out an official form according to the reign-name system; simply by hearing the fact that it is Heisei 11, Heisei 21, Heisei 31, or Reiwa 1; or especially by a change in reign names. The reign-name system is a form of soft nationalism. When the new reign name, Reiwa ("Beautiful Harmony"), was announced around noon on 1 April 2019, it was as though Japan came to a stop. What followed was a discussion about the meaning and appropriateness of the new reign name.[1]

The end of an imperial era results in a flood of commentary about the reign, and commentators often ask three questions: From whence Japan? Where is Japan at the moment? And whither Japan? Some retrospectives limit themselves to the happenings of the imperial house during that reign, whereas others try to match a narrative about the evolution of Japan to a particular reign. This does not always work well, for important economic, social, cultural, and political turning points in history do not necessarily correspond to imperial reigns.

The Shōwa era lasted so long and encompassed two periods so dramatically different that it became common to reference two Shōwas, the Shōwa that was largely characterized by war (1926–45), and the postwar or peaceful Shōwa (1945–89). The Heisei era (1989–2019) was half as long as the Shōwa era. It corresponded to approximately one generation, providing no firm reason to discuss two Heisei eras. There were many fascinating developments in the imperial house during the Heisei era, but is it possible to periodize the history of Japan within the Heisei era?

FIGURE 32. Chief Cabinet Secretary Suga Yoshihide holds up a sign with the new reign name, Reiwa, 2019. (Photograph Courtesy Kyodo News Service.)

Curiously, the beginning of the Heisei era coincided with momentous developments on the international and domestic stages, namely, the end of the Cold War and the collapse of Japan's Bubble Economy. The death of Hirohito corresponded to the end of the Cold War. A significant discontinuity from the previous era is that today there are few taboos inhibiting discussion about various aspects of the monarchy.

Many imperial taboos survived well into the 1980s, only to weaken and even disappear during the Heisei era. One of these was the issue of Hirohito's war responsibility, which inhibited a broader discussion about Japan's war responsibility because broaching the topic of war responsibility opened the door to the question of imperial responsibility. As the result of the recent analysis of imperial chamberlain Kobayashi Shinobu's diary, we now have evidence that the issue of war responsibility was very much on Hirohito's mind in the years before his passing.

Nonetheless, the broader taboo remained in effect even as the emperor privately struggled. Thus, Hirohito's death, combined with the end of the Cold War, resulted in widespread reexamination of various issues related to Japan's modern history, including war responsibility and, in a broader sense, responsibility for imperialism. Emperor Akihito took a strong personal interest in trying to heal various wounds of the past, a topic discussed later.

The collapse of the Bubble Economy was traumatic, so much so that eventually the phrase "lost decades" was coined to describe the subsequent period of economic stagnation. "Lost decades" is a problematic phrase because Japan continued to evolve, including in many positive ways, during the post–Bubble Economy decades. The country became much more tolerant toward and accommodating of people with disabilities. Women won the right to pursue careers on terms approaching equality with men (in spite of the fact that by various measures of women's participation in society, Japan continues to score low). An LGBTQIA movement emerged and began to gain acceptance, although there is much work yet to be done in this area.

Nonetheless, the suffering of many Japanese during the post-Bubble era was real, and at a broader level a basic sense of social security seems to have been undermined among a large portion of the population during the Heisei era. This is one negative legacy. In addition, the economic stagnation required a rethinking of Japan's place in the world—a fact driven home in 2011 when China surpassed Japan to become the second largest economy in the world. Some of Japan's politicians continue to suffer from a hangover from the 1980s, by which I mean they have never come to terms with the fact that Japan did not go on to become a superpower and make the twenty-first century "Japan's century." The Japanese should prepare themselves going forward, as they are likely to be passed by countries like India and Brazil in terms of national economy size. This relative repositioning (rather than "decline") of Japan may be painful for some politicians, but most Japanese are more interested in quality of life issues rather than superpower status.

As the Heisei era drew to a close, the world political situation was unsettled. Might the end of the era also correspond, coincidentally, to major economic, political, cultural, and social changes? I write too close to this ending to draw any conclusions, but here are some tentative thoughts. If we end up looking back at 2018 as the year the United States abrogated its role of supporting the international system of free trade, then it is indeed possible the Heisei era will be bookended with significant global turning points. In spite of much rhetoric claiming that we are living through a momentous shift in the international order, it is nonetheless too early to judge whether this will be remembered as a major juncture. After all, well into the mid-1990s many people assumed that Japan's economy would bounce back. Only after it had still not recovered by the latter part of that decade did it become clear that 1991–92 was truly a major turning point and the economy and society had entered a new era.

When my earlier book on the monarchy in postwar Japan was published in 2001, in English, I did not imagine that soon thereafter the Japanese translation (*Kokumin no tennō*) would come to enjoy a large and loyal readership. In addition, I could not have possibly imagined that the translated version would be awarded a prize as prestigious as the Osaraji Jirō rondanshō (Osaragi Jirō Prize for Commentary presented by the *Asahi* newspaper, Japan's equivalent of the Pulitzer Prize). Over and over, Japanese have told me that "no Japanese could have written such a book about the monarchy."

I remain thoroughly unconvinced about the correctness of that statement. There are many superb Japanese scholars who write about the imperial house, many of whom I count among my friends and colleagues. What those who voiced this opinion seemed to mean was that in reference to a topic as ideologically divisive as the emperor system when I researched the book, it is sometimes useful for an outsider who has no particular stake in the issue to undertake an analysis. In terms of national history, there are occasions when it is useful for an outsider to analyze topics that are taboo or profoundly divisive for citizens of that particular nation-state. Although overall my study received a positive reception in Japan, it is with a touch of pride that I report that parts of the book aggravated representatives of the political right, whereas other parts aggravated some on the political left.

I argued that the Heisei-era monarchy represented the thorough realization of the concept of the "people's emperor." The Heisei monarchy was in its fifteenth year when the Japanese translation of my book was published. Looking back on the three decades of the Heisei era now that it has concluded, I am all the more convinced of the appropriateness of the phrase "people's emperor." Perhaps it would have been better if I had also explicitly referenced the "people's empress" as well, so important was Empress Michiko to the Heisei monarchy, but the concept of the people's emperor was intended to apply to the whole imperial family, especially those members raised under the Postwar Constitution. "People's monarchy" or "people's imperial house" also would have been appropriate terms.

The selection of "people's emperor" as the title of the earlier version of this book took place several years after I returned to the United States from conducting research in Japan. It directly resulted from a three-hour phone conversation with an American friend, John Urda, who was then in the publishing industry. Together we bounced around numerous possible titles until settling on "the people's emperor." But the seeds of this title were planted much earlier. Over and over during my field research in Japan, I bumped into examples of what I eventually called the people's emperor.

Permit me to recount one anecdote that is mildly embarrassing for me but relates well to the concept of the people's emperor. When I arrived in Japan in 1994 to research my dissertation on the monarchy in Postwar Japan, I had Japanese language skills but knew little about many aspects of the monarchy. Not too long after I began my research, Takahashi Hiroshi of Kyodo News, who had spent several years in the Imperial House Press Club, introduced me to Kyodo's representative in the Imperial House Press Club at that time. Twenty-five years later, I cannot recall the name of the young journalist, but perhaps it is just as well that he remain anonymous.

I was trying to understand the role the mass media played in transmitting and shaping the image of the monarchy, specifically the role it played as an intermediary between the imperial house and the people. I asked the young journalist the following question, which seems naive in retrospect: "Do imperial family members read any of the newspaper and magazine articles that are published about them?" The journalist was well mannered, but he had trouble suppressing a look that suggested he was surprised that someone researching the monarchy would ask a question so patently simplistic.

After he recovered his composure, he politely informed me that not only do the imperial family members read almost everything published about them, there also was a section in the Imperial Household Agency specifically charged with clipping newspaper and magazine articles and forwarding them to the appropriate imperial family members. Imperial family members regularly "perform" in public for the people. Their performances are then rated by the people, and it would be cause for concern to the family if its overall performance was judged poorly by the public. Thus, imperial family members gauge in part through the media how their performances are playing out at the popular level.

Of course, the Constitution of Japan provides the underlying framework for the people's emperor. Only in the postwar era did the basic survival of the monarchy become a question that was open to debate, along the lines of, "Shall the imperial house be maintained?" However eagerly conservative scholars might have liked to have read the constitution differently, there really is no way to wiggle around the following interpretation.

The fact that the Japanese people enjoy popular sovereignty means, in constitutional terms, that the future of the monarchy depends on the people wanting to maintain the imperial house. Hypothetically, if the Japanese people were to turn against the imperial house and insist on its abolition, elected politicians would have to respond. If elected officials initially declined to respond to the will of an overwhelming majority of the citizenry in reference to this issue, the people could then elect politicians committed to abolishing the throne. In practical terms, it would require a sustained movement at the popular level to realize the abolition of the throne. But there is no way to interpret the present constitution other than to conclude that the future of the throne rests in the hands of the sovereign people.

For this reason, the imperial house must keep its finger on the pulse of the public and operate in a way that is in tune with the wishes of the people. In 1987, Crown Prince Akihito acknowledged this during a press conference: "The present imperial house must operate as the countrymen want it to operate."[2] Akihito and his astute wife, Michiko, seemed to have embraced the concept of a people's emperor and a people's empress not simply out of necessity but also because they found it satisfying and meaningful to share various joys and sorrows with the people.

For a time in 2004, the public had a window into the complex calculations among imperial family members that normally happen behind closed doors in reference to balancing their personal hopes and aspirations with the public duties expected of them. The combination of his wife's mental breakdown and the confusion regarding Princess Aiko's (2001–) future were likely two of several factors that explain Crown

Prince Naruhito's blunt remarks during his press conference in May 2004 before leaving, alone, to attend royal weddings in Denmark and Spain: "There were developments that denied Masako's career as well as her personality."[3]

At the time, I interpreted Naruhito's remarks as an indictment of the notion that Crown Princess Masako's primary duty was to serve as a womb to produce a male heir and as a call for action to change the law to permit Princess Aiko to ascend to the throne. But in a broader sense, this incident, which soon embroiled other members of the imperial family, spoke to the question of what it means for imperial family members to serve dutifully the nation. What does it mean to be a people's emperor? The fact that Naruhito's remarks continued to reverberate for months after he made them was evidenced at Prince Akishino's (Akishino became next in line to be emperor when Naruhito became emperor on 1 May 2019) press conference on the occasion of his birthday (30 November) later that year. Akishino voiced regret that his older brother, without first conferring with the emperor, lashed out at unspecified people for denying Masako's personality.

Akishino elaborated, "Identifying what is official work is also a very difficult matter, I think. Naturally, we, members of the Imperial Household, are expected to perform a variety of duties of an official nature. As far as I am concerned, personally, I'm not going to create official jobs for my own sake. In other words, I have many things that I personally want to pursue, but whether or not they are official work is a different matter. In my view, official duties are rather passive in nature. We're going to hold this or that event, people say, and they ask us to attend them. If we think a given event is very valuable, then we accept the request as required. Personally, that's how I understand the process, and that's how I have been going about my responsibilities."[4] The latter remark came across to some, whether or not it was intended in this manner, as a rebuke of Naruhito and especially Masako for whining about limited opportunities to travel abroad.

If a television journalist seeking sound bites asked 100 average Japanese, "Do you think that the Imperial Household Agency should allow the imperial family members more freedom?," I suspect that a large majority would answer along the lines of "Yes, definitely!" Criticizing the Imperial Household Agency for over-regulating royal family members' lives became a fashionable pastime in postwar Japan. But do the Japanese people really want royal family members to do as they please while enjoying a privileged lifestyle financed by tax money?

Akishino's remark reflected the following interpretation held by many inside the palace. The reason many Japanese support the imperial house to a greater or lesser extent is that they view royal family members as unselfish people who, although they are denied a host of simple pleasures such as the freedom to take casual strolls in the neighborhood, nonetheless faithfully carry out their duties on behalf of the people and the country. The Imperial Household Agency definitely wants royal family members to be perceived as putting duty before happiness, or at the very least as not putting personal happiness before duty.

Later in 2004, during the annual press conference marking his birthday (23 December), Akihito referenced Naruhito's blunt public comments in a way that demonstrated how surprised and puzzled he was by them, even after repeatedly asking his son for an explanation. Curiously, though, without defending Naruhito's remarks, Akihito offered a critically important interpretation of public duties carried out by imperial family members that sought to reconcile interpretations offered by his sons:

> Since the Crown Prince's statement in May, there has also been much discussion about the Crown Prince and Crown Princess' official duties. I think that the statement made by Prince Akishino that "official duties are passive in nature" and the statement by the Crown Prince about "new official duties in step with a particular era" are not necessarily contradictory in nature. The Empress and I have learned during the long years since our marriage that new official duties would have very little real meaning if they did not reflect individual hopes or interests, and, at the same time, official duties could newly emerge in the course of diligently carrying out the duties of one's assignment.[5]

This comment was an admission that each emperor and empress put their particular stamp on the throne. The definition of duty evolves, and imperial family members play a role in defining their public duties. However, these public duties also must resonate with people.

One of the best ways to understand the concept of the people's emperor is to examine the opposition to it that has been expressed through examples of "bashing" the imperial house. There is a type of imperial house bashing that is fundamentally a critique of the postwar democratic system. This type of bashing periodically surfaced from the time the Occupation ended, intensified after Crown Prince Akihito's engagement to Michiko, and continues to take place today. Not all bashing of imperial family members is a critique of the democratic system (e.g., this was not the case with some of the bashing of Crown Princess Masako), but there is a significant anti–postwar democratic system thread that runs through much of it.

Abuse was directed toward Komuro Kei, fiancé of Princess Mako (1991–), from 2017 until the time this book went to press. Some of the attacks were directed at the postwar democratic system because certain critics were clearly sneering at the notion that an imperial princess would marry into a family that has money troubles. This raised the specter that Princess Mako might need to work after marriage, contributing to the family income in the same way that many wives do so in Japan. Democratic, sure, but for elements of the far right nostalgic for an imperial house that was above the clouds and commanded rather than won the hearts of the people, Princess Mako's engagement to someone who is not of means was a painful reminder that the imperial house operates within a democratic system. As I write, it is not clear that this marriage will in fact happen, not so much because of Komuro's limited income but because of the taint of scandal involving whether a loan his family received from the ex-fiancé of his mother should be repaid.

Consider also literary critic Etō Jun's (1932–99) bitter diatribe at the time of the Kobe earthquake in 1995. Reacting to images of how the imperial couple had consoled victims of the disaster, Etō fumed in *Bungei shunjū:*

> It is not necessary [for the imperial couple] to kneel down. It is not necessary [for the imperial couple] to be at the same line of sight as the victims. If one views it from the perspective of the emperor having a special position according to the Constitution, then it would make no difference if they stood. It would be fine if they were on top of a horse or in a car [for the visit]. There is no necessity whatsoever for the imperial couple to try to be loved by the people.[6]

Nihon keizai shinbun journalist Inoue Makoto interpreted Etō's critique of the Heisei monarchy as fundamentally an attack on the postwar democratic system, an accurate assessment in my estimation.[7] In the ten-page essay, Etō used, in a critical manner, the phrase "postwar democracy" (*sengo minshushugi*) nine times. The imperial couple simply served as a convenient surrogate for his criticism of postwar democracy overall.

The "people's emperor" so loathed by elements of the right wing but celebrated by an overwhelming majority of the population came to full fruition under Akihito and Michiko. So much has the people's emperor developed these past decades that as the abdication approached in early 2019, the Heisei monarchy seemed "natural" to many; in other words, it may almost have seemed that the monarchy has always operated in this way. For many Japanese, this assumption was challenged only by the deluge of programming by NHK and other networks and the flood of commentary in the print media that outlined antecedents to the Heisei monarchy, including historical accounts of the sacrosanct throne under the Meiji Constitution.

As much as the present imperial couple have tried to narrow the distance between the royal house and people, it would be incorrect to include Japan's royal house (or that of Great Britain, for that matter) in the category of the particularly informal bicycle monarchies of Scandinavia and also other continental European royal houses. This level of informality is still not typically the case in Japan or, for that matter, in terms of how the British royal house operates. This is true even though Naruhito's occasional jogs around the perimeter of the imperial palace certainly brought to mind a more informal style.

To understand the agenda Akihito and Michiko pursued during the Heisei era, it is important to revisit Akihito's formative life experiences. Akihito was a boy of eleven when Japan surrendered in August 1945. He was old enough to remember the devastation the war brought to his country (and extrapolate what he witnessed to imagine the experiences of Japan's adversaries), but young enough to spend his formative educational years under the postwar system, which emphasized democracy and peace. He spent his formative years, with the assistance of various tutors, studying how a monarch constitutionally defined as the national symbol under popular sovereignty should exercise his role.

Akihito was born in 1933, the year Japan withdrew from the League of Nations in protest of the acceptance of the Lytton Report that condemned Manchukuo as an illegitimate puppet state. Beginning with the Manchurian Incident of 1931, which led to a wave of nationalism throughout the empire, Japan turned its back on cooperation with imperialist powers such as the United States and United Kingdom and instead pursued a policy of autonomous imperialism in Asia. Japan's quest for an expanded empire resulted in full-scale war with China before the future emperor was four years old.

When Akihito was six, and thus likely old enough to maintain some memories of events into adulthood, his country engaged in one of the most extensive mass celebrations of the imperial nation-state ever to take place: the 2,600th anniversary of the Empire of Japan.[8] Since the anniversary celebrations in 1940 represent the sort of national chauvinism that Akihito seems to find distasteful, it is worth highlighting these mass celebrations that, at a broad level, bear comparison with the Nuremberg rallies of Nazi Germany. Much about Japan's wartime cult of the emperor also makes one think of the cult of Mao, which reached its apex during the Great Proletarian Cultural Revolution (1966–76), and of the cult of the Kim dynasty in North Korea under Kim Il Sung (1912–94), Kim Jong Il (1941–2011), and now Kim Jong Un (1984–).

The young crown prince spent the months leading up to Japan's surrender, as did many children at the time, in the countryside to avoid the air attacks on the cities. He returned to a Tokyo flattened by air raids. As heir apparent, Akihito was shielded from the worst of the wartime and postwar suffering, but he witnessed his country's humiliation and his countrymen's misery. Furthermore, his education from age twelve onward (which continued long past his investiture as crown prince) placed overwhelming stress on the role he would play as a national symbol in the postwar democratic system. Akihito was aware of his role as a symbol outside of the formal political process in an uncompromised way that is different from his father's experience.

Hirohito was raised under the Meiji Constitution, which gave him sweeping political authority, and he spent half his life (about one-third of his reign) under the Meiji Constitution. Overnight the Postwar Constitution redefined the emperor's position and role, but Hirohito had his way of doing things. For example, he expected to be briefed regularly about government affairs—about politics, in other words—by a wide array of government ministers and officials. He was not shy about expressing his opinions during these briefings, and the emperor's opinion mattered to officials conditioned to show utmost deference to him.

In contrast to his father, Akihito has thoroughly embraced his constitutional role as a symbol. He was briefed by the prime minister and occasionally by other ministers or government officials throughout his reign. In the years after Akihito ascended to the throne, journalists affiliated with the Imperial House Press Club assured me that he often actively asked questions during these briefings (there is every reason to assume that Naruhito now does the same). Akihito was well aware that his constitutional position does not provide him with anything more than a ceremonial role in the formal political process, and this is equally true of Naruhito.

Unlike his father, Akihito was never *genshu* (sovereign head of state) according to the meaning of this term under the Meiji system, and this provided briefings during the Heisei era with less of an aura and significance than before. Although observers of the throne expect that now that Akihito has abdicated (or after his death), anecdotes shedding light on his personal opinions recorded by those who served him in the role of chamberlain or those who briefed him will come to light, although there is less interest in this topic than there was for his father. Few people familiar with briefings during the Heisei monarchy believe that Akihito, who embraced his role as symbol, exerted much influence through these briefings.

The Heisei Agenda

It is nonetheless important to understand that Akihito was no automaton. How could a living national symbol be no more than a robot? The most common symbol of a nation-state, a flag, passively flies from a pole, but a symbol emperor walks and talks. Crown Prince Akihito addressed this fundamental tension directly at a 1969 press conference to mark the tenth anniversary of his wedding: "Constitutionally, in a sense, it would be best for the imperial family members to be robots, but I don't think it would be best for us to be robots. That's the difficult part."[9] Akihito, no robot, left his imprint so evidently on the monarchy and society that it is worth recalling how surprised some commentators were to learn that the new emperor had his own way of doing things when he ascended to the throne.

As the result of the campaign spearheaded initially by the U.S. occupying forces (SCAP) and thereafter by the palace to absolve Hirohito of war responsibility, by 1989 many people had come to accept the adage that emperors were no more than stage props. But precisely their symbolic role affords the imperial family some social influence. The same is true of representatives of other symbolic monarchies, ranging from Britain to Bhutan.

For example, when Princess Diana (1961–97) removed her glove before shaking hands with an AIDS patient in 1987, she called, in a way that resonated widely, for an end to the discrimination directed at individuals suffering from AIDS in the early years of the epidemic. There is an equally striking example from Bhutan, where the 2008 constitution transformed the monarchy from the previous hands-on version to a symbolic one, of the sort of social influence that a symbolic monarch can bring to bear. During a twenty-five-day domestic tour in 2009 that included visits to remote villages, King Jigme Khesar Namgyel Wangchuck (b. 1980; r. 2006–) demonstrated his belief that certain superstitions are harmful and should be discarded.

Walking between two remote villages in March, the king met Tashi Wangmo, a woman ostracized in her community as a "poison giver." In certain rural villages in Bhutan, families have been ostracized for generations because they are seen as being cursed, and thus fellow villagers refuse to receive food or drink from them. Someone from the king's entourage who had scouted ahead notified the king not to receive anything from this woman.

Instead, the king reached out to Tashi Wangmo by presenting her with a rosary and asking her to pour some *ara* (locally brewed alcohol) into his cup, which he drank. He asked her to tell her fellow villagers that the king had drunk from the so-called poison giver, which proved to be a life-changing event for her. By this simple act, the king had broken the curse that had plagued this woman's family for generations. It was the sort of benevolent act with tremendous symbolic resonance from a young king to which people in Bhutan are quickly becoming accustomed.[10]

Japan's imperial couple has made targeted use of its societal prestige as well. In Japan, individual emperors, while obviously subject to manipulation, can still shape the throne in significant ways. It is important to recognize not only that the monarchy under Akihito and Michiko differed dramatically from the pre-1945 monarchy, but also that in many significant ways it was a departure from the postwar monarchy under Hirohito and Nagako. It is also abundantly clear that Akihito and Michiko (who herself was far more than a stage prop) had an agenda in mind before Akihito ascended to the throne in 1989. Their agenda directly relates to the concept of the people's emperor, because we must ask ourselves how this elite institution, the monarchy, has succeeded at perpetuating itself when its survival is dependent on the good will of the sovereign people.

The agenda or symbolic essence of Akihito and Michiko was characterized by five themes, which sometimes overlap: (1) an unabashed support of the postwar system, including the values inherent in the Postwar Constitution; (2) efforts to compress the margins of society by reaching out to the most vulnerable members of society and by extending a hand to others marginalized by geography and other factors; (3) efforts to bring closure to the postwar era by trying to heal the festering wounds of the war and of the imperial era in a more general sense; (4) demonstrations of pride in the best that Japan has to offer, but a pride tempered with a cosmopolitanism that clashed with simplistic nationalism, including in reference to views of Japan's history; and (5) the unusually active and important role played by Michiko. Key words that one could use to describe the Heisei imperial couple's agenda include peace, culture, tolerance (*kanyō*), and sincerity (*shinshi*). There were also some noticeable absences, especially in comparison with monarchies around the world, in the Heisei imperial couple's symbolic essence that must be discussed.

In terms of the imperial couple's embrace of the postwar system, one can begin with the fact that Akihito's basic style was more informal than that of his father. When he was ready to make a prepared statement, he simply retrieved it from his pocket rather than having a chamberlain present it to him, as was customary under Hirohito. In addition, the Heisei imperial couple narrowed the distance between themselves and the people to the extent that images of Michiko hugging victims of natural disasters are widely cited as iconographic, precisely the sort of informality and closeness to the people that results in fits of rage among far-right critics of the postwar democratic system.

Akihito made numerous public statements in support of the postwar system, leaving little doubt as to how thoroughly he was aligned with it. In 1974, Crown Prince Akihito referenced the generational influence on his commitment to culture and peace: "Terms such as 'Peace Country' and 'Culture Country' that were widely used immediately after the war make people of my generation nostalgic. I would like to give those concepts another try."[11] Akihito may have felt a particularly strong attachment to these concepts because his father popularized these terms in the immediate postsurrender period.

In 1987, during the regular press conference on his birthday, Crown Prince Akihito spoke in support of free speech: "When all is said and done freedom of expression is crucial."[12] Although circumstances did not allow him to play the sort of heroic, hands-on role of steering his country from a dictatorship to a democratic system of government as King Juan Carlos did for Spain during the late 1970s and early 1980s, the emperor nonetheless made clear his resolute support for democracy and peace.

With this foreshadowing in Akihito's comments, it should have come as little surprise that he began his reign with a ringing pledge to carry out his duties in accordance with the Postwar Constitution and specifically referenced peace and social welfare.[13] It is sometimes said that the pre-1945 emperor system was laden with ideology, but it is not as though the Heisei monarchy has been free of it. It may seem natural, almost invisible, but a complex web of ideology underlies the postwar democratic system, no less so than the ideology that was linked to the imperial system (1868–1945). Akihito and Michiko learned how to "operate" within the postwar democratic system, and during the Heisei era, they made clear their fervent support of the values, of the ideology, inherent in this system.

What does it mean to say that the Heisei imperial couple sought to compress the margins of Japanese society? Throughout the modern era (1868–present), imperial family members have sponsored charitable causes on behalf of the disadvantaged. Previously this sponsorship typically took the form of, for example, helping provide facilities that kept those suffering from various conditions comfortable but in a setting isolated from mainstream society. In contrast, Akihito and Michiko worked to integrate as much as possible previously marginalized groups into mainstream society. The Heisei imperial couple regularly lent its prestige to people who did not fit easily into mainstream society to bring them in from the margins. The definition of marginalized is multifold, ranging

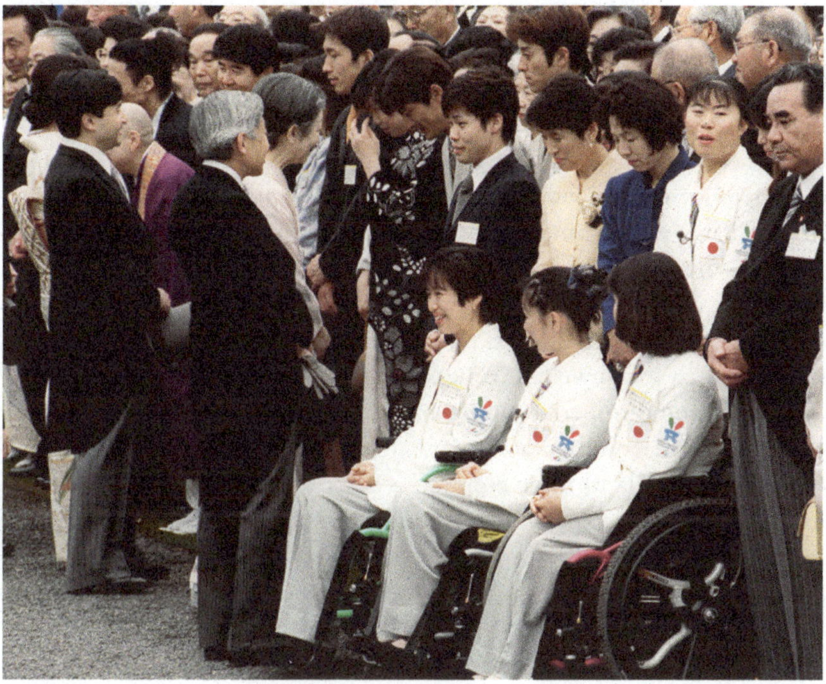

FIGURE 33. Akihito and Michiko talk with Nagano Paralympics gold medalists during a spring garden party at the Akasaka Imperial Gardens, 27 April 1998. (Photograph Courtesy Kyodo News Service.)

from those who suffered discrimination because of physical handicaps to those who might feel marginalized for geographic or historical reasons.

Long before they became emperor and empress, Akihito and Michiko lent imperial prestige to people who face particular challenges in their daily lives. When the Paralympics were first held in Japan, in the aftermath of the 1964 Tokyo Summer Olympics, Crown Prince Akihito adopted them as one of his causes. At the time, disabled people in Japan were typically encouraged to play sports only for rehabilitation.

According to Watanabe Makoto (1936–), who served as grand chamberlain from 1996 to 2007, the present emperor quickly embraced a different view, namely, that "handicapped individuals should play sports for the same reason that everyone else plays them."[14] Today social values have evolved to the point that such an interpretation seems natural, but it is no exaggeration to say that a common view of the handicapped in 1964 was that they should be hidden away, kept separate from mainstream society. There are degrees of marginalization, and certainly individuals with disabilities continue to face many challenges, but they are far less marginalized than they used to be, and imperial prestige played a role in this process.

In 1999, the Imperial Household Agency published a book titled *Michi* (Path) to commemorate Emperor Akihito's tenth year on the throne.[15] Obviously, it was an uncritical examination of the monarchy, but it was useful for understanding Akihito and Michiko's agenda. One of the points that stood out is how often the Heisei imperial couple lent its support to social welfare issues. Unlike members of the British royal family, Japanese imperial family members do not establish their own charities. Some commentators have described Prince Charles as having developed a "philanthropic empire," a description that would not apply to any member of Japan's imperial family. It is accepted practice for Japan's imperial family members to provide a stamp of approval, by serving as honorary chair or something along those lines, for philanthropic institutions (ranging from social welfare organizations to those supporting the arts),[16] but not with the remarkable frequency and range of British royal family members, including in the area of fundraising.

In a way appropriate to the context of Japan, Akihito and Michiko were tireless advocates of social welfare, whether by making statements at conferences devoted to improving the lives of the most disadvantaged or through countless visits to social welfare institutions. This has been so much the case that it is appropriate to think of them as the "social welfare imperial couple." It is telling to cite comments Akihito made about this role, in this case on the tenth anniversary of his enthronement: "I think that it is very important work to reach out to individuals with disabilities and the elderly, as well as individuals who have suffered natural disasters, as well as to individuals working on behalf of such people."[17]

Consider the regrettable history of individuals in Japan with Hansen's disease, who until recently were kept isolated for no medical reason long after this was necessary. In the 1940s, a revolutionary drug named Promin (sodium glucosulfone) was invented that cured Hansen's disease. However, until the Leprosy Prevention Law was repealed in 1996, the Japanese government continued the policy of forcibly isolating patients (the government eventually paid reparations and also apologized). Even after the law was repealed, many of the patients in sanitoriums had spent so many years there that it was difficult for them to imagine living anywhere else, even if social discrimination had instantly disappeared (which it had not).

Between 1968 and 2014, over a period of forty-six years, Akihito and Michiko visited each of the fourteen sanitoriums in Japan for people with Hansen's disease. By design, these facilities were located in remote areas. In addition, on 28 January 2015, Akihito and Michiko hosted for an audience at the imperial palace people affected with leprosy from Japan and five overseas countries (India, the United States, the Philippines, Indonesia, and Ethiopia). Vargavathali Narusappa (age forty-six), president of the Association of People Affected by Leprosy, India, remarked of his experience of meeting the emperor and empress: "The experience we had today is incredible. Their Majesties shook my hands while even my family had never done so. I was diagnosed with leprosy at the age of 9, ousted from my family and village and have continued to taste the bitterness of life. Today I feel that all my agonizing past has been erased."[18]

Akihito and Michiko's efforts to reach out to the most disadvantaged have been praised by people at different poles of the political spectrum. The Mainichi Newspaper Company published a book of the text of a debate between Kobayashi Yoshinori (1953–), famous for his illustrated novellas that take up historical and contemporary societal issues, representing the conservative viewpoint, and Inoue Tatsuo (1954–), representing the liberal one. This book is useful for understanding many of the basic fault lines between the right and the left in Japan. But one point of agreement between Kobayashi and Inoue was their interpretation that among the powerful in Japan, only the emperor speaks for the weak. Kobayashi particularly stressed the emperor's critically important role in looking out for the most disadvantaged members of society.[19] Ogawa Eiichi, president of the Japanese Federation of Organizations of Disabled Individuals (established 1958), credited Akihito and Michiko with having been one of the few constant sources of support for his organization's initiatives in his speech at the ceremony to mark the twentieth anniversary of Akihito's accession to the throne.[20]

On at least one occasion, Akihito played a worthwhile role in the area of social welfare even while dealing with a life-threatening illness.

Immediately after having been diagnosed with prostate cancer in December 2002, Akihito asked his doctors to make this information public, thereby undermining another taboo surrounding the imperial house. Doctors promptly disclosed details of the subsequent operation to remove the cancer. Akihito's openness about his battle with prostate cancer drew important attention to this health issue that affects many men. With early diagnosis, a high percentage of men who develop prostate cancer can be cured.[21] Akihito's frankness about his condition may have encouraged men in Japan to seek appropriate early testing for and treatment of this disease.

It is fair to conclude that Akihito and Michiko encouraged society-wide tolerance for differences by showing tolerance themselves. Nonetheless, the imperial couple was not able to or chose not to extend its prestige to all members of society on the margins. For example, in spite of all the visits that the present imperial couple has made to social welfare institutions, they steered clear of institutions housing the mentally ill. One cannot help but wonder if Empress Masako might take up the cause of mental illness, working to erase its shame and encouraging those suffering from it to seek professional treatment. It might be too much to ask of her, especially because to be effective it might be best for her to explain frankly what mental health issues have caused her own problems. But this would be an area where she could arguably make a meaningful difference because her message would be reinforced by her personal experiences. In the case of the British monarchy, Prince William (1982–) and Prince Harry (1984–) have spoken frankly about their struggles with mental health to encourage others who may need professional help.

Akihito and Michiko also did not take up the cause of LGBTQIA rights in the way that, for example, Queen Elizabeth II (who is older than Akihito and Michiko) has done during the past two decades or so. In a 2017 speech opening Parliament, Queen Elizabeth II pledged, "My government will make further progress to tackle the gender pay gap and discrimination against people on the basis of their race, faith, gender, disability, or sexual orientation."[22] In June 2019, Prince William responded to a question about how he would react if any of his three kids came out as gay by stressing that he would be fine with that possibility if also a bit concerned because of the barriers they might face (and also because, as royals, such a coming out would draw immense attention).

Mainstream Japan's acceptance of LGBTQIA rights by the time that Akihito abdicated, in spite of progress made in recent decades, is arguably nowhere nearly as far along as that of certain Western European societies, including Great Britain. Perhaps for this reason, Akihito and Michiko did not make this one of their causes. Whether or not Emperor Naruhito and Empress Masako adopt LGBTQIA rights as one of their issues probably partly depends on how the issue evolves in Japan.

Even if Akihito and Michiko were not able to take up every social issue, there is little argument about the extent to which they exerted themselves to reach out regularly to areas of Japan that are geographically marginalized (e.g., remote islands) with visits. In fact, Akihito specifically referenced such visits in his 2016 televised address explaining why he would like to abdicate:

> Ever since my accession to the throne . . . I have spent my days searching for and contemplating on what is the desirable role of the Emperor, who is designated the symbol of the State by the Constitution of Japan. . . . I have felt that my travels to various places throughout Japan, in particular, to remote places and islands, are important acts of the Emperor as the symbol of the State and I have carried them out in that spirit.[23]

Here it is important to understand that as some monarchies have evolved away from ruling to reigning within a democratic polity, their functions have also changed. According to historian David Cannadine, a term that describes well the contemporary British royal family is "peripatetic." He stresses how this is a contemporary development: "But the practice whereby, on any given weekday, many members of the royal family will be found undertaking public duties in towns and cities across the length and breadth of the country is a relatively recent development, and it seems likely that it is connected with the near-simultaneous extension of the franchise [right to vote]."[24]

"Peripatetic" could also be used to describe Akihito and Michiko and Japan's imperial family in general. In his opening address at the ceremony to celebrate the twentieth anniversary of Akihito's accession to the throne, parliamentarian Hiranuma Takeo (1939–) noted with precise statistics just how peripatetic Akihito had been: "Up until Heisei 19 [2008] His Majesty has made 180 regional visits, including to each of the forty-seven prefectures, and including remote islands he has visited 514 cities, towns, and villages, and has been welcomed by 7,700,000 people. He is the first emperor to have visited all the country's prefectures."[25] To understand the Heisei era and grasp the agenda of Akihito and Michiko, it is unquestionably necessary to analyze their various travels, as journalist Inoue Makoto did with his recent book *The Travels of the Symbol Emperor*.[26]

For example, Akihito long took a particular interest in spiritually integrating Okinawa, which for geographic and historical reasons was the most estranged of the forty-seven prefectures in the postwar era, more fully into the national community. This was demonstrated by the repeated visits he and Michiko made to that prefecture since its reversion from U.S. military occupation to Japan in 1972 and the interest they have shown in Okinawan culture. In March 2018, Akihito and Michiko completed their eleventh and final official trip to Okinawa. Close observers of these visits pointed out that it was not just the number of visits but Akihito and Michiko's insistence during each visit to go to the sites of the most intense battles and take an interest in the accounts of survivors that left such an impression. Akihito's interest in Okinawa was also related to his effort to bring closure to the postwar, a topic discussed below.

Akihito and Michiko also took on the role of chief consolers and encouragers of countrymen who found their lives turned upside down as the result of natural disasters. The first visit to a disaster area made by Crown Prince Akihito after his marriage to Michiko was in October 1959 (Michiko was pregnant at the time), to the Ise Bay area, which had been devasted by a typhoon. This role as consolers and encouragers only clearly came to the forefront after Akihito ascended to the throne. There were numerous natural disasters during the Heisei era, from volcano eruptions to typhoons and flooding to earthquakes to the triple disaster of 11 March 2011.[27] Negative memories of the Heisei era mostly revolve around the natural disasters, with economic stagnation also weighing on people's minds.

In the early years of the Heisei era, postdisaster visits by Akihito and Michiko resulted in scenes, captured with the photos included in Chapter 6, that evidenced just how committed the new emperor and empress were to mixing with the people on as equal terms as possible. Precisely this sort of down-to-earth style is what Etō Jun castigated. The triple disaster of 2011 (earthquake, tsunami, nuclear meltdown) produced no dramatic variations of the imperial couple's informal style of mixing with the people. But it did result in the first major address to the Japanese people by an emperor since Hirohito's announcement of Imperial Japan's surrender.

Akihito's address included these moving and exhortatory comments: "I have been told that many overseas media are reporting that, in the midst of deep sorrow, the Japanese people are responding to the situation in a remarkably orderly manner, and helping each other without losing composure. It is my heartfelt hope that the people will continue to work hand in hand, treating each other with compassion, in order to overcome these trying times."[28] The role of the imperial couple as consoler and encourager after disasters has become so routinized, so seemingly traditional (!), that it is difficult to imagine how Emperor Naruhito and Empress Masako could abruptly break with this "tradition" in the Reiwa era.

For most Japanese, the frequent use of the term "postwar" (*sengo*) is so customary that most individuals presumably do not pause to think how curious it is that nearly three-quarters of a century after the end of the war, the word remains so commonly used in Japan. Whether it is appropriate to think of Japan today as still in the postwar era is in the eye of the beholder, but there is some meaning to the fact that the word remains so common. When Akihito ascended to the throne, he seemed hopeful of soothing lingering wounds that were legacies of the imperial era (1868–1945), and thereby helping bring closure to the postwar era. Evaluating his record in this area is not without difficulty, in no small part because there was only so much that Akihito (or any single person) could do to heal divisions between, for example, Japan and China. After all, these divisions resulted from two wars and nearly uninterrupted tension between these countries during the latter part of the nineteenth century and first half of the twentieth century.

Akihito nonetheless endeavored to address troubling legacies of the imperial era. Only sixteen months into his reign, he issued what up to that point was the most forthright apology by any official representative of Japan to Korea for the colonial era, to Korean President Roh Tae Woo during his visit to Japan in May 1990. This was the earliest explicit indication of Akihito's intent to confront head on various painful legacies, both domestic and international, related to Japan's imperial era. His efforts became a major theme of the Heisei era. By all accounts, Akihito himself insisted that this be a major component of his public duties.

It would be difficult to say that issues regarding the past between Japan and Korea, most notably in reference to comfort women, were more resolved by the time of Akihito's abdication than they were when he came to the throne. The reasons for the lack of a full-fledged reconciliation between the countries are complex and hardly one-sided. Many observers of the Republic of Korea (and of North Korea for that matter) have noted, for example, that anti-Japanese nationalism remains too useful a unifying force to be discarded. This raises the legitimate question of what (if anything) the Japanese side could do to earn forgiveness.

The efforts of Akihito to bring about reconciliation have not gone unnoticed in the Republic of Korea, however. I asked Nam Eui Young, a Korean national who is finishing a doctorate at Tokyo University, to investigate how the mass media in Korea was evaluating Akihito as the date of his abdication approached. Nam was herself surprised at the uniformity with which the media in Korea, representing the full range of the political spectrum from left to right, held Akihito in high regard. The Korean mass media repeatedly praised Akihito's commitment to peace, his contrite interpretation of the colonial era as evidenced by his statement to Roh in 1990, and his generally friendly view toward Korea as evidenced by his December 2001 remark that he "felt a kinship for Korea" (this remark is discussed below). But it is telling that Akihito's long-standing wish to visit Korea was not realized during his reign.

Along the same lines, in spite of Akihito's efforts, the past continues to weigh heavily on relations between Japan and China. During a September 1992 visit to China, Emperor Akihito issued an apology to China. But in the twenty-five years since he made those remarks, numerous historical issues ranging from the Rape of Nanjing to the gruesome germ warfare and human experimentation conducted by Unit 731 have continued to roil Sino-Japanese relations. A retired advisor of Akihito who preferred not to be named told me in June 2019 that whereas Akihito was satisfied with his other international trips, even then he occasionally asked people their views about the trip to China, possibly suggesting that he was troubled by whether it produced the results he desired.

In China, anti-Japanese nationalism is a conveniently unifying glue that is proving difficult to discard for the Chinese Communist Party (CCP), which had to seek new means of legitimacy after abandoning revolutionary socialism. Similar to the two Koreas, this raises the question of what (if anything) Japan could do to put to rest this anti-Japanese sentiment in light of the fact that it has become a pillar of the CCP's legitimacy in the postrevolutionary era. Because China's mass media is not free, I did not commission a study of how Akihito was portrayed there around the time of his abdication because it would reveal nothing beyond official propaganda.

Akihito and Michiko's efforts to address the wounds of the imperial era and the war with countries other than China and Korea and on the domestic front were arguably more successful. As with other aspects of his agenda, before ascending to the throne, Akihito foreshadowed the importance he placed on remembering the war dead. On 7 August 1981, Crown Prince Akihito was asked during a press conference to comment on the significance of the upcoming 15 August anniversary of Japan's surrender. After strongly expressing his view that such a war must never be repeated, Akihito explained that there were four days that "must be remembered at any cost in Japan": 23 June, when the Battle of Okinawa concluded; 6 August, when an atomic bomb was dropped on Hiroshima; 9 August, when an atomic bomb was dropped on Nagasaki; and 15 August, the day Imperial Japan surrendered. The prince explained, "I observe a moment of silence on those days. And then I treasure the preciousness of peace."[29]

As with so many aspects of the Heisei monarchy, the imperial couple's repeated examples of praying for the war dead and generally seeking to heal the wounds of the war became so customary after thirty years that they seemed "traditional." It is thus especially important to point out that Hirohito never made similar efforts in this area. Although Akihito and Michiko traveled in 1994 to Iwo Jima, the site of ferocious fighting between Japanese and U.S. forces in early 1945 that left almost all of the 21,000 Japanese defenders and 7,000 U.S. marines dead, to pray for the war dead, it was in 1995 that it became especially clear just how much importance the imperial couple put on remembering those (including noncombatants) who were victimized by the war.

During the fiftieth anniversary of the end of World War II, Akihito and Michiko took a tour that brought them to Nagasaki, Okinawa, Hiroshima, and the memorial in Tokyo that commemorates victims of the air raids, at each place praying for the war dead. In addition, at the annual ceremony held on 15 August to commemorate the war dead that year, for the first time Emperor Akihito specifically expressed his hope, in short remarks, that such a tragedy would not be repeated.

As horrific as the conventional air raids on Tokyo and other Japanese cities and the atomic bombings were, there are aspects to the tragedy of Okinawa that serve as reminders that during much of Japan's modern history, this prefecture's experiences diverged from those of the rest of the country. At the annual birthday press conference in 1975, the year of his first visit to Okinawa that had included a Molotov cocktail being thrown at him and the crown princess by left-wing protesters, Crown Prince Akihito remarked, "It is important for all Japanese to confront head on how painful the history of Okinawa is. This must not be avoided."[30] The Molotov cocktail incident occurred when the prince and princess were visiting a monument to the Himeyuri Corps. During the Battle of Okinawa, 222 female high school students and their 18 teachers were conscripted into a nursing unit. All of the teachers and more than half of the students perished, some taking their own lives rather than face what they had been told would be horrible fates should they be captured by the U.S. forces.

Even in postwar Japan, emperors tend to speak in broad terms. Various details of Okinawa's history were almost surely known by Akihito, who has been a student of history, even if he did not explicitly reference them in his remarks in 1975. These details included the fact that some of the estimated 160,000 Okinawan civilians who lost their lives during the Battle of Okinawa, the only area of Japan proper to have experienced a land invasion, were killed at the hands of the Japanese military. Some Japanese military personnel viewed Okinawans, who had a different dialect, with suspicion, perhaps as possible spies for the Americans. The killings of Okinawan civilians by the Japanese military are a particularly difficult historical chapter for patriotic Japanese to digest because they fundamentally challenge the notion of a unified national community.

There is credible evidence that Hirohito played an active role after Japan's surrender in arranging for the United States to maintain control of Okinawa after the rest of the country was to regain independence. Hirohito's diplomatic intervention led some Okinawans to question why they should feel a common bond with the rest of Japan when the prefecture was used as a sacrificial lamb again in the immediate aftermath of the war. In remarks that were particularly candid about the marginalization that Okinawa had experienced, Crown Prince Akihito expressed his hope in 1983, the year of his second visit to the prefecture, that "All the people of Okinawa can think it was good to have rejoined [reverted to] Japan."[31]

The Heisei imperial couple understood the challenge of thoroughly integrating Okinawa into the national community, which explains why Akihito and Michiko returned there many times. Akihito's extraordinary efforts to bring Okinawa more fully into the national community included his appreciation for traditional Ryūkyūan poetry, which requires an understanding of a language that is close to Japanese in terms of linguistic roots but still essentially a foreign language, especially in comparison to contemporary Japanese. As Akihito's abdication approached, the *Okinawa Taimusu* (Okinawa Times) newspaper conducted a public opinion poll indicating that 87 percent of residents of Okinawa had positive feelings toward the emperor. This was in contrast to the 53 percent who had positive feelings when this newspaper conducted a similar survey in February 1989, a month after Akihito assumed the throne.[32]

Akihito and Michiko's efforts to honor the war dead and console the bereaved took them beyond Japan. For the sixtieth anniversary of the end of the war, in 2005, the imperial couple visited the U.S. territory of Saipan to pay their respects to the war dead. Saipan, now popular among Japanese tourists, was the scene of savage fighting between Japanese and U.S. forces in 1944. The Japanese side suffered more than 29,000 dead, with almost no survivors. The last 3,000 or so Japanese troops, out of supplies, perished in largely futile suicidal mass attacks on the U.S. lines. The Japanese war dead included hundreds of civilians who loyally killed themselves in mass suicides by jumping off seaside cliffs rather than surrender (note the cover image of this book). While in Saipan, the imperial couple changed its schedule midstream to pay its respects at a memorial to Korean war dead, most of whom had been forced laborers. This is the sort of gesture that symbolizes Akihito's efforts to bring comprehensive closure to the postwar era.

We now know that Akihito was thinking about abdication years before his August 2016 televised address to the nation. Even putting aside the question of abdication, he must have sensed during the previous five years or so that his especially active years on the throne were drawing to an end. This fact, perhaps combined with societal and political developments around him, seemed to stiffen his resolve to pay his respects to the war dead whenever possible and remind the living of the horrors of war. This latter theme included reminding his countrymen that Japan bore particular responsibility for having caused so much of the suffering.

In 2015, Akihito seemed to "up his game" in drawing attention to the suffering caused by the war. In April, he and Michiko made their second overseas trip to honor the war dead (from all sides), to Palau. Palau was the site of ferocious fighting between Japanese and U.S. forces that left approximately 16,000 Japanese and 2,000 Americans dead. During the visit, Akihito repeated a statement about the war dead that he has stressed over and over: "They must never be forgotten."

At the annual 15 August ceremony to commemorate the war dead that year, Akihito adopted stronger wording for his ritualistic statement, wording he repeated at subsequent ceremonies held on 15 August (the key new phrase is italicized): "Reflecting on our past and bearing in mind the feelings of *deep remorse* over the last war, I earnestly hope that the ravages of war will never be repeated. Together with all of our people, I now pay my heartfelt tribute to all those who lost their lives in the war, both on the battlefields and elsewhere, and pray for world peace and for the continuing development of our country."[33]

Any doubt that by 2015 Akihito was gravely concerned that memories of the horrors of the war were fading from the consciousness of his countrymen was erased when he made the following remark during his annual birthday press conference in December: "With each passing year, we will have more and more Japanese who have never experienced war, but I believe having thorough knowledge about the last war and deepening our thoughts about the war is most important for the future of Japan."[34] Akihito's insistence on continually drawing attention to the tragedy of the war, a role he continued during the imperial couple's trip to the Philippines in 2016, their trip to Vietnam in 2017, and by his use of the word "remorse" in his final appearance in 2018 at the annual 15 August ceremony, stood in contrast to the efforts of Prime Minister Abe Shinzō (b. 1954; prime minister, 2006–7, and 2012–) to relegate the war to part of the distant past and blur the extent of Japan's responsibility. Abe seemed to find the endless references to the war and claims that Japan bore a special responsibility bothersome to his efforts to make Japan great again.

Tellingly, Akihito finished his reign without once visiting Yasukuni Shrine, thus following the precedent of his father. Hirohito made it clear to his advisors that he considered the 1978 decision by the chief priest of Yasukuni to enshrine Class A war criminals a mistake (in signing the San Francisco Peace Treaty of 1952, Japan pledged to accept the verdict of the Tokyo War Crimes Tribunal). Hirohito expressed his displeasure by making no further visits there. At the time I write, it has been nearly a half century, a period of time corresponding to the Meiji era (1868–1912) that so shaped modern Japan, since an emperor last visited Yasukuni (1975), and there is no reason to think that Naruhito will change directions in this area. In the fall of 2018, Yasukuni Shrine formally invited Akihito to attend a celebration to mark the 150th anniversary of the establishment of the shrine, citing the fact that emperors attended the 50th and 100th anniversary celebrations, but the Imperial Household Agency declined. Even if the problem of the war criminals' enshrinement were resolved, one wonders if the overall historical view of Yasukuni, including the Japan-never-did-anything-wrong version of history put forth at the Yūshūkan Museum on site, is so estranged from the historical consciousness of the imperial family members that they would continue to decline to visit.

Far less controversial than issues such as Yasukuni Shrine is the imperial house's role in the area of culture. One need only visit the page of the Imperial House Agency's website (http://www.kunaicho.go.jp/e-culture/) titled "Traditional Culture" to be reminded of the imperial family's role as the protector, carrier, and champion of Japanese culture. This is demonstrated by sponsorship of events ranging from the Imperial New Year's Poetry Reading (Utakai hajime) to the performances of Imperial Court Music and Dance (Gagaku), and by practices that go on somewhat less publicly, such as the empress's cultivation of silkworms on the small farm in the imperial palace and the Imperial Household Agency's management of collections of national treasures like those housed in the Shōsōin. It is hardly surprising that the imperial household should play such a role in the area of culture.

What is notable about Akihito and Michiko is not so much that they have with their countrymen a justifiable pride in all that is good about Japan, including demonstrating pride in far less high-brow examples of Japan's culture, such as the country's fine agricultural products. Rather, what stands out is that they pointedly declined to lend their prestige to expressions of national pride that were not tempered with cosmopolitanism. Perhaps the most obvious demonstration of the imperial couple's cosmopolitanism was the numerous overseas trips they made and their sincere interest before, during, and in between these trips in foreign cultures and world history.

On at least two occasions Akihito delivered powerful statements that directly undermined the sort of simplistic, chest-thumping nationalism of the variety promoted throughout the postwar era, mostly by the far to the extreme right and more recently to some extent by the Abe administration and its supporters. In 2002, Japan and South Korea cohosted what was a very successful FIFA World Cup. It was an example of how these two countries, when they choose to do so, can work well together in spite of tension about how to interpret the past.

On the occasion of his annual birthday press conference in December 2001, Akihito responded in dramatic fashion to a tame question about his feelings about Korea (and implicitly Japan–Korea relations) in advance of the cohosting of the World Cup. The question, submitted in advance as is customary, was as follows: "Next year Japan and the Republic of Korea will co-host the global event, the 2002 FIFA World Cup. As the tournament draws ever nearer, exchange on a person-to-person level between the two countries is intensifying. Could Your Majesty tell us of any interests or thoughts you have concerning the Republic of Korea, which both historically and geographically is Japan's close neighbor?" The emperor could have answered this question with the typical diplomatic blather about having warm feelings for Korea and hoping for a successful event, but instead he launched into a history lesson:

> That the people of Korea and Japan have from ages past had deep interchange is recorded in detail in the *Nihon Shoki* [Chronicles of Japan, compiled in 720], among other historical records. Those who immigrated or were invited to come to Japan from Korea introduced culture and technology. Of the musicians in the Music Department of the Imperial Household Agency, some are direct descendants of musicians who came over to Japan from Korea at that time, and have inherited the music for generations and still perform the Gagaku [Imperial Court Music] on various occasions. It was truly fortunate that such culture and technology was brought to Japan through the enthusiasm of Japanese people and the friendly attitude of the

> Korean people. I also believe that it contributed greatly to Japan's subsequent development. I, on my part, feel a certain kinship with Korea, given the fact that it is recorded in the *Shoku Nihongi* [Chronicles of Japan, compiled in 797], that the mother of Emperor Kammu [r. 781–806] was of the line of King Muryong [r. 501–23] of the Kingdom of Paekche.[35] King Muryong had strong relations with Japan, and it was from his time that masters of the Five Chinese Classics [books compiling the teaching of Confucianism] were invited to Japan one after another to teach Confucianism. King Song Myong [r. 523–54], son of King Muryong, is recognized as the one who introduced Buddhism to Japan.
>
> It is regrettable however that Japan's exchanges with Korea have not all been of this kind. This is something that we should never forget.
>
> The FIFA World Cup 2002 is an event that is further energizing exchange between the peoples of the two countries. In order that this course be followed through, I believe that it is important that the people of both countries try to understand correctly the individual course of events that their respective countries have followed and that they each understand on a person-to-person basis the other's position. I hope that the World Cup will, through cooperation between the two peoples, run smoothly and that this will result in enhancing understanding and mutual trust between the Japanese and Korean people.[36]

It may seem innocent enough that Akihito made clear he felt "a certain kinship for Korea" because the mother of Emperor Kammu (736–806, r. 781–806) was from a royal family that sought refuge in Japan as the result of political upheavals on the Korean Peninsula many centuries ago. But the statement was actually flush with meaning in the context of Japan's mistreatment of Korea during the modern era, something Akihito also explicitly referenced in his remarks. In addition, the emperor's remark undermined theories of a "pure Japanese race" that were (and are still) bandied about in Japan by pointing out that there was Korean blood in the imperial line. Stalwart proponents of the concept of *bansei ikkei*, which stresses the primacy of the supposedly unbroken male bloodline, would likely go out of their way to stress that this was female blood and thus of little consequence, but for many people, blood is blood.

Katō Mari, a Japanese college student interviewed in 2002 when she was nineteen years old, summed up the meaning of the emperor's remark about Emperor Kammu's mixed lineage: "I was surprised by what the Emperor said. It means that the imperial line is not purely Japanese." When one remembers that Japanese exploitation of Koreans (including the use of Korean women as comfort women, providing sex to imperial military personnel) during the colonial period (1910–45) resulted in part from Japanese views of themselves as an exalted race and Koreans (and other Asians) as lower beings, the significance of the emperor's remarks becomes clearer. Indeed, South Korean Foreign Minister Han Seung Soo publicly praised Akihito's remarks as an important step forward in relations between the two countries.

Palace officials were unwilling to talk on the record about what Akihito was trying to accomplish with his remarks, even insisting that there was no particular agenda. "Emperor Akihito is a very scientific man, and he was simply acknowledging what he considers to be a historical fact," one leading palace official (who wished to remain anonymous) stressed to me at the time. One of the strategies of the palace is to leave enough ambiguity that those of different perspectives can interpret imperial happenings, including public statements, in myriad ways. In spite of efforts by palace officials to suggest that Akihito just happened to make the remarks, the emperor's statement, into which considerable preparation surely went, was not to the liking of far-right supporters of the throne.

The far right (and many other Japanese, for that matter) still argue that membership in the national community (at least full membership) should be reserved for members of the "Japanese race." As a result of Japan's demographic time bomb, with an aging and shrinking population, arguably at no previous time has the notion that Japanese citizenship should be defined by blood been under more strain, yet it remains surprisingly tenacious. It is fair to say that Akihito's remark served to undermine the notion that there is a pure Japanese race.

It is ironic that although the far right appoints itself the guardian of the throne's dignity, Akihito, through additional statements, has aligned himself with positions that blatantly contradicted the far-right worldview. The far right has long insisted that the prescription for Japan's present ills is a heavy dose of emperor-centered nationalism, a stance adopted to some extent by the Abe administration with its close links with Nippon Kaigi (Japan Conference), but it is by no means clear that Akihito ever concurred with this viewpoint. The first decade of the twenty-first century witnessed efforts by politicians in Japan to shore up nationalism by requiring displays of nationalism in public schools. At least one architect of this policy seems to have wrongly interpreted himself as having the emperor's backing for his efforts.

When Tokyo Board of Education member and famous *shōgi* player Yonenaga Kunio (1943–2012), at the 28 October 2004 imperial garden party, proudly informed Akihito that he had helped push through the requirement that public schools in Tokyo raise the national flag and sing the national anthem, the emperor bluntly retorted, "It is desirable that [such activity] is not compulsory" (*kyōsei de wa nai koto ga nozomashi*). The exchange was caught on film and subsequently broadcast widely. Palace officials and even Prime Minister Koizumi Junichirō (b. 1942; prime minister, 2001–6) insisted that the emperor's remarks were apolitical. But was there really any doubt that Akihito was aligning himself with opponents of Tokyo Governor Ishihara Shintarō's (1932–) policy of making displays of patriotism in Tokyo's public schools compulsory?

Although there was confusion about what protocol public schools throughout Japan should follow in reference to the flag and the national anthem, Tokyo's policy of requiring these rituals seemed at odds with an admittedly ambiguous policy by which the Ministry of Education since 1989 had called on (but not necessarily required) schools to perform these rituals. Perhaps the dissonance between the national and local policies as well as having been witness to the disaster that befell his country as the result of policies driven in part by hypernationalism motivated Akihito to express his personal misgivings about forcing nationalism on anyone. In any case, it is difficult with this remark in particular to interpret it as anything but a slap in the face to anyone convinced that Japan's problems will be solved by requiring more rote displays of nationalism.

Of course, anyone who respects the Constitution of Japan should consider whether as a result of this statement the emperor's position as symbol has been stretched in ways that clearly overlap with politics. In practice, it is impossible to perfectly maintain the neutrality of a national symbol who walks and talks, but the ideal of neutrality should be strived for all the same. Consistent maintenance of the firewall between the emperor and politics protects the left and the right from unfair political use of the emperor, however tempting it is to let slip actions and comments by the emperor that support one's own agenda. Although much of the left came to delight in certain symbolic acts and statements by Akihito that seemed to support its agenda, the left would do well to uphold the constitution, which requires the emperor be kept outside of the formal political process except for ceremonial acts. Otherwise, this could boomerang in the same way that the conservatives who favored an expanded public role for the emperor after the establishment of the Postwar Constitution could have never imagined that such an expanded role would eventually include making apologies to neighboring countries.

Constitutional issues aside, it is nonetheless interesting to consider the following question. Did Akihito served as a brake on Japan experiencing the sort of distasteful populism plaguing Europe and the United States in the second decade of the twenty-first century? Populism is of course a broad topic (for starters, there is no agreement on the precise definition of the term) that I cannot address in depth here, although I have been thinking at length about why Japan has thus far escaped the sort of populism that has roiled Europe and the United States and shaken the global system (e.g., the international system of free trade). If one analyzes the cases of populism that have taken hold in various European countries and in the United States, arguably the central driving force for each of the populisms is nativism.

In Japan's case, there are many significant factors that explain why the country is not experiencing a spasm of nativist populism, including the fact that for the most part Japan has not opened itself to immigrants (as of 1 April 2019, a new law allowed for expanded immigration, but the results are not yet clear). Therefore, there is no easy scapegoat for populist anger about what ails contemporary Japan. Of course, this also means that Japan concomitantly has not derived the various benefits that come from accepting immigrants. I want to be especially careful not to exaggerate the significance of Akihito having possibly served as a brake against populism. If in fact he played this role, it was only one factor among many that has allowed Japan to escape the scourge of populism as defined by, for example, Federico Finchelstein.[37]

It bears remembering that the imperial house has been used in the past as a symbol for a particularly nasty form of jingoism, and it could be used for distasteful nativism again. In fact, there definitely have been individuals and groups in the postwar era that have tried to use the imperial line as a nativist symbol, but during the Heisei era such efforts faced a significant roadblock. That barrier was an emperor and empress who repeatedly went out of their way to express distaste for nativism and show support for cosmopolitanism.

Akihito, whose political views were formed early in life and changed little through the decades, seemed to come across as left of center at times. This likely explains why observers of the imperial house sometimes lost track of certain details. First, even in comparison with his father, Akihito carried out various Shinto palace rituals expected of the emperor with studious seriousness throughout his reign. Second, it is likely that Akihito considers his greatest success to have been the continuation of the imperial line, the fact that the institution enjoyed overwhelming popular support when he turned it over to his son. If this stance seems contradictory, one might ask how an emperor could possibly carry out as active an agenda as Akihito did without believing in the value of the imperial institution. If professors believe in the value of universities, even with all their downsides, and journalists believe in the value of a free press, for all its foibles, one should not be surprised that Akihito was of the opinion that the imperial house should continue and that it had an important role to play.

No empress in the modern era had the same degree of a public role as Michiko had. In fact, one could argue that no previous empress in the modern era has even come close in this area, especially when one considers the degree to which Michiko's public role came to extend beyond Japan. Part of the explanation for this is that Japan's imperial family members have become far more peripatetic in general, as is required of a symbolic monarchy dependent on the good will of the people. But it is also true that Michiko has brought skills that have accentuated her public role.

The significance of Michiko's public role was symbolized in the showing of a videotaped speech about her experiences of reading books in her childhood at the 1998 meeting of the International Board on Books for Young People (IBBY) in New Delhi, India. This role was augmented by her making a solo trip to Switzerland to deliver an address at the 2002 meeting of the IBBY in Basel, marking the fiftieth anniversary of the organization's founding. Michiko is a product of her generation to be sure. She majored in English literature, an especially appropriate major

FIGURE 34. Michiko helps Akihito find the correct page of his address at the ceremony marking the thirtieth year of his reign, in February 2019. Akihito became confused about the order of the pages of his speech in the middle of his remarks, and Michiko immediately came to his aid. In the past, such a role likely would have been played a chamberlain. (Photograph Courtesy Kyodo News Service.)

for an aspiring housewife at the time. No doubt her focus on children's literature and her resolute commitment to playing a supporting role to her husband leaves certain Japanese feminists uninspired.

Nonetheless, one must recognize the extent of her role. She was almost always by Akihito's side, reinforcing his agenda. One wonders if there was a comparable partnership as successful as that of Akihito and Michiko among any other contemporary royal couples. Historian Hara Takeshi, whom I hold in the highest regard, used the photo in figure 34 as the cover image for his book-length study of the Heisei monarchy to emphasize what he believes to be its defining feature—the partnership between Akihito and Michiko.[38]

In fact, Michiko's role was so prominent that one of the main questions about the future of the monarchy Japanese were asking as the Heisei era drew to a close was, "How will the monarchy function with an empress (Masako) who seems unlikely to be able to play anything close to the sort of public role that Empress Michiko has played?" Journalists who have covered the imperial house cite Michiko's power of communication (*hatsugen nōryoku*) and her empathy for the human condition, especially for the weaker members of society, as factors that have made her so influential.

Throughout Japan, especially in areas that have experienced disasters, one finds monuments inscribed with short poems that Michiko offered to console and encourage her countrymen and -women. Many people believe that in quality her *waka* (short poems) approach those of respected full-time poets, and they have been translated into several languages. If Akihito in particular believed, for example, in the tremendous importance of trying to heal the wounds of the war, in the case of the imperial couple's efforts to reach out to vulnerable members of society, Michiko at least has been an equal partner. One close advisor to Akihito pointed out that while the emperor emeritus has a big heart, it was Michiko who helped show him how to demonstrate that. We may learn later that Michiko in fact played the defining role in shaping this part of the overall agenda, which might have been part of what Akihito was referencing when he referred to Michiko as having opened a window for him.

Michiko's empathy for the human condition was very much evidenced in her 1998 video address to the IBBY. Consider, for example, the following passage:

> Reading gave me opportunities to ponder over joy and sorrow. It was through reading books, with the many kinds of grief delineated in them, that I could come to know how deeply people other than myself can feel, or that I could perceive the many hurts they bear. When I think that there are children who go through so many griefs and pains beyond comparison with mine, maybe I should refrain from saying that in my own sheltered childhood, too, there were such things as sorrows. But, in any life whatever, there is pain and sorrow.[39]

The theme of empathy was also evident in her 2002 IBBY speech, delivered in person. She was speaking of her experiences reading as a child in wartime Japan:

> There were also two volumes of "Masterpieces of World Literature for Boys and Girls" which I relished. They contained stories, excerpts from novels—not abridgements—poems and letters of outstanding writers from many lands including even some from our enemy countries at that time. These two volumes taught me there were many sorrows in the world that I had not known, and I learned how intensely people other than myself could feel, and how deeply they could be hurt. I also came to realize that in order to live, one has to bear life's complexities. Together with this, reading brought me a real spiritual uplift. It planted seedlings within me that would grow reaching out towards joy. Indeed, while living in the countryside during the war time, I was meeting both my remote ancestors and strangers from other lands on *the bridge of children's books*. How fortunate I was to have someone who slipped a book or two into my hands when he visited me at our place of wartime evacuation.[40]

Although in both cases Michiko spoke in English, her addresses were later broadcast by NHK with Japanese subtitles. Japanese versions of the texts of the addresses were eventually published. Through these means and as the result of the general mass media coverage of her lectures, many Japanese became further aware of the degree of Michiko's empathy and her skills as a communicator. Although it is not clear whether this was Michiko's intention, her 2002 solo trip to Switzerland and her prominent public role in a more general sense explicitly called into question the notion that only men are fit to serve as Japan's national symbol. If the Japanese eventually decide to fix the inherent structural problems that make imperial heirs in contemporary Japan scarce enough to threaten the future of the imperial line by changing the system to allow women to serve as *tennō*, some of the foundation for that change will have been laid by Michiko's remarkable public role during the Heisei era.

Mixed Messages and Absences

There have been more facets to the Heisei monarchy beyond the five themes I analyzed here. For example, in spite of Masako's struggles, the imperial family still largely maintains its image as a model family. No imperial marriages in Japan have been torn apart by sordid affairs detailed in the tawdriest way by the tabloid press, as has happened to the British royal family. The lack of sex scandals has clearly contributed to the dutiful image of the imperial house, an image that is critically important because otherwise why should Japanese taxpayers finance this elite institution?

But there was at least one aspect of the present imperial couple's agenda that was mildly problematic, although at the same time I can understand why the emperor and empress took an interest in this issue. Akihito and Michiko made a special point, particularly during their visits to foreign countries, of reaching out to overseas Japanese who are now citizens of other countries (e.g., Brazil). Although this attention to *nikkeijin* was evident during their 2016 trip to the Philippines, it was especially on display during their trips to Brazil (1967, 1978, and 1997) and other countries in the Americas where many Japanese emigrated during the twentieth century. More recently, the visit by Prince Akishino and Princess Kiko (1966–) to Hawaii in June 2018 to mark the 150th anniversary of the arrival of the first Japanese immigrants there as well as Princess Mako's trip to Brazil that next month to help commemorate the 110th anniversary of Japanese immigration there suggests that the focus on Japanese emigrants may outlive the present imperial couple. Princess Mako also visited Peru and Bolivia in July 2019 to mark the 120th anniversary of Japanese immigration to these two countries. Foreign trips by imperial family members only take place if the agenda supports the policy of the government of Japan. It is difficult to understand to what extent individual family members agree with efforts to reach out to overseas Japanese. Regardless, the outreach is supportive of official policy in this area.

At first glance, the imperial family's special attention to *nikkeijin* may seem natural and appropriate, especially if one considers the following factors. In Imperial Japan, there was often an official hand promoting and backing Japanese emigration overseas. Although in the end these emigrants went abroad on their own volition, the Japanese government was substantially involved in the process. Arguably it would have been remiss in the postwar period for the Japanese government, including the emperor, to simply ignore these overseas Japanese.

In addition, these emigrants faced many challenges, sometimes trials beyond those that all immigrants face because of factors such as racial discrimination. In spite of these challenges, there are many examples of Japanese immigrants succeeding in their adopted countries to the extent that they have made societal contributions disproportionate to the size of their population. One example of this would be the contributions that those of Japanese descent made to the development of agriculture in Brazil. Finally, *nikkeijin*, wherever in the world they are, have often served as bridges between their adopted country and their ancestral country. They are well suited to play this role if they become bilingual and develop fluency in the cultural ways of their adopted country and their ancestral country.

Finally, in defense of efforts by the imperial family to reach out to overseas *nikkeijin*, I should mention that at a broad level, this bears similarity to one reason the British royal family continues to maintain close ties with the many countries that make up the Commonwealth: the populations of many of these countries include people whose ancestors emigrated from the British Isles. Moreover, King Juan Carlos of Spain reached out to overseas individuals of Spanish descent. In reference to a 1978 visit to Mexico by Juan Carlos, biographer Paul Preston wrote:

> In Mexico, he put further distance between himself and Franco's policy of maintaining the festering divisions of the Civil War. Many thousands of Republicans had been given refuge by Mexico immediately after the Spanish Civil War and had made their lives there, making a very significant contribution to intellectual, artistic, educational and economic life. Juan Carlos's olive branch of reconciliation to the exiles was symbolized by his generous words to Dolores Rivas Cherif, the widow of the Republican President Manuel Azaña (1880–1940): "Your husband and you yourself are as much part of the history of Spain as I am."[41]

So why might one take issue with the imperial couple's special interest in overseas Japanese? The reason is that this sort of attention reinforces the notion that when all is said and done, membership in the Japanese national community continues to be based on race (blood), even while there are various minority groups in Japan who could benefit from additional attention from the imperial family to overcome the fact that they are not "racially Japanese" in their efforts to be accepted into the national community, most notably the Korean minority. In recent decades the government of Japan has made significant efforts to mobilize Japanese Americans, first and foremost because they have Japanese ancestry, as spokesman for Japan and for the United States–Japan relationship by means of bringing prominent members of this community on junkets to Japan (the official term for these visits is the Japanese American Leadership Delegation, a program that began in 2000).

This heightened interest on the part of the government of Japan in overseas Japanese brings to mind similarly problematic efforts by the government of Imperial Japan to leverage overseas Japanese in the Americas during the 1930s and early 1940s as propaganda agents. Representatives of Imperial Japan frequently proclaimed that all individuals of Japanese ancestry worldwide were loyal subjects of the emperor, regardless of the hopes and wishes of the overseas *nikkeijin* who found themselves in various local environments.[42] Obviously, with the rise of China, the government of Japan has become especially concerned with maintaining (indeed, tightening) its alliance with the United States. But these overtures to overseas individuals of Japanese ancestry are also almost surely related to the fact that Japan's population is shrinking.

In 1990, Japan's fertility decline exploded into the public consciousness in that country. That was the same year that the government of Japan extended special visa preferences to second- and third-generation overseas individuals of Japanese descent to welcome them back to Japan (then facing a labor shortage). Initial responses to the specter of a shrinking national community have included efforts to nationalize overseas individuals of Japanese descent, an initiative that continues today.

Sadly, private organizations in the United States have been complicit in this racialist initiative. The U.S.-Japan Council (est. 2009), has become a central actor in the effort to mobilize Japanese Americans in support of the U.S.-Japan Alliance. During sponsored visits to Japan, Japanese Americans are told all that is good about Japan and taught about the importance and inviolability of the United States–Japan relationship. Clearly the Japanese government hopes they will become emboldened as spokespeople for Japan and about the sanctity of the international partnership after their introduction to the official view on various topics. But one wonders if as many Japanese Americans would agree to participate in such delegations if they were aware that by doing so they were indirectly supporting, supposedly in the name of international friendship, a definition of citizenship in Japan that contributes to discrimination against those who are not racially Japanese. Will such organizations be remembered for having partnered with the government of Japan to use Japanese

Americans to help maintain a race-based definition of citizenship that inflicts precisely the sort of harm on minorities in Japan that individuals of Japanese ancestry experienced in the United States well into the post-war era? The parallels are significant.

I personally subscribe to the notion that what should define membership in the national community is legal citizenship, plain and simple. An individual's race, religion, or other such factors should not matter. Membership in the national community should be predicated on legal citizenship combined with an acceptance of the basic values of one's country (e.g., a willingness to uphold the constitution), not on some racial, ancestral link.

The stories of Japanese immigrants who overcame incredible challenges to succeed in places like Brazil are unquestionably moving. For that matter, so are the stories of various immigrants to Japan who overcame considerable challenges, including discrimination (in the case of Koreans, for example), to make lives for themselves in Japan and contribute to their adopted country in many ways. Japan has its own aboriginal and immigrant communities seeking full acceptance in the national community. Whether Japan can move away from its race-based definition of citizenship may well determine how well the country navigates the demographic time bomb it faces. Unless Japanese are willing to suffer the consequences that will almost surely accompany as much as a one-third drop in population in the coming decades if they do not open the doors to immigrants, they shall face integrating more newcomers into the national community in the coming years. This will require moving beyond racial definitions of citizenship, rather than seizing on the surface solution of trying to nationalize individuals of Japanese descent wherever they can be found.

Going forward, the new emperor and empress may want to privilege the role of helping existing minorities and new immigrants to Japan gain acceptance as full members of the national community over the role of reaching out to overseas Japanese, or at least give this domestic task no less attention than the case of people who left Japan. Overseas Japanese largely are not, after all, Japanese citizens. They are citizens of countries such as Brazil, Peru, and the United States. With few exceptions, at this point in history they tend to be well integrated and respected in their adopted countries. In contrast, there are many citizens and people who would like to be citizens in Japan whose acceptance into the national community could be facilitated by symbolic acts by the emperor, empress, and other imperial family members.

To be fair, in his last annual birthday press conference, Akihito connected the issue of overseas *nikkeijin* with that of more and more immigrants seeking to make Japan their home:

> This year marked 150 years since the beginning of Japanese emigration overseas. Over the years many Japanese people who emigrated have continued to work hard, with the help of the people in their newly settled countries, and they have come to play important roles in the societies there. Thinking of the efforts of those people of Japanese ancestry, we have made a point of meeting with them as much as possible when visiting those countries. Meanwhile, many foreign nationals have come to work in Japan in recent years. When the Empress and I visited the Philippines and Viet Nam, we met individuals who were making efforts towards their goals of working in Japan one day. Bearing in mind that the people of Japanese ancestry are living as active members of society with the help of the people in their respective countries, I hope that the Japanese people will be able to warmly welcome as members of our society those who come to Japan to work here. At the same time, the number of international visitors to Japan is increasing year by year. It is my hope that these visitors will see Japan with their own eyes and deepen their understanding of our country, and that goodwill and friendship will be promoted between Japan and other countries.[43]

Emperor Akihito's emphasis on the parallels between those Japanese who went abroad as immigrants and recent newcomers to Japan is most welcome. But in my view it is a different interpretation of the lessons to be drawn from the experiences of overseas *nikkeijin* than the one held by the Foreign Ministry and other elements of the Japanese government. The Foreign Ministry and Cabinet Affairs Office see in overseas Japanese not simply lessons for a diversifying Japan trying to understand how to welcome newcomers but potential spokespeople for Japan's official policies as somewhat curious overseas and noncitizen members of the national community because of their racial lineage.

There was another near absence from the Heisei imperial couple's agenda where there might be some shift in approach as generational change takes place in the imperial house, extraordinarily delicate though this topic is in Japan. It is an absence that may seem natural to many Japanese, but it contrasts dramatically with other symbolic monarchies. Japan's imperial house is disconnected from the national armed forces (the SDF), to a degree that is unthinkable in almost all other symbolic monarchies. These symbolic monarchies, incidentally, exist in fellow pluralistic democracies, but ones with different histories. Of course, there is also one example of close connections between the monarchy and the military that anyone who values democracy would avoid emulating: the case of Thailand. For more than half a century, the Thai royal house has been complicit in repeatedly supporting military coup d'états and repressive rule by regimes led by the military (often by different factions within the military). In recent years, yet another military regime in Thailand has taken extraordinary measures against anyone, including scholars researching ancient history, deemed guilty of infringing on the dignity of the royal house.

Whether readers think the estrangement of their imperial house from the SDF is a good or a bad thing, or something in between, will likely depend on their political views. Earlier in the book I detailed the comprehensive postdefeat campaign to distance Hirohito and the imperial house from the war. It also must be remembered that after 1945, many Japanese came to define democracy as including peace. The Postwar Constitution is commonly referred to as the "Peace Constitution," not as the "Democratic Constitution." This definition of democracy including peace is arguably specific to postwar Japan; people in other liberal democracies do not define democracy as including peace. Of course, the definition of peace and how to maintain it are questions open to debate. Individuals representing the pacifist end of the spectrum may be in favor of outright elimination of the armed forces, whereas some proponents of peace might argue that in fact the single most likely way to maintain peace is to prepare oneself for war so as to deter one's enemies.

In any case, it is clear how delicate the relationship between the imperial house and the SDF remains more than seventy years after the end of the war. It is not as though there is no interaction. One point that stood out about Akihito's address to the nation on 16 March 2011, after the triple disaster, was that the SDF were the first of the various agencies providing relief efforts to be acknowledged: "I wish to express my appreciation to the members of the Self-Defense Forces." It is also true that during the Heisei era, Akihito and Michiko regularly met with members of the SDF in the imperial palace to thank and honor them for their service to the nation. In addition, while on visits to disaster areas, the imperial couple occasionally received briefings from representatives of various agencies, including the SDF.

But consider the following. The peripatetic Akihito and Michiko crisscrossed the archipelago, setting records for the number of localities visited. To the best of my knowledge these visits did not include a single stop at an SDF base. Members of the SDF make special sacrifices in their work on behalf of the country, the sort of public service that typically draws attention from the imperial couple. The emperor is no longer the head of the armed forces, and it is unthinkable that this position will be restored to him anytime soon. Nonetheless, even today, a visit by the emperor to a military base could remind Japanese, in a negative manner, of prewar military inspections presided over by the emperor. The imperial palace has been very cautious in this area, so much so that one wonders if the SDF feels abandoned by the symbol of the nation-state they are charged with defending.

The extent to which Japan is an outlier in this area becomes clearer when one compares it with three symbolic monarchies in Europe. To begin, consider the case of Spain. King Juan Carlos attended Spain's General Military Academy, and his tertiary education included stints at the Naval Military School and the General Academy of the Air. In a way that exceeded the roles of other symbolic monarchs in Europe who tend to have close links with the military, King Juan Carlos's personal ties with the military were actually crucial in keeping the military in check during Spain's bumpy transition to democracy. The king of Spain is constitutionally commander-in-chief of the armed forces. It is thus unsurprising that the education of the present king, Felipe VI (1968–), also included attendance at the General Military Academy and extensive military training.

The British monarch is also the commander-in-chief of the armed forces. Military education is a fundamental part of the upbringing for male members of the royal family (Queen Elizabeth II seems to have largely learned on the job in this area after serving in the military in World War II). Prince William and Prince Harry both graduated from the Royal Military Academy Sandhurst and continue to maintain close ties to the military, as does their father, Prince Charles. The other European symbolic monarchies also tend to link themselves to the military, including cases where the monarch is a woman. Historian Gunnar Leistikov wrote of Denmark:

> In European monarchies tradition demands that male members of the royal families become officers in the national defense forces. But what to do when the heir apparent is a woman? Princess Margrethe found a solution. She became a member of the Women's Auxiliary Flying Corps, the Danish equivalent of the WAAF [Britain's Women's Auxiliary Air Force]. She participated in much military drill, various sports, learned jiu-jitsu and was at the time of her succession a major in the Danish WAFC.[44]

Although it seems unlikely that Prince Hisahito, who is second in line for the throne after his father, Prince Akishino, might do a short stint at the National Defense Academy of Japan, one wonders if the new emperor might draw more regular attention to those who serve their country through the SDF. The fact that the Abe administration, as I write, remains stubbornly committed to constitutional revision, including of Article 9, makes it unlikely that there will be any new public outreach to the SDF until the issue of constitutional revision is settled. Emperor Naruhito and his advisors almost surely want to avoid the slightest hint that he supports revision of Article 9, one of the most volatile political issues in Japan today.

The sort of work done by SDF personnel, especially the rank and file, is broadly similar to the work done by those in social welfare, even if it lacks the "feel-good" aura. The imperial house maintains a carefully measured distance, at least in public, from the SDF, which provides another window into how heavily the war still weighs on Japan and how the concept of the postwar still resonates as we approach the seventy-fifth anniversary of the end of the war. It is up to the Japanese to decide to what extent they want to maintain the firewall between their emperor and the SDF. Although the distance between them is largely a rejection of generalissimo side of the emperor that was constructed during the Meiji era and was particularly on display when Hirohito was the symbol of Japan's aggressive militarism, it is also important to remember that for most of the long history of the imperial line (especially when one focuses on the history of the imperial line supported by empirical evidence and ignores, say, the supposed military exploits of emperors such as Jimmu), the emperor was kept separate from military affairs. The Meiji conception of the emperor as the supreme commander of the armed forces was a discontinuity from previous practices.

When one compares Japan's imperial house to symbolic royal houses elsewhere, one is also reminded of some absences from the present imperial couple's agenda that have no doubt been welcomed by the emperor and his handlers. For example, the monarchs in Spain and Belgium must devote themselves to keeping their countries unified in the face of significant regional and linguistic divisions. Preston wrote of King Juan Carlos:

> The 1980s would see the conversion of Spain into a semi-federal state through the evolution of what came to be called the State of Autonomies. This had significant implications for the King who took extremely seriously the crown's constitutional role as 'symbol of the unity and permanence' of the Spanish State. He worked extremely hard to elaborate and popularize the idea of a Spain that was pluralistic and multicultural while remaining united.[45]

Although Japan has never been as homogeneous as some commentators have claimed, it is nonetheless true that the country does not face strong regional, linguistic, or cultural challenges to its basic unity. Even the case of Okinawa does not rise to the level of some of the regional divisions Spain continues to face. The centrifugal forces present in Spain were evidenced by the recent unsuccessful and traumatic bid for independence by Catalonia. The few divisions in Japan are also minimal compared with those that continuously lurk beneath the surface in Belgium as the result of this nation-state constituting an amalgam of citizens who speak three different languages.

The Reiwa Era

We now understand that Akihito and Michiko put a significant stamp on the monarchy. Emperor Naruhito and Empress Masako will do the same. We look back on comments that Akihito, as crown prince, made during press conferences and understand how much he was foreshadowing the direction of his reign. Thus, it behooves us also to pay attention to what Naruhito said during his press conferences as crown prince. At the February 2018 press conference marking his birthday (23 February), Crown Prince Naruhito stressed, "I think . . . what people expect in official duties will change according to social changes, and it would be important to respond to new demands. I would like to sincerely perform official duties accordingly."[46] More recently, at his 2019 birthday press conference, his last as crown prince, Naruhito made clear that the issues of diversity and tolerance are on his mind. He described the Heisei era as an "age that witnessed greater diversity in the lifestyles and value systems held by the people." He went onto to stress, "It will be important to accept that diversity with a spirit of tolerance while seeking to further develop it through the mutual encouragement of each other."[47]

In this chapter thus far, I have imagined some possible areas to which the new emperor and empress might turn their attention in a way that would differentiate them from the previous imperial couple. Below I discuss more. It is likely that there will be more basic continuity between the Heisei era and the Reiwa era than was the case between the Shōwa and Heisei eras for one simple reason. Although Hirohito reigned long into the postwar era, he was nonetheless the product of the prewar era, accustomed to the Meiji Constitution. In contrast, Akihito spent his most formidable years under the postwar system, and Naruhito has spent his whole life under the postwar system. Akihito once described the education of the heir to Japan's throne as *shōchōgaku* (the study of being a symbol), a telling comment reflecting how much Naruhito is a product of postwar Japan. The new era will continue to be fundamentally a constitutional symbolic monarchy under popular sovereignty.

Of the five themes characterizing the Heisei era that I analyzed above, there is good reason to think that four will be features of the next imperial era, if perhaps not to the same extent: (1) support of the postwar system; (2) efforts to compress the margins of society; (3) efforts to bring closure to the postwar era; and (4) demonstrations of pride in the best that Japan has to offer, a pride tempered with a cosmopolitanism. We must also hold out the possibility that Masako could surprise many by being an active empress, even if it will be difficult for her to match Michiko's role. The early signs since Masako became empress have in fact been very promising, with her regularly appearing at official functions and exuding energy, and this has not gone unnoticed by her countrymen and -women.

Even if these themes continue to be important, we should expect adjustments. After all, if Emperor Naruhito and Empress Masako adopt all the public duties considered important by Akihito and Michiko, how will they add additional "public acts in the position of symbol" that might be of greater meaning to them and more in tune with the trends of the times? For example, unlike his father, Naruhito has no direct, personal memory of the war (although he has referenced how frequently his parents spoke to him about it). In addition, those Japanese who experienced the war firsthand are rapidly dying off. It simply may not be possible for Naruhito to bring the same sort of passion that his father did to the issues of healing wounds of the war and reminding people of the horrors of war. Even if he attaches to these issues the same sort of importance, with fewer and fewer Japanese with personal memories of the war (that number could approach zero in the next imperial era), the societal response to this theme could be quite different.

The symbolic contours of Naruhito and Masako were delayed from taking better shape as a result of the heir problem, combined with Masako's adjustment disorder, which dates from December 2003. Masako became empress still lacking an uncompromised, positive image. Although her health has been improving in recent years, allowing her to undertake more public duties, to the extent that she had a "symbolic essence" (*shōchōsei*) when she became empress it still included vestiges of being seen as a victim of the inflexible imperial house by some or condemned as a whiny former career woman unwilling to gracefully accept the duties of her role (which, according to the present system, included providing a male heir to the throne) by others—not the sort of image befitting an imperial family member.

In contrast, Naruhito's symbolic essence gradually developed during his time as crown prince and included some noticeable departures from previous generations. Consider the topic of gender roles. Commentators writing about gender tend to focus largely on women even though it has been well documented that male roles are also shaped in part by cultural expectations. When Princess Aiko was born in 2001, I wrote an opinion piece querying whether the Imperial Household Agency might release a photo of Naruhito changing a diaper, to symbolize his role as a hands-on father. This did not happen, but at the same time Naruhito emerged as a symbol of a new definition of fatherhood.

In July 2002, images of Naruhito carrying Princess Aiko on his back were widely disseminated; indeed, at one point the little princess managed to grab her father's hair, and Naruhito responded with a laugh. During a February 2003 press conference, the crown prince remarked, "Through giving the princess a bath, taking her for walks, or giving her baby food, I myself feel a strong bond with my child." He further commented, "The help of fathers in raising children whenever possible not only lightens the burden on mothers, but it is also a very good way for fathers to strengthen their relations with their children."[48]

Claims of sexism against women in Japan are of course legitimate; in too many areas Japan remains a patriarchal society. But I have long empathized equally with those men, especially the postwar generations who worked themselves to the bone (and sometimes literally to death), who never got to be hands-on fathers because that role was not seen as "manly" (and because they were kept so incredibly busy in their "manly" roles as salarymen that they literally had no time to be hands-on fathers). Thus, one should not underestimate the symbolic significance of Naruhito explicitly being a hands-on father. Incidentally, after Prince George, third in line to the British throne, was born on 22 July 2013, it was Prince William who changed the baby's first diaper, to highlight his role as a hands-on father.

Continuing on the topic of gender, it is true that some women have been disappointed that Masako, who gave up a career as an elite diplomat to marry, has not been able to reform the palace in any noticeable way since her marriage in 1993. These hopes were largely misplaced, because a crown princess, with the exception of raising the heir to the throne, structurally has very little power in the palace. Her adjustment disorder has defined Masako far more so than the Imperial Palace would like. But it should be remembered that Naruhito has resolutely lived up to the vow he made at the time of his marriage proposal—to protect her with all his strength. Such a supporting role in Japan is more typically associated with the wife, so in this area Naruhito is again blurring traditional gender roles.

Masako is now empress. It is not fair to expect her to turn her attention first and foremost to redefining gender roles for women. But if she wanted to make a difference in this area, there are simple things she could do. For example, the next time a Japanese schoolgirl wins a significant prize related to math and science, the empress could attend the awards ceremony, lending imperial legitimacy to the notion that it is appropriate for girls to excel in math and science rather than in just the arts. She could also attend professional women's luncheons from time to time to validate the notion that women can have careers outside the home. There are many other causes she could adopt beyond those suggested by her career background. She has given clear hints that she values a role of looking out for people in a "weak position," thus carrying on in an area that was particularly important to Michiko.

One obvious break with the immediate past is that, at least according to how the Imperial House Law stands as of 2019, Empress Masako and Emperor Naruhito will not raise the heir to the throne. Since the birth of their son Prince Hisahito, Prince Akishino and Princess Kiko have been catapulted into additional prominence. Princess Kiko has long represented the "good wife, wise mother" (*ryōsai kenbo*) model of womanhood. But this image of her obscures the fact that in many ways she has come to play the role as the champion of new definitions of the roles of women in society that many people inside and outside of Japan expected Masako to play. Just to provide one example, Kiko lends her symbolic prestige to an initiative by the Japan Promotion of Science to encourage women researchers to restart their research activities after giving birth. According to the Imperial Household Agency's website, Kiko often attends presentations by these researchers.

Kiko is obviously the central figure in raising Prince Hisahito, which could be her most important role in the imperial system. Whatever additional tutoring in the area of "learning how to be a symbol" that Prince Hisahito may receive from others, including his uncle the emperor, Crown Prince Akishino and Crown Princess Kiko will surely influence Prince Hisahito most of all and thus shape the future of the imperial house, if he becomes emperor. How this story unfolds will be a new and interesting thread in the story of the monarchy in modern Japan.

Although this fact is sometimes lost in the coverage devoted to the dizzying number of international trips that Akihito and Michiko undertook, Emperor Naruhito's background is actually more international than that of his father. Naruhito spent two years as a graduate student at Oxford University, living as much like a regular student as his royal status allowed him to do. He visited forty-one countries while crown prince. Along the same lines, Masako's background, which included stints at Harvard and Oxford, is also more international than was that of Michiko.

Emperor Naruhito's interest in a variety of issues related to water apparently goes back to his childhood, and his graduate studies at Oxford helped internationalize his interest in this issue. The topic of water may seem mundane for people who have regular access to clean water. But it is a consuming issue for the billion-plus individuals around the world for whom accessing clean water is a daily challenge. There are billions of people whose basic livelihoods are still threatened when, for example, the annual rains are insufficient on one hand or torrential on the other.

Whether not enough of it (especially in clean form) or too much of it at once, water is often a cause of poverty worldwide (and it can certainly be the cause of wars). Although everyone in Japan has access to clean water and most Japanese today can only imagine what it is like to go at length without food, 2018 was a year when water-related storms, possibly strengthened by climate change, caused unusually extensive damage in Japan. This possibly served as a reminder that the issue of water is truly one of critical importance to the whole world, a point Naruhito has been stressing for decades. A collection of Naruhito's speeches on water was published in Japan just in advance of his enthronement.[49] With his basic concern for environmental issues, Naruhito is following in the footsteps of his grandfather and father, but with more of an international focus.

Naruhito's focus on issues related to water has been perhaps best highlighted by him having served as honorary president of the United Nations Secretary General's Advisory Board on Water and Sanitation from 2007 through 2015. Throughout the postwar era, Japanese have tended to rate the significance of the United Nations far greater than, for example, Americans have, giving extra cachet to Naruhito's association with it. In his 18 November 2015 keynote lecture to the United Nations Special Thematic Session on Water and Disasters in New York City, Naruhito stressed, "There is no topic of greater importance to our common future than water, nor one with deeper links to our common humanity."[50] He went on to describe, citing Japanese poems through the centuries, the joys and sorrows that result from humankind's interconnectedness with water, including examples of droughts and floods. His lecture also addressed scientific breakthroughs in water management and what a difference these can make in the lives of people worldwide.

FIGURE 35. Then-Crown Prince Naruhito delivers a speech about "Water and Natural Disasters" at the World Water Forum held in Brasilia, Brazil, 19 March 2018. (Photograph Courtesy Kyodo News Service.)

Naruhito has given broad hints that water will remain one of the issues to which he devotes his attention. Emperor Akihito devoted himself to cultivating international goodwill through trips and hosting international guests to Japan, and he was a tireless advocate of peace. But it is fair to say that he never adopted a specific issue at the international level along the lines of Princess Diana dramatically taking up the cause of the disposal of land mines, or in the more studious way that Naruhito has taken up the cause of water. Thus, Naruhito's attention to water as a global problem marks a new departure for the imperial house. Although it is too early to conclude this with certainty, it is likely that in the same way that his father and mother devoted much of their reign to lending their prestige to vulnerable members of Japanese society, Naruhito intends to lend his prestige to some of the most vulnerable members of global society, for example, those individuals who cannot take access to water for granted.

If Naruhito seemed overly cautious and soft-spoken at times as crown prince and to have been less active overall than some Japanese might have liked, it might be worth mentioning that having a bold, strong-minded crown prince like Charles of Britain brings its own problems. To his credit, Prince Charles has made some tangible contributions to British society, including programs to help the underprivileged. But nearly no one in Japan today, where there is a consensus that imperial family members must stay away from openly political issues, can imagine the corollary of a crown prince behaving along the lines of the following description of Prince Charles in a recent biography:

> Charles's other principal crusade, his two-decades-long advocacy of alternative medicine, intensified during the early years of the twenty-first century. In May 2003 his Foundation for Integrated Health announced a five-year effort to put complementary therapies on an equal basis with traditional medicine in the NHS [National Health Service]. He tenaciously lobbied senior government officials, all the way up to [Prime Minister] Tony Blair, to block the adoption in Britain of European Union rules restricting the sale of unproven herbal nostrums including Chinese and Ayurvedic remedies. Charles wrote a long letter to the prime minister following a conversation in March 2005. In stating his unequivocal demands for action, he reminded Blair that they had agreed that EU regulations were "using a sledgehammer to crack a nut." Blair promised to delay the implementation for another six years. It was a further example of Charles finding a way to advance his agenda, no matter the constitutional implications.[51]

There are many sides to this description of Prince Charles that would shock Japanese. First there is the issue of a crown prince forcefully supporting a cause that many in the medical profession consider to be little more than quackery (and readers unfamiliar with Prince Charles should understand that he has backed several other causes far outside the mainstream and had experts in those areas shaking their heads in distress). There is also the issue of the prince so blatantly involving himself in politics. Add into the equation the fact that the Prince Charles's sponsored Foundation for Integrated Health was dissolved in 2010 after a public scandal resulting from the chief financial officer embezzling large sums of money, and most Japanese would shake their heads in near disbelief and conclude that it is just as well that their imperial family, including the crown prince, chooses its causes and associates with great care. The collapse of the Foundation for Integrated Health was one of the negative side effects of Prince Charles overseeing a "philanthropic empire" that by 2005 involved him "pulling in more than $150 million a year for his seventeen 'core' charities."[52]

It is difficult to imagine that members of Japan's imperial family will develop philanthropic empires in the future. The most fundamental challenge the next imperial couple faces is maintaining the high degree of unity that Japan, relative to many nation-states, enjoys in the face of all sorts of centrifugal forces. Ahead of a visit to Malaysia in 2017, Crown Prince Naruhito credited that country with achieving success based on diversity and tolerance. Some observers would take issue with Naruhito's rosy view of Malaysia in this area, but in any case, it was one of several comments suggesting just how much he was mulling over the issue of how to forge unity out of diversity.

No one should underestimate the sort the challenges that diversity in all forms can present, ranging from diversity caused by greater socioeconomic differences among members of society to diversity created by immigrants coming into Japan. In many ways, one of the fundamental challenges of all nation-states is to try to maintain a common center to which the citizens feel loyal. This is true of nation-states whether or not they have monarchies, but in those that have monarchies, the monarchy often acts as a centripetal force. How can the next emperor and empress do so?

One might pose a question that will no doubt come as a great shock to certain self-appointed traditionalists in Japan. Japan has always been far less homogeneous, including in the area of religion, than some commentators would have us believe. In addition to preexisting heterogeneity, Japan's population is in the process of racially and religiously diversifying. Thus, might it be time to rethink the various Shinto rituals (*saishi*) that fill the emperor's schedule? Should the national symbol so obviously privilege one faith over another in a multireligious nation-state? This question is worth asking, even as one must respect the personal freedom of imperial family members to pursue a religion of their choice. The point here is that there is nothing necessarily "natural" about these Shinto rituals, many of which date from the Meiji era and not earlier and some of which do not allow participation by women. Before the Meiji era, the imperial house was arguably more associated with Buddhism than with Shinto. If many of these rituals were invented or reinvented during the Meiji era, then they can certainly be adjusted going forward.

For example, Prince Charles, for all his faults, has been thinking about the issue of "faith" at great length in reference to Britain. The British monarch is Supreme Governor of the Church of England, also known as the Anglican Church. In her biography of Prince Charles, Sally Bedell Smith wrote of the future king: "On becoming king, he would, like his mother, be called upon to take the coronation oath, pledging to be 'Defender of the Faith.' Instead, Charles said he 'would much rather see it as Defender of *Faith*, not *the* Faith.' . . . He gave equal weight to 'Catholic subjects of the sovereign' as well as the 'Islamic subjects or the Hindu subjects or the Zoroastrian subjects.'"[53]

The term "multicultural" is beloved by some and despised by others these days. Those in favor of multiculturalism no doubt applaud Prince Charles's sensitivity, whereas others may view him as throwing his country's Anglican traditions under the bus. I am by no means opposed to multiculturalism. At the same time, one must address the following issue in reference to multicultural nation-states. How does one hold the center? In other words, how does one keep a multicultural nation unified? Anyone living in the United States under President Donald Trump cannot fail to recognize that debates over multiculturalism are one of many factors contributing to an extreme polarization of political views among Americans. Trump has sought to profit politically by exploiting and deepening various divisions, rather than trying to bridge them.

My point is that multiculturalism and national unity are complicated issues; in fact they sometimes can be in tension with each other. How does one respect diversity? At the same time, how does one forge unity out of diversity? The answer to the latter question tends to include unceasing effort, not to mention defining the commonalities that should unite a nation. The single greatest challenge, at the broad level, that Emperor Naruhito and Empress Masako face is respecting and honoring diversity on one hand while maintaining unity on the other.

CHAPTER 8

The Abdication of Emperor Akihito and the Fragility of the Imperial Line

In recent decades, several monarchies have been in the news more so than usual because a new generation of royalty has come to the forefront, in several cases because of abdication, and in other cases because of deaths. Between 2000 and 2014, there were abdications in Luxembourg, Bhutan, the Netherlands, Qatar, Belgium, and Spain. Emperor Akihito had close personal relationships with three of the monarchs who abdicated (Grand Duke Jean [1921–2019; r. 1964–2000] of Luxembourg, Queen Beatrix [b. 1938; r. 1980–2013] of the Netherlands, and King Juan Carlos of Spain). Akihito's abdication in 2019 should be contextualized within this broader wave of abdications. The circumstances surrounding these abdications and the accession ceremonies for the new monarchs shed light on the challenges faced by royal houses to remain relevant in the twenty-first century.

Consider the case of Bhutan. In 2005, King Wangchuck (b. 1955; r. 1972–2006), a hands-on ruler, shocked his countrymen by declaring he would abdicate in favor of his eldest son even as the country transformed into a parliamentary democracy with a symbolic monarch. To understand the useful role a symbolic king can undertake, a government think tank in Bhutan invited me and other experts on monarchy to come to Bhutan in 2009 and explain how symbolic monarchies work elsewhere. The Bhutanese, who have friendly relations with Japan, were especially interested in Japan's symbolic monarchy as a model.

Since 2006, the new young king of Bhutan, Jigme Khesar Namgyel Wangchuck, has dutifully carried out his role as a symbolic monarch, showing no inclination of reclaiming a hands-on role from the democratically elected National Assembly.[1] But according to Article 2.6 of the Constitution of Bhutan, upon reaching sixty-five years of age he must step down and turn over the throne to the crown prince or crown princess, as long as the heir has come of age. This provision is unusual among the remaining symbolic monarchies, but arguably suitable for a time when people live much longer on average.

In 2011, Prince Akishino suggested that Japan's imperial line needed a mechanism for retirement, but no subsequent action has been taken to institutionalize such measures. Before he was named next in line to be emperor when Naruhito (his older brother) ascended to the throne, Prince Akishino often voiced opinions about necessary reforms to bring the imperial house in line with contemporary society. That does not mean that the politicians responded; they often ignored such suggestions. Crown Prince Akishino, Crown Princess Kiko, and Prince Hisahito visited Bhutan in August 2019 in what was Hisahito's first overseas trip, providing a chance for Japanese royals to take stock of Bhutan's symbolic monarchy, based to some extent on Japan's system, but an updated version.

The case of the royal transition in the Netherlands was interesting for the views expressed by the departing queen and the new king about the role of a monarch in the national community in the twenty-first century. In her abdication speech in 2013, Queen Beatrix said that hereditary authority did not give substance to a contemporary monarchy; rather, this was earned through "the will to serve the country."[2] In addition, the new king, Willem-Alexander (b. 1967), said that he does not expect to be called "His Majesty" by his countrymen or others, stressing that people can "address me as they wish."[3] Dispensing with the title "His Majesty" or "Your Majesty" takes the Dutch example of what experts call the bicycle monarchies of continental Europe another step closer to the people.

The Scandinavian monarchies in particular, but also other continental European monarchies, are sometimes referred to as "bicycle monarchies" because it is not unusual for one of the monarchs in these countries to hop on a bike and ride to a local café for an impromptu cup of coffee with their compatriots. In the case of bicycle monarchies, the distance between the throne and the people is especially small. I should stress that the term "bicycle monarchy" does not apply to the royal houses of Britain or Japan.

King Willem-Alexander dispensing with his title raises a fundamental question regarding monarchies that survive in democratic polities. If a royal house does not maintain some sort of elevated societal position, how can it perform a meaningful role? If it is not even newsworthy, for example, that a royal family member would visit a social welfare institution, how can the monarchy play the role of drawing attention to such issues as the challenges faced by the disabled? How can a royal house be among the people yet maintain enough special status to provide themselves with a meaningful role in society? These are the sorts of equations pondered by royals and their advisors in democratic polities around the world.

Just a few months after the Netherlands crowned a new king, in neighboring Belgium the way Philippe (b. 1960) took the oath of office after Albert II's (b. 1934; r. 1993–2013) abdication epitomized the centripetal force that monarchies hope to play in modern nation-states. Philippe swore his oath in the country's three official languages, Dutch, French, and German.[4] Arguably the most important role of the monarch in Belgium is to endeavor to keep this multilingual, multiethnic state unified in the face of significant centrifugal forces. When Emperor Akihito abdicated on 30 April 2019, he was the sixth monarch worldwide to abdicate since 2006. It is possible that later evidence will become available to support my suspicion that his decision to step down was influenced by these global trends.

The Abdication in Historical Context

Abdications by emperors were common throughout much of Japan's history. According to scholar of legal history Mizubayashi Takeshi, 60 of the verifiable 102 emperors before Akihito abdicated.[5] However, a provision for abdication was left out of the modernized legal codes implemented in the Meiji era, arguably representing a break with long-standing traditions. Reasons abdication did not appear in the Meiji-era Imperial House Law, as well as the postwar version, included a concern that the dual presence of a retired emperor and a sitting emperor might weaken the authority of the emperor. Or even worse, there was the possibility that divisive political factions could develop behind competitors to the throne, be they a retired emperor, a sitting emperor, or other claimants, as has happened before. In addition, there was the concern that an emperor might be forced to abdicate by people around the throne with ill motives.

Nonetheless, after Japan's catastrophic defeat in 1945, the possibility of Hirohito abdicating became an issue and was broached several times in the subsequent years. Japan's modern imperial project included various wars waged in the name of the emperor. This meant that after surrender, Hirohito found himself in a perilous position. The U.S. Occupation authorities were adamant about maintaining the monarchy, particularly the anticommunist Hirohito. General MacArthur made clear his opposition to Hirohito abdicating, which played a big role in the emperor putting to rest a question that had been on his mind.

Even some conservative Japanese, especially when Japan regaining independence in 1952 corresponded with Akihito coming of age, questioned whether it would be better for Hirohito, stained with responsibility for the war, to step aside. After all, in many ways Akihito seemed better suited to represent postwar Japan. Akihito was born in 1933, but his most formative childhood years were spent under the new, reformed system. This made him arguably more in tune with the postwar system, characterized by democracy and pacifism, than was his father, who was raised under the Meiji system and in whose name fifteen years of war were waged.

The question of who was better suited to symbolize postwar Japan, Hirohito or Akihito, led to a memorable exchange in January 1952 in the Diet between Nakasone Yasuhiro and Yoshida Shigeru regarding the potential of Hirohito abdicating. The abdication proposed by Nakasone in 1952 would have been as logistically complicated then as what happened after Emperor Akihito's August 2016 address in which he suggested his desire to abdicate. The revised, postwar Imperial House Law does not include a clause for abdication. It would not have been so easy for Hirohito to abdicate, although surely it could have been arranged if necessary.

It is almost certainly the case that a clause permitting abdication was left out of the postwar Imperial House Law in part to protect the anticommunist, pro-U.S.–Japan alliance Hirohito. After all, the U.S. Occupation authorities found Hirohito to be very useful in legitimizing various reforms. But it is also true and almost surely more important that the no-abdication policy followed the precedent of the Meiji-era Imperial House Law. In many areas, including the Imperial House Law and in reference to the various imperial rituals related to State Shinto (even if State Shinto was disestablished), the general tendency of the Japanese side (especially when the Americans were not paying too much attention) was to maintain as many continuities with Imperial Japan as possible.

One can draw several conclusions about the abdication of Akihito. First, the driving force behind this was definitely Akihito himself, another reminder that individual emperors put their stamp on the imperial house. Akihito chose to abdicate. We now know that he started to discuss abdication with people around him in 2010, six years prior to his August 2016 television address, when he laid out his reasons for wanting to step down. During those six years, Akihito tenaciously held to his desire to abdicate until he was finally allowed to make his case to the people.

In the interim, apparently a tense political struggle was waged between the Imperial Household Agency and the Office of the Prime Minister, the latter of which resisted abdication. This struggle continued in reference to every detail about the abdication, including the question of when the new reign name would be announced. What preceded (and very likely prompted) Akihito's televised address was a July 2016 scoop by NHK revealing the emperor's desire to step down. This story resulted from a leak by someone close to the emperor, and it is not clear whether the televised address the next month would have taken place without the NHK report. Unsurprisingly, an overwhelming majority of Japanese got behind abdication in the aftermath of the televised address, making the abdication at that point virtually guaranteed. For this reason, some constitutional scholars questioned the validity of the emperor being allowed to make his case to the people about what was, after all, a political matter.

Second, although strictly speaking "abdication" is the correct legal term to describe what Akihito did, the word "retirement" more accurately captures the overall situation. By the time Emperor Akihito turned the throne over to his son, he had served as emperor for thirty years and as crown prince for thirty-seven years before that. This was not a case of someone shirking his basic duties.

Perhaps the most famous case of abdication in modern times was that by Edward VIII (1894–1972; r. 20 January–11 December 1936) of the United Kingdom in 1936. That was a true abdication, so traumatic that according to historian David Cannadine the term "abdication" still makes British royal family members shudder, most notably Queen Elizabeth II. Edward VIII was seen as brazenly putting his private desires before public duty by insisting on marrying an American divorcée, which was out of tune with the mores of the time and led to his abdication.

It almost certainly goes beyond personal preference that even though Queen Elizabeth II is over age ninety, she has not abdicated. Such is the painful memory of the case of Edward VIII in the British royal house. But in other areas, much has changed about the British royal family. Prince Harry's (1984–) 2018 marriage to Meghan Markle (1981–) demonstrated that it was okay for a British royal to marry an American divorcée, one who also happens to be of mixed race, which is arguably more dramatic in terms of evidencing change than the fact that she was previously married.

Few Japanese interpreted Akihito's desire to retire along the lines of him putting his private interests before public ones, although a faction of conservatives viewed it critically in this manner. The third point to understand regarding Akhito's abdication is that there is no evidence that he abdicated to rebuke the Abe administration. Many people on the left make such a claim, but there is simply no evidence to support that thesis. Akihito's political views formed decades ago. It was a coincidence that he happened to end his reign side by side with a prime minister whose political views did not accord with his own.

There are two primary reasons Akihito wanted to step down. First, in his public position as national symbol, he pursued a rigorous schedule that had him and the empress reaching out to the people in numerous ways. Akihito was aware he could not maintain such a schedule as he aged. At the same time, he believed these various public acts in his position as symbol to be fundamental to the role of the emperor, whose survival is dependent on the good will of the people.

Second, he understood the importance, in terms of the imperial house maintaining its relevance to the people, of avoiding the scenario whereby one senior citizen would have been succeeded as emperor by another senior citizen. Naruhito was fifty-nine years old when he ascended to the throne on 1 May 2019. If Akihito had continued on the throne for another six years—a likely scenario (in fact, he plausibly could have continued as emperor for several years beyond that)—Japan would indeed have witnessed a senior citizen taking over as emperor. Imperial family members understand that the monarchy must keep the imperial house relevant to the people and reach out to the people regularly. Akihito concluded it was time for the next generation to take its turn. Probably no one understood better the basic fragility of the imperial line more so than Akihito, and he viewed passing it on to his son while Naruhito was in the prime of his life as a way to stabilize the system. In addition, by abdicating, Akihito was able to draw attention to the need for measures to address the heir crisis, which is arguably the most immediate threat to the future of the throne.

It is also the case that Akihito was traumatized by what he considered the inhumane treatment of his father as his death approached (e.g., daily announcements of excruciatingly minute details about his condition). He wanted to avoid a similar scenario. Akihito was well aware that his mother (Nagako) suffered from dementia in her later years. He could not help wondering if he would suffer the same fate, and he did not want to be emperor while suffering from this condition.

Although there is no evidence that Akihito abdicated to rebuke the Abe administration, it is nonetheless true that in some areas Akihito's views were (and are, although it is unlikely that there will be opportunities that remind us of this situation) out of tune with much of the political right. They were so much out of step that we have moved away from the previous dichotomy whereby it was said that the political right worshiped the throne and the political left was either against the emperor system or supported it in only a measured manner.

If a new dichotomy developed during the Heisei era, it was characterized by some of the political right feeling a lot of (largely unspoken) unease about Akihito, and the political left celebrating Akihito the person (but not necessarily the monarchy itself). Frankly, in terms of respecting the constitution, elements of the left behaved irresponsibly by repeatedly using Akihito's viewpoints to point out shortcomings with the Abe administration. Akihito successfully neutralized much of the previously fierce opposition against the emperor system by elements of the left. It was notable that by the end of the Heisei era, the JCP had dropped its opposition to the throne. The JCP participated amicably in high-level talks in the legislature about how to arrange for Akihito's abdication. Areas where Akihito was out of tune with much of the present political right include that he respects the Postwar Constitution and believes that Japanese need to reflect on and show contrition for their historical mistakes, especially those made during the imperial era. Nonetheless, I suspect that opposition from the left continues to exist just under the surface and could reignite easily in the future depending on imperial developments.

The political right reacted to Akihito's stated wish to abdicate with a variety of views. One must distinguish between true feelings and what representatives of the political right were willing to say in public, especially after the Akihito's August 2016 address, when public opinion polls showed overwhelming support for the government taking the necessary action to allow the emperor to step down. It is also important to remember that as one moves further to the right in Japan, the worry was not simply whether abdication, if adopted as precedent, might undermine the stability of the throne. Rather, there was another grave concern: that the discussion over abdication would drift toward the question of why women are not allowed to serve as the national symbol.

For the Abe administration, abdication was an annoying distraction, although of course no one representing the government said as much publicly. But one member of Abe's brain trust, Momochi Akira (1946–), spoke frankly. In August 2016, Momochi stressed, "For the first time since the war's end, there is a chance for the Japanese people to revise the constitution that was forced upon them by Occupation forces. Frankly, I worry we will lose the ability to achieve this."[6] But Momochi was willing to concede with great reluctance to a special provision to allow Akihito to abdicate. This was also the stance of the Association of Shinto Shrines. However, Momochi and the Association of Shinto Shrines recommended that measures be taken to ensure that the unbroken male bloodline continue.

Some members of Abe's brain trust not only came out in opposition to abdication, they apparently managed to denigrate Akihito's conception of how a symbolic emperor should spend his time by suggesting that all that mattered was that the emperor pray on behalf of the nation. Akihito, after all, was the first emperor to be enthroned under the Postwar Constitution. Thus, his role in defining the duties of a symbolic emperor was especially significant, and he interpreted the role of a symbol emperor in expansive terms.

Akihito did not disagree with the assertion that one important role of the emperor was praying for nation. In fact, to the concern of scholars who stress the necessity of maintaining a strict separation between religion and the state, as required by the constitution, Akihito indicated in his televised 2016 address that one important duty of the emperor was praying for the safety and happiness of the people. In the process of explaining his reasons for abdicating, Akihito provided the single most comprehensive explanation of his interpretation of the proper role of a symbol emperor.

According to the constitution, religious acts by the emperor are to be carried out only in the emperor's private position. However, Akihito's reference to them in his televised address seemed to conflate them with his public duties, to the concern of some scholars. For his part, Akihito took issue with the interpretation by a different group of scholars, mostly conservative ones, who argued that in terms of the emperor's duties nothing much beyond such prayers was particularly necessary. Meanwhile, historian Watanabe Osamu argued that the entire category of public acts in the emperor's position of symbol—the category that allowed for the expansive interpretation of the role of a symbol emperor that Akihito embraced and put into practice—was fundamentally unconstitutional.[7] There can be numerous competing interpretations among Japanese regarding any detail involving the imperial house.

The special government commission established to study the question of abdication (the official name of the commission referred to examining the issue of lightening the public duties of the emperor and other matters; 2016–17) hosted short presentations by experts whose political views spanned the political spectrum. But a disproportionate number of conservative commentators were called to testify. This may have represented the Abe administration's way of appeasing those who opposed abdication while also giving Akihito a slap on the hand for insisting on it, even after eventually approving it in the face of overwhelming public support. The conservative faction included Hirakawa Sukehiro (emeritus professor at Tokyo University; 1931–) and Watanabe Shōichi (emeritus professor at Sophia University at the time of testimony; 1930–2017). Hirakawa and Watanabe were of the same opinion regarding the fundamental role of the imperial house, which they viewed as simply continuing to exist, and in reference to the emperor's most basic duty, which they saw as praying for the people and the country.

Watanabe stressed in his testimony: "The work of the emperor, the primary work of emperors from past times, was to pray on behalf of the country, on behalf of the people."[8] He went on to say that although it was okay that the present emperor endeavored to show himself to the people through his many outings, that was not the least bit necessary. Akihito viewed this interpretation of the proper role of the national symbol as a negation of the active role he and his empress have played on various fronts. It is nonetheless true that Akihito vigorously leveraging his prestige behind certain causes and regularly interacting with the people was precisely his particular view of what role a symbolic monarch should play. The term "symbol" is inherently vague and the proper role of a symbol emperor is open to various interpretations, especially in light of the fact that the constitutional basis for the category of "public acts in his position as symbol" is less than firm.

In her testimony to the government commission, journalist Sakurai Yoshiko (1945–) agreed that praying on behalf of the people and the nation-state was the emperor's single most important function. She proceeded to denounce the Postwar Constitution because, according to standard interpretations, the emperor serves as the high priest of Shinto only in his private capacity, not in a public one. Throughout the postwar era, elements of the Shintoist far right have had Article 20, which provides separation of religion and the state, in their sights for revision. Sakurai also stressed that the 2,700-year tradition of an unbroken male lineage must be preserved, an interesting stance for this woman journalist that reminds us that not all women in Japan are in favor of allowing women to serve as the national symbol. The "2,700-year tradition" refers to the mythical version of the origins and history of the imperial line. No one who values empirical evidence accepts the notion that the imperial line dates back to Emperor Jimmu, but this account is used to support the notion that it is an unbroken male bloodline.

Several of the conservatives who testified to the commission on abdication spoke glowingly about how Emperor Shōwa (Hirohito) had continued his duties up until his passing, suggesting that Akihito was less an emperor for wanting to retire. They repeated panegyrics to Hirohito. Over and over they glorified his intervention to end the war while ignoring all his other political interventions, including his delay of the surrender in the hope that the Imperial Military could score a decisive victory so that a negotiated surrender rather than an unconditional one could be achieved. Hirohito was no monster, but he certainly was no hero either. In their unreserved praise of him, certain conservatives seemed to suggest that the present emperor did not measure up to his father. Perhaps this criticism had more to do with Akihito's progressive positions rather than his desire to abdicate.

One underlying worry for conservatives gravely concerned about protecting the future of the imperial line, especially because there are so few eligible heirs, was the following corollary. If an emperor can abdicate, can a crown prince decline to be emperor? Or can an emperor, after only a few years as the national symbol, decide that the role does not suit him and abdicate? These are legitimate questions. Conservatives repeatedly made comments that suggested their concern for continuing the imperial line at all costs extended to disregard for imperial family members as individuals. Yagi Hidetsugu (Reitaku University; 1962–) testified: "If one recognizes abdication according to personal will, then one recognizes that the next generation can refuse to be enthroned, or that it has the right to abdicate shortly after having been enthroned, and this shakes the stability of the imperial line, thus putting in danger the survival of the imperial system."[9]

It is difficult to fault the logic behind Yagi's imaginings about possible future scenarios. But he did not validate the notion that the personal desires of imperial family members might also have legitimacy. Yagi is a staunch supporter of male lineage, stressing in recent remarks, "Historically speaking, the succession principle based only on male lineage has firmly established the status of emperors. Will a future emperor with female lineage be considered legitimate? We should not confuse imperial succession with modern society's trend toward gender equality and women's empowerment."[10] Yagi is the main peddler of a pseudo-scientific theory that gives particular importance to the Y chromosome for shaping a lineage, and this view sadly enjoys some popularity in Japan.

In the August 2019 issue of the Japanese monthly *WiLL*, Yagi, who is a member of Prime Minister Abe's brain trust in reference to matters concerning the imperial house, accused me and the *Asahi* newspaper (publisher of my Japanese-language account of the Heisei monarchy) of conspiring to put a mixed-race emperor on the throne by advocating for a change in the law to allow women to serve as *tennō* (and to permit matrilineal succession). To the extent that logic backed up this accusation, it rested on the notion that a woman in line to be *tennō* might marry a foreigner (the child of such a union would be the mixed-race emperor). This slanderous attack was greeted by even most conservatives in Japan with distaste and amazement. But there is a segment of Japanese who, as the world around them evolves rapidly, are taking refuge in racialist views. Japanese who were embarrassed by Yagi's jingoistic chest-beating pointed out that there would be nothing wrong with having a mixed-race emperor down the road in any case.

From the moment Akihito was permitted to give a televised address suggesting his desire to step down, there was not much doubt that the abdication would take place. In June 2017, the Diet passed a special law permitting a one-time abdication. A resolution attached to this legislation called on the government to study how to stabilize the imperial line, including through the possibility of enlarging the pool of collateral families by changing the law whereby female imperial family members lose their royal status when they marry. On the day the special measure passed, Chief Cabinet Secretary Suga remarked in the Upper House of the Diet: "The number of imperial family members is decreasing because of the marriage of female members and other reasons. Considering the ages of the imperial family members, this is an important problem that we cannot shelve." At the same time, Suga stressed that the Abe administration "will firmly maintain" the system of male-only succession. During that same session of the Upper House, Representative Matsuzawa Shigefumi called for reestablishing the collateral families whose royal status was ended during the Occupation-era reforms as a way to solve the heir crisis.[11]

Nearly two years after the passage of the special law, Akihito formally abdicated. His short remarks on the occasion of his abdication included two statements that were representative of the Heisei monarchy. First, he stressed, "I sincerely thank the people who accepted and supported me in my role as the symbol of the state." Second, when articulating his hopes for the next era, he reminded his compatriots of the remarkable partnership he and Michiko had formed when he said, "*Together with the Empress*, I wish from the bottom of my heart that the new Reiwa era that begins tomorrow will be peaceful and fruitful" (emphasis added). It came as little surprise to those who followed the Heisei era that Akihito emphasized peace in his final remarks as emperor. In retirement, he may be able to pursue one of his lifelong passions, the study of the small goby

FIGURE 36. Akihito catching gobies in Saroma Lake, Hokkaido, 10 September 1985. (Photograph Courtesy Kyodo News Service.)

fish. His duties as emperor left little time for his research in this area, which has resulted in several respected publications.

In his first remarks as emperor, Naruhito stressed his intention to stay the course with the previous reign. He also promised to "devote myself to self-improvement," the sort of humility and devotion to life-long learning that is prized by his countrymen and -women.

The Fragility of the Imperial Line

Even before the issue of abdication, Japan's imperial system was fragile. It is a ticking time bomb in terms of having insufficient heirs. There will almost certainly not be a male heir at some point. Once Naruhito ascended to the throne with only a daughter, his younger brother, Akishino, became next in line. Second in line is Prince Hisahito (son of Akishino and Kiko), and no further children can be expected from

Prince Akishino and Princess Kiko). There are no more boys among the current generation of imperial children. Strictly speaking, Prince Masahito (1935–) is third in line, although in light of his advanced age, this is hardly reassuring in terms of providing for the continuation of the imperial line. Thus, it is fair to say that unless the current imperial system is changed, the future of the line rests squarely on the shoulders of Prince Hisahito. The unfolding imperial story will include the awkward specter of Emperor Naruhito having to help tutor Hisahito in the art of being the national symbol even as Naruhito's daughter, Princess Aiko, will lose her imperial status if and when she marries.

There are various questions regarding this situation that Japanese discuss in hushed tones behind closed doors. What if Prince Hisahito should die in an accident or by some disease before he produces an heir? What if Hisahito is not inclined to marry a woman, preferring other sorts of relationships? What if Hisahito does marry a woman but they are unable to have children or do not produce a boy? What if Prince Hisahito and his future wife have only one boy? This would mean that for another generation the imperial line would rest on one pair of shoulders, a tenuous situation even if it is better than some of the alternatives.

Why not fix the situation now? The issue of reforming the system to address the heir crisis was taken up during the administration of Prime Minister Koizumi Junichirō (b. 1942; prime minister, 2001–6) when there was still not a single boy among the current generation of imperial children. The report issued in November 2005 by the Commission to Study the Imperial House Law, a regular law that can be amended by a simple majority in the Diet, covered most of the possible ways to resolve the crisis. These included allowing women to serve as *tennō* and to permit matrilineal succession (at present, only males with patrilineal lineage are eligible).

It also proposed that first-born children, regardless of sex, be first in line for succession. Opposition to allowing women to serve as *tennō* among many LDP representatives in the Diet was the key factor in Koizumi never introducing legislation to institute this reform. The birth of Prince Hisahito in 2006 provided a convenient excuse for lawmakers to delay addressing the heir crisis. The crisis has not been solved, only postponed. Furthermore, the delay has created a new problem. Addressing the crisis through changes in the imperial system now potentially includes a personal choice. Who should be *tennō* down the road: Princess Aiko or Prince Hisahito?

Historically, two mechanisms have been necessary to maintain male bloodlines, and even with these in place sometimes it has not been possible to continue the line. The first is a system of concubines, which Japan had until it was abolished after the country's defeat in 1945. The second is a pool of collateral families eligible to provide an heir, and the pool was significantly decreased after the war. Even with these mechanisms, sustaining the imperial line historically required eight regnant empresses.

The eight regnant empresses (two of them served two separate stints) in the past are seen, especially by those who wish to maintain the tradition of men, as having been caretakers of the role. Furthermore, the unbroken blood line was preserved because each empress was of patrilineal lineage. This was true even when the daughter of Empress Genmei (r. 707–15) succeeded her as *tennō* (Empress Genshō, r. 715–24). After each empress, the line eventually reverted to a male of the patrilineal bloodline, thus keeping the line supposedly unbroken. There were six regnant empresses between the Sixth and Eighth centuries; then 859 years passed before there was another. The reign of the last regnant empress, Go-Sakuramachi, was from 1762 to 1771.[12]

In the postwar era, the practice of monogamy has been critically important to the imperial households maintaining their images as ideal families. Nonetheless, within the long history of the imperial line, monogamy is a strikingly recent innovation. The system of concubines has far more history than does the practice of monogamy. Only about half of all Japanese emperors were born to what would be considered the "empress." The others, including most recently the Taishō emperor, were born to concubines. In the centuries leading up the modern period, a remarkably high percentage of emperors were born to concubines. I have heard Japanese who are well versed in history joke that to restore tradition to the imperial house, it will be necessary to restore the ladies-in-waiting system. This could provide a solution to the heir problem but might make it especially difficult for those in line to be emperor to find wives. Many people cease to support change when presented with calls to maintain tradition (e.g., the male imperial bloodline), but many aspects of the imperial house that are now taken for granted (and are often seen as "traditional") are very recent developments.

Few Japanese women are unaware that Empress Masako was treated as a womb by those in the Imperial Household Agency who interpreted her most important duty to be the production of a male heir. If it were made expressly clear, by reinstituting the concubine system, that any princess who did not produce an heir might then have to accept her husband making use of ladies-in-waiting, the difficulty of male imperial family members finding brides could be compounded several times over. The reality of the situation is that restoring the concubine system at the palace is virtually out of the question.

The second mechanism required to maintain a male bloodline is a broad pool of collateral families eligible to produce an heir. Occupation-era reforms eliminated eleven collateral families, significantly reducing the pool of families eligible to provide heirs under the system of patrilineal succession. Reestablishing some or all of the collateral families abolished in 1947, at least those that still have heirs, is a slightly more conceivable option to address the crisis. But would it stand up to public opinion? In fact, very few people, including those close to the imperial line, favor this solution. The blood ties between most of these collateral families and the imperial family are extremely weak, with some of the families having diverged 600 years ago. To reintroduce them into the imperial family line seems to some as hardly any different than starting a separate line.

Furthermore, all but the most elderly members of these disestablished collateral families were born as commoners and have lived as commoners. Thus, to reintroduce people who now are commoners (whatever their lineage) into the imperial lineage seems to some to undermine the prestige of the line. There are five or so young male members of these collateral families alive today. The report released during the Koizumi administration said that it was not clear whether the surviving members of these collateral families favored a return to royal status, and the situation has not changed in the interim.

Should they be returned to royal status, single men from collateral families may face extra challenges in finding wives because Masako's experience would likely apply to their prospective spouses, too. This might be one reason that none of these candidates has expressed any interest in the opportunity. Moreover, considering the fact that few scholars take seriously the notion of an unbroken male bloodline dating back to Emperor Jimmu, why go to the extraordinary step of reestablishing collateral families when there is a simpler solution that preserves the direct lineage of the imperial family: allowing women to serve as *tennō*.

Strictly speaking, in light of the history of eight empresses, the notion of an occasional regnant empress is not the issue. The true issue is that in this day and age, it would almost surely be the case that a female imperial member in line to be *tennō* (should the law be changed) would marry a man who was a commoner (a separate worry often cited by commentators is whether a female imperial family member in line for the throne could find a husband willing to play a supporting role, additional testament to lingering patriarchy in Japan). There are really no other options for a spouse other than finding a commoner. The fundamental issue is that if a child from this union went on to become *tennō*, the unbroken patrilineal line would be broken.

There is another path to address the heir crisis: changing the law whereby female imperial family members lose their royal status on marriage and allowing them to establish "female collateral families" (*josei miyake*). Some see this as a compromise solution, a softer approach than directly permitting women to be *tennō*. But for diehard supporters of the unbroken male imperial bloodline, this option is hardly more attractive because it bumps into the same problem of matrilineal succession. These days, female members of the imperial family inevitably marry commoners. Thus, if one of these collateral families were to provide an heir down the road, the unbroken line would be broken by matrilineal succession. The reason it is a compromise solution is that it delays breaking the supposedly unbroken line further into the future than would the scenario of allowing a female *tennō*, thus postponing a scenario that the far right loathes.

As of September 2019, there are eighteen members of the imperial family (including the emperor emeritus and empress emerita), of which thirteen are women. Of these thirteen, six have yet to marry (Princess Mako is engaged, although it is unclear at this writing whether her marriage will proceed). The shrinking number of royals has resulted not only in an heir crisis but strain in terms of having enough royals to share the burden of official duties. Prince Akishino has publicly stressed that it may be necessary to reduce the number of public duties expected of royal family members because of declining numbers of their members.

Under the administration of Noda Yoshihiko (b. 1957, prime minister, 2011–12) during the short interlude that the Democratic Party of

Japan (DPJ) had displaced the LDP from the halls of power, it seemed possible that the Diet would change the Imperial House Law to allow for female collateral families. Once the DPJ fell from power, however, this proposal was shelved. It remains the most likely compromise solution because it is less blunt than immediately permitting a female *tennō*. Chief Cabinet Secretary Suga referenced the possibility of female collateral families in March 2019, in the lead-up to the transition of emperors. Then on 1 May, the day Naruhito was enthroned, Suga again mentioned the need for the government to take action to stabilize the imperial line, but only after the various formal accession ceremonies were completed in fall 2019.

Suga was referring to the ceremony on 22 October to proclaim and celebrate the enthronement of the new emperor, to which Japan has invited representatives of the 195 nation-states it recognizes, a parade in Tokyo, and the *Daijōsai* ritual of 14–15 November. There are many interesting threads to these upcoming ceremonies. Nomura Mansai II (1965–) is charged with arranging the entertainment for the main 23 October banquet, to be hosted by the prime minister. Nomura has also been tapped to choreograph the opening ceremonies to the 2020 Tokyo Summer Olympic games, and one wonders if the banquet entertainment will provide a prologue about what to expect at the Olympics opening ceremony. It has become common for host nations to tell an edifying version of their national history in the opening ceremonies (e.g., the Beijing Olympics of 2008), but will Nomura eschew a historical narrative (which could raise troubling questions about how to tell Japan's modern history, especially with neighboring countries paying very close attention) for a concentration on the arts?

Controversy also swirls around the *Daijōsai*, a Shinto ceremony performed by newly enthroned emperors that some Japanese, including Prince Akishino, believe should not be supported by public funds but should be a private ceremony financed only through the private budget of the imperial house (as are the other Shinto rituals typically carried out by imperial family members). The Abe administration, however, intends to proceed with sponsoring with public funds a grand *Daijōsai*. There are various nooks and crannies where the imperial house and Shinto rituals continue to intersect in ways that seem incongruent with the postwar system, even in the eyes of some imperial family members.

Meanwhile, the question of imperial succession lurks just under the surface. Where does the public stand on the issue of reforming the law regarding succession? A Kyodo News poll conducted in December 2018 showed 84 percent support for female *tennō*, and 76 percent support for the establishment of female branches or collateral families. Distinguished Japanese such as Sonobe Itsuo (1929–), a former Supreme Court justice who was an acting head of the expert panel on the Imperial Household Law during the Koizumi administration, have spoken out in favor of female *tennō*: "Without accepting women emperors or female branches, Japan could face the crisis of the imperial household's demise. Globally speaking, there are queens and female prime ministers. But Japan is still a male-centered society and it is discouraging."[13] After all, gender equality is becoming the global standard in the twenty-first century.

Observers who are puzzled as to why Japan's lawmakers have not acted to allow for women to serve as *tennō*, and to permit matrilineal succession, should not underestimate the influence of an intense minority that is adamant about preserving the male-only system. This faction insists that what makes Japan's imperial line unique, and therefore what makes Japan special, is the unbroken male imperial bloodline. This opposition to female *tennō* is in spite of the fact that one of the fundamental policies of the second Abe administration (2012–) has been to create "a society in which all women can shine" (*subete no josei ga kagayaku shakai zukuri*).

This broad policy apparently does not extend to the area of revising the Imperial House Law to allow women to serve as the national symbol, as female *tennō* (not just as caretaker regnant empresses, but as *tennō* who give birth to a child who then becomes *tennō*, passing down the imperial line matrilineally). At the time that I write, the percentage of the LDP representatives in the Diet who are women exceeds 10 percent only by the slightest of margins, a discouraging sign for the prospects of legislation that would bring gender equality to Japan's imperial house.

As the Reiwa era unfolds, it will require balancing traditions with new practices, and Japanese who are charged with making changes necessary to stabilize the imperial line might keep in mind that even among self-appointed, hard-core emperorists, the definition of "tradition" changes. For the first two decades of the postwar era, the far right indicted the Occupation-era reform of the emperor's position from national sovereign to symbol as an affront to Japanese tradition. But after their efforts to resurrect the Meiji Constitution had failed dismally, the far right eventually concluded that the emperor's postwar position as a symbol in fact represented a return to the "true" tradition of emperors playing a symbolic role outside of politics, as had been the case for most of the imperial line's history.

The point is that the romantic, nationalistic far right would almost surely live with, say, a woman in the role of national symbol (female *tennō*, or *jotei*) if that proves to be the only way to preserve the imperial line. Moreover, one can imagine that if Japan should get *jotei* in the future, the far right would change its tune and begin to claim that the true Japanese tradition included female *tennō*. In any case, in spite of periodic statements from representatives of the far right that it would be better for the imperial line to go extinct than for the male-only lineage to be abandoned, one might suspect that if directly faced with this option, the far right would choose the latter. But the survival of the imperial house is by no means written in stone. It may remain fragile even if various reforms are enacted to remedy the heir crisis. Hereditary monarchy and democracy are something of a tricky graft, in spite of several successful examples of this blend working.

Where do I stand about the monarchy in Japan? I have been asked this question over and over since publication of the first book, especially by Japanese. I am neutral, a stance that through the decades has pleased neither opponents nor supporters of the imperial system, but seems to be an advantage in analyzing the evolution of this institution. I have found the imperial house to be a useful window into understanding many aspects of modern Japan. But if the imperial house were abolished tomorrow, I would simply shrug. My indifference results from the belief that the Japanese would carry on fine without an imperial house.

At the same time, I disagree with those who see the abolition of the monarchy as a panacea for Japan's problems. To those who believe that abolishing the monarchy would eliminate nationalism and strike a fatal blow to the far right, I point out the near inevitability that far-right nationalists (not to mention nationalists in other parts of the political spectrum) would invent a new national icon around which they would continue to champion nationalistic policies with surprisingly little long-term disruption. Consider the example of France in this area. France has a vibrant far right today although almost no far rightists are committed to restoring France's monarchy. When Jean-Marie Le Pen (1928–), who established the far-right National Front political party, needed a potent symbol for his anti-immigration platform, he embraced Joan of Arc (1412–31) for her role in driving foreigners out of France.

Surely Japanese nationalists could devise a new rallying symbol if the necessity arose. At the same time, as long as Japan continues to have a monarchy, it is best that royal family members perform useful societal roles. These range from lending their prestige to the most vulnerable members of society to declining to lend their prestige to jingoistic chest thumping (a particularly powerful stance considering that the emperor is the national symbol!) to facilitating national unity in a fundamental sense.

Conclusion

Any serious examination of the Japanese monarchy, especially in the modern era, must take into account the "invention of tradition" paradigm. Although it is true that all traditions were invented at one time or another, critical historians delight in debunking the traditionality of the Japanese throne precisely because conservatives continue to trumpet it as the essence of timeless Japanese culture. The stress on invented tradition may give the impression to some readers that Japanese traditions are particularly inauthentic compared with those of other national communities. It has been well documented, however, that the invention of tradition was a significant feature in the construction of modern national identities throughout the world and was especially evident in reference to monarchies adjusting to modernity. During the modern era, the Japanese borrowed massively from abroad, mainly from European countries and the United States. The Japanese monarchy is emblematic of the tremendous cultural diffusion that has taken place globally over the past 200 years. However, a national symbol that is recognized explicitly as an amalgam of domestic practices, most of them of modern origin (or manipulated to suit the modern), and practices borrowed from abroad hardly suits the needs of those who champion the distinctiveness and timelessness of the Japanese national community.

In analyzing the history of Japan's symbolic monarchy, I face a problem encountered by historians studying ideology, culture, and memory, among other topics. Tracing the construction of various meanings attached to Japan's national symbol is considerably easier than the task of gauging their reception or consumption. The question of reception is equally relevant to studies of the prewar emperor system. Whenever possible, I attempted to bridge the gap between production and reception, or at least highlight the fact that such a gap typically exists. Nonetheless, the reader should understand, for example, that my analysis of the message put forth by weeklies at the time of Akihito and Michiko's engagement does not capture the full diversity of contemporary reactions. As much as I tried to trace the assortment of postwar views about the throne, this diversity was likely more extensive than what is portrayed here.

This study was designed to be broad and comprehensive, but some aspects of the postwar monarchy could not be addressed in sufficient depth. The topic of the Imperial Household Agency, in particular, is worthy of a separate book. I suspect that a careful analysis of the agency, far from showing the omniscience of this bureaucratic gatekeeper to the throne, would discover numerous internal divisions on a variety of policies related to handling the imperial family throughout the postwar period. In fact, I think that in some cases officials of the Imperial Household Agency were as surprised at the success of a particular policy in projecting a desired image of the throne as they were by the failure of others. In addition, although the Imperial Household Agency enjoys an almost legendary reputation for conservatism, which is sometimes justified regarding some issues, I nonetheless suspect that a study of this agency would show that in other areas its reputation for conservatism is off the mark. The royal house needs to stay in tune with changing societal trends, after all, and that task falls to the Imperial Household Agency. Nor do I address the topic of the Shinto rituals (*saishi*) that are a significant (and controversial) component of the imperial house in anything approaching the depth that this topic deserves. This could possibly be the basis for yet another book.

I would like to have analyzed more extensively the political right in postwar Japan, but this topic is also deserving of a separate book. Even though I used terms such as "left" and "right," this study has shown that it is often difficult to draw a strict boundary between them. This is true in no small part because neither the left nor the right has been monolithic or static during the past seventy-five years. In terms of political parties' views of the monarchy, the division between the JCP and all other parties was often more stark than the division between the LDP on the one side and the JSP and JCP on the other. In the early 1990s, however, the most right-wing faction of the LDP lined up with the JSP and JCP against the rest of the LDP to oppose imperial apologies as unconstitutional, an example that reminds us to be careful in classifying the Japanese political spectrum. After all, it is no small matter that in the postwar era virtually the entire Japanese political right, as has been the case with the political right in Western Europe since the end of World War II, has come to accept parliamentary democracy. This book will no doubt be seen as first and foremost a study of the monarchy in postwar Japan, but in my mind it is also an account of how Japanese made nationalism compatible with democracy in the postwar period, a critically significant development.

A detailed study of the postwar political right, not just political parties but also intellectuals and civil organizations (including New Religions), with regard to a host of issues, from anticommunism to nuclear armament to the environment to "traditional values" to political tactics, would better our understanding of Japan over the past seventy-five years by showing the right's plurality and fluidity and by muddling accepted divisions between the left and the right. Any comprehensive examination of the postwar political right should include social histories of populist movements from the right (including the important role played by women) that avoid the assumptions that such political action (1) is aberrational and transitory; and (2) originates from atrophying social groups that have missed the train to "modernity," in other words, the progression of history toward a rational and secular world. If this study addressed the right not only in the postwar era but throughout the twentieth century, it would be all the more valuable, if quite a tall task.

As problematic as facile divisions between the left and the right in analyzing Japan are frameworks that implicitly or explicitly privilege the people (or civil society) as progressive and the "state" as not only regressive but also particularly powerful. Many aspects of the postwar monarchy have been society-driven, and the result has made neither the political left or the political right entirely happy. If one points to popular support for the constitution as the critical explanation for the failure of the constitutional revision movement, as many scholars do, one also must take note of popular support for Foundation Day and the reign-name system to understand why these imperial practices were reestablished. To credit the people with the wisdom to maintain the progressive constitution while blaming the state for reestablishing nationalistic symbols provides a misleading portrayal of the dynamics of Japanese society and politics. The majority of the Japanese came to support the Postwar Constitution, but they also wanted Foundation Day and the reign-name system, if in different forms from those of Imperial Japan. Society-driven politics have been a critical feature not only of postwar Japan but of Japan throughout the modern period, even during the 1930s. The 2,600th anniversary celebrations staged in 1940 are typically portrayed as having been orchestrated in a top-down fashion by the government, but the governmental committee charged with planning the celebrations was influenced by lobbying from civil organizations (of course, the context of wartime Japan was different from postwar democratic Japan, but even the wartime state was pervious to societal input). The 2,600th anniversary celebrations are one example of how, even during this authoritarian period, the state was open to societal influence.

In the context of historical writing about postwar Japan, particularly in the United States, there is a need to stress the importance of the post-Occupation decade in shaping Japan as we know it today. The reason for this lies in the dominance, at least until recently, of studies about the Occupation that lacked nuance in measuring this period's role in the "remaking" of Japan. Numerous studies in the past decades have shown the importance of transwar continuities, and it is also evident not only that the postwar political settlement occurred in the decade after independence but also that the sweeping transformation of the lives of all the Japanese began in earnest then.

The Occupation reforms were reviewed in the 1950s and early 1960s, to be legitimated in some cases and discarded in others. The 1947 Constitution was the most important reform to survive. In contrast, the educational and the policing systems were recentralized after having been decentralized, American-style, during the Occupation. In the case of the monarchy, it became evident only in the years after Japan regained independence that the throne's role would remain symbolic, as defined by the Postwar Constitution. The constitutional principle that politics should be carried out in the name of the people was a fundamental change from the imperial prerogative of Imperial Japan.

It was conservative Cabinets that, in interpreting the emperor's position and role under the new constitution, continued ministerial briefings, maintained the emperor as Japan's external representative, and broadened the emperor's public role. They also defined the postwar imperial decoration system, reestablished Foundation Day, perpetuated the reign-name system, and developed and studiously maintained the myth of the pacifistic emperor, thus putting their conservative stamp on the symbolic monarchy. The boundary between the symbolic and the political can be quite artificial, of course, and the conservative politicians who have enjoyed power for most of the postwar period continued to try to use the monarchy for political ends. Yet one must remember that however much conservative Cabinets might have attempted to manipulate the symbolic monarchy, they were constrained by constitutional limits and a variety of watchdogs, from opposition parties to the mass media. The environment in which conservative Cabinets sought to manage the throne is representative of many areas of postwar Japanese politics, the reason one must speak of the political "predominance" instead of "dominance" of the LDP and its antecedents. The word "predominance" is semantically weaker than "dominance" and serves to remind us not only that conservative parties have had to compete in a political system characterized by free elections, but that they have had to contend with surveillance from a variety of quarters.

Inasmuch as the symbolic valence of the throne is measured by the extent to which it represents popular values, one must understand that the monarchy of the masses was very much a product of social evolution, especially the dramatic changes of the late 1950s and early 1960s. Although the role played, for example, by Crown Prince Akihito and Crown Princess Michiko in helping define, as though they were "natural," certain gender roles should not be overlooked, the fact remains that for the most part social change was pushing the monarchy, rather than the monarchy driving social change. Akihito's engagement to Michiko and the middle-class image of the young imperial couple provided reassurance to the Japanese that their society was egalitarian. The fact that Akihito married a commoner and that Japanese housewives enjoyed many of the same electrical kitchen appliances as their crown princess was hardly a valid measure of whether Japanese society was egalitarian, but it is nonetheless significant that the throne was linked to this middle-class ideal by the late 1950s. The imperial house often faced the challenge of keeping up with the dramatic evolution of society, a task made more difficult by Hirohito's longevity, which kept an emperor educated for a different era on the throne for more than four decades into the postwar era.

Various postwar values, including the principle of international cooperation, have come to be accepted widely by the Japanese, but nationalism has by no means disappeared in the postwar era. In the context of the international system of nation-states, postwar Japan indeed would be unique if nationalism had been absent. The "neo-nationalism" of the 1990s that has continued into the twenty-first century, although new in the sense that it addressed issues of concern to the Japanese in a rapidly evolving world, has antecedents that can be traced back decades. What is important to understand is the plurality of the forms of nationalism that have existed in postwar Japan and the context in which they have operated. The far-right Association of Shinto Shrines articulated, especially in the post-Occupation decade, "reactionary nationalism" by calling for a return to the Meiji system, but this form of nationalism drew minimal popular support. Almost all the citizens who testified to the Foundation Day Commission in 1966 expressly indicated their support for the Postwar Constitution and Foundation Day. This is a strange combination perhaps, but it is no more odd than various examples of nationalistic expression found in many other democratic nation-states. Whether called "democratic nationalism," or simply nationalism in the context of a democratic system, forms of nationalism in postwar Japan that resonated with the people were those that accepted (or at least did not oppose) democracy, an important change from Imperial Japan, especially in the 1930s.

Massification has both weakened and extended the roots of the monarchy. There is no doubt that the present-day monarchy is much weaker than its wartime counterpart. It is no longer an inviolate symbol of the state. This evisceration has led certain elements of the political right to belittle the popularized throne. The monarchy, however, is firmly embedded in democratic, mass consumer culture. Its popularity not only has protected the monarchy from calls for abolition but has also maintained the imperial house's social influence, even in the twenty-first century.

Although the symbolic monarchy is regularly subjected to manipulation, it is nonetheless true that the agency of individual emperors matters considerably, a point that became abundantly clear during Akihito's reign. Emperor Hirohito has been the subject of several biographies, most of which focused on his wartime role. At present, however, there is no English-language biography of Emperor Akihito. A book-length study of Akihito, or of Akihito and Michiko, with a particular focus on their active roles in shaping the monarchy, would be a valuable contribution. The notion that Japan's emperor is "only a symbol" masks how powerful a societal role the emperor can still play.

The value of such a biographical account would be increased if it included a detailed analysis of imperial rituals, such as the delivery of betrothal presents to imperial brides, that provide special drama to the stories of imperial family members, especially the emperor and empress. Each generation of Japanese learns through the mass media, on an imperial engagement, of the "tradition" of betrothal presents, but just how traditional is it for an imperial bride to receive two freshly caught sea bream, six bottles of sake, and five bolts of silk? Finally, if the biography included carefully referenced comparisons to the practices and initiatives of members of the twenty-seven other royal houses who were contemporaries of Akihito and Michiko, that would make it all the more significant. The surviving royal houses keep close tabs on each other, including what practices are helping them ensure survival (e.g., abdication to allow a new generation to take over). Meanwhile, we shall watch to see whether politicians in Japan take action to stabilize the imperial line, or if they prefer the path that representatives of the far right have bombastically articulated on numerous occasions, namely, that it would be better for the imperial line to go extinct than for the unbroken male lineage to be broken.

Notes

For complete author names, titles, and publication data for works cited here in short form, see the Works Cited list at the back of the book.

Introduction

1. It is problematic to use the term "emperor" to describe the monarch throughout most of Japanese history. As Joan R. Piggott reminds us in *The Emergence of Japanese Kingship*, "The term *empire* is strongly associated with a martial political formation founded on conquest" (8). For most of Japanese history, Japanese monarchs did not preside over empires.

The monarchs of Imperial Japan (1890–1945) *did* rule over an empire that came to include numerous overseas possessions, however. In the case of Hirohito (r. 1926–89), he ascended to the throne as the sovereign of an empire, and thus the term "emperor" is an appropriate title for him for the period from 1926 to 1945. Strictly speaking, the term "emperor" does not describe Japan's monarch since 1945, for Japan no longer has an empire and the monarch does not even remain sovereign. In the end, however, I decided to use the term "emperor" (as well as terms such as "monarch") for the postwar period in part because it seemed confusing to switch back and forth between "emperor" for the prewar period and, say, "king" for the postwar period, and also because it served to highlight one of the most important transwar continuities regarding the Japanese throne: Hirohito, who ascended to the throne with the mindset of a sovereign emperor, remained on the throne even as the Japanese empire collapsed and the politico-legal system defining his position underwent sweeping reform.

2. Mori followed this remark with another gaffe a few weeks later when he accused the Japan Communist Party of being incapable of protecting Japan's *kokutai*. In prewar Japan this word, unknown to many Japanese today (as evidenced by the extensive explanatory commentary that accompanied mass media coverage of the prime minister's remark), was used to describe the national polity centered on imperial sovereignty.

3. The bill passed by the Diet not only made the *Kimigayo* the national anthem but formally made the *Hinomaru* (the "Rising Sun"), the same flag used in modern Japan from 1870 until 1945, the official national flag. The decision regarding the flag was more controversial on the international stage (for some Asians, in particular, the *Hinomaru* symbolizes Japan's brutal imperialism and wars of aggression), but domestically the adoption of the *Kimigayo* was seen as equally if not more significant, for students now will be made to sing lines about the eternal reign of the imperial house. For information, see Tanaka Nobumasa, *Hinomaru Kimigayo no sengoshi*.

4. On the phenomenon of "self-restraint" (*jishuku*), see Watanabe Osamu, "The Sociology of Jishuku and Kicho." In contrast to Watanabe's stress on the extent of "self-restraint," many other commentators noted the number of Japanese citizens who refrained from self-restraint during the period of the emperor's illness.

5. The mass media reported comments from members of village youth groups indicating that young adults believed that the crown prince's marriage would help them overcome parental resistance to love matches. See Matsushita Keiichi, "Zoku-taishū tennōseiron," 115–16.

6. English-language scholarship about the postwar monarchy that focuses mainly on the Occupation era includes Dower, *Embracing Defeat*; Bix, "Inventing the 'Symbol Monarchy' in Japan, 1945–52"; Bix, "The Showa Emperor's 'Monologue' and the Problem of War Responsibility"; Titus, "The Making of the 'Symbol Emperor System' in Postwar Japan" (Titus addresses the post-Occupation decade to some extent as well); Nakamura Masanori, *The Japanese Monarchy*; Watanabe Osamu, "The Emperor as a 'Symbol' in Postwar Japan"; and K. Takeda, *The Dual-Image of the Japanese Emperor*.

For biographies of Hirohito, see Bix, *Hirohito and the Making of Modern Japan*; D. Irokawa, *The Age of Hirohito*; and Large, *Emperor Hirohito and Showa Japan*.

Works that address aspects of the post-Occupation monarchy include Lebra, "Self and Other in Esteemed Status"; Titus, "Accessing the World"; T. Fujitani, "Electronic Pageantry and Japan's 'Symbolic Emperor'"; and Field, *In the Realm of a Dying Emperor*.

I began research for this book in 1993 and prepared my manuscript at the same time that Bix was studying Emperor Hirohito's political role. I read and profited from his works as they came out. However, with the exception of those points at which I cite his work directly, to the extent that our interpretations overlap in the first section of Chapter 4 of this book is a reflection of my independent reading of some of the same sources. Our main concerns differ, for Bix traced Emperor Hirohito's political role whereas I analyze the remaking of the postwar monarchy as an institution.

7. These messages were reprinted in Supreme Commander for the Allied Powers, Government Section, *Political Reorientation of Japan*, 2: 414–15.

8. Ibid., 413.

9. The text of this debate, "Tennōsei shiji ka, hitei ka," was reprinted in *Gendai no esupuri*, no. 45 (Oct. 1970).

10. The other participants were promonarchist Kiyose Ichirō (1884–1967), and liberal Makino Ryōzō (1885–1961), who also supported the monarchy.

11. The acronym SCAP refers to the chief executive of the Allied Occupation (General Douglas MacArthur, 1945–51; General Matthew B. Ridgway, 1951–52) or, more broadly, to the Occupation bureaucracy or administration.

12. Dower, *Empire and Aftermath*, 319.

13. Supreme Commander for the Allied Powers, Government Section, *Political Reorientation of Japan*, 2: 657.

14. The new constitution was promulgated on 3 November, birthday of Emperor Meiji and a prewar holiday. The Japanese government chose this day to stress continuity.

15. Fellers submitted various memoranda to MacArthur urging the retention of the throne and Hirohito. As Herbert Bix has shown, Fellers's view of the throne and Hirohito as impediments to communization was evident in a conversation that he had with former prime minister Yonai Mitsumasa (1880–1948) in March 1946. Fellers argued: "The

national policy of the Soviet Union in particular aims to bring about communization of the entire world. Consequently, the Japanese emperor system and the presence here of MacArthur have become major obstacles for them." See Bix, "Inventing the 'Symbol Monarchy' in Japan, 1945–52," 343.

16. See Nachmani, "Civil War and Foreign Intervention in Greece, 1946–1949."

17. In 1946, Minister of State Kanamori Tokujirō (1886–1959), speaking for the government during an interpellation in the Diet about the reign-name system, insisted that the 1868 edict establishing the practice that an era would correspond to one emperor's reign provided the legal basis for continued use of the system. This interpretation was questionable, however. In 1950, for example, Okuno Ken'ichi (1898–1984), director of the Cabinet Legislation Bureau, denied that the 1868 edict was still in effect under the Postwar Constitution. He also voiced the opinion that since there was no legal mechanism for establishing a new reign name, when the present emperor died the reign-name system would die with him. For Kanamori's interpretation, see *Daikyūjūkai teikoku kizokuin kōshitsu tenpan tokubetsu iinkai sokkiroku*, 6. For Okuno's interpretation, see Sangiin jimukyoku, *Dainanakai kokkai sangiin monbu iinkai kaigiroku*, no. 6, 2–3.

18. Kokuritsu kokkai toshokan chōsa rippō kōsakyoku, *Kigensetsu mondai ni kansuru shiryōshū*, 23.

19. Kigensetsu hōshukukai, *Kigensetsu hōshukukai koshi*, 9–10. See also Woodard, *The Allied Occupation of Japan 1945–1952 and Japanese Religions*, 143–47.

20. One of the most comprehensive descriptions of postwar values was provided by the immensely popular cartoonist Kobayashi Yoshinori in his biting critique of these very values; see his *Shin gomanizumu sengen supesharu sensōron*.

Chapter 1

1. Webb, *The Japanese Imperial Institution in the Tokugawa Period*, 1–64.

2. I have borrowed the phrase "officiant in the rice harvest rituals" from Emiko Ohnuki-Tierney, "The Emperor of Japan as Deity (Kami)," 199.

3. Curiously, during the Meiji era (1868–1912), even as a descendant of the Northern Dynasty held the throne, the government elevated fourteenth-century supporters of Emperor Go-Daigo's Southern Dynasty into national heroes.

4. Webb, *The Japanese Imperial Institution in the Tokugawa Period*, ix.

5. Bob Tadashi Wakabayashi, *Anti-Foreignism and Western Learning in Early-Modern Japan*, 149.

6. Takagi Hiroshi, *Kindai tennōsei no bunkashiteki kenkyū*, 267.

7. Takagi Hiroshi, "Kindai ni okeru shinwateki kodai no sōzō," 24–25.

8. Hobsbawm, "Introduction: Inventing Traditions," 1.

9. The Japanese term for this system is *issei ichigensei*. This system, too, was borrowed from China, where beginning in the Ming dynasty (1368–1644) a system of one emperor, one reign name was employed.

10. See Togashi Junji, *Nihon no kunshō*, esp. 91–105, 202. Until 1940, recipients of the Order of the Golden Kite enjoyed a pension for life. After 1940 recipients were awarded a lump-sum payment. By the time the Order of the Golden Kite was abolished in 1946, more than 108,000 individuals had received this award linking them to Emperor Jimmu's military exploits.

11. T. Fujitani, *Splendid Monarchy*, 12.

12. Kokuritsu kokkai toshokan chōsa rippō kōsakyoku, *Kigensetsu mondai ni kansuru shiryōshū*, 4.

13. N. Hozumi, *Ancestor-Worship and Japanese Law*, 81.

14. Iwamoto Tsutomu, *"Goshin'ei" ni junjita kyōshitachi.*

15. For the construction of State Shinto during the Meiji period, see Hardacre, *Shintō and the State, 1868–1988.*

16. Archeologists doubt the validity of almost all ancient imperial tombs; see Takagi Hiroshi, "Bunkazai no kindai," 311.

17. Ibid.

18. T. Osamu, "How Radicals in the Popular Rights Movement Viewed the Emperor."

19. "Teishitsuron" is reprinted in Koizumi Shinzō, ed., *Fukuzawa Yukichi zenshū*, 5: 261–92; "Sonnōron," in 6: 2–29. Both essays are reprinted in Fukuzawa Yukichi, *Nihon kōshitsuron.*

20. Fukuzawa Yukichi, "Teishitsuron," in *Fukuzawa Yukichi zenshū*, 261.

21. Ibid.

22. Ibid., 263.

23. Bagehot, *The English Constitution*, 90.

24. Fukuzawa, "Teishitsuron," 265.

25. Ibid., 281.

26. For prewar court finances, see Titus, *Palace and Politics in Prewar Japan*, esp. 64–70. The standard Japanese work on this topic is Kuroda Hisata, *Tennōke no zaisan.*

27. Itō Hirobumi, *Commentaries on the Constitution of the Empire of Japan*, 2–3.

28. Yoshimoto Yanase, *Genshu to kikan*, 3–4, 11.

29. Titus, *Palace and Politics in Prewar Japan*, 313.

30. The official translation of the Imperial Rescript on Education appears in Gauntlett, *Kokutai no hongi*, Appendix IV.

31. Baelz, *Awakening Japan*, 115–16.

32. Chamberlain, *The Invention of a New Religion*, 3–4.

33. Ibid., 5.

34. Gluck, *Japan's Modern Myths.*

35. For an analysis of debates regarding Nogi's suicide, see ibid., 221–25.

36. During a ministerial briefing in 1967, Minister of Transport Nakasone Yasuhiro, in an unusual break with protocol, asked the emperor if he might ask a question. When Emperor Hirohito assented, Nakasone proceeded to inquire about the truth of accounts that portrayed Hirohito as listening intently to General Nogi's entire complex lecture about emperorship even though his younger brothers had ceased to pay attention. Hirohito's response indicated that the accounts were basically correct. See Iwami Takao, *Heika no goshitsumon*, 9–13.

37. The so-called party cabinets never consisted completely of members of the dominant party because, at the very least, the army and navy each supplied at least one cabinet minister.

38. For an exhaustive study of Minobe's constitutional theories, see Miller, *Minobe Tatsukichi.*

39. Quoted in Banno Junji, "Foreword," iii.

40. Nagata Hidejirō, *A Simplified Treatise on the Imperial House of Japan*, 111.

41. Ibid., 111–13.

42. Nagako was fifteen at the time of the couple's engagement in 1918.

43. See Takahashi Hiroshi, "Shōwa Tennō no jokan kaikaku," 251–64.

44. See ibid.

45. "Theses on the Situation in Japan and the Tasks of the Communist Party," *International Press Correspondence*, no. 23 (26 May 1932), 467. See also Appendix F in Beckmann and Okubo Genji, *The Japanese Communist Party, 1922–1945*, 332–51. Beckmann and Okubo edited the original English-language version for style. For the Japanese version, see Kominterun, "Nihon ni okeru jōsei to Nihon kyōsantō no ninmu ni kansuru teze."

46. Fujitani, *Splendid Monarchy*, 19–20.

47. Gordon, *Labor and Imperial Democracy in Prewar Japan*, 317.

48. Kigen nisen roppyakunen shukuten jimukyoku, *Kigen nisen roppyakunen shukuten giroku*, 11: 48.

49. See Chou, "The Kōminka Movement in Taiwan and Korea"; and Kim, *Lost Names*, esp. 98–115.

50. Kenneth J. Ruoff, *Imperial Japan at Its Zenith.*

51. Kigen nisen roppyakunen shukuten jimukyoku, *Kigen nisen roppyakunen shukuten giroku*, 11: 12.

52. See Furukawa Takahisa, *Kōki, banpaku, orinpikku*, for information on the bottom-up lobbying. The number of proposals linked to the anniversary celebrations that did not succeed were almost equal to the thousands of celebrations that did take place. One of the more famous failed proposals involved the Olympics. In 1930, Tokyo mayor Nagata Hidejirō proposed that his city host the 1940 Olympics as part of the anniversary celebrations. For an account of the attempt by Nagata and others to bring the Olympics to Tokyo in 1940, see Hashimoto Kazuo, *Maboroshi no orinpikku*, esp. 8–17.

53. Kigen nisen roppyakunen hōshukukai, *Tengyō hōshō*, 138. The Association to Celebrate the 2,600th Anniversary (Kigen nisen roppyakunen hōshukukai) was a semi-governmental, semi-civil group that worked closely with the Cabinet-level 2,600th Anniversary Celebration Bureau (Kigen nisen roppyakunen shukuten jimukyoku). For an analysis of the *Nihon bunka taikan*, the officially commissioned study of Japanese culture, see Miyachi Masato, "'Nihon bunka taikan' henshūshimatsu-ki."

54. For information on the "movement to recognize [or gain recognition of] sacred vestiges [of Jimmu]," including accounts of competition between villages, see Suzuki Ryō et al., *Nara-ken no hyakunen*, 203–5. While conducting research in Kashihara Shrine's archives, I came across numerous pamphlets published by villages to stake their claim as locations of sacred vestiges of Jimmu.

55. See Kigen nisen roppyakunen hōshukai, *Tengyō hōshō*, 237–40; and Suzuki et al., *Nara-ken no hyakunen*, 205.

56. The chart on the back of the monument that lists the numbers of volunteers and their origins is damaged, but it simply reproduces information included in many accounts of the volunteers' efforts. See, for example, Fujita Munemitsu, *Kashihara Jingū gokenkoku hōshitai*, 31. The expansion of the Kashihara Shrine compound in 1940, as had earlier, smaller-scale expansions (as well as projects to sanctify the area surrounding Jimmu's mausoleum), required that entire villages be moved. Not just the villagers themselves, but the remains of their ancestors were moved to make way for the expanding compound. On a visit to Kashihara City in June 2000, I had a conversation with Fukumoto Tsurue

(b. 1909), a resident of Kashihara City who had been a member of one of the villages that had been moved. Mrs. Fukumoto, who after the war joined a women's group (Keishin fujinkai) that devotes itself to assisting the Kashihara Shrine, refused to criticize the official decision to move her village. Other representatives of relocated villages, looking back on the forced relocation, have expressed outrage against the government, however.

57. The competition included a prize of ¥4,000, no doubt a significant motivation for many people. Earlier, the 2,600th Anniversary Celebration Bureau had commissioned two faculty members of the Tokyo School of Music to write and compose what was clearly a more official song in commemoration of the 2,600th anniversary. Today far-right groups that still celebrate Foundation Day along prewar lines use the song selected in the national competition, titled *Kigen 2,600*, for their annual ceremony. For the official history of both songs, see Kigen nisen roppyakunen shukuten jimukyoku, *Kigen nisen roppyakunen shukuten giroku*, 8: 659–718. There is also a song titled *Kigensetsu*, which predates both of the songs composed for the 2,600th anniversary celebrations. It also continues to be used in right-wing celebrations of Foundation Day.

58. *Kigen nisen roppyakunen*, a magazine intended for popular audiences issued from 1938 until shortly before Japan's surrender (later issues appeared under the name *Chōkoku seishin*) by the semi-governmental, semi-private Association to Celebrate the 2,600th Anniversary, carried a wealth of practical information for would-be visitors to imperial tombs, shrines, and vestiges of Emperor Jimmu. Individuals specifically interested in visiting sacred sites related to Jimmu could consult the thirty-five-page guidebook *Jimmu tennō no goseiseki* (Nihon ryokō kyōkai, 1940). For imperial shrines, the guidebook titled *Jinja* (Kigen nisen roppyakunen shukuten jimukyoku, 1939) was useful. These are just a small sample of the numerous guides available.

59. The figures of 1.25 million and 700,000 are from Suzuki et al., *Nara-ken no hyakunen*, 209–10.

60. Quoted in Tolischus, *Tokyo Record*, 15.

61. Cook and Cook, *Japan at War*, 376.

62. Roger W. Purdy, "Imperial Presence, Symbols and Surrogates: The Image of the Emperor in Japan's Wartime Newsreels," paper presented at the Association for Asian Studies 1996 Annual Meeting.

Chapter 2

1. *New York Times*, 25 Sept. 1945.

2. Minobe Tatsukichi, "Minshushugi to waga gikai seido."

3. Ibid., 21.

4. Ibid., 23.

5. The Matsumoto draft had the support of the Shidehara Cabinet. It made what SCAP interpreted as only superficial changes in the emperor's position—imperial sovereignty was to be maintained, for example—and it was in reaction to this that the Government Section soon thereafter drafted what became the Constitution of Japan.

6. Suprême Commander for the Allied Powers, Government Section, *Political Reorientation of Japan*, 2: 619.

7. Miyamoto Kenji, "Tennōsei hihan ni tsuite," 6.

8. For one account of the Tsuda Incident at Tokyo University, see "Tsuda Sōkichi hakushi no koto," in Maruyama Masao and Fukuda Kanichi, *Kikigaki*, 236–58.

9. Tsuda Sōkichi, "Kenkoku no jijō to bansei ikkei no shisō." This essay was republished, under a different title, in Tsuda's collected writings; see Tsuda Sōkichi, "Nihon no kokka keisei no katei to kōshitsu no kōkyūsei ni kansuru shisō no yurai," in *Tsuda Sōkichi zenshū*, 3: 439–73. For the letter, see "Tsuda hakushi 'Kenkoku no jijō to bansei ikkei no shisō' no happyō ni tsuite."

10. Tsuda, "Nihon no kokka keisei no katei to kōshitsu no kōkyūsei ni kansuru shisō no yūrai," 451.

11. Ibid., 456.

12. In fact, Tsuda was not the first Japanese person in the postwar era to use the term *shōchō* to describe the emperor's historical role. For example, in an essay published in December 1945, Kubokawa Tokuji used essentially the same term, *shōchōsha*, several times to describe the emperor's role throughout Japan's history; see Kubokawa, "Tennōsei to Nihon demokurashii."

13. Tsuda, "Nihon no kokka keisei no katei to kōshitsu no kōkyūsei ni kansuru shisō no yurai," 467.

14. Ibid., 469.

15. Ibid., 471, 473.

16. "Tsuda hakushi 'Kenkoku no jijō to bansei ikkei no shisō' no happyō ni tsuite," 131.

17. Nosaka (1892–1993) was a leader of the JCP who after the war called for his party to tread softly on the question of the monarchy, and Yamakawa (1880–1956) was a leading figure on the socialist/communist left.

18. "Tsuda hakushi 'Kenkoku no jijō to bansei ikkei no shisō' no happyō ni tsuite," 133.

19. Takakura Teru, "Tennōsei narabi ni kōshitsu no mondai."

20. Bellah, "Japan's Cultural Identity," 579.

21. Karube Tadashi, *Hikari no ryōkoku*, 195.

22. See Watsuji Tetsurō, "Hōken shisō to shintō to kyōgi," reprinted in Watsuji, *Kokumin tōgō no shōchō*, 3–26.

23. For a more detailed account of the debate between Sasaki and Watsuji, see Titus, "The Making of the 'Symbol Emperor System' in Postwar Japan," esp. 542–49.

24. Watsuji Tetsurō, "Kokutai henkōron ni tsuite Sasaki hakushi no oshie o kou," in Watsuji, *Kokumin tōgō no shōchō*, 100.

25. Ibid., 102.

26. Ibid., 105.

27. Ibid., 113.

28. Ibid., 118–19.

29. The petition is reprinted in Maruyama Masao and Fukuda Kanichi, *Kikigaki*, 255–58.

30. Ishii Ryōsuke, *Tennō*, 216. Snippets of Ishii's interpretation of the emperor's role throughout history are available in English in Ishii, *A History of Political Institutions in Japan*.

31. In the imperial house's first centuries of existence, there were several reigning empresses (six between 593 and 793). Thereafter, there were only two other reigning empresses, one in the seventeenth century and another in the eighteenth century.

32. Ishii, *A History of Political Institutions in Japan*, 7.

33. Ishii, *Tennō*, 224.

34. Ibid., 233.

35. Ibid., 248–49.

36. Koseki Shōichi, *The Birth of Japan's Postwar Constitution.*

37. For a chart showing the proposals of the major parties and other organizations in 1946 regarding the proper constitutional position for the emperor, see *Jurisuto* 933 (1–15 May 1989), 251.

A team of Japanese constitutional scholars has compiled the complete known documentary record of the making of the Constitution of Japan. Volumes 1 and 2 contain numerous documents pertaining to the drafting of the chapter on the emperor. For the draft constitution of the nongovernmental Constitutional Research Association (Kenpō kenkyūkai), which of all the Japanese proposals most closely matched, on the question of the emperor, the draft produced by the U.S. authors, see Ashibe Nobuyoshi et al., *Nihonkoku kenpō seitei shiryō zenshū*, 2: 344–52. A group of little consequence in the eyes of the Japanese authorities, the Constitutional Research Association attracted favorable attention from SCAP with its draft constitution.

38. Historian Nakamura Masanori (*The Japanese Monarchy*, 94) has argued that the Statute of Westminster (1931) was one of the sources used by the U.S. drafters. The preamble of the Statute of Westminster defined the crown as the "symbol of the free association of the members of the British Commonwealth of Nations." The Statute of Westminster formally recognized the legislative independence of members of the dominion such as Canada, but maintained these nations in a voluntary commonwealth whose unifying symbol was the crown. Nakamura's assertion seems reasonable, if only because the drafters used the British monarchy as their model, but Nakamura was not able to provide concrete evidence to support his hypothesis.

39. Supreme Commander for the Allied Powers, Government Section, 1: 103, 114.

40. Ibid., 144.

41. Telephone conversation with Richard A. Poole, 8 Oct. 1997.

42. Bradford, *George VI*, 277.

43. The "return to tradition" interpretation was not absent entirely from the Diet debates. Theodore H. McNelly ("Domestic and International Influences on Constitutional Revision in Japan, 1945–1946," 272–73) has pointed out that the extremely conservative Progressive Party, in a radical reversal of its earlier position regarding imperial sovereignty, endorsed the emperor's position in the constitutional draft as being in accordance with the emperor's role throughout most of Japanese history.

44. Shimizu Shin, *Chikujō Nihonkoku kenpō shingiroku*, 1: 165. Hereafter cited as Shimizu.

45. The constitutionalist Odaka Tomoo was one of a few scholars to argue Kanamori's line, but his thesis never gained acceptance. See Titus, "The Making of the 'Symbol Emperor System' in Postwar Japan," esp. 537–41. Other works addressing the debates over the locus of sovereignty include K. Inoue, *MacArthur's Japanese Constitution*; Cornwall, "Japanese Political Reaction to Constitutional Revision 1945–46"; and K. Okubo, *The Problems of the Emperor System in Postwar Japan.*

46. The letters about this topic exchanged by Yoshida and MacArthur are reprinted in Supreme Commander for the Allied Powers, Government Section, *Political Reorientation of Japan*, 2: 679–80.

47. Minobe Tatsukichi, "Watakushi wa omou," 1.

48. Minobe Tatsukichi, *Shinkenpō no kihon genri*, 69.

49. Miyazawa Toshiyoshi, *Kenpō*, 179.

50. Katsube Mitake, "Tennō wa Nihonjin ni totte hitsuyō ka," 5.

51. See Titus, "The Making of the 'Symbol Emperor System' in Postwar Japan," esp. 537–42.

52. Nakamura Mutso, "Kokuji kōi naishi tennō no kōteki kōi," 115.

53. Supreme Commander for the Allied Powers, Government Section, *Political Reorientation of Japan*, 1: 102.

54. Shimizu, 507.

55. Suzuki Shizuko, "Tennō gyōkō to shōchō tennōsei no kakuritsu," 59. The emperor's trip took place 12–15 Nov. 1945.

56. Shimizu, 452.

57. Ibid., 640–41.

58. This is from the private papers of Satō Isao, who, as an official in the Cabinet Legislation Bureau, served as secretary to the meetings. This unpublished document was given to me by Professor Takami Katsutoshi of Hokkaido University, who first came across it in a meeting of the Tōkyō daigaku hōgakubu senryō taisei kenkyūkai.

59. For a description of how the emperor's role in the opening ceremony is carried out according to precedent, see Sangiin jimukyoku, *Sangiin senreiroku*, 35; and Shūgiin jimukyoku, *Shūgiin senreishu*, 33–34.

60. One of the few individuals who immediately raised strenuous objections to the tours was not a Japanese national but the head of the Russian mission in Japan, Lieutenant General K. Derevyanko. In a 10 April 1946 letter to MacArthur, Derevyanko wrote: "Definite expressions of political activities by the Japanese Emperor have been noticed. In particular they were expressed by several trips of a demonstrative and political nature through the country" (letter from Lieutenant General K. Derevyanko, U.S.S.R. Member of the Allied Council for Japan, to Chairman of the Allied Council for Japan and Supreme Commander for the Allied Powers, General of the Army, Douglas MacArthur, 10 April 1946. Located in R6–5, B.110, F. 1, "Russian Mission Corres., Feb. 28, '46–Dec. 12, '47," Archives, General Douglas MacArthur Memorial, Norfolk, VA).

61. For an English translation of the Imperial House Office Law, see Supreme Commander for the Allied Powers, Government Section, *Political Reorientation of Japan*, 2: 960.

62. "Tennō ni kansuru hōkokusho," 24. This is an excellent summary of the Commission on the Constitution's investigation into legal matters relating to the emperor.

63. Hōgaku kyōkai, *Chūkai Nihonkoku kenpō*, 1: 51.

64. Ibid., 102–3.

65. *New York Times*, 3 Dec. 1948.

66. *Asahi shinbun*, 4 Dec. 1948.

67. Shūgiin jimukyoku, *Daiyonkai kokkai shūgiin gaimu iinkai giroku* 2, 1.

68. Ibid.

69. Ibid.

70. Shūgiin jimukyoku, *Daiyonkai kokkai shūgiin gaimu iinkai giroku* 4, 1.

71. Yokota Kisaburō, *Tennōsei*, 63.

72. Tsunetō Kyō, "Waga kuni ni wa genshu ga sonzai suru ka."

73. Watanabe Osamu, *Sengo seijishi no naka no tennōsei*, 175–79. The official Commission on the Constitution (1956–64) examined the decisionmaking process by

which the form of the letters of accreditation under the Postwar Constitution was decided. The records of the commission contain an example of one such letter; see Kenpō chōsakai jimukyoku, *Shingikai nado ni okeru kenpō kankei rongi oyobi kenpō kankei jitsurei, senrei, tsūdatsushū*, 3–4.

74. Yamanouchi Kazuo and Asano Ichirō, *Kokkai no kenpō rongi*, 222, continued on 233. For the complete record of the exchange, see Shūgiin jimukyoku, *Daijūgokai kokkai shūgiin gaimu iinkai gijiroku*, 1–2.

75. For newspaper coverage of the government's interpretation of the legal nature of the crown prince's trip, see "Kokuji kōi de nai," *Asahi shinbun*, 3 Dec. 1952.

76. Hōgaku kyōkai, *Chūkai Nihonkoku kenpō*, 1: 96.

77. Kuroda Satoru, "Tennō no kenpōjō no chii," 2–3.

78. Ibid., 14.

79. Here Hasegawa was referring to a visit the emperor made to the Ise Shrine on 2 June 1952 to report to the imperial ancestors that Japan had regained its independence.

80. Hasekawa Masayasu, "Shōchō no hōteki imi naiyō," 27. Paragraph 3 of Article 20 of the constitution reads: "The State and its organs shall refrain from religious education or any other religious activity."

81. Kiyomiya Shirō, *Kenpō*, 114–15.

82. See Yamanouchi Kasuo and Asano Ichirō, *Kokkai no kenpō rongi*, 240–71.

83. The third paragraph of Article 14 of the constitution specifies that honors are purely symbolic, however: "No privilege shall accompany any award of honor, decoration or any distinction, nor shall any such award be valid beyond the lifetime of the individual who now holds or hereafter may receive it."

84. Millions of individuals received awards for their contributions to the war. Beginning in 1942, the families of all soldiers killed in action were given certificates specifying the award earned by the soldier through his death.

85. Sōrifu shōkunkyoku, *Shōkunkyoku hyakunen shiryōshū*, 2: 200. This volume, which runs nearly 1,000 pages, contains all the official documents, including records of Diet debates, about the imperial decoration system in Postwar Japan. Volume 1 addresses the prewar system.

86. Ibid., 185.

87. Ibid., 279.

88. Quoted in Kitagawa Yoshihide, "Senryō hōki," 450.

89. Fifty-six percent of respondents to the question "Do you think that the emperor's authority should be strengthened, or do you think that the present situation is good?" supported the status quo; cited in Nishihira Shigeki, "Tennō, gengō, kokka, kokki," 83.

90. Quoted in Kishimoto Hideo et al., "Zadankai," 7.

91. Inoue Kiyoshi, "Saigunbi to shintennōsei," in Inoue, *Tennōsei*, 238. Originally published in *Kaizō*, April 1952.

92. Kishimoto Hideo et al., "Zadankai," 9.

93. Ibid., 10.

94. A passage in one textbook that linked Fukuzawa's "get-out-of-Asia" thinking to Japan's imperialism was rejected by the Ministry of Education during a review in 1992, leading to litigation by one of the authors. Takashima Nobuyoshi, a former student of Ienaga Saburō (who spent much of the postwar period engaged in litigation against the government regarding the Ministry of Education's screening of textbooks), was part of

team of authors of a textbook about contemporary Japanese society. During the screening process, the Ministry of Education demanded changes in several passages, including one that highlighted Fukuzawa's "Datsuaron" (Get out of Asia) as an example of Japanese colonialist thought. In response, Takashima quit the team and filed suit against the government. But Takashima's legal challenges were dismissed by the courts over and over. For information on the textbook passage in question and the lawsuit, see Yokohama kyōkasho soshō o shiji suru kai, *Yokohama kyōkasho soshō*. I am grateful to Professor Inokuchi Hiromitsu of the University of East Asia for sending me materials about this topic.

95. The essay, "Fukuzawa Yukichi no teishitsuron," is reprinted in Koizumi Shinzō, *Jooji goseden to teishitsuron*, 98–101.

96. This line is from Fukuzawa's "Sonnōron."

97. In a short essay in the appendix of a glossy collection of photographs of the imperial family published in 1952 as part of the campaign to remake the imperial house to suit New Japan, Takahashi Seiichirō (1884–1982), who served as minister of Education in the first Yoshida Cabinet (1947), also invoked Fukuzawa's paradigm of the monarchy in arguing that the emperor as symbol was the true Japanese tradition; see Takahashi Seiichirō, "Tennō to Nihon kokumin" in Nihon yoron chōsa kenkyūjo, *Tennō: Album of the Human Emperor*, 286–87.

98. Tsuda Sōkichi, "Nihon no kōshitsu."

99. Ibid., 8. Tsuda stressed that the Occupation authorities had *inadvertently* returned the emperor to his traditional position.

100. Jinja shinpōsha seikyō kenkyūshitsu, *Tennō, shintō, kenpō*, 9.

101. The proposal is reprinted in Jiyūminshutō kenpō chōsakai, *Jiyūminshutō kenpō chōsakai shiryō*, vol. 2.

102. Mitsuma testified on 6 June 1954. See Mitsuma Shingo, "Nihonkoku kenpō ni okeru tennō no chii to kokutairon," 71.

103. Hiraizumi testified on 30 June 1954. See Hiraizumi Kiyoshi, "Nihon rekishi no ue kara mita tennō no chii," 91.

104. Ibid., 92. The literal translation of *minpon* is "people as the base." This term was used by scholars on both the left (Yoshino Sakuzō; 1878–1933) and the right (Uesugi Shinkichi; 1878–1929) in prewar Japan to describe politics for the people under imperial sovereignty.

105. Ibid., 93–94.

106. Ibid., 96.

107. Jiyūminshutō kenpō chōsakai, *Jiyūminshutō kenpō chōsakai shiryō*, 2: 24–25.

108. Oguchi Iichi, "Tennō genshuron no jittai," 138.

109. "Tennō futatabi kumo ni noritamau," 76.

110. The poll results appeared in Saitō Dōichi, "Seron chōsa ni miru tennō-kan," 169.

111. For poll results showing support for constitutional revision, see Cole and Nakanishi, *Japanese Opinion Polls with Socio-Political Significance, 1947–1957*, 1: 444–63.

112. Jiyūminshutō kenpō chōsakai, *Jiyūminshutō kenpō chōsakai shiryō*, 2: 25–26.

113. Mitsuma Shingo, "Tennō to kenpō chōsakai," 23.

114. Mitsuma had made the same point in his 1952 monograph *Sokoku fukkō*. This book was reissued in 1970; see *Sokoku fukkō*, 166.

115. Nanjō Hiroshi, "Riyō sareta 'tennō no ishi,'" 40–41.

116. Ibid., 41.

117. Ibid., 41–42.

118. Sangiin jimukyoku, *Dainijūkai kokkai sangiin yosan iinkai kaigiroku*, 3.

119. Nanjō Hiroshi, "Riyō sareta 'tennō no ishi,'". 43.

120. Cited in Saitō Dōichi, "Seron chōsa ni miru tennōkan," 169. Various polls show the same trends; see "Kōshitsu ni kansuru hitobito no iken"; and Nishihara Shigeki, "Seron kara mita tennōsei to daikyūjō." The most systematic study of popular consciousness about the constitution is Kobayashi Naoki, *Nihon ni okeru kenpō dōtai no bunseki*. In Chapter 4, Kobayashi addressed changing views of the symbolic monarchy. Polls showed that reactionary views regarding the emperor were only slightly more common in rural areas than in urban areas.

One poll conducted by the *Mainichi shinbun* before the constitutional draft had been released in 1946 showed that 45 percent of respondents favored a unpoliticized monarchy. This oft-cited result (see Kobayashi, *Nihon ni okeru kenpō dōtai no bunseki*, 121–22) suggests that a high level of support for a symbolic monarchy already existed among the Japanese prior to SCAP drafting of the constitution.

121. Saitō Dōichi, "Seron chōsa ni miru tennōkan," 169.

122. Ibid., 169–70. A series of polls probing this and other issues were conducted by the government in the early 1960s.

123. K. Takayanagi, "Some Reminiscences of Japan's Commission on the Constitution," 74.

124. Kenpō chōsakai jimukyoku, *Kenpō unyō no jissai ni tsuite no dai-san iinkai hōkokusho*, 29.

125. Ibid., 81–82.

126. Takayanagi Kenzō, "Shōchō no genshu, tennō." For a significantly abridged English version of this essay, see "The New Emperor System."

127. Takayanagi Kenzō, "Shōchō no genshu, tennō," 13.

128. Bonner F. Fellers, "Memorandum to the Commander-in-Chief," 2 Oct. 1945. Located in RC-5, Box 2, Folder 2, Official Correspondence, July–December 1945, MacArthur Archives, Norfolk, VA. Fellers wrote: "It is a fundamental American concept that the people of any nation have the inherent right to choose their own government. Were the Japanese given this opportunity, they would select the Emperor as the symbolic head of state."

129. Takayanagi Kenzō, "Shōchō no genshu, tennō," 13.

130. Bagehot, *The English Constitution*, 93–94.

131. See Satomi Kishio, *Nihonkoku no kenpō*, 420–73; the article in question appears on 425.

132. For a more detailed analysis of the various opinions of the members of the commission, see Maki, *Japan's Commission on the Constitution*.

133. Kenpō chōsakai jimukyoku, *Kenpō chōsakai daihyakuikkai sōkai gijiroku*, 1.

134. Ibid., 3.

135. I have profited greatly from Watanabe Osamu's analysis of Nakasone's views on the emperor. For further details, see his *Sengo seijishi no naka no tennōsei*.

136. The task of managing the system fell to the Awards Bureau of the Office of the Prime Minister (Sōrifu shōkunkyoku). In 1964, the Ikeda Cabinet also decreed that certificates designating decorations earned by soldiers who died in action were to be distributed

as soon as possible, and the Ministry of Health and Welfare began the task of processing the cases of the approximately two million deceased soldiers whose files had not been cleared at the time the system was suspended. Since the circumstances of death influenced the rank of award to be granted, each case had to be investigated individually. As an act in matters of state, the emperor issued these certificates to the families of the dead soldiers.

137. A useful guide to the contemporary decoration system is Sōrifu shōkunkyoku, *Nihon no kunshō, hōshō seido.*

138. See Takagi Hiroshi, *Kindai tennōsei no bunkashiteki kenkyū,* esp. 22–69, 141–64.

Chapter 3

1. See Titus, *Palace and Politics in Prewar Japan.*

2. Ihara Yoriaki, *Zōho kōshitsu jiten,* 71–74. I am grateful to Professor Takami Katsutoshi for directing me to this source.

3. Okada Keisuke, *Okada Keisuke kaikoroku,* 95–96.

4. Ziegler, "Churchill and the Monarchy," 198.

5. For an example of the orthodox interpretation, see the dictionary of prewar and wartime Japan's political system compiled by Itō Takashi (editor) and Momose Takashi: *Jiten. Shōwa senzenki no Nihon.*

6. In addition to Large's biography of Hirohito, see his "Emperor Hirohito and Early Shōwa Japan."

7. The Monologue was first published in December 1990 in the magazine *Bungei shunjū* and later issued in book form. For the book, see Terasaki Hidenari and Mariko Terasaki Miller, *Shōwa tennō dokuhakuroku.* In 1996, NHK journalist Higashino Makoto discovered an abridged English-language translation of the Monologue in the files of General Bonner Fellers, who served as secretary to MacArthur from 1944 to 1946. For the English-language translation as well as further analysis of the Monologue, see Higashino Makoto, *Shōwa tennō futatsu no dokuhakuroku.*

8. Large, *Emperor Hirohito and Showa Japan,* 39.

9. Ibid., 70.

10. Awaya Kentarō, "Emperor Shōwa's Accountability for War." Awaya stresses that "the portrayal of Emperor Shōwa as a constitutional monarch and a pacifist has been widely propagated since the defeat, but it is the greatest political myth of postwar history" (396).

11. Irokawa, *The Age of Hirohito,* 86.

12. Ibid., 87.

13. Quoted in Bix, "The Showa Emperor's 'Monologue' and the Problem of War Responsibility," 353–54.

14. Hirohito made this comment during an interview with *Newsweek*'s Bernard Krisher shortly before the emperor undertook his historic trip to the United States. Krisher's question was: "Could Your Majesty compare your prewar and postwar roles?" See "A Talk with the Emperor of Japan," *Newsweek,* 29 Sept. 1975, 56.

15. Kojima Noboru, "Nihon senryō," 349. The details of this meeting have never been confirmed by the release of documents thought to be held by the Foreign Ministry. Kojima, however, claims to have examined the documents surreptitiously in the Foreign Ministry.

16. *New York Times,* 7 May 1947.

17. *New York Times*, 9 May 1947.

18. Kojima, "Nihon senryō," 346–47.

19. Irie Tametoshi, *Irie Sukemasa nikki*, 5: 169, entry for 10 Sept. 1975.

20. See the chapters "Imperial Democracy: Driving the Wedge" and "Evading Responsibility" in Dower, *Embracing Defeat*, 277–301, 319–45.

21. Katayama naikaku kinen zadan, *Katayama naikaku*, 299.

22. The chamberlain was Kinoshita Michio (1887–1974), and the memo first became public with the publication of Kinoshita's papers after the death of the emperor in 1989; see Kinoshita Michio, *Sokkin nisshi*, 218–20.

23. Ibid., 218.

24. Shindō Eiichi, *Ashida Hitoshi nikki*, 2: 13–14.

25. Ihara Yoriaki, *Zōho kōshitsu jiten*, 71–74.

26. Shindō Eiichi, *Ashida Hitoshi nikki*, 2: 14.

27. Quoted in Irokawa, *The Age of Hirohito*, 99.

28. Irie, *Irie Sukemasa nikki*, 5: 419.

29. Hariu Seikichi and Yokota Kōichi, *Kokumin shuken to tennōsei*, 261.

30. Eldridge, "Shōwa Tennō to Okinawa."

31. Katō Kanjū was minister of Labor and Nomizo Masaru was chair of the Local Finance Committee.

32. Shindō Eiichi, *Ashida Hitoshi nikki*, 2: 72.

33. According to Sebald's diary, Terasaki told him in November 1948 that "the Emperor was anxious over [the] China situation"; see K. Okamoto, "William J. Sebald," 27.

34. Titus, "The Making of the 'Symbol Emperor System' in Postwar Japan," 565.

35. The exchange rate in 1940, before the outbreak of war between Japan and the Allies, was approximately four yen to the dollar; in prewar dollars the imperial house was worth nearly $400 million.

36. The term *honsha* refers to the main house that controlled a financial clique.

37. The memorandum, dated 14 Nov. 1945, was reprinted in Ashibe Nobuyoshi and Takami Katsutoshi, *Nihon rippō shiryō zenshū 7: Kōshitsu keizaihō*, 65–67.

38. An English translation of the Imperial House Economy Law can be found in Supreme Commander for the Allied Powers, Government Section, *Political Reorientation of Japan*, 2: 849–50.

39. On the finances of the British monarchy, see Hall, *Royal Fortune*; and Bogdanor, *The Monarchy and the Constitution*, esp. chap. 7, "The Financing of the Monarchy."

40. Takahashi Hiroshi, *Shōchō tennō*, 90.

41. Quoted in Titus, *Palace and Politics in Prewar Japan*, 42.

42. The Imperial Family Council consisted of all adult male members of the imperial family who were eligible to become regent.

43. Takayanagi Kenzō et al., *Nihonkoku kenpō seitei no katei*, 1: 394. The conversation reprinted here is from SCAP records cited in this volume.

44. Shindō Eiichi, *Ashida Hitoshi nikki*, 1: 87–88, entry for 5 Mar. 1946.

45. Ibid., 90.

46. For an English translation of the 1889 Imperial House Law, see McLaren, *Japanese Government Documents*, 1: 145–53. This collection of documents was published originally in 1914. For an English translation of the postwar Imperial House Law, see Supreme

Commander for the Allied Powers, Government Section, *Political Reorientation of Japan*, 2: 846–48.

47. For information on the making of the postwar Imperial House Law, see Ashibe Nobuyoshi and Takami Katsutoshi, *Nihon rippō shiryō zenshū 1: Kōshitsu tenpan.*

48. Shindō Eiichi, *Ashida Hitoshi nikki*, 2: 90, entry for 6–8 Apr. 1948.

49. Ibid., 118, entry for 28 May 1948.

50. Irie Tametoshi, *Irie Sukemasa nikki*, 2: 229, entry for 29 May 1948.

51. Shindō Eiichi, *Ashida Hitoshi nikki*, 2: 107, entry for 10 May 1948.

52. Ibid., 121.

53. Iwami Takao, *Heika no goshitsumon*, 30–31.

54. Togashi Junji, *Tennō to tomo ni gojūnen*, 171.

55. "Fukkatsu shita seijō sōjō."

56. Iwami Takao, *Heika no goshitsumon*, 86.

57. Mitani Takanobu, *Kaikoroku*, 249.

58. The message was sent via Sebald; see Hata Ikuhiko, *Hirohito tennō itsutsu no ketsudan*, 247.

59. Roberts, "The 'Japan Crowd' and the Zaibatsu Restoration," 403.

60. Hata Ikuhiko, *Hirohito tennō itsutsu no ketsudan*, 249.

61. Toyoshita Narahiko, *Anpo jōyaku no seiritsu*, 201–4. Toyoshita suggests that Emperor Hirohito, by offering U.S. diplomats his support for proposals for a security treaty between the two countries, in fact undermined Prime Minister Yoshida's bargaining power. Toyoshita himself admits that he has no proof for his hypothesis, however.

62. Ridgway, *Soldier*, 227.

63. The Imperial House Press Club is one of the numerous press clubs that developed in Japan between 1890 and 1910.

64. Tanaka Minoru, "Tennō ichi-nichi no seikatsu," 81. Tanaka had been a member of the Imperial House Press Club before the surrender.

65. I asked Takahashi Hiroshi, who served in the Imperial House Press Club and who has written extensively about the imperial house, if there were a possibility that Tanaka could not have known about the briefings. Takahashi responded that there was not (personal correspondence, 15 May 1995).

66. Ibid.

67. See Freeman, *Closing the Shop*, 108–9, 149–53, 191–93.

68. See Pimlott, *The Queen*, esp. 252–88.

69. Nicolson, *King George the Fifth.*

70. Koizumi Shinzō, "Aru kokuō no shōgai," 192.

71. Koizumi Shinzō, "Kunshu no yūraku," 118.

72. Togashi Junji, *Tennō to tomo ni gojūnen*, 172.

73. Iwami Takao, *Heika no goshitsumon*, 170–71.

74. Itō Takashi and Watanabe Yukio, *Zoku Shigemitsu Mamoru shuki*, 732.

75. When David Titus was conducting research in the early 1960s for his book *Palace and Politics in Prewar Japan*, he once asked Irie Sukemasa if the emperor met with Prime Minister Ikeda. Titus remembers Irie responding, "Yes, all the time." Titus then asked why they met, given that the emperor no longer was supposed to have a political role. Irie responded: "They like each other" (personal correspondence from David A. Titus, 7 Jan. 1998).

76. Kishi Nobusuke et al., *Kishi Nobusuke no kaisō*, 58.
77. Koizumi Shinzō, "Teishitsuron."
78. Ibid., 114.
79. Ibid., 120.
80. Itō Takashi, *Satō Eisaku nikki.*
81. See, for example, ibid., 4: 318, entry for 23 Apr. 1971.
82. Iwami Takao, *Heika no goshitsumon*, 151–54.
83. Itō Takashi, *Satō Eisaku nikki*, 4: 153.
84. Ibid., 5: 25.
85. Iwami Takao, *Heika no goshitsumon*, 158.
86. Ibid., 159.
87. Ohsuga Mizuo, *Shushō kantei*, 101.
88. Irie Tametoshi, *Irei Sukemasa nikki*, 4: 372; entry for 7 July 1972.
89. Yamada Eizō, *Seiden Satō Eisaku*, 2: 137.
90. Irie Tametoshi, *Irei Sukemasa nikki*, vol. 4.
91. It was not uncommon for the Japanese to be moved deeply by meeting the emperor. In another incident that raised eyebrows in 1973, an officer in the Self Defense Forces (SDF) publicly commented in January that "he felt that he had received the imperial will (*seishi*)" after hearing the emperor tell him and other SDF officers during an audience that he "wished that they exert themselves in their work on behalf of the nation"; see "Nihon no shōchō o kangaeru," 171.
92. "Masuhara hatsugen ni miru tennō to seiji no kiken na kankei;" 18.
93. Masuhara was born in 1903. After graduating from Tokyo University's Faculty of Law in 1928, he joined the Home Ministry. In 1947, he was elected governor of Kagawa prefecture.

Masuhara had a knack for creating problems for the emperor whom he so respected. In 1950, Governor Masuhara hosted the emperor on one of his regional tours. During this time of continuing food shortages, Masuhara served the emperor eel (*unagi*), a delicacy in Japan. The emperor apparently thanked Masuhara profusely at the time, but after the press publicized the story of the emperor indulging in eel, the emperor thereafter refused for a few years to eat eel, although many other hosts tried to duplicate Masuhara's hospitality; see ibid.
94. See "Kyūchū enyūkai ni etsuzankai hachi-nin o shōtai shita shushō no senkyō-ku sabisu."
95. Ibid., 29.
96. "Hoshutō naikaku o yusaburu 'naisō' mondai no shōgeki," 19.
97. "Masuhara hatsugen ni miru tennō to seiji no kiken na kankei," 20.
98. Quoted in Yokota Kōichi, "Tennō to seiji," 188.
99. *Asahi shinbun*, 30 May 1973.
100. *Mainichi shinbun*, 30 May 1973.
101. Quoted in "'Nai mono wa nai' to kyōben shitsuzuketa shushō no 2-jikan 37-fun," 141.
102. Horikoshi Sakuji, *Sengo seiji 13 no shōgen*, 142.
103. "Masuhara hatsugen ni miru tennō to seiji no kiken na kankei," 21.
104. Irie Tametoshi, *Irei Sukemasa nikki*, 5: 27; entry for 29 May 1973.
105. Ibid., 27.

106. Ibid., 28; entry for 1 June 1973.
107. Thatcher, *The Downing Street Years*, 17–18.
108. See Yokota Kōichi, "Tennō to seiji."
109. Pimlott, *The Queen*, 329–32.
110. For King Juan Carlos's role in the political transformation of Spain, see Powell, *Juan Carlos of Spain*; and Bernecker, "Monarchy and Democracy."
111. Anderson, "Royal Affairs," 112.
112. Larsson, "Sweden, the Crown of State."
113. Kaarsted, "Denmark, a Limited Monarchy."
114. Ohsuga Mizuo, *Shushō kantei*, 101. The interpellation took place on 27 May 1988, in a meeting of the House of Councillors Budget Committee. In addition to the records of the Diet, another source for the exchange between Hashimoto and Takeshita is Nihon kyōsantō chūō iinkai shuppankyoku, *Tennōsei no genzai to kōtaishi*, 76–84.
115. I am grateful to Ohsuga Mizuo, a member of the team of reporters, for sharing his experiences with me at length.
116. Iwami Takao, *Heika no goshitsumon*, 82.
117. Ibid., 79.
118. Thatcher, *The Downing Street Years*, 208.
119. Iwami Takao, *Heika no goshitsumon*, 135–37.
120. Ibid., 89.
121. Quoted in ibid., 196.
122. Ibid.
123. Hashimoto was Japan's ambassador to China when Emperor Akihito made his historic visit there in 1992.
124. Iwami Takao, *Heika no goshitsumon*, 83–84.
125. Bagehot, *The English Constitution*, 111.
126. Ibid., 111–12.
127. D. Irokawa, *The Age of Hirohito*, 81.
128. I received a copy of a confidential, internal Imperial Household Agency document about briefings from a journalist who wished to remain anonymous. The source is titled "Sōri, kakuryō no naisō"; it is dated 14 Oct. 1993 and bears the name of an official of the Imperial Household Agency who also must remain anonymous. According to this source, for example, on 31 Aug. 1993 Prime Minister Hosokawa Morihiro (1938–), who just had returned from a visit to the United States, briefed the emperor about his meeting with President Bill Clinton.
129. The information that Emperor Akihito is no less active than his father in making comments and asking questions during briefings comes from several journalists who presently serve or have served in the Imperial House Press Club. Each of them heard it from sources inside the palace, and all of them wished to remain anonymous.

Chapter 4

1. I borrowed this term from Eric Conan and Henry Rousso's *Vichy: An Ever-Present Past.*
2. Cohen, "Beyond Nuremberg." I thank Professor Franziska Seraphim of Boston College for bringing this essay to my attention.
3. Supreme Commander for the Allied Powers, Government Section, *Political Reorientation of Japan*, 2: 413.

4. For a complete translation of the Imperial Rescript on Surrender, see Lu, *Japan: A Documentary History*, 2: 457–58.

5. Quoted in Bix, "The Showa Emperor's 'Monologue' and the Problem of War Responsibility," 302.

6. Emperor Hirohito reiterated his concern in parts of the radio address not quoted above.

7. For a contemporary translation of Higashikuni's address, see "Premier Prince Naruhiko Higashi-kuni's Address at the Eighty-Eighth Session of the Diet, September 5, 1945."

8. Ibid., 281.

9. This report was reprinted in *Jurisuto* 938 (15 July 1989): 176.

10. *Asahi shinbun*, 24 Nov. 1945.

11. Togashi Junji, *Heika no "ningen" sengen*, 4.

12. Ibid., 23.

13. For accounts of Hirohito's concern with preserving the *kokutai*, see Wetzler, *Hirohito and War*, esp. 196–99; and Drea, "Chasing a Decisive Victory."

14. Ono Noboru, *Ningen tennō*.

15. Notable photo collections with both Japanese and English text are San Nyūsu Futosu, *Tennō* (1948), the highlight of which is a picture of Hirohito, dressed in a suit and tie, reading a book in his study with a bust of Abraham Lincoln visible in the background; and the elegant Nihon yoron chōsa kenkyūjo, *Tennō: Album of the Human Emperor* (1952).

16. Takahashi Hiroshi, "Ningen tennō enshutsusha no keifu."

17. Ibid., 145. Ishiwatari was minister until 1 Jan. 1946.

18. Glynn, *A Song for Nagasaki*, 189.

19. Takakura Teru, "Tennōsei narabi ni kōshitsu no mondai," 11.

20. Quoted in Dower, *Embracing Defeat*, 344.

21. Ibid., esp. 277–345.

22. Hans Christian Andersen, "The Emperor's New Clothes."

23. See S. Kurihara, *Black Eggs: Poems by Kurihara Sadako*, especially the poems "Human Emperor, Meek and Mild," "His Majesty Has Donkey's Ears," and "Hiroshima and the Emperor's New Clothes."

24. No veteran was more active and persistent in reminding his countrymen of Hirohito's responsibility for the war than Okuzaki, the subject of Hara Kazuo's powerful and often disturbing documentary *The Emperor's Naked Army Marches On* (*Yukiyukite shingun*, 1987). For an account of Okuzaki's activities and the significance of this acclaimed film, see Ruoff and Ruoff, *The Emperor's Naked Army Marches On*.

For an interview of Hara Kazuo (1945–), director of this, see Ruoff and Ruoff, "Japan's Outlaw Filmmaker: An Interview with Hara Kazuo."

25. Shūgiin jimukyoku, *Daijūsankai kokkai shūgiin yosan iinkai gijiroku* 5, 19.

26. Iwami Takao, *Heika no goshitsumon*, 18.

27. Bix, "The Showa Emperor's 'Monologue' and the Problem of War Responsibility," 315–16.

28. Satō Tadao, "Hirohito no bishō," 199.

29. Quoted in Rousso, *The Vichy Syndrome*, 16.

30. Ibid., 100.

31. Paxton, *Vichy France*. Paxton, in a 22 Nov. 1997 letter responding to an inquiry

from me, wrote: "The death of de Gaulle was certainly one of the factors that combined in the years 1968–1972 to bring an end to the consensual postwar myths about Vichy and the Resistance. But other things probably contributed more: the arrival of the 'generation of 1968' and the impact of those demonstrations, Ophuls' film 'The Sorrow and the Pity,' President Pompidou's pardon of Paul Touvier in 1971, [and] the changing feelings of the Jewish survivors who no longer wished to keep a low profile, as in 1945."

32. "Intabyū: Tennō oyobi tennōsei ni tsuite: Kodama Yoshio," 216.

33. Kodama Yoshio, "Watakushi no uchinaru tennōsei," 83.

34. Ibid.

35. "Nakasone Yasuhiro-shi 'Waga tennōron,'" 136.

36. The text of Nakasone's comments in the Diet on 5 and 13 June was reprinted in Bunka hyōron henshūbu, *Tennōsei o tou*, 440–41.

37. "Nakasone Yasuhiro-shi 'Waga tennōron,'" 136.

38. See "Gakusha 100-nin ga gekiron no 'kunshusei shinpojiumu' o dō kangaeru."

39. Ibid., 22–27.

40. Morita Akio and Ishihara Shintarō, *"No" to ieru Nihon*. For an English edition, see Ishihara Shintarō, *The Japan That Can Say No*. The "no" refers to Japan standing up to the United States.

41. Ishihara Shintarō, "Ishihara Shintarō no seiji handan," 38.

42. Ibid.

43. The proposal was reprinted in Jiyūminshutō kenpō chōsakai, *Jiyūminshutō kenpō chōsakai shiryō*, 1: 496.

44. Under interpellation on 8 Mar. 1986 by JCP representatives questioning the need for an elaborate ceremony honoring Hirohito's sixtieth year on the throne, Prime Minister Nakasone vehemently defended the emperor from charges of war responsibility; see Shūgiin jimukyoku, *Daihyakuyonkai kokkai shūgiin yosan iinkai giroku* 20, 32–34.

45. Ueyama Shunpei et al., "Nihon no naka no tennō."

46. Ibid., 69.

47. *Süddeutsche Zeitung*, 10 Oct. 1971.

48. *Asahi shinbun*, 6 Oct. 1971, evening edition.

49. *Daily Mirror*, 6 Oct. 1971.

50. *Asahi shinbun*, 12 Oct. 1971.

51. *Mainichi shinbun*, 15 Oct. 1971.

52. *Japan Times*, 15 Oct. 1971.

53. *Asahi shinbun*, 15 Oct. 1971.

54. Quoted in "Tennō ga 'sengo shori' ni iyoku," 121.

55. "Tennō to heishi Yokoi no kikan," 32.

56. Ibid., 36.

57. Ibid., 32–39.

58. For the text of this press conference, see "Tennō no saigo no heishi 'sokoku' no itutsukan."

59. Yokoi Shōichi, "Hajimete akasu waga-tsuma, tennō, sensō," 33.

60. Ibid., 35.

61. "Tennō hatsugen e no Nihonjin 20-nin no iken," 18.

62. In a 1994 interview, famous fighter pilot Sakai Saburō made the following comments in reference to Hirohito: "Whose name was on the battle orders? Over three

million died fighting for the emperor, but when the war was over he pretended it was not his responsibility. What kind of man does that?" See the obituary of Sakai that appeared in *New York Times*, 8 Oct. 2000.

63. *Japan Times*, 8 Jan. 1989.

64. Ibid., 24 Sept. 1988.

65. While Hirohito was alive, his birthday was celebrated as a national holiday, as is Akihito's birthday, 23 December, now.

66. A collection of selected letters of the 7,300 sent to Motoshima was published in 1989; see *Nagasaki shichō e no 7300-tsu no tegami.*

67. *Asahi shinbun*, 8 Feb. 1989.

68. I was riding in the taxi with Kobayashi Naoki, emeritus professor of constitutional law at Tokyo University, and Takami Katsutoshi, professor of constitutional law at Hokkaido University.

69. The Japanese film *Pride: The Fateful Moment* (*Puraido: unmei no shunkan*, 1998), which provided an edifying account of Japan's motivations for launching the Pacific War, is typically cited as an example of right-wing revisionism, but curiously this film also drew attention to Emperor Hirohito's active wartime role so matter of factly that the viewer is left with the impression that the question of Hirohito's complicity in the war has been definitively settled.

70. At the official level, the myth of the pacifist emperor has proved surprisingly tenacious. Even socialist Murayama Tomiichi, when he served as prime minister between 1994 and 1995, doggedly upheld the interpretation separating Hirohito from the war, except in reference to the emperor's role in the cessation of hostilities.

71. The Japanese government's response to demands for monetary compensation from victims generally has been to insist that all claims for compensation were settled by the reparations Japan paid in accordance with the peace treaties signed with various Asian countries in the decades after the war.

72. "Tennō to 'seiji riyō,'" 123. This critical essay appeared anonymously but was authored by journalist Takahashi Hiroshi.

73. "It is indeed regrettable that there was an unfortunate past between us for a period in this century and I believe that it should not be repeated again."

74. *Asahi shinbun*, 15 May 1990.

75. "Tennō to 'seiji riyō,'" 122.

76. *Asahi shinbun*, 9 May 1990.

77. *Asahi shinbun*, 15 May 1990.

78. *Asahi shinbun*, 16 May 1990.

79. Ibid.

80. The official English version of the emperor's statement appeared in *Asahi shinbun*, 26 May 1990. On 7 Oct. 1998, at a banquet in honor of visiting South Korean President Kim Dae-jung, Emperor Akihito repeated his 1990 apology and then remarked, "The deep sorrow that I feel over this never leaves my memory."

81. Ibid.

82. See Takahashi Hiroshi, "Tennō, kōgō heisei jūnen no kiseki."

83. Shintō seiji renmei, *Seisaku suishin no kadai o kangaeru*, 15–20.

84. I came across this description of the battle over historical memory in Japan in Ueno Chizuko, "The Politics of Memory," 132.

85. In 1995, the Diet passed a resolution recognizing that Japan "carried out [instances of colonial rule and acts of aggression] in the past, inflicting great pain and suffering upon the peoples of other countries, especially in Asia." A translation of the resolution appeared in the 19–25 June weekly international edition of the *Japan Times*.

The conservative backlash against the "Japan was wrong" interpretation grew increasingly evident in the mid-1990s. Symbolic of the backlash are organizations such as the Liberal View of History Study Group and Society for the Making of New School Textbooks in History that were founded in 1995 and 1996, respectively, by Fujioka Nobukatsu (1943–) of Tokyo University. These organizations, which work in coalition with groups such as the Association of Shinto Shrines, believe that the role of history, especially at the secondary level, should be limited to fostering national pride. Thus, they seek the deletion from textbooks of references to negative behavior by the Japanese and the Japanese state in the past, most notably regarding the issue of the comfort women and other unpleasant aspects of Japan's attempt to dominate Asia militarily. See McCormack, "The Japanese Movement to 'Correct' History."

86. See Ishihara Shintarō, "Ooku no kokumin no fuan," 94–95.

87. Pimlott, *The Queen*, 507.

88. Ibid., 507–12.

89. It is fair to say that although Emperor Akihito has stressed collective national responsibility for the war, he certainly has not made any concrete judgments on individual accountability, including that of his father.

Chapter 5

Epigraphs: Hijikata Yoshio, "2-11 shikiten e no shushō shusseki o meguro dōkō," 11; "Hone-nuki shikiten ni kō-shita 'dai-hakkai kigensetsu hōshuku shikiten,'" 66.

1. Gluck, "The Past in the Present," 85.

2. On the contrary, this study should remind us that in the past fascist movements have used legal methods to achieve political power in democratic polities and that they could do it again. At the same time, I should stress that I do not interpret the ideology of many of the groups examined in this chapter to fit typical definitions of fascism.

3. Jürgen Habermas, in his study of the public sphere, wrote: "The public sphere of civil society stood or fell with the principle of universal access. A public sphere from which specific groups would be *eo ipso* excluded was less than merely incomplete; it was not a public sphere at all" (*The Structural Transformation of the Public Sphere*, 85). Scholars do not agree necessarily on the definition of "civil society," but many of the groups active in the Foundation Day reestablishment movement and reign-name legalization movement unquestionably were intermediary groups occupying the civil space between the state and the individual.

4. More than 81 percent of people polled in 1948 favored retention of the holiday, and in the intervening years before it was reestablished in 1966, polls showed only slightly lower levels of support for reestablishment. Polls taken by the government just before the bill reestablishing Foundation Day was passed by the Diet showed support for the measure at 71 percent. See Kigensetsu hōshukukai, *Kigensetsu hōshukukai koshi*, 91. One change was the declining level of support for celebrating the holiday on 11 February, a result of the campaign by historians and others to call into question the basis for celebrating Foundation Day on that day.

5. See, for example, the collection of essays published by historians and teachers in 1958, midway during the battle over reestablishment: Rekishi kyōikusha kyōgikai, *Kigensetsu: Nihon no shukusaijitsu I*.

6. See Jinja honchō kenshūjo, *Jinja honchō shikō* (Jinja honchō kenshūjo, 1989); and Teeuwen, "Jinja Honchō and Shrine Shintō Policy." I am grateful to Sugitani Masao of the Association of Shinto Shrines for providing me with numerous documents, published and unpublished, shedding light on the association's political activities.

7. Jinja honchō jimukyoku taisaku honbu, *Dentō kaiki e no chōryū*, 5. Representatives of the shrine world are quick to correct individuals who ask them if what they really want is renewed financial support from the state; they insist that they want the legitimacy of a renewed link with the state most of all, not simply financial support.

8. Woodard, *The Allied Occupation of Japan, 1945–1952*, 193.

9. An umbrella organization for women's groups in the shrine world.

10. Tanaka Takashi, "Takamatsu Tadakiyo gūji o shinobu," 5–16.

11. For a list of the organizations, see Kigensetsu hōshukukai, *Kigensetsu hōshukukai koshi*, 16–17.

12. The Japan Veterans Friendship League can be thought of as the postwar equivalent of the prewar Imperial Military Reserve Association (Teikoku zaigō gunjinkai), although the latter was much more influential in its time. The Japan Veterans Friendship League, founded in 1956, was the successor of the War Comrades' Association (Senyūkai). It claimed a membership of 1.5 million in 1964. Writing that year, journalist Murakami Hyōe ("Saigunbi o sasaeru 'gōyūren'") stressed that the organization's central office was impotent, but that the influence of the organization's branches at the local level was significant.

13. Seichō no ie was founded in 1930 by Taniguchi Masaharu. In 1980, it claimed three million members.

14. Quoted in Rekishi hyōron, "Kigensetsu fukkatsu mondai nenpu," 72.

15. Kigensetsu hōshukukai, *Kigensetsu hōshukukai koshi*, 12.

16. Jinja shinpō seikyō kenkyūshitsu, *Kindai jinja shintōshi*, 304. The authors of this book claim that more than 500,000 signatures were collected that year.

17. *Asahi shinbun*, 3 Jan. 1954.

18. It is likely that this journalist used as his source a pamphlet by Wakabayashi Yoshitaka titled *Kokumin no shukujitsu toshite 'kenkoku kinenbi' (Kigensetsu) o atarashiku seitei suru koto to no igi ni tsuite*. On page 19, in a section titled "Establishing Foundation Day Through a Citizens' Movement," Wakabayashi stressed that it was not desirable for the state or the government to take the lead in establishing the holiday. Wakabayashi wrote that if the people celebrated the holiday, then the government would follow their lead.

19. "Aogu kyō koso tanoshikere," 19. As the first mayor, Yoshikawa was instrumental in choosing the city's symbol: the Golden Kite.

20. "'Kenkoku no hi' o tsukuru hitobito."

21. *Kashihara-shi gikai kaigiroku* no. 5 (21, 27 Dec. 1956), n.p. Mayor Yoshikawa explained his motivations in a general speech to the assembly on 21 Dec.

22. For plans for the highway, see Suzuki Ryō et al., *Nara-ken no hyakunen*, 299–309.

23. Each year from 1957 until the holiday's reestablishment in 1966, the Yamato Parade was a leading story in the *Yamato taimusu*, a prefectural paper for Nara. The *Yamato*

taimusu's coverage of the Yamato Parade was extensive and favorable throughout the reestablishment movement.

24. Legendary hero of ancient Japan whose exploits are chronicled in the *Kojiki* and *Nihon shoki.*

25. "Aogu kyō koso tanoshikere," 19. For the Kigensetsu Dance, see "Daigaisha mo ashinami soroete," 32.

26. Professor Albert Craig of Harvard University suggested this analogy to me.

27. In a conversation with the author on 21 June 2000, Nishino used the term *karuku suru* to express his sentiment that the inclusion of Miss Foundation Day "made light" of the holiday's significance.

28. "Aogu kyō koso tanoshikere," 20.

29. Ibid., 16. In the prewar and wartime eras, schools were one of the main sites used by the state to inculcate the populace with the emperor-system ideology, and government-supervised school celebrations had ended with the suspension of the holiday in 1947.

30. *Asahi shinbun*, 12 Feb. 1956.

31. The interpellation took place on 14 Feb. 1956, in the House of Representatives Culture and Education Committee. For the text of the interpellation, see Rekishi kyōikusha kyōgikai, *Kigensetsu: Nihon no shukusaijitsu I*, 217–20.

32. See, for example, *Yomiuri shinbun*, 11 Feb. 1959.

33. "Daigaisha mo ashinami soroete," 29.

34. Ibid., 29–30.

35. Ibid., 31.

36. Local branches of national business organizations, such as the chambers of commerce and industry in Miyazaki and Nara prefectures, were active in the reestablishment movement, however.

37. Kimura Tokutarō (1886–1982), former chief of the National Defense Agency, served as chair of the Foundation Day Celebration Association. This association's successor, the Foundation Day Celebration Steering Committee (Kenkoku kinen no hi hōshuku un'ei iinkai), continues to sponsor annual celebrations of Foundation Day today.

38. Kigensetsu hōshukukai, *Kigensetsu hōshukukai koshi*, 33–34.

39. Ibid, 49.

40. Ibid., 57. In 1990, on the occasion of the 2,650th anniversary of the founding of the empire by Jimmu, another group of young men repeated this feat. See "Shinwa no furusato kara Tōkyō e."

41. Kigensetsu hōshukukai, *Kigensetsu hōshukukai koshi*, 40.

42. Nihon bunka kenkyūkai, *Jimmu tennō kigenron.*

43. Mikasa no Miya Takahito, "Kigensetsu ni tsuite no watakushi no shinnen." As early as 1956, there were indications that Prince Mikasa had deep reservations about reestablishing the holiday.

44. After Foundation Day was reestablished, Prince Mikasa continued to express his reservations about the holiday. In a 1974 discussion with historian Irokawa Daikichi, Prince Mikasa stressed that his greatest concern was that the holiday was celebrated on 11 February, a day that had no empirical basis. See Mikasa No Miya Takahito and Irokawa Daikichi, "Teiō to haka to minshu."

45. *Miyazaki konnichi*, 11, 12 Feb. 1963. Aikawa was a graduate of the Faculty of Law, Tokyo Imperial University.

46. Kigensetsu hōshukukai, *Kigensetsu hōshukukai koshi*, 50.

47. The Japanese name of this committee was Nara-ken kigensetsu hōshuku kyōgikai seiritsu junbi iinkai.

48. Kigensetsu hōshukukai, *Kigensetsu hōshukukai koshi*, 51.

49. Ibid., 61–63.

50. Ibid., 74.

51. Ibid., 70–72.

52. Ibid., 69.

53. "Kigensetsu Kanagawa hōshiki," *Sandē mainichi* (24 Jan. 1965), 23. Uchiyama was a member of the LDP faction headed by the then–prime minister, Satō Eisaku.

54. Ibid., 22.

55. "Dokusha wa ronsō suru," 13.

56. "Kenkoku kinen no hi o oiwai shimasho," 25.

57. Kigensetsu hōshukukai, *Kigensetsu hōshukukai koshi*, 84.

58. *Kumamoto nichinichi shinbun*, 11 Feb. 1965, evening edition.

59. *Miyazaki konnichi*, 12 Feb. 1966. The phrase *yamato damashii* was used widely in presurrender Japan to describe the supposedly unique spiritual qualities of the Japanese.

60. Professor Takami of Hokkaido University told me this story in early 1995.

61. *Jinja shinpō*, 26 Feb. 1966.

62. Kigensetsu hōshukukai, *Kigensetsu hōshukukai koshi*, 97.

63. Naikaku sōridaijin kanbō shingishitsu, *Kenkoku kinen no hi ni kansuru kōchōkai sokkiroku*, 72.

64. Ibid., 6.

65. Ibid., 7.

66. Ibid., 13.

67. Ibid., 58–62.

68. Ibid., 101–4.

69. Ibid., 100.

70. Ibid., 116.

71. Ibid., 31.

72. Ibid., 55.

73. Ibid., 55.

74. Ibid., 26.

75. Ibid., 26–30.

76. Ibid., 41–46.

77. Kenkoku kinenbi shingikai, *Kenkoku kinen no hi ni kansuru seron chōsa*, 3. Among those polled, 12.5 percent responded that "any day is fine."

78. "Aogu kyō koso tanoshikere," 16.

79. Ibid., 21.

80. Kigensetsu hōshukukai, *Kigensetsu hōshukukai koshi*, 134.

81. Ishikawa Masumi, "Kokkai giin anketo," 109–10.

82. Arita Michio, "Kenkoku kinen no hi," 97.

83. "Hone-nuki shikiten ni kō-shita 'dai hakkai kigensetsu hōshuku shikiten,'" 66.

84. Gojima was head of the Japan Chamber of Commerce and Industry at the time.

85. Hijikata Yoshio, "2–11 shikiten e no shushō shusseki o meguru dōkō," 11.

86. Nakasone clarified this point in response to a question by a JSP representative on 11 Mar. 1985 in the House of Councillors Budget Committee. See ibid., 12.

87. For the details of why the purist faction considered this break necessary, see "Kenkoku kinen no hi hōshuku no shoshin ni kaeri." *Sokoku to seinen* is the publicity organ of the far-right Japan Youth Council (Nihon seinen kyōgikai).

88. "2–11: Futatsu no kenkoku shikiten."

89. Titus, "Accessing the World," 83.

90. For information on the Imperial Household Agency's postwar policies regarding the imperial tombs, see Edwards, "Contested Access."

91. "Hone-nuki shikiten ni kō-shita 'dai-hakkai kigensetsu hōshuku shikiten.'"

92. See "'Kenkoku kinen no hi' hantai, fushōnin undō no nijūgonen."

93. Demonstrations of grassroots support were so visible that some scholars and journalists began to speak of a phenomenon new to Japan in the postwar era: mass movements from the right. The historian Miyachi Masato, looking back in 1980 on the movement to enact the Reign-Name Law, wrote that in the 1970s "right-wing-type movements began to assume the coloring of quasi-mass movements" ("Sengo tennōsei no tokushitsu," 33). The historian Watanabe Osamu (*Sengo seijishi no naka no tennōsei*, 339–50) concluded that the movement to win enactment of the Reign-Name Law was a mass movement but interpreted grassroots support from the right as a new phenomenon. Although the scale of such movements broadened in the 1970s, their history dates to the immediate post-Occupation period.

94. For more information on Tan'gi and the myth of Tan'gun, especially the use of this myth by nationalists in modern Korea, see Pai, *Constructing "Korean" Origins*. I thank Dr. Pai and Don Baker of the University of British Columbia for clarifying how the Republic of Korea has used the Tan'gun myth.

95. Later that year, Tanaka was appointed chief justice of Japan's Supreme Court.

96. Sangiin jimukyoku, *Dainanakai kokkai sangiin monbu iinkai kaigiroku* 6, 1. I also profited from the following study of the 1950 debate about the reign name system: Akazawa Shirō, "1950-nen no gengō rongi."

97. Sangiin jimukyoku, *Dainanakai kokkai sangiin monbu iinkai kaigiroku* 7, 1.

98. Ibid., no. 8, 4.

99. Ibid., 5.

100. Jinja honchō jimukyoku taisaku honbu, *Dentō kaiki e no chōryū*, 18–19.

101. *Tōkyō shinbun*, 1 Mar. 1950. A poll conducted by the *Asahi shinbun* showed that although 25 percent of respondents were in favor of adopting the Western calendar, 47 percent opposed this proposal (*Asahi shinbun*, 2 Mar. 1950).

102. Tsuda Sōkichi, "Gengō no mondai ni tsuite." Tsuda had expressed many of the ideas he put forth in this essay in a lecture in February, at the time the House of Councillors Education Committee was investigating the reign-name system.

103. Ibid., 74.

104. "'Fukeizai' fukkatsu mondai no uchimaku."

105. *Mainichi shinbun*, 6 Feb. 1961.

106. The society's founding can be dated to 1947. That year Emperor Hirohito granted a formal audience to founding members, thus establishing an immediate link between the organization and the palace. The Bereaved Society has been one of the most influential

pressure groups in postwar Japan, with a membership that still numbered 1.04 million dues-paying households in 1985 (this number decreases each year as the relatives of the war dead themselves die). Tanaka Nobumasa, Tanaka Hiroshi, and Hata Nagami (*Izoku to sengo*) have documented the plurality of views within this organization as well as among bereaved families in general (not all bereaved families are members of the Japan Society of War-Bereaved Families).

107. See, for example, Kokuritsu kokkai shokan chōsa rippō kōsakyoku, *Yasukuni jinja mondai shiryōshū*, 303–11.

108. Jinja shinpō seikyō kenkyūshitsu, *Kindai jinja shintōshi*, 338.

109. According to the calendar in use in the time, this took place on the eighth day of the ninth month; this corresponds to 23 Oct. on the solar calendar adopted later in the Meiji period.

110. Jinja honchō jimukyoku taisaku honbu, *Dentō kaiki e no chōryū*, 20–24.

111. *Asahi shinbun*, 17 Jan. 1968.

112. For a description of the planning process leading to the government-sponsored events, see Naikaku sōridaijin kanbō, "Meiji hyakunen kinen ni kansuru seifu no gyōji, jigyō nado ni tsuite." For information about public views of the Meiji Restoration centennial, see Naikaku sōridaijin kanbō, "Meiji hyakunen ni kansuru seron chōsa ni tsuite."

113. For an analysis of this phenomenon, see George, "The Comparative Study of Interest Groups in Japan."

114. Naikaku sōridaijin kanbō shingishitsu, *Gengōhō seitei no kiroku*, 136.

115. Publications of far-right groups such as the Japan Youth Council described the fiftieth anniversary celebrations of the emperor's accession to the throne as a movement (*undō*). The publicity organs of several far-right groups stressed the heavy participation in the fiftieth anniversary celebrations and noted that many of the same people participated in the reign-name legalization movement. See, for example, Nihon seinen kyōgikai, *Moeagare gengō hōseika undō no homura*, 2.

116. The preface to a pamphlet published by the Association of Shinto Shrines in 1975 titled "Aiming for Establishment of the Reign-Name System" begins, "This year the Association of Shinto Shrines welcomes the fiftieth year of Shōwa, and along with events celebrating the fiftieth anniversary of the emperor's enthronement, we are presently gaining the cooperation of each group [this refers to each group affiliated with the Association of Shinto Shrines, such as the National Shinto Youth Council] to [win] legalization of the reign-name system" (see Jinja honchō jimukyoku taisaku honbu, *Gengō seido no kakuritsu o mezashite*).

117. Jinja honchō jimukyoku taisaku honbu, *Dentō kaiki e no chōryū*, 33.

118. Those interested in the details of the main ceremony itself and the various commemorative events sponsored by the government can consult Naikaku sōridaijin kanbō, *Tennō heika zaii gojūnen kinen shikiten kiroku*.

119. See "Nihon sanka."

120. Jinja honchō jimukyoku taisaku honbu, *Dentō kaiki e no chōryū*, 40.

121. For a list of the groups participating in this rally, see Nihon seinen kyōgikai, *Moeagare gengō hōseika undō no homura*, 6.

122. Nihon seinen kyōgikai, *Heisei jidai no atarashii kuni-zukuri e*, 1. I am grateful to both Professor Furuya Jun of Hokkaido University and Professor Franzisca Seraphim of

Boston College for gathering further documents about the Japan Youth Council for me after I had returned from my field research.

123. Quoted in Jinja honchō jikyoku taisaku honbu, *Dentō kaiki e no chōryū*, 42.

124. Ibid., 12.

125. In other words, the petition is given to household A, which is then responsible for passing it along to household B, and so on.

126. One of the peculiarities of the circular petition method was that only heads of households were asked to express their opinion; other eligible voters in the household were given no chance to sign.

127. "Genchi rupo: Imari-shi gikai ketsugi e no ayumi," in Nihon seinen kyōgikai, *Moeagare gengō hōseika undō no homura*, 19–21.

128. Reprinted in Nihon seinen kyōgikai, *Moeagare gengō hōseika undō no homura*, 24.

129. This figure comes from an internal Association of Shinto Shrines' document from 1978. The Association of Shinto Shrines constantly was updating its charts and maps to keep track of which prefectures, cities, towns, and villages had passed resolutions, and which should be targeted in the future.

130. "Chihō gikai ketsugi jitsugen no hōhō," 1978. Document provided by the Association of Shinto Shrines.

131. Naikaku sōridaijin kanbō shingishitsu, *Gengōhō seitei no kiroku*, 175–76.

132. For a list of the organizations, see ibid. In addition to most of the far-right groups in Japan, the list includes many women's and youth groups, as well as several business federations and unions.

133. Jinja honchō jimukyoku taisaku honbu, *Dentō kaiki e no chōryū*, 49.

134. Naikaku sōridaijin kanbō shingishitsu, *Gengōhō seitei no kiroku*, 175–76.

135. See, for example, the ad titled "Gengō hōseika no koe wa zenkoku ni hirogatte imasu!" (Calls for legalization of the reign name spread throughout the country) that appeared in the *Sankei shinbun*, 20 Aug. 1978. By that time forty-three of the regional assemblies had passed resolutions.

136. For details about this second caravan's activities, see "Gengō dainiji kyaraban kita e kakeru."

137. Jinja honchō jimukyoku taisaku honbu, *Dentō kaiki e no chōryū*, 50.

138. *Asahi shinbun*, 18 Aug. 1978.

139. For details of this rally, see *Gengō shinbun*, no. 5 (17 Oct. 1978).

140. Previous polls had shown strong support for the continuation of the reign-name system but had not demonstrated this level of support for restoring the legal basis of the system.

141. Miyachi Masato, "Sengo tennōsei no gendankai," was particularly useful in the preparation of this section. It is especially valuable to read Miyachi's essay along with Akazawa's essay about the 1950 debates. I thank Professor Miyachi for allowing me to photocopy his collection of the records of the Diet covering debate about the Reign-Name Bill.

142. Aoki Tamotsu, *"Nihonbunkaron" no henyō*, esp. 81–125.

143. Shūgiin jimukyoku, *Daihachijūnanakai kokkai shūgiin kaigiroku* 15, 4.

144. Ibid., 3.

145. Ibid., 4

146. Ibid., 5.

147. Ibid.

148. In the late 1990s, Nakano emerged as one of the leaders of the newly formed Democratic Party of Japan (DPJ).

149. Shūgiin jimukyoku, *Daihachijūnanakai kokkai shūgiin kaigiroku* 15, 4, 8–9.

150. Ibid., 10.

151. Ibid., 11.

152. Mayor Tomino explained his policy to me when I spent the summer of 1992 working as an intern in Zushi City Hall and also confirmed the nature of the forms used in Zushi in an e-mail message to me on 11 Mar. 1999. For more information on Tomino's controversial policies as mayor, see Ruoff, "Mr. Tomino Goes to City Hall."

153. On the Christian Coalition and the history of the political right in the postwar United States, see Diamond, *Roads to Dominion.*

154. In an informal discussion that took place on 20 June 2000, six students in Professor Tomino Kiichirō's course on local government at Ryukoku University were at an utter loss when asked to identify what Foundation Day commemorates. One student suggested that it marked the day that Japan regained independence from the United States. Although by no means a scientific sample, it suggests how little Foundation Day means to many people in Japan.

155. See, for example, the text of the roundtable discussion between Aoki and Yamazaki published in the 17 July 2016 issue of *Sande mainichi.*

Chapter 6

1. Matsushita Keiichi, "Taishū tennōseiron." Although Matsushita used the term *taishū tennōsei*, or "emperor system of the masses," to describe the postwar Japanese monarchy throughout his essay, he also used the term *taishū kunshusei*, or "monarchy of the masses," to describe the British monarchy from the late nineteenth century to present.

2. I once asked a journalist assigned to the Imperial House Press Club how much imperial family members follow media coverage of themselves. He emphasized that they closely read almost everything published about themselves (officials in the Imperial Household Agency are charged with clipping all published accounts of the throne's activities).

3. Miyamoto Kenji, "Tennōsei hihan ni tsuite," 5.

4. For more information on the modernist interpretation of the emperor system, see Barshay, "Imagining Democracy in Postwar Japan."

5. Yokota, *Tennōsei*, 252–53.

6. Cannadine, "The Context, Performance and Meaning of Ritual," 101–2.

7. For a full translation of the rescript, see Gauntlett, *Kokutai no hongi*, Appendix VI. By opening the rescript with a recitation of the 1868 Charter Oath, Hirohito linked democracy in Japan to his grandfather, Emperor Meiji, in whose name the Charter Oath was issued. The Charter Oath's second clause, it is true, called for the establishment of an assembly and for all matters of state to be decided by public assembly, but Hirohito's interpretation of the roots of democracy in Japan inflated the significance of the Charter Oath to Japan's development while overlooking the authoritarian aspects of the Meiji state, not to mention his grandfather's total lack of interest in democracy.

8. Togashi, *Heika no "ningen" sengen*, 4.
9. Ibid., 60.
10. Ibid., 63.
11. Ibid., 24–25.
12. See Mosley, *Hirohito*, 56–57.
13. There were a few exceptions, notably the emperor's visit in 1951 to Kyoto University, where groups of students staged protests to direct attention to the emperor's role in the war.
14. Sakamoto Kōjirō, *Shōchō tennōsei e no pafomansu*, 105.
15. For further accounts of how the imperial house's image was remade in the decade after the war, see ibid.; Titus, "The Making of the 'Symbol Emperor System' in Postwar Japan"; and Bix, "Inventing the 'Symbol Monarchy' in Japan, 1945–52."
16. *Asahi shinbun*, 3 Dec. 1952.
17. Shimizu Ikutarō, "Senryōka no tennō," 22.
18. "Weekly Magazines: Keys to an Information Society," 9.
19. " 'Tōgū-san o' to kyōchō sareta Chichibu-miyasama," 5.
20. "Okaerinasai! Gokurōsama!," 8.
21. " 'Tōgū-san o' to kyōchō sareta Chichibu-miyasama," 8.
22. "Toei no kōtaishisama ni nozomu," 53.
23. Ibid., 54.
24. Prochaska, "George V and Republicanism, 1917–1919," 49.
25. Laski, *Parliamentary Government in England*, 330–31.
26. Bradford, *George VI*, 323.
27. Pimlott, *The Queen: A Biography of Elizabeth II*, 287.
28. Bruce Brenn, "A Window for the Emperor of Japan," lecture delivered at Portland State University, 17 May 2000. Bruce Brenn is a superb example of the fact that the Occupation was a dialectic process—that even as the U.S. Occupation forces were profoundly influencing various aspects of Japanese society, they (or their family members) were being influenced by the Japanese. Bruce's father was a general in the Occupation army, and that is what brought him to Japan for the first time. Vining introduced Bruce and his older brother to Crown Prince Akihito after observing them in class at the American School in Japan. After returning to the United States in 1951, Bruce eventually earned an M.A. in Japanese studies from the University of Michigan (1961) and achieved fluency in the Japanese language. Thereafter he pursued an international business career with companies including Citibank and Nike that included numerous extended stays in Japan.
29. Shimada Tatsumi, "Igirisujin to kōtaishi: mada aru senjichū no zōaku," 15.
30. " 'Tōgū-san o' to kyōchō sareta Chichibu-miyasama," 6.
31. Cannadine, "The Context, Performance and Meaning of Ritual," 153–54.
32. "Okaerinasai! Gokurōsama!," 6.
33. Quoted in "Kāten ni natta zuiintachi," 8.
34. See Mayuzumi Toshirō and Fujishima Taisuke, "Tennōsei no kiki o ureu."
35. Satomi Kishio, *Nihon no minshushugi*, 14.
36. Ibid., 87–88.
37. Ibid.
38. Vining, *Windows for the Crown Prince*, 300.

39. Jiyūminshutō kenpō chōsakai, *Jiyūminshutō kenpō chōsakai shiryō*, 3: 82; quoted in Watanabe Osamu, "The Emperor as a 'Symbol' in Postwar Japan," 121.

40. See Fujitani, *Splendid Monarchy*, 113–16.

41. For details, see ibid., 116–21.

42. See Kelly, "Finding a Place in Metropolitan Japan"; and Ivy, "Formations of Mass Culture."

43. Matsushita, "Taishū tennōseiron," 33.

44. Ibid., 32–33.

45. Akira Takahashi, "TV and the Imperial Wedding," 15.

46. Togashi Junji, *Chiyodajō*.

47. "Weekly Magazines: Keys to an Information Society," 9.

48. "Karuizawa no kōtu de," 6.

49. Ibid., 12.

50. Sonobe Eiichi, *Shintennōke no jigazō*, 35.

51. For a concise historical analysis of social and political changes in postwar Japan, see Andrew Gordon, "Society and Politics from Transwar through Postwar Japan."

52. "Denka, zubon ga futosugiru."

53. "Nihon ichi no nakōdo yaku," 10.

54. Koizumi Shinzō, "Rikken kunshusei," in Koizumi, *Jooji goseden to teishitsuron*, 16–21.

55. Ibid., 17–18. Without explaining that this was the reason that he was having Crown Prince Akihito read Nicolson's biography, Koizumi wrote almost the exact same description of King George V in a 1955 essay; see Koizumi, "Aru kokuō no shōgai," 188.

56. Matsushita, "Zoku-taishū tennōseiron," 115–16. In this later essay, Matsushita, in the face of intense criticism from elements of the left, qualified several of the assertions he made in his first essay. My tendency here is to highlight the qualifications that I found valuable while ignoring those that seemed unnecessary.

57. In the 8 Dec. 1958 edition of *Dokusho shinbun*, Murakami Hyōei, referring to the emperor's role in the war, wrote: "If the emperor is a symbol . . . I think that it is appropriate to say that he is a symbol of the suffering of the people."

58. Matsushita, "Taishū tennōseiron," 40.

59. Matsushita, "Zoku-taishū tennōseiron," 117.

60. Matsushita, "Taishū tennōseiron," 31.

61. Ibid.

62. Matsushita attributed this quote to the 28 Dec. 1958 morning edition of the *Kumamoto nichinichi shinbun*.

63. Matsushita, "Taishū tennōseiron," 32.

64. Ibid.

65. A special small building, most commonly found on school grounds, to hold the emperor's portrait. They often were built out of cement to prevent fires and possible destruction of the portrait. On special occasions, the building was opened to permit viewing of the portrait.

66. Matsushita, "Taishū tennōseiron," 32.

67. Ibid., 36.

68. Ibid., 44.

69. Ibid., 37.

70. Ibid., 37.
71. Ibid., 38.
72. *Yomiuri shinbun*, 27 Nov. 1958.
73. Matsushita, "Zoku-taishū tennōseiron," 116.
74. Matsushita, "Taishū tennōseiron," 45.
75. Ibid., 45.
76. Ibid., 38.
77. Matsushita, "Zoku-taishū tennōseiron," 116–17.
78. Matsushita, "Taishū tennōseiron," 46.
79. Matsushita, "Zoku-taishū tennōseiron," 126.
80. Inoue Kiyoshi, "Kōshitsu to kokumin," 34.
81. Ibid., 39.
82. Ibid., 40.
83. Quoted in "Kōtaishi no ren'ai o meguru kokkai rongi," 205. Hirai made this statement in the 6 Feb. 1959 meeting of the House of Representatives Budget Committee.
84. Mishima Yukio, "Bunka bōeiron."
85. Muramatsu Takeshi et al., "Zadankai: Kōtaishi 'shinnō.'"
86. Ibid., 219.
87. Vining, *Windows for the Crown Prince*, 49.
88. Ibid., 207.
89. Muramatsu et al., "Zadankai: Kōtaishi 'shinnō,'" 225.
90. Ibid., 225.
91. Ibid., 231.
92. Mayuzumi and Fujishima, "Tennōsei no kiki o ureu," 16.
93. Ibid., 23.
94. Ibid., 30.
95. Naikaku sōridaijin kanbō, *Tennō heika zaii gojūnen kinen shikiten kiroku*, preface (n.p.).
96. Fujitani, "Electronic Pageantry and Japan's 'Symbolic Emperor.'" The term "electronic pageantry" originally was used in England in reference to the 1981 wedding ceremony of Prince Charles and Diana.
97. On this point, see Satō Kōji, "Kokuji Kōi to seikyō bunri."
98. Yoshida Shigeto, "Ima, 'oku' wa dō natte iru ka," 162.
99. Naruhito Shinnō, *Temuzu to tomo ni.*
100. Ichimura Shin'ichi and Etō Jun, "Tennō," 28.
101. Kase Hideaki, interviewer, Mikasanomiya Tomohito Shinnō, interviewee, "Kōshitsu to kokumin," 105. I thank Takahashi Hiroshi for sending me this source.
102. Ibid., 102.
103. Sakamoto Kōjirō, "Shinshōchō tennō e no pafōmansu," 123.
104. Pimlott, *The Queen: A Biography of Elizabeth II*, 380.
105. Ibid., 392.
106. Eisenstodt, "Behind the Chrysanthemum Curtain," 22.
107. See Gordon, "My Student, the Princess."
108. *New York Times*, 20 Jan. 1993.
109. Quoted in Yoshida Shigeto, "Ima, 'oku' wa dō natte iru ka," 156.
110. Shintō seiji renmei, *Seisaku suishin no kadai o kangaeru*, 10–15.

Chapter 7

1. This discussion eventually extended to Nakanishi Susumu, the scholar credited with having put forward *reiwa,* calling on Prime Minister Abe to live up to the meaning of the new reign name, "beautiful harmony." See Nobuhiko Tajima, "Scholar Who Suggested Reiwa Asks Abe to Live Up to its Meaning," *Asahi shinbun*, 5 May 2019, http://www.asahi.com/ajw/articles/AJ201905050029.html (accessed 20 May 2019).

2. Yamashita Shinji, ed. *Tennō heika 100 no kotoba*, 30. Hereafter cited as Yamashita.

3. Accessed at the Imperial Household Agency official website, http://www.kunaicho.go.jp/e-okotoba/02/press/gaikoku-h16az-europe.html (accessed 15 April 2019).

4. Accessed at the Imperial Household Agency official website, http://www.kunaicho.go.jp/e-okotoba/03/press/kaiken-h16.html (accessed 15 April 2019).

5. Accessed at the Imperial Household Agency official website, http://www.kunaicho.go.jp/e-okotoba/01/press/gokaito-h16e.html (accessed 15 April 2019).

6. Etō Jun, "Kōshitsu ni aete tōu," 101.

7. Inoue Makoto, "Hatsugen suru 'Kokumin no kōgō," 186–87.

8. See my study of these celebrations, Ruoff, *Imperial Japan at Its Zenith.*

9. Yamashita, 14.

10. See Ruoff, "Lessons from Japan's Symbolic Monarchy."

11. Yamashita, 110.

12. Ibid., 34.

13. Ibid., 36.

14. Grand Chamberlain Watanabe generously answered various questions about the contemporary monarchy during a two-hour discussion we had in his office on 26 August 2002.

15. Kunaichō, ed., *Michi.*

16. For example, upon becoming empress, Masako took over as honorary president of the Japanese Red Cross Society from Michiko.

17. Yamashita, 88.

18. Accessed at http://leprosy.jp/english/topics/1955/ (accessed 2 Aug. 2018). Princess Diana also adopted the cause of leprosy victims and made headlines during a November 1989 visit to Indonesia. While visiting a leprosy hospital there, she shook hands with victims of the disease, including many children, helping reduce the stigma of the ailment. See Smith, *Prince Charles*, 247.

19. Inoue Tatsuo and Kobayashi Yoshinori, *Za Giron.*

20. http://www.houshuku.org/20th/en/h201219/syosai.html (accessed 15 May 2019).

21. Tomasz Beer, a researcher of prostate cancer on the faculty at the Oregon Health & Science University in Portland, Oregon, provided me with a short briefing on prostate cancer in an e-mail message on 21 August 2003. In the case of the United States, arguably the most important example of a public figure drawing attention to prostate cancer was the case of Andrew Grove (1936–2016), former CEO of Intel, who wrote a story titled "Taking on Prostate Cancer" that was featured in the 13 May 1996 issue of *Fortune.*

22. Accessed at https://www.townandcountrymag.com/society/tradition/a10207486/queen-elizabeth-lgbt/ (accessed 14 Aug. 2018).

23. Accessed at the Imperial Household Agency official website, http://www.kunaicho.go.jp/page/okotoba/detailEn/12#41 (accessed 15 April 2019).

24. Cannadine, "Monarchy: Crowns and Contexts, Thrones and Dominations," 52.

25. See http://www.houshuku.org/news/h201219/syosai.html (accessed 16 Aug. 2018).

26. Inoue Makoto, *Shōchō tennō no tabi.*

27. For a thorough study of the imperial couple's visits to disaster areas, see Asahi shinbun shakaibu, ed., *Inori no tabi.*

28. Accessed at the Imperial Household Agency official website, http://www.kunaicho.go.jp/e-okotoba/01/address/okotoba-h23e.html (accessed 15 April 2019).

29. For the original Japanese, see Yamashita, 120.

30. Ibid., 112.

31. Ibid., 122.

32. https://www.okinawatimes.co.jp/articles/-/415062 (accessed 30 June 2019).

33. Accessed at the Imperial Household Agency official website, http://www.kunaicho.go.jp/e-okotoba/01/address/okotoba-h27e.html (accessed 15 April 2019).

34. Accessed at the Imperial Household Agency's official website, http://www.kunaicho.go.jp/e-okotoba/01/press/kaiken-h27e.html (accessed 15 April 2019).

35. Paekche is one of three kingdoms of ancient Korea. It is said to have been established in 18 BCE and perished in 660 CE.

36. http://www.kunaicho.go.jp/okotoba/01/kaiken/kaiken-h13e.html (accessed 27 Aug. 2018).

37. Finchelstein, *From Fascism to Populism in History.*

38. Hara Takeshi, *Heisei no shūen.*

39. Accessed at the Imperial Household Agency's official website, http://www.kunaicho.go.jp/e-okotoba/01/address/koen-h10sk-newdelhi.html (accessed 15 April 2019).

40. Accessed at the Imperial Household Agency's official website, http://www.kunaicho.go.jp/e-okotoba/01/address/okotoba-h14sk-basel.html (accessed 15 April 2018); emphasis in original.

41. Preston, *Juan Carlos: A People's King*, 426.

42. See chapter 6, "Overseas Japanese and the Fatherland," of Ruoff, *Imperial Japan at Its Zenith.*

43. http://www.kunaicho.go.jp/page/kaiken/showEn/25 (accessed 30 June 2019).

44. Leistikow, "Queen Margrethe II of Denmark," 231.

45. Preston, *Juan Carlos: A People's King*, 505.

46. Accessed at the Imperial Household Agency's official website, http://www.kunaicho.go.jp/page/kaiken/show/18 (accessed 16 April 2019).

47. Accessed at the Imperial Household Agency's official website, http://www.kunaicho.go.jp/page/kaiken/show/26 (accessed 16 April 2019).

48. Accessed at the Imperial Household Agency's official website, http://www.kunaicho.go.jp/e-okotoba/02/press/kaiken-h15az.html (accessed 16 April 2019).

49. Naruhito shinnō, *Suiunshi kara sekai no mizu e.*

50. Ibid., 249 (2).

51. Smith, *Prince Charles*, 384.

52. Ibid., 414.

53. Ibid., 285.

Chapter 8

1. Ruoff, "Lessons from Japan's Symbolic Monarchy."

2. "Dutch Queen Beatrix Abdicates in Favour of Son," *BBC*, 30 April 2013, https://www.bbc.com/news/world-europe-22348160.

3. Ibid.

4. "Philippe Becomes New Belgian King as Albert II Abdicates," *BBC*, 21 July 2013, https://www.bbc.com/news/world-europe-23393963.

5. "Ritsuryō tennōsei ni nazoraeru na," *Asahi shinbun*, 10 June 2017.

6. Linda Sieg, "If the Pope Can Retire, Why Not Japan's Elderly Emperor?," *Reuters*, 1 August 2016, https://www.reuters.com/article/us-japan-emperor-abdication-idUSKCN10C3CJ.

7. See "Seijiteki kōi no kakuchō yurushita," *Asahi shinbun*, 7 March 2019.

8. The complete records of this committee are available online. For Watanabe's testimony, see http://www.kantei.go.jp/jp/singi/koumu_keigen/dai4/gijiroku.pdf (accessed 15 May 2019).

9. See http://www.kantei.go.jp/jp/singi/koumu_keigen/dai5/gijiroku.pdf (accessed 15 May 2019).

10. "Role of Women in Spotlight as Imperial Family Members Dwindle," *Kyodo News*, 5 May 2019.

11. Reiji Yoshida, "Diet Enacts Abdication Law for Emperor Akihito," *Japan Times*, 9 June 2017.

12. For more information on Japan's regnant empresses, see Kiyoko Takagi, *The Eight Female Emperors of Japan*.

13. "Role of Women in Spotlight as Imperial Family Members Dwindle."

Works Cited

The place of publication of Japanese works, unless otherwise noted, is Tokyo.

Letters

Derevyanko, K., Lieutenant General, U.S.S.R. Member of the Allied Council for Japan, to Chairman of the Allied Council for Japan and Supreme Commander for the Allied Powers, General of the Army, Douglas MacArthur, 10 Apr. 1946. Located in R6-5, B.110, F. 1, "Russian Mission Corres., Feb. 28,'46–Dec. 12, '47," Archives, General Douglas MacArthur Memorial, Norfolk, Virginia.

Fellers, Bonner F. "Memorandum to the Commander-in-Chief," 2 Oct. 1945. Located in RC-5, Box 2, Folder 2, Official Correspondence, July–Dec. 1945, Archives, General Douglas MacArthur Memorial, Norfolk, Virginia.

Paxton, Robert, to author, 22 Nov. 1997.

Takahashi Hiroshi to author, 15 May 1995.

Titus, David A., to author, 7 Jan. 1998.

Tomino Kiichirō to author (by e-mail), 11 Mar. 1999.

Interviews

Poole, Richard A. Telephone interview conducted 8 Oct. 1997.

Sugitani Masao, section chief, Division of Outside Affairs, Jinja honchō (Association of Shinto Shrines), Tokyo. 22 Mar. 1995.

Unpublished Sources

"Chihō gikai ketsugi jitsugen no hōhō." Jinja honchō, 1978.

Purdy, Roger W. "Imperial Presence, Symbols and Surrogates: The Image of the Emperor in Japan's Wartime Newsreels." Paper presented at the Association for Asian Studies 1996 Annual Meeting.

"Sōri, kakuryō no naisō." Kunaichō, 14 Oct. 1993.

Newspapers

Akahata

Asahi shinbun

Daily Mirror (London, England)

Dokusho shinbun

Gengō shinbun

International Press Correspondence (London, England)

Japan Times
Jinja shinpō
Kumamoto nichinichi shinbun (Kumamoto City, Japan)
Mainichi shinbun
Miyazaki konnichi (Miyazaki City, Japan)
New York Times
Sankei shinbun
Süddeutsche Zeitung (Germany)
Tōkyō shinbun
Yamato taimusu (Nara, Japan)
Yomiuri shinbun

Published Sources

"A Talk With the Emperor of Japan." *Newsweek*, 29 Sept. 1975, 56.
Akazawa Shirō. "1950-nen no gengō rongi." *Rekishi hyōron* 345 (Jan. 1979): 103–8.
Andersen, Hans Christian. "The Emperor's New Clothes." In Hans Christian Andersen, *Eighty Fairy Tales*, 64–68. New York: Pantheon Books, 1976.
Anderson, John Lee. "Royal Affairs: The Reign in Spain." *New Yorker*, Apr. 27 / May 4, 1998, 110–19.
"Aogu kyō koso tanoshikere." *Shūkan asahi*, 20 Jan. 1967, 16–21.
Aoki Tamotsu. *"Nihonbunkaron" no henyō*. Chūō kōronsha, 1990.
Arita Michio. "Kenkoku kinen no hi: hōshukukai no kiretsu." *Asahi jānaru*, 27 Feb. 1987, 96–99.
Asahi shinbun shakaibu, ed. *Inori no tabi: Tennō Kōgō hisaichi e no omoi*. Asahi shinbun, 2018.
Ashibe Nobuyoshi and Takami Katsutoshi, eds. *Nihon rippō shiryō zenshū 1: Kōshitsu tenpan*. Shinzansha, 1990.
———. *Nihon rippō shiryō zenshū 7: Kōshitsu keizaihō*. Shinzansha, 1992.
Ashibe Nobuyoshi, Takahashi Kazuyuki, Takami Katsutoshi, and Hibino Tsutomu, eds. *Nihonkoku kenpō seitei shiryō zenshū*. Vols. 1 and 2. Shinzansha, 1997, 1998.
Awaya Kentarō. "Emperor Shōwa's Accountability for War." *Japan Quarterly*, Oct.–Dec. 1991, 386–98.

Baelz, Toku, ed. *Awakening Japan. The Diary of a German Doctor: Erwin Baelz*. Bloomington: Indiana University Press, 1974.
Bagehot, Walter. *The English Constitution*. London: Collins, 1963.
Banno Junji. "Foreword." Special issue: The Emperor System in Modern Japan. *Acta Asiatica* 59 (1990): iii–x.
Barshay, Andrew E. "Imagining Democracy in Postwar Japan: Reflections on Maruyama Masao and Modernism." *Journal of Japanese Studies* 18.2 (Summer 1992): 365–406.
Beckmann, George M., and Okubo Genji. *The Japanese Communist Party, 1922–1945*. Stanford, CA: Stanford University Press, 1969.
Bellah, Robert N. "Japan's Cultural Identity: Some Reflections on the Work of Watsuji Tetsuro." *Journal of Asian Studies* 24.4 (Aug. 1965): 573–94.
Bernecker, Walther L. "Monarchy and Democracy: The Political Role of King Juan Carlos in the Spanish Transicion." *Journal of Contemporary History* 33.1 (1998): 65–84.

Bix, Herbert P. *Hirohito and the Making of Modern Japan*. New York: Harper Collins, 2000.
———. "Inventing the 'Symbol Monarchy' in Japan, 1945–52." *Journal of Japanese Studies* 21.2 (Summer 1995): 319–64.
———. "The Showa Emperor's 'Monologue' and the Problem of War Responsibility." *Journal of Japanese Studies* 18.2 (Summer 1992): 295–363.
Bogdanor, Vernon. *The Monarchy and the Constitution*. New York: Oxford University Press, 1995.
Bradford, Sarah. *George VI*. London: Weidenfeld and Nicolson, 1989.
Bunka hyōron henshubu. *Tennōsei o tou*. Shin Nihon shuppansha, 1986.

Cannadine, David. "The Context, Performance and Meaning of Ritual: The British Monarchy and the 'Invention of Tradition', c. 1820–1977." In *The Invention of Tradition*, ed. Eric Hobsbawm and Terence Ranger, 101–64. Cambridge: Cambridge University Press, 1996.
———. "Monarchy: Crowns and Contexts, Thrones and Dominations." In *Making History Now and Then: Discoveries, Controversies and Explorations*, ed. David Cannadine, 39–58. New York: Palgrave MacMillan, 2008.
Chamberlain, B. H. *The Invention of a New Religion*. Canton: Pan-Pacific Cultural Association, 1933 [1912].
Chou, Wan-yao. "The *Kōminka* Movement in Taiwan and Korea: Comparisons and Interpretations." In *The Japanese Wartime Empire, 1931–1945*, ed. Peter Duus, Ramon H. Myers, and Mark R. Peattie, 40–68. Princeton, NJ: Princeton University Press, 1996.
Cohen, David. "Beyond Nuremberg: Individual Responsibility for War Crimes." In *Human Rights in Political Transitions: Gettysburg to Bosnia*, ed. Carla Hesse and Robert Post, 53–92. New York: Zone Books, 1999.
Cole, Allan B., and Naomichi Nakanishi, comps. and eds. *Japanese Opinion Polls with Socio-Political Significance, 1947–1957*. Vol. 1. Williamston: Fletcher School of Law and Diplomacy, Tufts University; and Roper Public Opinion Poll Research Center, Williams College, 1959.
Conan, Eric, and Henry Rousso. *Vichy: An Ever-Present Past*. Hanover: University Press of New England, 1998.
Cook, Haruko Taya, and Theodore F. Cook. *Japan at War: An Oral History*. New York: Free Press, 1992.
Cornwall, Peter G. "Japanese Political Reaction to Constitutional Revision, 1945–46." In *Studies in Japanese History and Politics*, ed. Richard K. Beardsley, 39–70. Ann Arbor: University of Michigan Press, 1967.

"Daigaisha mo ashinami soroete." *Nihon shūhō*, 5 Feb. 1960, 28–33.
Daikyūjūkai teikoku kizokuin kōshitsu tenpan tokubetsu iinkai sokkiroku 3 (18 Dec. 1946).
"Denka, zubon ga futosugiru." *Shūkan shinchō*, 5 Sept. 1960, 28–34.
Diamond, Sara. *Roads to Dominion: Right-Wing Movements and Political Power in the United States*. New York: Guilford Press, 1995.
"Dokusha wa ronsō suru." *Asahi jānaru* 7.8 (21 Feb. 1965): 13–18.
Dower, John W. *Embracing Defeat: Japan in the Wake of World War II*. New York: W. W. Norton and New Press, 1999.

———. *Empire and Aftermath: Yoshida Shigeru and the Japanese Experience, 1878–1954*. Cambridge, MA: Council on East Asian Studies, Harvard University, 1988.
Drea, Edward J. "Chasing a Decisive Victory: Emperor Hirohito and Japan's War with the West (1941–1945)." In *In the Service of the Emperor*, ed. Edward J. Drea, 169–215. Lincoln: University of Nebraska Press, 1998.

Edwards, Walter. "Contested Access: The Imperial Tombs in the Postwar Period." *Journal of Japanese Studies* 26.2 (Summer 2000): 371–92.
Eisenstodt, Gale. "Behind the Chrysanthemum Curtain." *Atlantic Monthly*, Nov. 1998, 20–36.
Eldridge, Robert D. "Shōwa tennō to Okinawa: 'Tennō messēgi' no saikōsatsu." *Chūō korōn*, Mar. 1999, 152–71.
Etō Jun. "Kōshitsu ni aete tōu." *Bungei shunjū*, 73.4 (April 1995).

Field, Norma. *In the Realm of a Dying Emperor*. New York: Pantheon, 1991.
Finchelstein, Federico. *Populism in History*. Berkeley: University of California Press, 2017.
Freeman, Laurie A. *Closing the Shop: Information Cartels and Japan's Mass Media*. Princeton, NJ: Princeton University Press, 2000.
Fujita Munemitsu. *Kashihara Jingū gokenkoku hōshitai*. Keishin hankyū dentetsu, 1940.
Fujitani, Takashi. "Electronic Pageantry and Japan's 'Symbolic Emperor.'" *Journal of Asian Studies* 51.4 (Nov. 1992): 824–50.
———. *Splendid Monarchy: Power and Pageantry in Modern Japan*. Berkeley: University of California Press, 1998.
"'Fukeizai' fukkatsu mondai no uchimaku: 'Kōshitsu o omamori suru tame ni' makareta panfuretto." *Shūkan shinchō*, 27 Nov. 1961, 30–33.
"Fukkatsu shita seijō sōjō." *Shūkan asahi*, 13 Sept. 1953, 12–13.
Fukuzawa Yukichi. *Nihon kōshitsuron*. Commentary by Tōyama Motokazu. Shimazu shobō, 1987.
Furukawa Takahisa. *Kōki, banpaku, orinpikku*. Chūō kōronsha, 1998.

"Gakusha 100-nin ga gekiron no 'kunshusei shinpojiumu' o dō kangaeru." *Shūkan posuto*, 3 Aug. 1973, 22–27.
Gauntlett, John O., trans. *Kokutai no hongi* (*Cardinal Principles of the National Entity of Japan*). Ed. Robert K. Hall. Cambridge, MA: Harvard University Press, 1949.
"Gengō dainiji kyaraban kita e kakeru." *Sokoku to seinen* 33 (Feb. 1978): 52–62.
George, Aurelia. "The Comparative Study of Interest Groups in Japan: An Institutional Framework." Australia-Japan Research Centre Research Paper #95. Canberra, Dec. 1982.
Gluck, Carol. *Japan's Modern Myths: Ideology in the Late Meiji Period*. Princeton, NJ: Princeton University Press, 1985.
———. "The Past in the Present." In *Postwar Japan as History*, ed. Andrew Gordon, 64–95. Berkeley: University of California Press, 1993.
Gordon, Andrew. *Labor and Imperial Democracy in Prewar Japan*. Berkeley: University of California Press, 1991.
———. "My Student, the Princess." *New York Times*, 17 Mar. 1993, A21.

———. "Society and Politics from Transwar through Postwar Japan." In *Historical Perspectives on Contemporary East Asia*, ed. Merle Goldman and Andrew Gordon, 272–96. Cambridge, MA: Harvard University Press, 2000.
Glynn, Paul. *A Song for Nagasaki*. Hunters Hill, Australia: Catholic Book Club, 1988.

Habermas, Jürgen. *The Structural Transformation of the Public Sphere*. Trans. Thomas Burger with the assistance of Frederick Lawrence. Cambridge, MA: MIT Press, 1995.
Hall, Phillip. *Royal Fortune: Tax, Money & the Monarchy*. London: Bloomsbury, 1992.
Hara Takeshi. *Heisei no shuūen: taii to tennō to kōgō*. Iwanami shinsho, 2019.
Hardacre, Helen. *Shintō and the State, 1868–1988*. Princeton, NJ: Princeton University Press, 1989.
Hariu Seikichi and Yokota Kōichi. *Kokumin shuken to tennōsei*. Hōritsu bunkasha, 1983.
Hasekawa Masayasu. "Shōchō no hōteki imi naiyō." *Kōhō kenkyū* 10 (1954): 23–28.
Hashimoto Kazuo. *Maboroshi no orinpikku*. NHK Bukkusu # 709. NHK, 1994.
Hata Ikuhiko. *Hirohito tennō itutsu no ketsudan*. Kōdansha, 1984.
Higashino Makoto. *Shōwa tennō futatsu no dokuhakuroku*. Nihon hōsō shuppan kyōkai, 1998.
Hijikata Yoshio. "2-11 shikiten e no shushō shusseki o meguru dōkō." *Shinchihei*, Apr. 1985, 10–12.
Hiraizumi Kiyoshi. "Nihon rekishi no ue kara mita tennō no chii." In *Tennōron ni kansuru mondai*, ed. Jiyūtō kenpō chōsakai. 77–102. Jiyūtō kenpō chōsakai jimukyoku, 1954.
Hobsbawm, Eric. "Introduction: Inventing Traditions." In *The Invention of Tradition*, ed. Eric Hobsbawm and Terence Ranger, 1–14. Cambridge: Cambridge University Press, 1983.
Hōgaku kyōkai. *Chūkai Nihonkoku kenpō*. Vol. 1. Yūhikaku, 1948.
———. *Chūkai Nihonkoku kenpō*. Rev. ed. Vol. 1. Yūhikaku, 1953.
"Hone-nuki shikiten ni kō-shita 'dai-hakkai kigensetsu hōshuku shikiten.'" *Zenbō*, Apr. 1992, 66.
Horikoshi Sakuji. *Sengo seiji 13 no shōgen*. Asahi shinbun, 1989.
"Hoshutō naikaku o yusaburu 'naisō' mondai no shōgeki." *Sandē mainichi*, 17 June 1973, 16–23.
Hozumi, Nobushige. *Ancestor-Worship and Japanese Law*. Hokuseido Press, 1940.

Ichimura Shinichi and Etō Jun. "Tennō." *Shokun*, Dec. 1987, 26–39.
Ihara Yoriaki. *Zōho kōshitsu jiten*. Hozanbō, 1937; reissued in 1979.
Inoue Kiyoshi. "Kōshitsu to kokumin." *Chūō kōron*, May 1959, 34–48.
———. *Tennōsei*. Tōkyō daigaku shuppankai, 1952.
Inoue, Kyoko. *MacArthur's Japanese Constitution: A Linguistic and Cultural Study of Its Making*. Chicago: University of Chicago Press, 1991.
Inoue Makoto. "Hatsugen suru 'Kokumin no kōgō." In *Kōgō yondai no rekishi*, ed. Mori Yōhei and Kawanishi Hideya, 181–203. Yoshikawa kōbunkan, 2018.
Inoue Makoto. *Shōchō tennō no tabi: Heisei ni kizukareta kokumin to no kizuna*. Heibonsha, 2018.
Inoue Tatsuo and Kobayashi Yoshinori. *Za Giron*. Mainichi shinbun, 2016.
"Intabyū: Tennō oyobi tennōsei ni tsuite: Kodama Yoshio." *Ryūdō*, Oct. 1971, 210–16.

Irie Tametoshi, ed. *Irie Sukemasa nikki*. 6 vols. Asahi shinbunsha, 1990.
Irokawa, Daikichi. *The Age of Hirohito: In Search of Modern Japan*. Trans. Mikiso Hane and John K. Urda. New York: Free Press, 1995.
Ishihara Shintarō. "Ishihara Shintarō no seiji shindan: Nihon wa, doko e iku." *Shūkan gendai*, 31 Aug. 1978, 38–39.
———. *The Japan That Can Say No*. Trans. Frank Baldwin. New York: Simon & Schuster, 1991.
———. "Ooku no kokumin no fuan." *Bungei shunjū*. Oct. 1992, 94–103.
Ishii Ryōsuke. *A History of Political Institutions in Japan*. University of Tokyo Press, 1980.
———. *Tennō*. Kōbundō, 1950.
Ishikawa Masumi. "Kokkai giin anketo: anata wa heika o keiai suru ka." *Asahi jānaru*, 13–20 Aug. 1976, 102–10.
Itō Hirobumi. *Commentaries on the Constitution of the Empire of Japan*. Igirisu Hōritsu gakko, 1889.
Itō Takashi, ed. *Satō Eisaku nikki*. Vols. 1–6. Asahi shinbunsha, 1997–98.
Itō Takashi, ed., and Momose Takashi. *Jiten. Shōwa senzenki no Nihon: seido to jittai*. Yoshikawa kōbunkan, 1990.
Itō Takashi and Watanabe Yukio, eds. *Zoku Shigemitsu Mamoru shuki*. Chūō kōronsha, 1988.
Ivy, Marilyn. "Formations of Mass Culture." In *Postwar Japan as History*, ed. Andrew Gordon, 239–58. Berkeley: University of California Press, 1993.
Iwami Takao. *Heika no goshitsumon: Shōwa tennō to sengo seiji*. Mainichi shinbunsha, 1992.
Iwamoto Tsutomu. *"Goshin'ei" ni junjita kyōshitachi*. Otsuki shoten, 1989.

Jinja honchō jimukyoku taisaku honbu, ed. *Dentō kaiki e no chōryū: gengō hōseika undō no seika*. Jinja honchō jimukyoku taisaku honbu, 1979.
———. *Gengō seido no kakuritsu o mezashite*. Jinja honchō jikyoku taisaku honbu, 1975.
Jinja honchō kenshūjo. *Jinja honchō shikō*. Jinja honchō kenshūjo, 1989.
Jinja shinpō seikyō kenkyūshitsu. *Kindai jinja shintōshi*. Jinja shinpōsha, 1986.
Jinja shinpōsha seikyō kenkyūshitsu, ed. *Tennō, shintō, kenpō*. Jinja shinpōsha, 1954.
Jiyūminshutō kenpō chōsakai. *Jiyūminshutō kenpō chōsakai shiryō*. Vols. 1–3. Jiyūminshutō kenpō chōsakai, 1983.

Kaarsted, Tage. "Denmark, a Limited Monarchy." *Res Publica* 33.1 (1991): 41–48.
Karube Tadashi. *Hikari no ryōkoku: Watsuji Tetsurō*. Sōbunsha, 1995.
"Karuizawa no kōtu de." *Sandē mainichi*, 7 Dec. 1958, 4–12.
Kase Hideaki, interviewer, Mikasanomiya Tomohito Shinnō, interviewee. "Kōshitsu to kokumin." *Bungei shunjū*, July 1993, 94–114.
Kashihara jingūchō. *Kashihara jingūshi bekkan*. Kashiwara jingūchō, 1982.
Kashihara-shi gikai kaigiroku no. 5 (21, 27 Dec. 1956).
Katayama naikaku kinen zadan, ed. *Katayama naikaku: Katayama Tetsu to sengo no seiji*. Katayama naikaku kiroku kankōkai, 1980.
"Kāten ni natta zuiintachi." *Sandē mainichi*, 18 Oct. 1953, 4–11.
Katsube Mitake. "Tennō wa Nihonjin ni totte hitsuyō ka." In *Tennōsei*, ed. Katsube Mitake, 5–42. Shibundō, 1970.

Kelly, William W. "Finding a Place in Metropolitan Japan: Ideologies, Institutions, and Everyday Life." In *Postwar Japan as History*, ed. Andrew Gordon, 189–216. Berkeley: University of California Press, 1993.

Kenkoku kinenbi shingikai. *Kenkoku kinen no hi ni kansuru seron chōsa.* Kenkoku kinenbi shingikai, 1966.

"'Kenkoku kinen no hi' hantai, fushōnin undō no nijūgonen." *Rekishi hyōron* 502 (Feb. 1992): 51–83.

"Kenkoku kinen no hi hōshuku no shoshin ni kaeri—dokuji shikiten kaisai e: naze dokuji shikiten o kaisai shinakereba naranakatta no ka." *Sokoku to seinen*, Feb. 1988, 18–34.

"Kenkoku kinen no hi o oiwai shimasho." *Risō sekai*, 10 Feb. 1965, 25.

"'Kenkoku no hi' o tsukuru hitobito." *Shūkan shinchō*, 21 Jan. 1957, 22.

Kenpō chōsakai daiichi bukai. *Zenbun, tennō, sensō no hōki, kaisei, saikō hōki ni kansuru hōkokusho.* Kenpō chōsakai daiichi bukai, 1964.

Kenpō chōsakai jimukyoku. *Kenpō chōsakai daihyakuikkai sōkai gijiroku.* Kenpō chōsakai jimukyoku, 1963.

———. *Kenpō unyō no jissai ni tsuite no dai-san iinkai hōkokusho.* Kenpō chōsakai jimukyoku, 1961.

———. *Shingikai nado ni okeru kenpō kankei rongi oyobi kenpō kankei jitsurei, senrei, tsūdatsushū.* Kenpō chōsakai jimukyoku, 1958.

Kigen nisen roppyakunen hōshukukai. *Tengyō hōshō.* Naikaku insatsukyoku, 1943.

Kigen nisen roppyakunen shukuten jimukyoku. *Jinja.* Naikaku insatsukyoku, 1939.

———. *Kigen nisen roppyakunen shukuten giroku.* Vols. 1–17. Naikaku insatsukyoku, 1943.

Kigensetsu hōshukukai. *Kigensetsu hōshukukai koshi.* Kigensetsu hōshukukai, 1968.

"Kigensetsu Kanagawa hōshiki." *Sandē mainichi*, 24 Jan. 1965, 22–26.

Kim, Richard E. *Lost Names: Stories from a Korean Boyhood.* Berkeley: University of California Press, 1998.

Kinoshita Michio. *Sokkin nisshi.* Bungei shunjū, 1990.

Kishi Nobusuke, Yatsugi Kazuo, and Itō Takashi. *Kishi Nobusuke no kaisō.* Bungei shunjūsha, 1981.

Kishimoto Hideo et al. "Zadankai: Tennō wa dōtoku no chūshin ka." *Nyūeiji* 4.1 (Jan. 1952): 6–16.

Kitagawa Yoshihide. "Senryō hōki." *Bessatsu Jurisuto* 144 (Oct. 1994): 450.

Kiyomiya Shirō. *Kenpō.* Yūhikaku, 1957.

Kobayashi Naoki. *Nihon ni okeru kenpō dōtai no bunseki.* Iwanami shoten, 1963.

Kobayashi Yoshinori. *Shin gomanizumu sengen supesharu sensōron.* Gentosha, 1998.

Kodama Yoshio. "Watakushi no uchinaru tennōsei." *Seiron*, Aug. 1975, 82–88.

Koizumi Shinzō. "Aru kokuō no shōgai: jooji goseden." *Bungei shunjū*, Jan. 1955, 182–92.

———. *Jooji goseden to teishitsuron.* Bungei shunjū, 1989.

———. "Kunshu no yūraku." *Bungei shunjū*, Mar. 1955, 118–30.

———. "Teishitsuron." *Bungei shunjū*, Jan. 1960, 114–20.

Koizumi Shinzō, ed. *Fukuzawa Yukichi zenshū.* Vols. 5–6. Iwanami shoten, 1959.

Kojima Noboru. "Nihon senryō: yonkaime no kaiken." *Bungei shunjū*, Jan. 1978, 338–57.

Kokuritsu kokkai shokan chōsa rippō kōsakyoku, ed. *Yasukuni jinja mondai shiryōshū.* Kokuritsu kokkai shokan chōsa rippō kōsakyoku, 1976.

Kokuritsu kokkai toshokan chōsa rippō kōsakyoku. *Kigensetsu mondai ni kansuru shiryōshū*. Kokuritsu kokkai toshokan chōsa rippō kōsakyoku, 1965.
Kominterun. "Nihon ni okeru jōsei to Nihon kyōsantō no ninmu ni kansuru teze." In *Tennōsei*, ed. Katsube Mitake, 263–73. Shibundō, 1970.
Koseki Shōichi. *The Birth of Japan's Postwar Constitution*. Ed. and trans. Ray A. Moore. Boulder, CO: Westview Press, 1997.
"Kōshitsu ni kansuru hitobito no iken." *Chūō kōron*, July 1959, 112–17.
"Kōtaishi no ren'ai o meguru kokkai rongi." *Chūō kōron*, Apr. 1959, 205–6.
Kubokawa Tokuji. "Tennōsei to Nihon demokurashii." In *Nihon ni okeru demokurashii*, ed. Mainichi shinbunsha, 28–36. Mainichi shinbunsha, Dec. 1945.
Kunaichō, ed. *Michi: Tennō heika gosokui j¯unen kinen kirokush¯u*. Nihon hōsō shuppankai, 1999.
Kurihara, Sadako. *Black Eggs: Poems by Kurihara Sadako*. Trans., with an Introduction and Notes, Richard H. Minear. Ann Arbor: Center for Japanese Studies, University of Michigan, 1994.
Kuroda Hisata. *Tennoke no zaisan*. Sanichi shinsho, 1966.
Kuroda Satoru. "Tennō no kenpōjō no chii." *Kōhō kenkyū* 10 (1954): 1–19.
"Kyūchū enyūkai ni etsuzankai hachi-nin o shōtai shita shushō no senkyō-ku sabisu." *Shūkan asahi*, 25 May 1973, 27–30.

Large, Stephen. "Emperor Hirohito and Early Shōwa Japan." *Monumenta Nipponica* 46.3 (Autumn 1991): 349–68.
———. *Emperor Hirohito and Shōwa Japan: A Political Biography*. London: Routledge, 1990.
Larsson, Torbjorn. "Sweden, the Crown of State." *Res Publica* 33.1 (1991): 49–60.
Laski, Harold J. *Parliamentary Government in England: A Commentary*. New York: Viking Press, 1947.
Lebra, Takie Sugiyama. "Self and Other in Esteemed Status: The Changing Culture of the Japanese Royalty from Showa to Heisei." *Journal of Japanese Studies* 23.2 (Summer 1997): 257–89.
Leistikow, Gunnar. "Queen Margrethe II of Denmark." *American-Scandinavian Review* 60.3 (1972): 22–32.
Lu, David. J. *Japan: A Documentary History*. Vol. 2. Armonk, NY: M. E. Sharpe, 1997.

Maki, John M. *Japan's Commission on the Constitution: The Final Report*. Seattle: University of Washington Press, 1980.
Maruyama Masao and Fukuda Kanichi, eds. *Kikigaki: Nanbara Shigeru kaikoroku*. Tōkyō daigaku shuppankai, 1989.
"Masuhara hatsugen ni miru tennō to seiji no kiken na kankei." *Shūkan asahi*, 15 June 1973, 18–22.
Matsushita Keiichi. "Taishū tennōseiron." *Chūo kōron*, Apr. 1959, 30–46.
———. "Zoku-taishū tennōseiron." *Chūo kōron*, Aug. 1959, 115–26.
Mayuzumi Toshirō and Fujishima Taisuke. "Tennōsei no kiki o ureu." *Roman*, May 1973, 14–32.
McCormack, Gavan. "The Japanese Movement to 'Correct' History." *Bulletin of Concerned Asian Scholars* 30.2 (1998): 16–23

McLaren, W. W., ed. *Japanese Government Documents*. Vol. 1. Washington, DC: University Publications of America, 1979.

McNelly, Theodore H. "Domestic and International Influences on Constitutional Revision in Japan, 1945–1946." Ph.D. dissertation, Columbia University, 1952.

Mikasa no Miya Takahito. "Kigensetsu ni tsuite no watakushi no shinnen." *Bungei shunjū*, Jan. 1959, 72–83.

Mikasa No Miya Takahito and Irokawa Daikichi. "Teiō to haka to minshu." *Ushio*, Apr. 1974, 80–96.

Miller, Frank O. *Minobe Tatsukichi: Interpreter of Constitutionalism in Japan*. Berkeley: University of California Press, 1965.

Minobe Tatsukichi. "Minshushugi to waga gikai seido." *Sekai*, Jan. 1946, 20–31.

———. *Shinkenpō no kihon genri*. Kokuritsu shoin, 1947.

———. "Watakushi wa omou." In *Shinkenpō to shuken*, ed. Kenpō kenkyūkai, 1–3. Eimi shobō, 1947.

Mishima Yukio. "Bunka bōeiron." In Mishima Yukio, *Mishima Yukio zenshū*, 33: 366–401. Shinchōsha, 1976.

Mitani Takanobu. *Kaikoroku*. Hibaihin (published but not offered for sale), 1980.

Mitsuma Shingo. "Nihonkoku kenpō ni okeru tennō no chii to kokutairon." In *Tennōron ni kansuru mondai*, ed. Jiyūtō kenpō chōsakai, 41–76. Jiyūtō kenpō chōsakai jimukyoku, 1954.

———. *Sokoku fukkō*. Yōhan shuppan, 1970.

———. "Tennō to kenpō chōsakai." *Minshu kōron*, 10 Oct. 1957, 22–25.

Miyachi Masato. "'Nihon bunka taikan' henshū shimatsu-ki: Tennōsei fashizumu ni okeru bunkaron." In *Nihon bunkaron hihan*. ed. Nihon kagakusha kaigi, 186–223. Suiyōsha, 1991.

———. "Sengo tennōsei no gendankai: kokkai no gengō rongi o tegakari toshite." *Rekishi hyōron* 358 (Feb. 1980): 3–19.

———. "Sengo tennōsei no tokushitsu." *Rekishi hyōron* 364 (Aug. 1980): 24–35.

Miyamoto Kenji. "Tennōsei hihan ni tsuite." *Zen'ei* 1 (Feb. 1946): 4–9.

Miyazawa Toshiyoshi. *Kenpō*. Yūhikaku, 1949.

Morita Akio and Ishihara Shintarō. *"No" to ieru Nihon: shin Nichi-bei kankei no kado*. Kobunsha, 1989.

Mosley, Leonard. *Hirohito: Emperor of Japan*. Englewood Cliffs, NJ: Prentice Hall, 1966.

Murakami Hyōe. "Saigunbi o sasaeru 'gōyūren.'" *Ekonomisuto bessatsu*, 10 Apr. 1964, 68–73.

Muramatsu Takeshi et al. "Zadankai: Kōtaishi 'shinnō.'" *Ryūdō*, Oct. 1971, 218–34.

Nachmani, Amikam. "Civil War and Foreign Intervention in Greece, 1946–1949." *Journal of Contemporary History* 25.4 (1990): 489–522.

Nagasaki shichō e no 7300-tsu no tegami. Komichi shobō, 1989.

Nagata Hidejirō. *A Simplified Treatise on the Imperial House of Japan*. Trans. Henry Satoh. Hakubunkwan, 1921.

Naikaku sōridaijin kanbō. "Meiji hyakunen kinen ni kansuru seifu no gyōji, jigyō nado ni tsuite." *Toki no hōrei* 618 (23 Sept. 1967): 2–15.

———. "Meiji hyakunen ni kansuru seron chōsa ni tsuite." *Toki no hōrei* 651 (23 Aug. 1968): 41–51.

———. *Tennō heika zaii gojūnen kinen shikiten kiroku*. Naikaku sōridaijin kanbō, 1977.

Naikaku sōridaijin kanbō shingishitsu. *Gengōhō seitei no kiroku*. Naikaku sōridaijin kanbō shingishitsu, 1980.

———. *Kenkoku kinen no hi ni kansuru kōchōkai sokkiroku*. Naikaku sōridaijin kanbō shingishitsu, 1966.

"'Nai mono wa nai' to kyōben shitsuzuketa shushō no 2-jikan 37-fun." *Sandē mainichi*, 24 June 1973, 139–41.

Nakamura Masanori. *The Japanese Monarchy: Ambassador Grew and the Making of the "Symbol Emperor System," 1931–1991*. Armonk, NY: M. E. Sharpe, 1992.

Nakamura Mutso. "Kokuji kōi naishi tennō no kōteki kōi." *Jurisuto* 933 (1–15 May 1989): 112–18.

"Nakasone Yasuhiro-shi 'Waga tennōron.'" *Sandē mainichi*, 24 June 1973, 135–39.

Nanjō Hiroshi. "Riyō sareta 'tennō no ishi': tennō no shukuhakujo ni kansuru kengikai no rongi." *Jinbutsu ōrai*, May 1957, 40–43.

Naruhito Shinnō. *Temuzu to tomo ni: Eikoku no ninenkan*. Gakushūin kyōyō shinsho, 1993.

Naruhito shinnō. *Suiunshi kara sekai no mizu e*. NHK Shuppan, 2019.

Nicolson, Harold. *King George the Fifth: His Life and Reign*. London: Constable & Co, 1952.

"2-11: Futatsu no kenkoku shikiten." *Sokoku to seinen*, Mar. 1988, 22–32.

Nihon bunka kenkyūkai. *Jimmu tennō kigenron*. Tachibana shobō, 1958.

"Nihon ichi no nakōdo yaku." *Sandē mainichi*, 14 Dec. 1958, 4–10.

Nihon kyōsantō chūō iinkai shuppankyoku. *Tennōsei no genzai to kōtaishi*. Nihon kyōsantō chūō iinkai shuppankyoku, 1988.

"Nihon no shōchō o kangaeru: Shin–Yoshida Shigeru kara Masuhara zen-chōkan made." *Josei jishin*, 23 June 1973, 168–71.

Nihon ryokō kyōkai, ed. *Jimmu tennō no goseiseki*. Nihon ryokō kyōkai, 1940.

"Nihon sanka: 'Tennō heika gozaii gojūnen hōshuku gyōji ni sanka shite.'" *Risō sekai*, Feb. 1977, 48–54.

Nihon seinen kyōgikai. *Heisei jidai no atarashii kuni-zukuri e*. Nihon seinen kyōgikai, 1990.

———. *Moeagare gengō hōseika undō no homura: gengō hōseika undō kirokushū*. Nihon seinen kyōgikai, 1977.

Nihon yoron chōsa kenkyūjo. *Tennō: Album of the Human Emperor*. Toppan, 1952.

Nishihara Shigeki. "Seron kara mita tennōsei to daikyūjō." *Jiyū*, May 1962, 54–61.

———. "Tennō, gengō, kokka, kokki." *Jiyū*, Oct. 1980, 82–96.

Oguchi Iichi. "Tennō genshuron no jittai." *Kaizō*, Dec. 1955, 137–40.

Ohnuki-Tierney, Emiko. "The Emperor of Japan as Deity (Kami)." *Ethnology* 30.3 (1991): 199–215.

Ohsuga Mizuo. *Shushō kantei*. Asahi sonorama, 1995.

Okada Keisuke. *Okada Keisuke kaikoroku*. Mainichi shinbunsha, 1950.

"Okaerinasai! Gokurōsama!" *Shūkan yomiuri*, 25 Oct. 1953, 4–14.

Okamoto, Koichi. "William J. Sebald: The United States Political Adviser for Japan." *Waseda Journal of Asian Studies* 19 (1997): 15–39.

Okubo, Kenji. *The Problems of the Emperor System in Postwar Japan*. Japan Institute of Pacific Studies, 1948.
Ono Noboru. *Ningen tennō*. Ichiyōsha, 1947.

Pai, Hyung Il. *Constructing "Korean" Origins: A Critical Review of Archaeology, Historiography, and Racial Myth in Korean State-Formation Theories*. Cambridge, MA: Harvard University Asia Center, 2000.
Paxton, Robert O. *Vichy France: Old Guard and New Order, 1940–1944*. New York: Knopf, 1972.
Piggott, Joan R. *The Emergence of Japanese Kingship*. Stanford. CA: Stanford University Press, 1997.
Pimlott, Ben. *The Queen: A Biography of Elizabeth II*. New York: John Wiley & Sons, 1996.
Powell, Charles. *Juan Carlos of Spain*. New York: St. Martin's, 1996.
"Premier Prince Naruhiko Higashi-kuni's Address at the Eighty-Eighth Session of the Diet, Sept. 5, 1945." *Contemporary Japan*, Apr.–Dec. 1945, 280–88.
Preston, Paul. *Juan Carlos: A People's King*. New York: Harper Collins, 2004.
Prochaska, Frank. "George V and Republicanism, 1917–1919." *Twentieth Century British History* 10.1 (1999): 27–51.

Rekishi hyōron, ed. "Kigensetsu fukkatsu mondai nenpu." *Rekishi hyōron* 93 (Feb. 1958): 72–77.
Rekishi kyōikusha kyōgikai. *Kigensetsu: Nihon no shukusaijitsu I*. Tanro shobō shinsha, 1958.
Ridgway, Matthew B. (as told to Harold H. Martin). *Soldier: The Memoirs of Matthew B. Ridgway*. New York: Harper & Brothers, 1956.
Roberts, John G. "The 'Japan Crowd' and the Zaibatsu Restoration." *Japan Interpreter* 12.3 (Summer 1979): 384–414.
Rousso, Henry. *The Vichy Syndrome: History and Memory in France since 1944*. Cambridge, MA: Harvard University Press, 1991.
Ruoff, Jeffrey, and Kenneth Ruoff. *The Emperor's Naked Army Marches On*. Wiltshire, UK: Flicks Books, 1998.
Ruoff, Kenneth J. *Imperial Japan at Its Zenith: The Wartime Celebration of the Empire's 2600th Anniversary*. Ithaca, NY: Cornell University Press, 2010.
———. "Lessons from Japan's Symbolic Monarchy." In *Monarchy & Democracy in the 21st Century*, ed. Bhutan Centre for Media and Democracy, 75–83. Bhutan: Paro, 2010.
———. "Mr. Tomino Goes to City Hall: Grass roots Democracy in Zushi City, Japan." In *The Other Japan: Conflict, Compromise, and Resistance Since 1945*, ed. Joe Moore, 320–42. Armonk, NY: M. E. Sharpe, 1997.
Ruoff, Kenneth, and Jeffrey Ruoff. "Japan's Outlaw Filmmaker: An Interview with Hara Kazuo." *Iris: A Journal of Theory on Image and Sound* 16 (Spring 1993): 103–14.

Saitō Dōichi. "Seron chōsa ni miru tennōkan." *Gendai no me*, Feb. 1966, 160–71.
Sakamoto Kōjirō. "Shinshōchō tennō e no pafōmansu." *Chūō kōron*, Jan. 1991, 115–23.

———. *Shōchō tennōsei e no pafomansu*. Yamakawa Shuppansha, 1989.
Sangiin jimukyoku. *Dainanakai kokkai sangiin monbu iinkai kaigiroku* 6 (21 Feb. 1950).
———. *Dainanakai kokkai sangiin monbu iinkai kaigiroku* 7 (28 Feb. 1950).
———. *Dainanakai kokkai sangiin monbu iinkai kaigiroku* 8 (2 Mar. 1950).
———. *Dainijūkai kokkai sangiin yosan iinkai kaigiroku* 10 (14 Mar. 1957).
———. *Sangiin senreiroku*. Sangiin jimukyoku, 1988.
San Nyūsu Futosu. *Tennō*. Toppan, 1948.
Sasaki Kazushi. "Tennō shikyo to Nihon kyōsantō no kenchi." *Zen'ei* 573 (Mar. 1989): 28–37.
Satō Kōji. "Kokuji Kōi to seikyō bunri." *Jurisuto* 933 (1–15 May 1989): 101–11.
Satō Tadao. "Hirohito no bishō." *Chūō kōron*, Sept. 1959, 194–99.
Satomi Kishio. *Nihonkoku no kenpō*. Kinseisha, 1962.
———. *Nihon no minshushugi*. Hokushinsha, 1954.
———. *Tennō no kagakuteki kenkyū*. Senshinsha, 1932.
Shimada Tatsumi. "Igirisujin to kōtaishi: mada aru senjichū no zōaku." *Shūkan asahi*, 7 June 1953, 14–15.
Shimizu Ikutarō. "Senryōka no tennō." *Shisō* 348 (1953): 4–22
Shimizu Shin, ed. *Chikujō Nihonkoku kenpō shingiroku* (*A Record of the Article-by-Article Debate of the Constitution of Japan*). Vol. 1. Yūhikaku, 1962.
Shindō Eiichi, ed. *Ashida Hitoshi nikki*. Vols. 1–2. Iwanami shoten, 1986.
Shintō seiji renmei. *Seisaku suishin no kadai o kangaeru*. Shintō seiji renmei, 1995.
"Shinwa no furusato kara Tōkyō e—Takachiho kara 2300 kiro: Kōki 2650-nen, goshinka daikōshin." *Zenbō*, Apr. 1990, 90.
"Shōchō tennōsei ni kansuru seron chōsa no hensen." *Jurisuto* 938 (15 July 1989): 210.
Shūgiin jimukyoku. *Daihachijūnanakai kokkai shūgiin kaigiroku* 15 (16 Mar. 1979).
———. *Daihyakuyonkai kokkai shūgiin yosan iinkai giroku* 20 (8 Mar. 1986).
———. *Daijūgokai kokkai shūgiin gaimu iinkai gijiroku* 5 (3 Dec. 1952).
———. *Daijūsankai kokkai shūgiin yosan iinkai gijiroku* 5 (31 Jan. 1952).
———. *Daiyonkai kokkai shūgiin gaimu iinkai giroku* 3 (6 Dec. 1948).
———. *Daiyonkai kokkai shūgiin gaimu iinkai giroku* 4 (14 Dec. 1948).
———. *Shūgiin senreishu*. Shūgiin jimukyoku, 1994.
Smith, Sally Bedell. *Prince Charles: The Passions and Paradoxes of an Improbable Life*. New York: Random House, 2017.
Sonobe Eiichi. *Shintennōke no jigazō*. Bungei shunjū, 1989.
Sōrifu shōkunkyoku. *Nihon no kunshō, hōshō seido*. Sōrifu shōkunkyoku, n.d.
———. *Shōkunkyoku hyakunen shiryōshū*. Vol. 2. Ōkurashō insatsukyoku, 1979.
Supreme Commander for the Allied Powers, Government Section. *Political Reorientation of Japan, September 1945 to September 1948*. Vols. 1–2. Washington, DC: U.S. Government Printing Office, 1948.
Suzuki Ryō et al. *Nara-ken no hyakunen*. Yamakawa shuppansha, 1985.
Suzuki Shizuko. "Tennō gyōkō to shōchō tennōsei no kakuritsu." *Rekishi hyōron* 298 (Feb. 1975): 53–66.

Takagi Hiroshi. "Bunkazai no kindai." *Nihon no kokuhō* 110 (11 Apr. 1999): 308–12.
———. "Kindai ni okeru shinwateki kodai no sōzō." *Jinbun gakuhō* 83 (Mar. 2000).
———. *Kindai tennōsei no bunkashiteki kenkyū*. Azekura shobō, 1997.

Takagi, Kiyoko. *The Eight Female Emperors of Japan*. Trans. Masako Hamada et al. Fuzambo, 2008.
Takahashi, Akira. "TV and the Imperial Wedding." In *Japanese Research on Mass Communication: Selected Abstracts*, ed. Hidetoshi Kato, 14–15. Honolulu: University of Hawaii Press, 1974.
Takahashi Hiroshi. "Ningen tennō enshutsusha no keifu." In *Hōgaku semina zōkan sōgō tokushū shirizu*, 144–52. Hōgaku seminā, 1986.
———. *Shōchō tennō*. Iwanami shinsho, 1987.
———. "Shōwa Tennō no jokan kaikaku." In *Kawai Yahachi, Shōwa shoki no tennō to kyūchū*, ed. Takahashi Hiroshi, Awaya Kentaro, and Otabe Yūji, 2: 251–64. Iwanami shoten, 1994.
———. "Tennō, kōgō heisei jūnen no kiseki." *Bungei shunjū*, Feb. 1998, 112–25.
Takakura Teru. "Tennōsei narabi ni kōshitsu no mondai." *Chūō kōron*, Aug. 1946, 7–28.
Takayanagi Kenzō. "The New Emperor System." *Japan Quarterly* 9.3 (July–Sept. 1962): 265–74.
———. "Shōchō no genshu, tennō." *Jiyū*, May 1962, 2–19.
———. "Some Reminiscences of Japan's Commission on the Constitution." In *The Constitution of Japan: Its First Twenty Years, 1947–67*, ed. Dan Fenno Henderson, 71–88. Seattle: University of Washington Press, 1968.
Takayanagi Kenzō, Ohtomo Ichirō, Tanaka Hideo, eds. *Nihonkoku kenpō seitei no katei*. Vol. 1. Yūhikaku, 1972.
Takeda, Kiyoko. *The Dual-Image of the Japanese Emperor*. London: Macmillan Education, 1988.
Tanaka Minoru. "Tennō ichi-nichi no seikatsu." *Bungei shunjū*, Oct. 1956, 80–83.
Tanaka Nobumasa. *Hinomaru Kimigayo no sengoshi*. Iwanami shoten, 2000.
Tanaka Nobumasa, Tanaka Hiroshi, and Hata Nagami. *Izoku to sengo*. Iwanami shoten, 1995.
Tanaka Takashi. "Takamatsu Tadakiyo gūji o shinobu." *Sumi no e* 135–36 (Mar.-Apr. 1975): 16–22.
Teeuwen, Mark. "Jinja Honchō and Shrine Shintō policy." *Japan Forum* 8.2 (1996): 177–88.
"Tennō futatabi kumo ni noritamau." *Bungei shunjū*, Oct. 1954, 64–78.
"Tennō ga 'sengo shori' ni iyoku." *Sentaku*, Dec. 1992, 118–21.
"Tennō hatsugen e no Nihonjin 20-nin no iken." *Shūkan asahi*, 10 Oct. 1975, 18–22.
"Tennō ni kansuru hōkokusho." *Hōritsu jihō* 33.14 (1961): 17–45.
"Tennō no saigo no heishi 'sokoku' no itutsukan." *Sandē mainichi*, 20 Feb. 1972, 16–22.
"Tennōsei shiji ka, hitei ka." *Gendai no esupuri* 45 (Oct. 1970): 158, 224, 238–39, 260–62, 276.
Tennōsei to kyōiku. Special issue. *Kikan kyōikuhō* 61.4 (1986).
"Tennō to heishi Yokoi no kikan." *Shūkan shinchō*, 12 Feb. 1972: 32–38.
"Tennō to 'seiji riyō.'" *Sentaku*, June 1990, 122–25.
Terasaki Hidenari and Mariko Terasaki Miller, eds. *Shōwa tennō dokuhakuroku—Terasaki Hidenari goyōgakari nikki*. Bungei shunjūsha, 1991.
Terasaki Osamu. "How Radicals in the Popular Rights Movement Viewed the Emperor: A Brief Analysis." *Acta Asiatica* 59 (1990): 18–37.
Thatcher, Margaret. *The Downing Street Years*. New York: Harper Collins, 1993.

Titus, David A. "Accessing the World: Palace and Foreign Policy in Post-Occupation Japan." In *Japan's Foreign Policy: After the Cold War*, ed. Gerald Curtis, 62–89. Armonk, NY: M. E. Sharpe, 1993.

———. "The Making of the 'Symbol Emperor System' in Postwar Japan." *Modern Asian Studies* 14.4 (1980): 529–78.

———. *Palace and Politics in Prewar Japan*. New York: Columbia University Press, 1974.

"Toei no kōtaishisama ni nozomu." *Shūkan sankei*, 22 Mar. 1953, 51–54.

Togashi Junji. *Chiyodajō: Kyūtei kisha yonjūnen no kiroku*. Kōbunsha, 1958.

———. *Heika no "ningen" sengen*. Dōwa shobō, 1946.

———. *Nihon no kunshō*. Daiippōki shuppan, 1965.

———. *Tennō to tomo ni gojūnen*. Mainichi shinbunsha, 1977.

" 'Tōgū-san o' to kyōchō sareta Chichibu-miyasama." *Sandē mainichi*, 5 Apr. 1953, 4–10.

Tolischus, Otto D. *Tokyo Record*. New York: Reynal & Hitchcock, 1943.

Toyoshita Narahiko. *Anpo jōyaku no seiritsu*. Iwanami shoten, 1998.

"Tsuda hakushi 'Kenkoku no jijō to bansei ikkei no shisō' no happyō ni tsuite." *Sekai*, Apr. 1946, 128–35.

Tsuda Sōkichi. "Gengō no mondai ni tsuite." *Chūō kōron*, July 1950, 70–82.

———. "Kenkoku no jijō to bansei ikkei no shisō." *Sekai*, Apr. 1946, 29–54.

———. "Nihon no kōshitsu." *Chūō kōron*, July 1952, 4–15

———. *Tsuda Sōkichi zenshū*. Vol. 3. Iwanami shoten, 1963.

Tsunetō Kyō. "Waga kuni ni wa genshu ga sonzai sura ka." *Kikan horitsugaku* 10 (1951): 44–50.

Ueno Chizuko. "The Politics of Memory: Nation, Individual and Self." *History and Memory* 11.2 (1999): 129–52.

Ueyama Shunpei, Umehara Takeshi, and Yano Tōru. "Nihon no naka no tennō." *Chūō kōron*, Oct. 1988, 64–79.

Vining, Elizabeth Gray. *Windows for the Crown Prince*. Philadelphia: J. B. Lippincott, 1952.

Wakabayashi, Bob Tadashi. *Anti-Foreignism and Western Learning in Early-Modern Japan*. Cambridge, MA: Council on East Asian Studies, Harvard University, 1986.

Wakabayashi Yoshitaka. *Kokumin no shukujitsu toshite 'kenkoku kinenbi' (Kigensetsu) o atarashiku seitei suru koto to no igi ni tsuite*. Kenkoku kinenbi (Kigensetsu) seitei sokushinkai sōhonbu, 1953.

Watanabe Osamu. "The Emperor as a 'Symbol' in Postwar Japan." *Acta Asiatica* 59 (1990): 101–25.

———. *Sengo seijishi no naka no tennōsei*. Aoki shoten, 1990.

———. "The Sociology of Jishuku and Kicho: The Death of the Showa Tenno as a Reflection of the Structure of Contemporary Japanese Society." *Japan Forum* 1.2 (Oct. 1989): 275–89.

Watsuji Tetsurō. *Kokumin tōgō no shōchō*. Keisō shobō, 1948.

Webb, Herschel. *The Japanese Imperial Institution in the Tokugawa Period*. New York: Columbia University Press, 1968.

"Weekly Magazines: Keys to an Information Society." *Japan Update*, Spring 1988, 8–11.
Wetzler, Peter. *Hirohito and War: Imperial Tradition and Military Decision Making in Prewar Japan*. Honolulu: University of Hawaii Press, 1998.
Woodard, William P. *The Allied Occupation of Japan 1945–1952 and Japanese Religions*. Leiden: E. J. Brill, 1972.

Yamada Eizō. *Seiden Satō Eisaku*. Vol. 2. Shinchōsha, 1988.
Yamanouchi Kazuo and Asano Ichirō, eds. *Kokkai no kenpō rongi*. Gyōsei, 1984.
Yamashita Shinji, ed. *Tennō heika 100 no kotoba*. Takarashimasha, 2017.
Yanase Yoshimoto. *Genshu to kikan*. Yūhikaku, 1969.
Yokohama kyōkasho soshō o shiji suru kai. *Yokohama kyōkasho soshō* (*soshō shiryōshū*, vol. 1). Yokohama: Yokohama kyōkasho soshō o shiji suru kai, 1993.
Yokoi Shōichi. "Hajimete akasu waga-tsuma, tennō, sensō." *Sandē mainichi*, 17 Dec. 1972, 32–36.
Yokota Kisaburō. *Tennōsei*. Rōdō bunkasha, 1949.
Yokota Kōichi. "Tennō to seiji." In *Kenpōgaku*, ed. Okudaira Yasuhiro and Sugihara Yasuo. 4: 177–88. Yūhikaku sōsho, 1977.
Yoshida Shigeto. "Ima, 'oku' wa dō natte iru ka." *Bungei shunjū*, Apr. 1993, 156–62.
Yoshimoto Yanase. *Genshu to kikan*. Yūhikaku, 1969.

Ziegler, Philip. "Churchill and the Monarchy." In *Churchill*, ed. Roger Blake and William Roger Louis, 187–98. London: Oxford University Press, 1993.

Index

Page numbers for figures are in italics.

Harvard East Asian Monographs
(most recent titles)

411. Jennifer E. Altehenger, *Legal Lessons: Popularizing Laws in the People's Republic of China, 1949–1989*
412. Halle O'Neal, *Word Embodied: The Jeweled Pagoda Mandalas in Japanese Buddhist Art*
413. Maren A. Ehlers, *Give and Take: Poverty and the Status Order in Early Modern Japan*
414. Chieko Nakajima, *Body, Society, and Nation: The Creation of Public Health and Urban Culture in Shanghai*
415. Pu Wang, *The Translatability of Revolution: Guo Moruo and Twentieth-Century Chinese Culture*
416. Hwansoo Ilmee Kim, *The Korean Buddhist Empire: A Transnational History, 1910–1945*
417. Joshua Hill, *Voting as a Rite: A History of Elections in Modern China*
418. Kirsten L. Ziomek, *Lost Histories: Recovering the Lives of Japan's Colonial Peoples*
419. Claudine Ang, *Poetic Transformations: Eighteenth-Century Cultural Projects on the Mekong Plains*
420. Evan N. Dawley, *Becoming Taiwanese: Ethnogenesis in a Colonial City, 1880s–1950s*
421. James McMullen, *The Worship of Confucius in Japan*
422. Nobuko Toyosawa, *Imaginative Mapping: Landscape and Japanese Identity in the Tokugawa and Meiji Eras*
423. Pierre Fuller, *Famine Relief in Warlord China*
424. Diane Wei Lewis, *Powers of the Real: Cinema, Gender, and Emotion in Interwar Japan*
425. Maram Epstein, *Orthodox Passions: Narrating Filial Love during the High Qing*
426. Margaret Wan, *Regional Literature and the Transmission of Culture: Chinese Drum Ballads, 1800–1937*
427. Takeshi Watanabe, *Flowering Tales: Women Exorcising History in Heian Japan*
428. Jürgen P. Melzer, *Wings for the Rising Sun: A Transnational History of Japanese Aviation*
429. Edith Sarra, *Unreal Houses: Character, Gender, and Genealogy in the* Tale of Genji
430. Yi Gu, *Chinese Ways of Seeing and Open-Air Painting*
431. Robert Cliver, *Red Silk: Class, Gender, and Revolution in China's Yangzi Delta Silk Industry*
432. Kenneth J. Ruoff, *Japan's Imperial House in the Postwar Era, 1945–2019*